INTERROGATING THE FUTURE

Studies in Critical Social Sciences Book Series

Haymarket Books is proud to be working with Brill Academic Publishers (www.brill.nl) to republish the *Studies in Critical Social Sciences* book series in paperback editions. This peer-reviewed book series offers insights into our current reality by exploring the content and consequences of power relationships under capitalism, and by considering the spaces of opposition and resistance to these changes that have been defining our new age. Our full catalog of *SCSS* volumes can be viewed at https://www.haymarketbooks.org/series_collections/4-studies-in-critical-social-sciences.

Series Editor
David Fasenfest (York University, Canada)

Editorial Board
Eduardo Bonilla-Silva (Duke University)
Chris Chase-Dunn (University of California–Riverside)
William Carroll (University of Victoria)
Raewyn Connell (University of Sydney)
Kimberlé W. Crenshaw (University of California–LA and Columbia University)
Heidi Gottfried (Wayne State University)
Alfredo Saad-Filho (Queen's University, Belfast)
Chizuko Ueno (University of Tokyo)
Sylvia Walby (Lancaster University)
Raju Das (York University)

INTERROGATING THE FUTURE

Essays in Honour of David Fasenfest

EDITED BY
TOM BRASS
RAJU J. DAS

Haymarket Books
Chicago, IL

First published in 2024 by Brill Academic Publishers, The Netherlands
© 2024 Koninklijke Brill NV, Leiden, The Netherlands

Published in paperback in 2025 by
Haymarket Books
P.O. Box 180165
Chicago, IL 60618
773-583-7884
www.haymarketbooks.org

ISBN: 979-8-88890-515-9

Distributed to the trade in the US through Consortium Book Sales and Distribution (www.cbsd.com) and internationally through Ingram Publisher Services International (www.ingramcontent.com).

This book was published with the generous support of Lannan Foundation, Wallace Action Fund, and the Marguerite Casey Foundation.

Special discounts are available for bulk purchases by organizations and institutions. Please call 773-583-7884 or email info@haymarketbooks.org for more information.

Cover design by Jamie Kerry and Ragina Johnson.

Printed in the United States.

Library of Congress Cataloging-in-Publication data is available.

*For Amanda, Anna, Ned, and Miles,
and in memory of my parents*
TOM BRASS

For the progressive scholars of the world
RAJU J. DAS

Contents

Acknowledgements IX
List of Illustrations X
Notes on Contributors XI

1 Introduction
   Interrogating the Future 1
      Tom Brass and Raju J. Das

PART 1

2 Interview with David Fasenfest 25
      Raju J. Das and Robert Latham

3 Thank You David
   A Tribute to a Mensch 32
      Lauren Langman

4 Critical Evaluation of a Critical Scholar
   David Fasenfest 35
      Rodney D. Coates

5 Marxist Sociology in Asia
   David Fasenfest's Engagement with the Global South and China 47
      Ngai Pun

6 The Politics of Coercion, the Coercion of Politics
   Thought Conversion in Pre-war Japan 54
      Hideo Aoki

7 Profile of an Insurgent Sociologist 79
      Ricardo A. Dello Buono

PART 2

8   Decolonizing Canons
    A Conversation with Chinese Sociologists   97
    Michael Burawoy

9   What Does Capitalism 'Know'? The Limits and Possibilities for Advancing Socialism in the 21st Century   112
    Robert Latham

10 The Centrality of Marx to the Global Periphery   134
    Raju J. Das

11 Crises in Neoliberalism
    Towards a Democratic Alternative   166
    Alfredo Saad-Filho

12 A Vanishing Army? Redefining the Industrial Reserve   186
    Tom Brass

13 Difference without End   219
    Kevin R. Cox

14 Capitalist Housing Regimes and Homeless People
    A Relative Surplus Population of the City   237
    Mahito Hayashi

PART 3

15 Postscript
    On the Continuing Necessity of (Marxist) Critique   267
    Tom Brass

    Author Index   291
    Subject Index   295

Acknowledgements

Following a conversation early in October 2022 between the two editors of this volume, it was decided that the record of work undertaken over the years by David Fasenfest merited recognition in the form of a *festschrift*, which would acknowledge the research and editorial role of the honorand. Not the least important aspect of this recognition was that all too often editorial tasks undertaken by an academic – considerable and continuing in his case – remain undervalued, both by the discipline concerned and frequently also by the institution in which the individual is based.

Despite it being customary to deploy tropes about the awfulness of a world beset by climate change, war, ethnic cleansing, mass population displacement and migration, the rise and consolidation of populism, all in a context where a seemingly unstoppable global capitalism licenses unimaginable disparities in wealth and poverty, both the honorand and the contributions to this volume remain optimistic about the capacity to effect progressive political change. Retaining this kind of positive outlook, especially in unpromisingly dark times, is crucial, in that evidence suggests so much of progressive opinion in academia has, to a large degree, given up on there being any systemic alternative to some form of capitalism.

Special thanks are due to the following people. To Judy Pereira of Brill Publishers, who guided the book through production; and to Anna Luisa Brass, who designed and drew the cover illustration. The dedication by one of the volume editors, Tom Brass, is to two sets of kin: his family: Amanda, and Anna, Ned and Miles; and also to the memory of his parents, Denis Brass (1913–2006), and Gloria Brass (1916–2012). That by the other editor, Raju Das, is to the progressive scholars of the world.

Illustrations

Figures

6.1 Process and form of *Tenkō*   72
14.1 Regulation of public space amid homelessness   246
14.2 Two metabolic circuits in public space   248

Photographs

7.1 Al Szymanski (on left) selling the journal   81
7.2 Artwork from the journal   82
7.3 Al Szymanski 1941–1985   85
7.4 David Fasenfest, mid-1970s   87
7.5 Mark Rudd and David Fasenfest, Shanghai University, 2018   93

Notes on Contributors

Hideo Aoki
is the Director of Institute of Social Theory and Dynamics in Japan. His research interests include homelessness, state and informality in Japan and the Philippines, and Japanese Marxism. Recent publications related to these interests are: *Japan's Underclass: Day Laborers and the Homeless*, (Trans Pacific Press, 2000); "The Global City Hypothesis" *Social Theory and Dynamics* 1 (2016); "Marxism and the Debate on the Transition to Capitalism in Prewar Japan," *Critical Sociology* (2020); "Marxism and the Debate on the Transition to Capitalism in Prewar Japan," *Critical Sociology* (2020); and "Urban Space of Exception and Urban Homo Sacer: Toward Embodying Critical Informality Theory," *Social Theory and Dynamics* 4 (2023).

Tom Brass
formerly lectured in the Social and Political Sciences Faculty at Cambridge University and directed studies in SPS for Queens' College. He carried out fieldwork research in Latin America and India during the 1970s and 1980s and is the second-longest serving editor of *The Journal of Peasant Studies* (1990–2008). His books include *New Farmers' Movements in India* (1995), *Free and Unfree Labour: The Debate Continues* (1997), *Towards a Comparative Political Economy of Unfree Labour* (1999), *Peasants, Populism and Postmodernism* (2000), *Latin American Peasants* (2003), *Labour Regime Change in the Twenty-First Century* (2011), *Class, Culture and the Agrarian Myth* (2014), *Labour Markets, Identities, Controversies* (2017), *Revolution and Its Alternatives* (2019), *Marxism Missing, Missing Marxism* (2021), and *Transitions* (2022).

Michael Burawoy
now Emeritus Professor, taught Marxism and sociology at the University of California, Berkeley for nearly 50 years. He has been an ethnographer of workplaces in the United States, Zambia, Hungary and Russia, developing theories of advanced capitalism, postcolonialism, state socialism and the transition from socialism to capitalism. His latest work tries to come to terms with the genius of W.E.B. Du Bois.

Rodney D. Coates
is a Professor in the Department of Sociology and Gerontology at Miami University (Ohio) and Director of the university's Black World Studies program. He specializes in the study of race and ethnic relations, inequality, critical race theory, and social justice. He has served on the editorial boards of the *American Sociological Review*; *Social Forces*; and *Race, Class and Gender*; on the executive boards of the Southern Sociological Society and Sociologists without Borders; and as Chair of the American Sociological Association's section on Race and Ethnic Minorities. He has published dozens of articles and several edited books, and frequently writes on issues of race and ethnicity, education and public policy, civil rights and social justice. His 2004 edited book, *Race and Ethnicity: Across Time, Space and Discipline* won the Choice award from the American Library Association. He is also a recipient of the Joseph Himes Career Award in Scholarship and Activism from the Association of Black Sociologists.

Kevin R. Cox
is Emeritus Distinguished Professor of Geography at The Ohio State University in Columbus. He is the author of numerous books, including *Making Human Geography* (2014), *The Politics of Urban and Regional Development and the American Exception* (2016), *Marxism and Human Geography* (2021), *Boomtown Columbus* (2021), and *Geography Indivisible* (2023). He has been a Guggenheim Fellow.

Raju J. Das
is Professor at York University, Toronto. He is on the Graduate Programmes in Social and Political Thought, Geography, Environmental Studies, and Development Studies. His teaching and research interests are in political economy, class relations, the state, uneven development, poverty, and politics of the Right and the Left. His recent books include *Marxist Class Theory for a Sceptical World* (2017), *Marx's Capital, Capitalism, and Limits to the State* (2022), *Contradictions of Capitalist Society and Culture* (2023), and *The Challenges of the New Social Democracy* (2023). He is currently working on a book titled, *A Marxist Theory of Dispossession: from Primitive Accumulation to Accumulation by Dispossession*.

Ricardo A. Dello Buono
is Professor of Sociology at Manhattan College in New York City. His work has spanned across a broad range of social problems and the sociology of development, with a regional emphasis on Latin America. He is active in the

Society for the Study of Social Problems (SSSP), the Association for Humanist Sociology (AHS), the International Sociological Association (ISA) and the Latin American Studies Association (LASA). He currently serves as Latin American and Caribbean Editor for the Sage journal *Critical Sociology*. His recent publications include "Elements for an Emancipatory Historical Sociology," in Andrea Borghini, ed., *Beyond Dogmatism: Studies in Historical Sociology*, Leiden/Boston: Brill, pp. 13–27, 2023 and "Emancipatory Thought in Latin America" (with José Bell Lara, FLACSO-CUBA), in D. Fasenfest, ed., *Marx Matters*, Leiden/Boston: Brill, pp. 157–180, 2022.

Mahito Hayashi
teaches urban studies and comparative Japanese studies in the Department of Global and Media Studies at Kinjo Gakuin University, Japan. His research focuses on poverty, labour, social movements, urban theory, and socio-spatial approaches to Marxist political economy. He is the author of *Rescaling Urban Poverty* (2023, Wiley) and *Homelessness and Urban Space* (2014, Akashi shoten, in Japanese), and has published widely in social science journals including *Critical Sociology*, *Antipode*, and the *International Journal of Urban and Regional Research*.

Lauren Langman
is emeritus professor of sociology at Loyola University of Chicago. He has long worked in the Marxist tradition of the Frankfurt School of Critical Theory, especially nationalism and reactionary movements, relationships between culture, identity and politics/political movements. He is the past Chair of Marxist Sociology of the American Sociological Association, where he recently received the Lifetime Achievement Award, and past President of Alienation Research and Theory Committee of the International Sociological Association, also a founding member of the Global Studies Association, and the International Herbert Marcuse Society. Recent publications include *Trauma Promise and Millennium: The Evolution of Alienation* (with Devorah Kalekin), *Alienation and Carnivalization* (with Jerome Braun), and a special issue of *Current Sociology* on the Arab Spring. His latest books are: *American Character* (with George Lundskow); *God, Guns, Gold and Glory* (Brill/Haymarket); and *Inequality in the 21st Century – Marx, Piketty and Beyond* (with David Alan Smith). He serves on the editorial boards of several journals, including *Critical Sociology*, *Current Perspectives in Social Theory*, and *Populism*.

Robert Latham
teaches in the Department of Politics at York University, Toronto. His recent publications include: "Organizing Anti-Capitalist Internationalism in Contemporary and Historical Perspective" (in *Rethinking Marxism*); *Challenging the Right, Augmenting the Left: Recasting Leftist Imagination* (co-edited); "Neoliberalism's Zeitgeist: The Untethered Disposition of Capitalism," (in *New Political Science*); "Contemporary Capitalism, Uneven Development, and the Arc of Anti-capitalism" (in *Global Discourse*); *The Radical Left and Social Transformation: Strategies of Augmentation and Reorganization* (co-edited); and "From Duty to Impulsion: Obstacles to Organising Future Revolutions" (in *Duty to Revolt: Transnational and Commemorative Aspects of Revolution*).

Ngai Pun
is Chair/Professor in Department of Cultural Studies, Lingnan University, Hong Kong. She obtained her Ph.D. from SOAS, University of London. She was honoured as the winner of the C. Wright Mills Award for her first book *Made in China: Women Factory Workers in a Global Workplace* (2005), which has been translated into French and Chinese. Her co-authored book *Dying for iPhone: Foxconn and the Lives of Chinese Workers* (2020) has also been translated into German, French, Italian, Spanish, Polish and Chinese. She is the author of *Migrant Labor in China: Post Socialist Transformation* (2016, Polity Press), and editor of seven volumes in Chinese and English.

Alfredo Saad-Filho
is Professor of Political Economy and International Development at King's College London; Distinguished Visiting Professor at the College of Business and Economics, University of Johannesburg, and Visiting Professor at the Department of Social Sciences, Lappeenranta-Lahti University of Technology. Previously, he was Professor of Political Economy at SOAS University of London, and Senior Economic Affairs Officer at the United Nations Conference on Trade and Development. He has taught in universities and research institutions in Belgium, Brazil, Canada, China, Finland, Germany, Italy, Japan, Mozambique, South Africa, Switzerland and the UK. His publications include 17 books, 80 journal articles, 60 book chapters, and 30 reports for the UN and other international agencies. His most recent books include *The Age of Crisis: Neoliberalism, the Collapse of Democracy, and the Pandemic* (London: Palgrave Macmillan, 2022) and *Progressive Policies for Economic Development: Economic Diversification and Social Inclusion after Climate Change* (London: Routledge, 2022).

CHAPTER 1

Introduction

Interrogating the Future

Tom Brass and Raju J. Das

1   From Detroit to Shanghai

This festschrift is unusual, in that it recognizes not only the scholarship of the honorand but also his achievement as a long-time editor, both of a major social science journal and of book series linked to this. For a quarter of a century, David Fasenfest has played a major editorial role in the social sciences. He has edited not just one of the most important social science journals, *Critical Sociology* (1998 to the present) published by SAGE, but also two book series: *Studies in Critical Social Sciences* (2000-) and *New Scholarship in Political Economy* (2019-), both published by Brill. To date, the latter series combined have produced around two hundred and seventy volumes, covering just about every aspect of social science research.

Accordingly, a major contribution to the world of radical thought, including especially Marxism, has been through his book series. Having founded one of the most successful book series in progressive social sciences, Fasenfest cofounded another book series produced by Brill: *New Scholarship in Political Economy* (NSPE). Already close to thirty volumes have been published in this series since 2020, which provides a platform for the work of doctoral students and early career scholars. Through this Fasenfest ensures that younger researchers with an interest in Marxism and progressive perspectives are empowered, receiving thereby a foothold in the domain of academic book publishing.

As editor of *Critical Sociology*, Fasenfest has ensured that it has become one of the most important journals in the social sciences. Not only does it continue to publish work by Marxists, but more generally it now has gained the status of 'socially engaged sociological scholarship' (or, 'critical sociological imagination', in a broad sense). Not the least important aspect of this achievement is its going against the grain politically, in a wider context where economic inequality is in the process of being consolidated and basic rights are under increasing attack from social forces on the political right.

Currently the Associate Professor of Sociology at Wayne State University in Michigan and Adjunct Professor at York University, Toronto, Canada, Fasenfest has also held research and visiting appointments at Shanghai University in China, Hamburg University in Germany, the Australian National University, and SOAS in the UK. His editorial board membership of other publications includes *Populism, New York Journal of Sociology, Cyberhood* (Urban Affairs Association), and the *Review of Radical Political Economics*. With an intellectual background in economics, urban sociology, and Chinese studies (BA from CUNY, MA and doctorate from Michigan University), his range of interests is large and impressive.[1] They extend from policy formation/implementation (urban redevelopment, human rights, planning, employment patterns and objectives, gender, poverty and inequality, environmental issues, social justice), via debates about theory (politics, democracy, Marxism, capitalism, neoliberalism, globalization, culture, race/class), to their application in and/or relevance to many different contexts, from Detroit to Shanghai.[2]

In addition to this, Fasenfest has contributed numerous conference presentations, as well as organized conferences and workshops. Together with his personal and editorial contributions, these sorts of contribution to the social sciences were recognized in 2016 with the accolade conferred on him by the American Sociological Association of a Lifetime Achievement award. What Fasenfest has managed to accomplish is all the more impressive when contextualized more broadly in terms of ongoing changes within academia, in particular the turbulent state of current debates in the social sciences, the impact on the latter of shifting political and intellectual opinion and fashion, plus the implications of all this for the role of journal editing.

As a journal and book series editor, Fasenfest is a 'bridge-builder' in two important ways. Whereas knowledge generated in academia is invariably left to collect dust and to 'the gnawing criticism of the mice' (to quote a long-dead European philosopher), he seeks to bridge the gap between academia and those outside it. That is to say, constructing links between academia and the non-academic world. Much that is intellectually and politically useful often remains locked within seemingly recondite academic debates, rarely surfacing to influence programmatic initiatives and policy. It is to counter this that

---

1 The broad intellectual nature of Fasenfest's own interests in terms of political economy is itself reflected in the correspondingly wide range of issues covered by the volume, as set out in the section below about themes.
2 Two points of interest are worth mentioning about the intellectual engagement by Fasenfest with the political economy of China. First, it predated what is now a bandwagon, whereby it is currently impossible to address any global issue without considering its impact on China, plus the outcome of this for the rest of the world. And second, his focus has been mainly on urban China, whereas that of much development studies analysis from the 1960s onwards has been on what was happening in the rural sector of the country.

Fasenfest emphasizes the necessity of a wider audience, both within and beyond the English-speaking world, for critical social science scholarship.³

Equally crucial is the second way in which Fasenfest is a 'bridge builder'. Not only is he a scholar in his own right, therefore, but he is also an exceptional *enabler* of scholarship of others: combining these two roles is itself no small achievement. A common academic trope is that in the world of critical and progressive sociology and social science scholarship more generally, there are many conflicting views about what is fundamentally wrong with existing society, what does a good society of the future look like, and how is one to get there. Unsurprisingly, therefore, disagreements about the latter frequently generate (sometimes acrimonious) polemical debate, with editors and journals supporting particular views to the exclusion of others. It is to his credit that Fasenfest has, his own Marxist politics notwithstanding, managed to follow a non-partisan editorial policy, allowing all sides a voice.

2   The Future of (Academic) Interrogation?

From the turn of the millennium, the kinds of difficulties facing journal editors over the changes occurring in social scientific discourse and paradigms have multiplied. Although there has always been debate, and with it disputes about what a journal should publish, it could be argued that currently this issue is polarized more so than ever before. At the centre of this issue is what exponents of the 'cultural turn' present as innovative, state-of-the-art theory, claims about which have emerged and achieved intellectual prominence over the past four decades.⁴ The result is that within the social sciences – and

---

3   A similar *cri de coeur* was encountered in another and much earlier sociological *festschrift*, for C. Wright Mills, which contained the following lament (Horowitz, 1964: 32, original emphasis): 'The same sociologists who are always impressing upon us the need for comparative study are often least cognizant of their own ethnocentric bias. How can you compare what you exclude from your range of vision? *You can no longer settle any major sociological problem within the boundaries of the United States*'. If that was true six decades ago, how much more so is it now.

4   Notwithstanding unpersuasive claims about 'newness', quite why the 'cultural turn' is – or should be – endorsed by so many sociologists, geographers, and anthropologists is a matter for conjecture. In the case of development studies, for example, the impact of this approach has been negative, in that the 'cultural turn' set out to deprivilege socialism, materialism and class as illegitimate Enlightenment/Eurocentric forms of 'foundationalism' inapplicable to the Third World. Quotidian resistance by (undifferentiated) peasants in defence of indigenous culture and tradition is instead seen as a legitimate part of the struggle against capitalism, a result being that rural struggle is no longer about class

indeed the humanities generally – Marxism has been marginalized, while a variety of concepts and approaches linked epistemologically to the 'new' populist postmodernism (subaltern studies, everyday-forms-of-resistance, global labour history, multitudes, empire, new social movements, ecofeminism, post-colonialism, post-Marxism, post-capitalism, etc.) have, in terms of intellectual fashion, become hegemonic.[5] The role played by academic journals in this displacement has not been negligible.

Curiously, academic publishing, and the respective weight given to Marxist/non-Marxist contributions, together with the reasons for such editorial privileging/depriviliging over time, remain possibly the most under-researched and undiscussed topics in the social sciences. This is ironic, given their centrality to the formation and reproduction of intellectual and political discourse; in a sense it is also an understandable absence, in view of the discomfort felt by many senior academics when an attempt is made to examine their political credentials and those of purportedly leftist publications. Easy to forget is what can happen – and indeed has happened relatively recently – when such a political shift occurs in the wider society: for example, how in the 1990s many Marxists were dismissed from their academic jobs following the break-up of Yugoslavia ('A doctor of philosophy as a homeless person, a doctor of sociology as a horoscope writer, a journalist as a fisherman: these are the fates of Croatian Marxists after the "End of History"').[6] In such circumstances, political

---

but identity politics. This recuperation of an essentialist peasant culture/economy leaves intact the existing class structure and reproduces the populist mobilizing discourse of the political right. It is, in short, a conservative form of anti-capitalism.

5   In many ways, the 'new' populist postmodernism adheres to a Tolstoyan concept of peasant society, as is evident from the following (Tolstoy, 1905: 273): 'The only books that are comprehensible to the people and according to their taste are not such are written for the people, but such as have their origins in the people, namely, fairy-tales, proverbs, collections of songs, legends.' In what is the mirror image of the Marxist view, Tolstoy seems to imply that the rural masses are unable to transcend their own ideology, being anchored permanently in longstanding discourses that never change and cannot be altered. The latter interpretation is little different from the postmodern view of culture, with the difference that postmodernism *celebrates* this inability-to-transcend as the 'authenticity' of grassroots popular culture. As has been argued elsewhere (Brass, 2003), the conservative nature of this celebration by the 'new' populist postmodernism of existing (= 'traditional') plebeian forms – invariably in the name of an empowering 'from below' process of subaltern 'resistance' – is that it simultaneously consecrates and declares immutable the class system which gives rise to such culture in the first place, very much as Tolstoy – an aristocratic landowner – did in Russia.

6   See 'The Lost Marxists: what happened to the academics made jobless by communism's collapse?', *New Statesman*, 23 November 2015, where – among many others – the following instances are recorded: 'Zvonko Šundov, a doctor of philosophy, got his last pay cheque 24 years ago … The years he spent as probably the most educated homeless person in Croatia have not broken him … In 1991 [he] was fired from [his academic post and] has

realignment signalled in journals and books can be seen as projecting the same kind of warning as the canary in the mineshaft.

It is testimony to *Critical Sociology* that it is one of the few social science publications still prepared to engage in debate about the basic theoretical and political issues central to Marxist theory – a transition to socialism remaining on its agenda – at a time when other purportedly leftist journals are no longer interested either in these issues or this kind of transformation, and indeed have closed down any attempts to discuss them. Paradoxically, *Critical Sociology* is itself quite broad church where theory and politics are concerned, an editorial approach consistent with a scholarly commitment to debate. As a Marxist-with-an-open-mind, Fasenfest has managed to achieve that most difficult of editorial balancing acts, obtaining a political mix of contributions/contributors that works, a theoretical/political inclusiveness which is rarely encountered elsewhere. This is not to say that there are no standards governing what is published: much rather the only criterion invoked editorially is that submissions be intellectually rigorous, displaying research endeavour, knowledge about the topic covered plus debates about this, and skilled argumentation. So many social science journals fail to sustain even a modicum of this approach, particularly once a new editorial regime takes over.

Underestimated, therefore, is both the fact and the outcome of what might be termed 'journal capture'.[7] A case in point is what occurred at one social science journal in 2008, when the editorial of a publication with a hitherto Marxist orientation (not absolute, however, as submissions following a populist line appeared from time to time) was replaced by one favouring a populist agenda.[8] Since 2009, however, not just Marxist critiques of populism but also

---

    never returned to the classroom – because his job no longer exists. He taught Marxism … Mira Ljubić Lorger, who has a doctorate in sociology, is another Marxist academic for whom the collapse of communism had dramatic personal consequences. Until 1990 she worked at the Social Sciences Research Centre in Split, a university institute which was, in the eyes of Croatia's new anti-communist government, a 'hotbed of Marxism'.

7   At times such journals resemble nothing so much as a collection of little kingdoms, each one of which becomes the domain of an individual warlord and his retainers, all of whom jealously guard access to their newly acquired property. For their part, publishers don't seem to mind, so long as the new regime brings in a larger audience, which it does by following fashion and discarding controversy.

8   The publication in question was *The Journal of Peasant Studies*. Much populist discourse, historically and currently, is simply about the desirability of reproducing a category of empowered petty commodity producers, who may or may not own the land they cultivate, a crucial distinction that often remains unclarified. This obscures the presence of what are in many rural contexts antagonistic class positions. Petty commodity producers who employ labour can be – and often are – as harsh employers as a landlord, not least because they in turn are subject to the most acute forms of market competition (and thus

their contributions to debate have been marginalized.[9] With much the same kind of braggadocio as the mid-1970s dismissal by cliometric historiography of earlier interpretations which categorized slavery as oppressive/exploitative, current populist academics declare Marxism banished from debate about the role of peasants in development.[10] This populist view is based on a combination of shortcomings: an absence of knowledge about what constitutes Marxism; an unquestioning adherence to populist ideology; and – like cliometric historiography – a failure to interrogate the methods and assumptions informing both its own epistemology and that of the sources cited.[11] By contrast, Marxist views continue to flourish in the journal and book series edited by Fasenfest, where critiques informed by this approach still have an important place. This has ensured not just that Marxism retains a central position in social science debate, as indeed it should, but also that populist claims are challenged.

3 Themes

It is clear from the individual contributions to this volume that Fasenfest is held in high esteem by his colleagues and friends, not least for his editorial role as an enabler of scholarship. This *festschrift* volume consists of fifteen chapters, including an introduction, an interview with the honorand, and a postscript. It is divided into three parts, the first of which is formed of context-specific contributions (Chapters 2–7), and contains accounts that not only celebrate

---

have to keep their costs to a minimum). For their part, landless workers seek to improve both pay and conditions, and for this reason are frequently in conflict with employers per se. This distinction is obscured by conflating petty commodity producers and landless workers in the same populist category of 'the rural poor'.

9 Details about this are provided elsewhere (Brass, 2023).

10 See, for example, the erroneous claim (Levien, Watts, and Hairong: 2018: 853–54) that 'much of this debate – and in fact a good deal of the earlier peasant studies research of the 1960s and 1970s – has reached something of an impasse. In part the impasse arises because new empirical work addressing the complex contemporary patterns and conjunctures of global agrarian capitalism, and because new and generative theoretical reconstructions of Marxism itself, offer exciting new analytical horizons.' What are termed 'exciting new analytical horizons' frequently turn out to be nothing of the sort, recycling old populist tropes recuperated unknowingly by present-day adherents of the same theory.

11 Problematic methods were central to the forensic dismantling by Sutch (1975) of the revisionist case about the non-oppressive nature of plantation slavery in the antebellum south made by the cliometric historiography of Fogel and Engerman (1974). For a critique of methods used in support of similar kinds of claims made by agrarian populism concerning Russia and India, see Brass (2020).

the achievements of Fasenfest himself, but also delineate his contribution to the study of Japan and China. The second part (Chapters 8–14) is composed of essays dealing mainly with theory, Marxist and non-Marxist, an additional field of interest where Fasenfest is concerned. The final part (Chapter 15) comprises a single contribution returning to the issue of critique, a theme that surfaces in many of the earlier chapters and is again a subject in which Fasenfest has an interest.

Part 1 commences with a conversation that places the honorand in his own time and space. Accordingly, Chapter 2 consists of an interview with David Fasenfest, conducted by Raju Das and Robert Latham, covering the salient aspects of the honorand's experience, both as an academic and as editor of the journal *Critical Sociology* and the two book series published by Brill. Traced is the history of Fasenfest's peripatetic career, his escape from the confines of the academic discipline, his approach to sociological research, and the manner in which he has built up both journal and book series, the objectives driving this process, and the international network of scholars established as a result.

Lauren Langman pens a short but personal tribute to David Fasenfest in Chapter 3, recounting how in his editorial capacity he has assisted many of those who submit articles to *Critical Sociology*. Outlining this input to and influence over his own work, Langman highlights the provision by Fasenfest of the kind of mentoring assistance that is rarely made available, and equally rarely acknowledged where editorial work is concerned. Over the years, moreover, Fasenfest has ensured that *Critical Sociology* has ascended the hierarchy of academic journal influence to the position it occupies currently, a – if not the – major publication in the sphere of the social sciences. An additional, and important, point made by Langman is that all this has come at a personal cost to the honorand: Fasenfest has poured much of his efforts into the work of others at the expense of his own writing, again an aspect of journal and book editing that goes unrecognized.

Many of the same points surface in Chapter 4, where Rodney Coates traces some of the issues raised and covered by Fasenfest over the years, underlining thereby not just their variety but also the political consistency of the approach. Emphasized is how, in his editorial role, Fasenfest has supported a sociology that is politically committed, the focus of which is on social justice, in the process challenging the fashionable and pervasive nostrums of neoliberalism that underwrite capitalist expansion based on *laissez-faire* policies. The impact of the latter is assessed in relation to the US over the post-war era, both domestically in terms of issues such as race, migration, sexuality, and poverty, and also internationally, where an undeniably imperial project has licensed foreign interventions and conflicts across the globe. A result, internally as externally, has been the rise of populism, as people everywhere increasingly perceive the hollowness of promises made by their elected politicians. Significance is also attached to the negative impact all this has had on academia, in terms not just of funding cutbacks in the social sciences but also in the kinds of topics deemed suitable for research. All the while, and against the grain, Fasenfest has continued to promote a radical agenda, advocating and conducting the study of emancipatory political alternatives to the accumulation process.

In Chapter 5 Ngai Pun assesses and also celebrates the approach, contribution, and influence of Fasenfest to current sociological research and scholarship informing the study of the Global South generally, and China in particular. Outlined is how a focus on Marxism as a useful lens through which to examine the political, social, and economic changes occurring in these contexts has been – and is – encouraged by Fasenfest in his role as editor of *Critical Sociology* and the Brill book series. This sort of engagement with Marxist theory is expressly important with respect to analyses dealing with Hong Kong, China, and other Asian nations, not least in challenging Eurocentric discourse, although Marxist views about European capitalism are still considered important guides to the broader patterns that accumulation may take. Of special relevance is an understanding of the contribution made by neoliberal policies to the interrelated processes of wealth concentration, income inequality, and poverty throughout the Global South. Where China's foreign policy is concerned, therefore, not the least important issue raised is the extent to which its development path, involving as it does programmes such as the Belt and Road Initiative, will manage to avoid repeating the exploitative/oppressive history of European colonialism. Domestically, Chinese infrastructural capitalism emphasizes combined public/private enterprise, overseen and coordinated by the state apparatus; although this can be seen as socialism with 'special characteristics', it is nevertheless that such an approach has generated much working-class opposition.

A coercive form of conversion therapy exercised by the pre-war Japanese state is examined by Hideo Aoki in Chapter 6. The process known as *tenkō* (changing direction), one that was designed to secure and embed a change of mind in its subject, was targeted principally at members of the Japanese communist party. The latter were arrested, prosecuted, imprisoned, and tortured in large numbers, during the course of which state authorities submitted victims to an enforced re-education programme ('thought war'), the object of which was to 'turn' communists by making them discard their existing beliefs and then adopt one that were antithetical. This entailed a transfer of political allegiance from socialism and revolution to an endorsement of *kokutai*, or upholding private property, the Japanese state, nationalism, and the Emperor system.

In this way, the communist self was reconstituted as an imperial subject, an object pursued both inside and outside prison. Coercion, reinforced by appeals to family, nation, and Emperor, was aided by difficulties within the communist party; under Stalin, Comintern required Japanese communists immediately to oppose the Emperor system and imperialism, notwithstanding the lack of popular support for such a programme. This generated ideological uncertainty within the communist membership, aiding the *tenkō* process.

In Chapter 7, Ricardo A. Dello Buono traces the journal history of what started out as the *Insurgent Sociologist* and became, under Fasenfest's long-term editorial role, *Critical Sociology*. Emerging from a background of critical/alternative/radical scholarship in sociology, the *Insurgent Sociologist* was born out of a dual opposition: both to the war in Vietnam, and to the kind of social science approach linked to the American Sociological Association. Its founding editor, Albert Szymanski, published Marxist theory gaining attention at the time, including the work of Harry Braverman, Poulantzas, Althusser, and Erik Olin Wright. However, the downturn in revolutionary politics after 1968 coincided with (and may have led to) the death of notable radical sociologists (among them Poulantzas and Szymanski himself), due in part to political and institutional difficulties encountered in academia. Like other initially radical journals, *Insurgent Sociologist* experienced a similar move away from its leftist politics, due in part to a shrinking readership and commercial viability. This led to the search for a new editor and publisher, from which emerged Fasenfest who, having moved from economics to sociology, pursued interests in critical urban development, and Sage. Since that date, *Critical Sociology* (as the *Insurgent Sociologist* had now become) under his editorship has flourished and consolidated its reputation as a leading sociological journal.

The first contribution in Part 2 is by Michael Burawoy, who in Chapter 8 considers how the broad tendency currently towards decolonization – questioning the past oppressions based on race, gender, and slavery – are generating a process of institutional introspection, not least in academia, where it is leading to calls for decolonizing the canons, or re-examining the meaning of what is taught, and why. Questioning the applicability of universals, which now extends to sociological theory, requires a fourfold response taking the form of restoration, rejection, revolution, and reconstruction. Some, like postcolonial theorists, simply reject the canon, while others advocate that to the list of canonical figures of Weber, Durkheim, and Marx – privileged historically by US sociologists – is now added the name and ideas of W.E.B. Du Bois. However, since the canon is foundational, its principles (freedom, equality, solidarity) cannot be abandoned, only reinterpreted and reconstructed. Hence the current focus of sociological theory can be complemented and amended by being put into conversation with Du Bois and others. In China, where the canon is still much influenced by Western sociological theory, this challenge might offer a reflexive approach combining global, historical, moral, and utopian perspectives, with the object of reconstructing sociology as a public science, by and for everyone.

Addressed by Robert Latham in Chapter 9 is the political question of what kind of anti-capitalist mobilisation is possible nowadays, given the way the capitalist system itself has developed and changed over time. History shows not just that capital possesses a capacity to wage counter-struggle against those opposed to its effects and oppressions, but learns from such a process, developing and deploying its multiple defences and weapons accordingly. The object of capital has been, and remains, to frustrate/prevent any advance leading to socialism, and thus toward its own demise. For this reason, the stronger the opposition to capitalism, the stronger becomes the counter-struggle of the latter, conducted historically and currently against any/all opponents. From the post-war era onwards, such counteraction has taken many shapes, extending from opinion-forming 'soft' power (sportswashing, greenwashing, stakeholder capitalism), via disinformation/disruption (surveillance, cyber/digital and psychological warfare) to violence. The anarchy of the market notwithstanding, this has involved the transformation of initially progressive developments (the internet) into projects supportive of accumulation. This can be resisted only by internationally coordinated social movements, combining different strategies from general strikes to state capture. Given that capital is now an international order, struggle against it must of necessity itself possess a global reach.

Drawing a contrast between on the one hand the focus of Marxism on the urban industrial proletariat in metropolitan capitalism as the subject of history, and on the other the fact that as a model of political and economic growth it has generated larger political support in the less-developed rural periphery, Raju Das in Chapter 10 asks whether Marxist theory about revolution and socialism is still applicable to the latter sort of context. The continued relevance of a Marxist approach lies in the way core and periphery combine dialectically to form a single economic process, a dynamic enabling the reproduction of what is now a global accumulation process without meaningful boundaries. For this reason, it is possible to analyse both periphery and core with the same Marxist concepts. Furthermore, it is in the periphery that capital searches for ever cheaper sources of labour-power, and such spaces are the locus where accumulation is able to operate super-exploitation, since wages are below levels needed to cover the reproduction of the worker. As important today on the global periphery as in the core, therefore, is the potential for political opposition to capitalism. Without support from petty commodity producers in the periphery, workers there cannot effect revolutionary change. Nor can the latter be achieved without the larger political unity between workers in the centre and those at the periphery.

Focussing on many of the same concerns, the wide-ranging conspectus by Alfredo Saad-Filho in Chapter 11 underlines how many seemingly disparate socio-economic problems are an effect of *laissez-faire* capitalism, emphasizing thereby that currently there is no area of social life anywhere in the world untouched by the negative impact of neoliberalism. An integrated analysis reveals the extent of the linkages between underdevelopment, stagnation, financialisation, and economic crises on the one hand, and on the other systemic damage to politics, health, social reproduction, and the environment. Contradictions stemming from neoliberalism involve a double paradox: economic and political, in that free market depends on a strong state and undermines democracy. Under increasingly authoritarian neoliberal regimes, therefore, deindustrialisation, employment precarity, declining wages/conditions, welfare erosion, have been combined with and accompanied by increasing wealth/income disparities, declining political representation/participation, and rising instances of nationalism, racism, and fascism. So much so that neoliberalism has in effect spread the process of dispossession from the means of production to the means of life. What this in turn suggests is the requirement for an alternative to the project of capital accumulation, one consists of a democratic economic strategy, based on state planning, sustainable growth, employment, welfare and basic needs provision.

In Chapter 12, Tom Brass outlines how and why an epistemological and political shift in the meaning of the industrial reserve army, an important concept of political economy generally and Marxism in particular, has taken place from the nineteenth century onwards. For early Marxists, therefore, an effect of the globalization of the labour regime was that, by encouraging competition for jobs, surplus labour could regulate the market on behalf of capital, keeping wages down, and discouraging class solidarity and organization. Although recognizing the deleterious impact on worker unemployment and impoverishment of a growing industrial reserve, liberals such as Beveridge advocated greater state intervention (regulation, social insurance) in order to save capitalism and prevent socialism. Subsequent leftists such as Kalecki, Sweezy, and Dobb also regarded the industrial reserve as negative, warning that because capital opposed full employment, it would always seek access to foreign labour, an objective increasingly made possible by globalization and deregulation. Currently, the latter permits employers either to outsource production to where labour is cheaper, or insource labour itself, allowing them to restructure their workforce. By contrast, much postmodern theory views the industrial reserve as unproblematically benign and positive, arguing that as open-door migration is a 'human right', borders – a legacy of colonialism – should be abolished. Unlike Marxism, which perceives the industrial reserve as disempowering for the existing workforce, a weapon used against the latter by employers, postmodernism regards it as a revolutionary source of anti-capitalist mobilisation.

Examining the connection across time and space between capitalism and the notion of identity difference, Kevin Cox in Chapter 13 emphasizes its significance to Marxist geography, arguing that the capitalism/difference relationship is not contingent but central. Underlying identity politics, the idea of difference is problematic when viewed in terms of class and labour organization. Crucially, it is capitalism which creates and reproduces its many manifestations, and the way the latter change. Hence all the forms of difference that permeate the working class – along the lines of ethnicity, gender, division of labour, and citizenship – are not innate, but linked both conceptually and ideologically to the kinds of identity fostered by the capitalist state, not least those of national belonging and claims about its egalitarian nature. Aspects such as culture, values, and work – all of which are the product of a totality of social processes – combine and recombine to ensure that national identity matters, leading to circumstances where old differences simply acquire new impetus.

Utilizing a binary opposition between populations that are housed and those that are homeless, in Chapter 14 Mahito Hayashi examines Marxist/neo-Marxist contributions to long-standing and more recent debates about city development through the lens of urban geography, with particular reference to the work of Engels and Lefebvre, among others. This entails a consideration of the multiple ways in which ideological construction of meanings have been and are applied to urban space in general, plus the related and complex understandings informing its political interpretation. The latter concern methods of local/national state regulation/deregulation, capitalist housing regimes, and social control in particular. These processes combine, and are contextualised ethnographically, to form disjunctions between housed/homeless perceptions of space and their meaning in urban Japan. The analysis concludes by reflecting on the prospects for politically radical social movements composed of relative surplus populations that are 'the homeless.'

Finally, in Part 3, Chapter 15, Tom Brass considers both the fact of and the reasons for the vanishing from academia in general, and the social sciences in particular, of critique based on Marxist theory. Despite appearances to the contrary, Marxism appears under siege in journals and books, its concepts and framework deemed irrelevant or Eurocentric when applied to explanations of present-day accumulation, as such challenged or discarded even by publications ostensibly sympathetic to its aims. Marxist analysis is increasingly replaced by supposedly fresh paradigms, a change driven in part by academic competition, involving a search for relevance, popularity, and funding. Such non- or anti-Marxist alternatives, often formulated by ex-Marxists (Laclau, Mouffe), deprivilege class, revolution, and socialism, advocating instead a 'new' populist postmodern approach privileging discourse about national/ethnic politics. This is justified by postmodern theory on the grounds that, as these are innate kinds of identity, such authentic ideologies are consequently more progressive and empowering for those at the grassroots. It is argued that this epistemological shift can be traced, again in part, to the post-1960s entry into academic posts of Marxists, many of whom transferred their political allegiance to the 'new' populist postmodernism, misinterpreting hegemony exercised by 'the people' as unmediated progressive voice.

References

David Fasenfest: A Select Bibliography

Books

Fasenfest D and Meyer P (eds.) (1991) *Comparative Politics of Local Economic Development*, Policy Studies Organization, Greenwood Press.

Fasenfest D (ed.) (1993) *Community Economic Development: Policy Formation in the U.S. and U.K.*, London: Macmillan Press and New York: St. Martin's Press.

Fasenfest D and Reese L (eds.) (2004) *Critical Perspectives on Local Development Policy Evaluation*, Detroit: Wayne State University Press.

Fasenfest D (ed.) (2009) *Engaging Social Justice: Critical Studies of 21st Century Social Transformation*, Leiden: Brill. Paperback edition published by Haymarket 2011.

Fasenfest D and Dello Buono R (eds.) (2010) *Social Change, Resistance and Social Practice*, Leiden: Brill. Paperback edition published by Haymarket 2012.

Fasenfest D (ed.) (2022) *Marx Matters*, Leiden: Brill. Choice Award, Outstanding Academic Title of 2022. Paperback edition published by Haymarket 2023.

Articles, Reviews, Book Chapters

Fasenfest D (1978) China's Post Mao Economic Future, in *China's Post Mao Economy, Joint Economic Committee of the U.S. House and Senate*, Vol. 1, January, pp. 3–47. (with Robert Dernberger).

Fasenfest D (1983) Gender and Class Formation: Female Clerical Workers, *Review of Radical Political Economy*, Special Issue on the Political Economy of Women, 16:1 (Spring): 69–103. (with Heidi Gottfried).

Fasenfest D (1986) Using Incentives to Achieve Social Objectives, *Policy Studies Review Symposium on Markets and Public Policy*, 5:3(Feb): 634 642.

Fasenfest D (1986) Community Politics and Urban Redevelopment: Poletown, Detroit and General Motors, *Urban Affairs Quarterly*, 22:1(Sept): 101 123.

Fasenfest D (1987) Urban Policies, Social Goals, and Producer Incentives: Are Market Mechanisms and Policy Objectives Compatible? in Richard C. Hula (ed.), *Market Based Public Policy*, pp. 137–157, New York: Macmillan.

Fasenfest D (1988) Municipal Capital Budgeting and Public Policy, *Proceedings of the Second Conference on Interdisciplinary Perspectives in Accounting*, (July): 2:155–80. (with Penelope Ciancanelli).

Fasenfest D (1988) Public Costs and Private Benefits: The Pitfalls of Capital Budgeting for Reindustrialization, *Journal of Urban Affairs*, 10:3:291 307. (with Penelope Ciancanelli).

Fasenfest D (1989) Race, Class, and Community Redevelopment: A Comparison of Detroit's Poletown and Chicago's Goose Island, in Jerry Lembcke (ed.), *Race, Class and Urban Social Change*, pp. 107–133, Greenwich, CT: JAI Press.

Fasenfest D (1989) A Typology of Suburban Economic Development Policy Orientations, *Economic Development Quarterly*, 3: 4 (Nov): 301–311. (with John Pelissero).

Fasenfest D (1989) The Comparative Politics of Local Economic Development: Introduction to the Symposium, *Policy Studies Review* (now *Review of Policy Research*), 10:2:79–80. (with Peter Meyer).

Fasenfest D (1991) Comparative Local Economic Development: Policy Emulation and Transfer, Symposium on the Comparative Politics of Local Economic Development, *Policy Studies Review* (now *Review of Policy Research*), 10:2:80–86.

Fasenfest D (1993) Local Policy Formation: Setting an Agenda for Development, in David Fasenfest (ed.), *Community Economic Development: Policy Formation in the U.S. and U.K.*, pp. 3–13, London: Macmillan Press and New York: St. Martin's Press.

Fasenfest D (1993) On the Possibility of Proactive Community Development, in Peter B. Meyer (ed.), *Comparative Studies in Local Economic Development: Problems in Policy Implementation*, pp. 169–178, Greenwich, CT: Greenwood Press.

Fasenfest D (1993) Cui Bono? Public Subsidies and Business Locations Strategies, in Charles Craypo and Bruce Nissen (eds.), *Grand Designs: Corporate Strategies and Their Effects on Unions, Workers and Communities*, pp. 119–137, Ithaca, NY: Cornell University ILR Press.

Fasenfest D (1994) Changes in Occupation and Income, 1979–1989: An Analysis of the Impact of Race and Place, *International Journal of Contemporary Sociology*, 31:2:203–233. (with Robert Perrucci).

Fasenfest D (1995) (Re) Structuring Urban Poverty: The Impact of Globalization on Its Extent and Spatial Concentration, in Dan Chekki (ed.) *Research in Community*

Sociology, Vol V: Urban Poverty, pp. 35–61, Greenwich, CT: JAI Press. (with Jens Dangschat).

Fasenfest D (1996) More of the Same: A Research Note on Local Development Practices Over Time, *Economic Development Quarterly*, 10:3:280–289. (with Laura Reese).

Fasenfest D (1996) Local Economic Development Policy in Canada and the US: Similarities and Differences, *Canadian Journal of Urban Research*, 5:1:97–118. (with Laura Reese).

Fasenfest D (1997) *Review: Coal, Class and Community: The United Mineworkers of New Zealand 1880–1960*, by Len Richardson, 1995, Auckland: Auckland University Press, in *Capital and Class*, 63:139–141.

Fasenfest D (1997) Economic Development Yes, But on Whose Behalf? in Richard Bingham and Robert Mier (eds.) *Dilemma of Urban Economic Development*, pp. 284–288, Newbury Park, CA: Sage Publications.

Fasenfest D (1997) Values, Exchange and the Social Economy: Framework and Paradigm Shift in Urban Policy, *International Journal of Urban and Regional Research*, 21:1:7–22. (with Penelope Ciancanelli and Laura Reese).

Fasenfest D (1997) Value, Valuation, Evaluation: Limits of Theory on Evaluation, *Economic Development Quarterly*, 11:3:217–221. (with Laura Reese).

Fasenfest D (1997) What Works Best? Values and the Evaluation of Local Economic Develop Policy, *Economic Development Quarterly*, 11:3:195–207. (with Laura Reese) Reprinted in John Blair and Laura Reese, eds., *Approaches to Economic Development*, pp. 278–292, Thousand Oaks: Sage Publications.

Fasenfest D (1998) Cities Down Under: Urban Development Politics and Policies in Australia, *Review of The Perils of Urban Consolidation*, by Patrick N. Troy, 1996, Sydney: The Federation Press, *Australian Cities: Issues, Strategies and Policies for Urban Australia in the 1990s*, Patrick N. Troy (ed.), 1995, Cambridge: Cambridge University Press, and *Technological Change and the City*, Patrick N. Troy (ed.), 1995, Sydney: The Federation Press, in *Environment and Planning C: Society and Space*, 16:3:373–378.

Fasenfest D (1999) Public Policy and Poverty, in Larry Joseph (ed.) *Families, Poverty and Welfare Reform in Illinois*, pp. 93–98, Chicago: University of Chicago Center for Urban Research and Policy Studies and the University of Illinois Press. (with Cedric Herring).

Fasenfest D (1999) Critical Perspectives on Local Economic Development Policy Evaluation, *Economic Development Quarterly*, 13:1:3–8. (with Laura Reese).

Fasenfest D (2000) Border Crossing: Local and Regional Economic Development on the US/Canadian Border, *International Journal of Economic Development*, 2:3:355–359. (with Laura Reese).

Fasenfest D (2001) Revival and Change in the Automobile Industry of Southeastern Michigan in Ralf Dahlberg (ed.), *Entrepreneurship, Firm Growth and Regional*

Development in the New Economic Geography, pp. 257–282, Uddevalla, Sweden: University of Trollhattan/Uddevalla. (with Jim Jacobs).

Fasenfest D (2002) Review: Stories Employers Tell: Race, Skill and Hiring in America, by Phillip Moss and Chris Tilly, 2001, New York: Russell Sage Foundation, in *Contemporary Sociology*, 31:5:512–513.

Fasenfest D (2002) The State of Local Economic Development Policy, in *The 2002 Municipal Year Book*, pp 5–9, ICMA: Washington. (with Laura Reese and Raymond Rosenfeld).

Fasenfest D (2002) Preparation for The New Economy: What the Supply Side Tells Us, in Ralf Dahlberg (ed.), *Regional Economies in Transition*, pp. 233–246, Uddevalla, Sweden: University of Trollhattan/Uddevalla. (with Jim Jacobs).

Fasenfest D (2002) Region und Unternehmen in der globalen Wirtschaft: Das Beispiel Detroit und Ford Motor Company, in Ulrich Muekenberger and Marcus Menzl (eds.) *Der Global Player und das Territorium*, pp. 155–170, Leske + Budrich: Opladen.

Fasenfest D (2003) Planning for Development: An Evaluation of the Economic Development District Planning Process, *Economic Development Quarterly*. 17:3:264–279. (with Laura Reese).

Fasenfest D (2003) The Automobile Industry of Southeast Michigan: An Anatomy of Change and Transition, *Small Business Economics Journal*, 21/2 (August): 153–172, (with Jim Jacobs).

Fasenfest D (2004) Evaluating Local Development Outcomes: Lessons from a Critical Perspective, in L. Reese and D. Fasenfest (eds.), *Critical Perspectives on Local Development Policy Evaluation*, Detroit: Wayne State University Press. (with Laura Reese).

Fasenfest D (2004) Planning for a Change: An Assessment of EDA's Local Planning Initiative, in L. Reese and D. Fasenfest (eds.), *Critical Perspectives on Local Development Policy Evaluation*, Detroit: Wayne State University Press. (with Laura Reese).

Fasenfest D (2004) Autonomy and Insecurity: The Status of Women Workers in the United States, *JOSEI ROUNDOU KENKYU* <46> (*Bulletin of the Society for the Study of Working Women*) Tokyo. (with Heidi Gottfried, Stephen Rose and Heidi Hartmann).

Fasenfest D (2004) Expectations for opportunities following prison education: A discussion of race and gender, *Journal of Correctional Education*, 55: 1: 24–39. (with Patricia Case).

Fasenfest D (2005) Living Together: A New Look at Racial and Ethnic Integration in Metropolitan Neighborhoods, 1990–2000, in A. Berube, B. Katz, and R. Lang, (eds.), *Redefining Urban and Suburban America: Evidence from Census 2000, Volume III*. Washington: Brookings. (with Jason Booza, and Kurt Metzger).

Fasenfest D (2005) Providing Educational Support for Female Ex-inmates: Project PROVE as a Model for Reintegration, *Journal of Correctional Education*, 56: 2: 146–157. (with Case, Patricia, Rosemary Sarri, and Anna Phillips).

Fasenfest D (2005) Enforcement Mechanisms Discouraging Black–American Presence in Suburban Detroit, *International Journal of Urban and Regional Research*, 29: 4: 960–971. (with Tim Bates).

Fasenfest D (2005) A Model for a Pro-Active and Progressive University-Community Partnership, *Professional Development: The International Journal of Continuing Social Work Education*, 8: 2/3: 24–39. (with Larry Gant).

Fasenfest D (2006) Critical Sociology, in Clifton D. Bryant and Dennis L. Peck (eds.), *Handbook of 21st Century Sociology*, Sage Publications: California.

Fasenfest D (2007) Race, Ethnicity and Place: New Patterns of Integration in Metropolitan Neighborhoods, 1970–2000, in Philip J. Davies and Iwan Morgan, (eds.) *Americas Americans: The Populations of the United States*, London: Institute for the Study of the Americas Press. (with Jason Booza).

Fasenfest D (2009) Scholarship from a Critical Perspective, in Graham Cassano and Richard Dello Buono (eds.) *Crisis, Politics and Critical Sociology*, Brill Academic Press: Leiden and Boston. (with Rhonda Levine).

Fasenfest D (2009) Review: The Good Temp, by Vicky Smith and Esther B. Neuwirth, Ithaca, NY: Cornell University Press, in *Work and Occupations*, 36:1.

Fasenfest D (2010) A Touch of Class, with Layers of Race and a Sprinkling of Gender, *Critical Sociology*, 36:1:5–8 (Jan).

Fasenfest D (2010) Global Economy, Local Calamity, *Critical Sociology*, 36:2:195–200 (Mar).

Fasenfest D (2010) The Global Crisis and the Politics of Change, *Critical Sociology*, 36:3:363–368 (May).

Fasenfest D (2010) A Political Economy of Knowledge Production, *Critical Sociology* 36:4:483–487 (July).

Fasenfest D (2010) Neoliberalism, Globalization and the Capitalist World Order, *Critical Sociology*, 36:5:627–631 (Sept).

Fasenfest D (2010) Government, Governing, and Governance, *Critical Sociology*, 36:6:771–774 (Nov).

Fasenfest D (2011) Capitalism's Shell Game, *Critical Sociology*, 37:1:3–6 (Jan).

Fasenfest D (2011) The Return to Culture Wars and the Politics of Culture, *Critical Sociology*, 37:2:147–150 (Mar). (with Graham Cassano).

Fasenfest D (2011) Good for Capitalists, Not So Much for Capitalism, *Critical Sociology*, 37:3: 259–262 (May).

Fasenfest D (2011) Terrorism, Neo-Liberalism and Political Rhetoric, *Critical Sociology*, 37:4:379–382 (July).

Fasenfest D (2011) Assault on Workers' Rights, *Critical Sociology*, 37:5:507–511 (Sept).

Fasenfest D (2011) The Politics of Economic Change: Are We in a Brave New World? *Critical Sociology*, 37:6:715–717 (Nov).

Fasenfest D (2011) Review: The Elgar Companion to Social Economics, John B. Davis and Wilfred Dolfsma (eds). Edward Elgar: Cheltenham, UK and Northampton, MA, USA, in *International Sociology*, 26:2:225–228.

Fasenfest D (2012) The 21st Century Urban Landscape: Plus ça change, *Critical Sociology*, 38:1:3–5 (Jan).

Fasenfest D (2012) The Importance of a Perspective from Abroad, *Critical Sociology*, 38:2:147–149 (Mar).

Fasenfest D (2012) Globalization and its Discontents, *Critical Sociology*, 38:3:343–346 (May).

Fasenfest D (2012) Racial Politics and the Right, *Critical Sociology*, 38:4:463–465 (July).

Fasenfest D (2012) Where Will Change Come From? *Critical Sociology*, 38:5:623–625 (Sept).

Fasenfest D (2012) Political Leadership and Social Transformation, *Critical Sociology*, 38:6:771–772 (Nov).

Fasenfest D (2013) Old Wine, Old Bottles, *Critical Sociology*, 39:1:3–6 (Jan).

Fasenfest D (2013) Marxist Sociology and Human Rights, in David L. Brunsma, et al. (eds) *Handbook of Sociology and Human Rights*, pp 440–448, Herndon, VA: Paradigm Publishers.

Fasenfest D (2013) Review: Nancy DiTomaso (2013) The American Non-dilemma: Racial Inequality without Racism, New York, NY: Russell Sage Foundation, in *Choice*,51: 1 (September).

Fasenfest D (2013) Neoliberalism, 2013, in Vicki Smith (ed) *The Sociology of Work: An Encyclopedia*, pp 619–621, SAGE.

Fasenfest D (2013) Globalization, 2013, in Vicki Smith (ed) *The Sociology of Work: An Encyclopedia*, pp 333–337, SAGE.

Fasenfest D (2013) The Health of Societies and Bodies, *Critical Sociology*, 39:3:315–316 (May).

Fasenfest D (2013) Profits of Doom, *Critical Sociology*, 39:5:651–653 (Sept).

Fasenfest D (2014) Critical Sociology after 40 Years: Looking Back, Looking Forward, *Critical Sociology*, 40: 1: 3–6 (January).

Fasenfest D (2014) Review: DETROIT: Race Riots, Racial Conflicts, and Efforts to Bridge the Racial Divide, by Joe T. Darden and Richard W. Thomas, in *City and Community*, 13:1 (March).

Fasenfest D (2014) Global Economy, Global Dialog, *Critical Sociology*, 40: 2 (March): 171–172.

Fasenfest D (2014) Considerations on Submitting and Getting Published, *Critical Sociology*, 40: 3 (May): 323–325.

Fasenfest D (2014) Review: Roithmayr Daria (2014) Reproducing Racism: How Everyday Choices Lock In White Advantage, New York, NY: New York University, in *Choice* 51: 11 (July).

Fasenfest D (2014) The Legacy of Debt, *Critical Sociology*, 40: 5 (September): 651–653.

Fasenfest D (2014) Dangerous Times, *Critical Sociology*, 40: 6 (November): 811–813.

Fasenfest D (2014) Review: Eric Avila (2014) The Folklore of the Freeway: Race and Revolt in the Modernist City, Minneapolis, MN: University of Minnesota Press, in *Choice* 52: 4 (Dec).

Fasenfest D (2014) Foreword, in Mohammad Chaichian, *Empire and Walls: Globalization, Migration, and Colonial Domination*, Leiden: Brill, pp xix–xxi.

Fasenfest D (2015) Western Societies and Islam, *Critical Sociology*, 41:1 (January): 3–4.

Fasenfest D (2015) Social Sustainability and Urban Inequality: Detroit and the Ravages of Neoliberalism, pp 15–27, in Faranak Miraftab, Ken Salo and David Wilson (eds) *Cities and Inequalities in a Global and Neoliberal World*, London: Routledge.

Fasenfest D (2015) Descent into the Maelstrom, *Critical Sociology*, 41:4/5: 575–578.

Fasenfest D (2015) Race and the Politics of Institutional Violence, *Critical Sociology* 41:6: 825–827.

Fasenfest D (2015) Review: Aaron Schutz and Mike Miller (2015) People Power: the community organizing tradition of Saul Alinsky, Nashville, TN: Vanderbilt University Press, in *Choice* 53: 1 (Sept).

Fasenfest D (2015) Review Essay: The Strange Fruit of Racist Violence, *Critical Sociology*, 41:6:913–920 (September).

Fasenfest D (2015) Review: Trouble at Work, by Ralph Fevre (2012), Duncan Lewis, Amanda Robinson and Trevor Jones. London and New York, NY: Bloomsbury Academic, in *Contemporary Sociology*, 44:5:659–661.

Fasenfest D (2015) Dumbing and Numbing of the American Electorate (with Naida Simon), *Critical Sociology* 41: 7/8: 999–1002.

Fasenfest D (2015) The Cooperative City: Building Economic Democracy, in Michael Peter Smith and Lucas Owen Kirkpatrick (eds.), *Reinventing Detroit, Volume 11, Comparative Urban and Community Research*, Piscataway, NJ: Transaction Books.

Fasenfest D (2016) Class Politics and the Reactionary Electorate, *Critical Sociology*, 42:1:3–5.

Fasenfest D (2016) Emergency Management in Michigan: Race, Class and the Limits of Liberal Democracy (with Theodore Pride), *Critical Sociology*, 42:3: 331–334.

Fasenfest D (2016) Marx, Marxism and Human Rights, *Critical Sociology*, 42: 6: 777–779.

Fasenfest D (2016) Megacities, in George Ritzer (ed). *Wiley-Blackwell Encyclopedia of Sociology*, London: John Wiley & Sons.

Fasenfest D (2016) A Fascination with China, Foreword in Horst Helle, *China: Promise or Threat*, Leiden: Brill, pp vii–x.

Fasenfest D (2017) The Struggle Continues, *Critical Sociology*, 43: 2: 161–165.

Fasenfest D (2017) Review: William Goldsmith (2015) Saving Our Cities: A Progressive Plan to Transform Urban America, Ithaca, NY: Cornell University Press, in *Choice* 54: 10 (June).

Fasenfest D (2017) Rust Belt Cities, in Douglas Richardson (ed) *The International Encyclopedia of Geography: People, the Earth, Environment, and Technology*, London: John Wiley & Sons (revised and updated 2018).

Fasenfest D (2017) Monsieur Le Capital and Madame La Terre on the Brink (with Penelope Ciancanelli) pp 37–55 in Molly Scott Cato and Peter North (eds) *Towards Just and Sustainable Economies: Comparing Social and Solidarity Economy in the North and South*. Bristol: Policy Press.

Fasenfest D (2017) Checks, (Bank) Balances and Death Panels, *Critical Sociology*, 43: 4–5: 521–523.

Fasenfest D (2017) The Downward Healthcare Slide: Tearing the Social Fabric, *Critical Sociology*, 43: 6: 815–818.

Fasenfest D (2017) Review: John Joe Schlichtman, Jason Patch, and Marc Lamont Hill (2017). Gentrifier Toronto in *Choice* 55: 4 (Dec).

Fasenfest D (2018) Review: Thomas Angotti, ed (2017) Urban Latin America: inequalities and neoliberal reforms, ed. Rowman & Littlefield, in *Choice* 55: 8 (April).

Fasenfest D (2018) Emergency Management in Michigan: A Misguided Policy Initiative, in Ashley Nickels and Jason Rivera (eds) *Community Development and Public Administration Theory: Empowerment through the Enhancement of Democratic Principles*, London: Routledge.

Fasenfest D (2018) Network priorities for social sustainability research and education: Memorandum of the Integrated Network on Social Sustainability Research Group, *Sustainability: Science, Practice and Policy*, 12: 1: 16–21.

Fasenfest D (2018) Review: Dikeç, Mustafa (2018). Urban Rage: the Revolt of the Excluded. Yale, CT: Yale University Press in *Choice* 55: 10 (June).

Fasenfest D (2018) Marx and the Global South (with Raju Das), *Global Dialogue: Magazine of the International Sociological Association*, Vol 8, Issue 1 (April).

Fasenfest D (2019) Review: Hecht, Bennett L, (2018) Reclaiming the American Dream: Proven solutions for creating economic opportunity for all, Washington, DC: Brookings in *Choice* 56: 7 (March).

Fasenfest D (2019) わりゆく世界の中で連帯を築く (Building Solidarity in a Changing World), translated by 沙羅 朴 (Sara Park), in 理論と動態, 11号 (*Theory and Dynamics* 11), 社会理論・動態研究所 (Institute of Social Theory and Dynamics), Hiroshima, Japan.

Fasenfest D (2019) A Neoliberal Response to an Urban Crisis: Emergency Management in Flint, MI. *Critical Sociology* 45: 1: 33–47.

Fasenfest D (2020) Constructing the Conceptual Tools for the Global South. in Håkon Leiulfsrud and Peter Sohlberg (eds) *Constructing the Research Object in Social Science*, Leiden: Brill.

Fasenfest D (2021) Neoliberalism, Urban Policy and Environmental Degradation, in Graham Cassano and Terressa Benz (eds) *Geographies of Neoliberal Indifference: Environmental Racism in Flint and Beyond*, Leiden: Brill.

Fasenfest D (2021) Global Poverty: A Marxian Analysis, (with Alfredo Saad-Filho) in ВОПРОСЫ ПОЛИТИЧЕСКОЙ ЭКОНОМИИ (*Problems in Political Economy*), Moscow: Institute of Economics, Russian Academy of Sciences, 25:1:65–77.

Fasenfest D (2021) Review: Nickels, A E, Power, Participation, and Protest in Flint, Michigan: Unpacking the Policy Paradox of Municipal Takeovers, 2019, Philadelphia: Temple University Press, in *Journal of Urban Affairs*, 43:1:218–220.

Fasenfest D (2022) Sociology and Marxism in the USA (with Graham Cassano), in Beverley Skeggs, Sara R. Farris, and Alberto Toscano (eds) *Handbook of Marxism*, London: Sage Vol 3, pp 1013–1028.

Fasenfest D (2022) The Challenge for Sociology: The Value of the Critique, *Critical Sociology*, 48: 2: 189–192.

Fasenfest D (2022) The Importance of International Cooperation, *Social Theory and Dynamics*, 3: 3–5.

Fasenfest D (2022) Spiking the Sociological Canon, *Critical Sociology*, 48: 4/5: 549–552.

Fasenfest D (2022) The Once and Future Marx, Chapter 1 in Fasenfest D (ed.) *Marx Matters*, Leiden Brill.

Fasenfest D (2023) Marxism or Economic Sociology, Chapter 5 in Milan Zafirovski (ed) *Routledge International Handbook of Economic Sociology*, New York: Routledge.

Fasenfest D (f2023) Marxism or Economic Sociology, Chapter 5 in Milan Zafirovski (ed) *Routledge International Handbook of Economic Sociology*, New York: Routledge.

Fasenfest D (forthcoming) 海外全球学研究期刊的梳理与介绍 (Introduction to Global Research Journals), with Xiaoxiao Xie, *Chinese Global Studies Review*, Shanghai University, China.

Fasenfest D (forthcoming) The Making of the Journal Critical Sociology, in Clyde W. Barrow (ed). *Encyclopedia of Critical Political Science*, Cheltenham: Edward Elgar Publishing.

Fasenfest D (forthcoming) Fallacies of Neoclassical Economic Knowledge, in Fran Collyer (ed) *Research Handbook for the Sociology of Knowledge*, London: Edward Elgar Publishing.

Other References

Brass T (2003) On Which Side of What Barricade? Subaltern Resistance in Latin America and Elsewhere. In Brass T (ed.) *Latin American Peasants*, pp. 336–399, London: Frank Cass Publishers.

Brass T (2020) Is Agrarian Populism Progressive? Russia then, India now. *Critical Sociology* 46(7–8): 987–1004.

Brass T (2023) Critical Agrarian Studies as Populist Land-Grab. *Critical Sociology* 49 (3): 563–573.

Fogel RW, Engerman SL (1974) *Time on the Cross: Volume I – The Economics of American Negro Slavery*. London: Wildwood House.

Horowitz IL (ed.) (1964) *The New Sociology: Essays in Social Science and Social Theory in Honor of C. Wright Mills*. New York: Oxford University Press.

Levien M, Watts M, Hairong Y (2018) Agrarian Marxism, *The Journal of Peasant Studies* 45(5–6): 853–883.

Sutch R (1975) The Treatment Received by American Slaves: A Critical Review of the Evidence Presented in Time on the Cross, *Explorations in Economic History* 12(4): 335–438.

Tolstoy L Count (1905) The School at Yásnaya Polyána, in *Pedagogical Articles* (edited and translated by Leo Wiener), London: G.J. Howell & Co.

PART 1

CHAPTER 2

Interview with David Fasenfest

Raju J. Das and Robert Latham

Raju Das:[1] David Fasenfest, currently Professor at Wayne State University in the US, and Adjunct Professor at York University, Toronto, Canada, is by training a sociologist and economist with an interest in urban sociology and Marxist theory. He is the author and editor of many books, too numerous to list, the most recent being Marx Matters, which received the Choice Award for Outstanding Academic Title in 2022. So, David, could you say a little about yourself, your parents and childhood, and how you became interested in the social sciences.

David Fasenfest: My father was a Jewish survivor of the concentration camps, my mother lived through the carpet bombing and privations of war-time Germany, where I was born. We moved to the US when I was not quite a year old. This is by way of saying that my earliest memories were anti-fascist ones, albeit not understanding at the time what that meant politically. I began my education as a chemical engineer, and then moved into economics, becoming interested in the French Revolution and Marxism, which I studied with Richard Wolff, a young professor at CCNY. After graduation, I toured Europe for several years, on foot and by motorcycle, my backpack containing two volumes of Marx's theories of surplus value that, perhaps optimistically, I intended to work through on my travels. Whilst in Europe I became interested in the Russian Revolution, reading accounts written by Lenin and Trotsky, and placing Marx in a more contemporary setting. Further travels took me to the Middle East, and I returned to the States with a greater appreciation of Third World development issues. Around the early 1970s I became interested in China, entering an MA and then the PhD programme at the University of Michigan – where Marx was not part of what one studied – undertaking research into the Shanghai commune. During that time, I joined the editorial board of the *Review of Radical Political Economics*, becoming involved in editorial work over a four- or five-year period. It was in mid-1970s Washington that I was made aware that one was unable to do research on China unless it was

---

1 The interview with David Fasenfest was conducted by Raju Das and Robert Latham in the newly formed Marx Center at York University, Toronto.

via the CIA. I was working at a DC research firm as part of a team analyzing the PRC economy. In that capacity I went along to a meeting in the CIA headquarters and wondered how someone like me who had been arrested in demonstrations against Nixon would be there except under duress. The discussion focused on how the US could transfer technology to China without enabling them to become independent of US control, so I decided that was not for me, and left. At Michigan I encountered Marxists such as Thomas Weisskopf and worked with Charles Tilley, who encouraged me to focus away from economics and on sociology. As significant was the important question I was asked at that time by some African students: is there nothing wrong with your country that you're spending so much time studying ours. That forced me into thinking about urban society in the United States, so that by the mid-1980s a combination of sociology, Marxism, and critical political economy was pointing me in the direction of urban social processes.

Over the past decades your work has covered many different topics, all very important, among which are poverty, class, race, social inequality, political protest, social justice, and socialism. What are the major problems faced by society, and how are they addressed in your writings?

One of the things that I learned early on, and stayed with me ever since, was the analytical importance of locality. All that I have written, whether on urban sociology, race, or community development, has centred on the place I happened to be at the time. When I was at Purdue and Detroit, my work addressed projects and problems in Indianapolis and Chicago. As a postgraduate, my interest focused on Namibia – then still a colony – when I carried out a study of African labour and various relevant workforces. Hence for me, the nature of power, its accompanying causes and effects, manifests itself on the ground, so to speak. One of my first publications was an analysis of economic development policy in Detroit, where a whole community was dismantled in order to build a GM plant in Poletown. I also investigated homelessness, asking my students why the homeless are not asked where to build low-income housing, any more than workers are asked when employers fix wage levels. What confronted me directly when moving to Detroit, therefore, was the political situation in Indianapolis and racism in Chicago. My research always starts from the ground up, examining a locality to understand the economic, political, and social dynamics at play. This is a materialist approach informed by Marxism. In order to critique something, one has to begin by understanding what it is. Until we know what capitalism is, how it functions as a system, and why it is prone to crises, we cannot hope to transform it.

Robert Latham: About this local framing, how do you go about incorporating into your approach the various levels that are at play in the local, and responsible for the concrete nature of the conditions that are found there?

This question about methodology requires contextualizing. My peripatetic employment history is due in part to an interdisciplinary approach: sociologists maintain that I'm an economist, whereas economists say that my work is political science. Mine is an approach that doesn't fit easily within the formal structures of a university department, a situation that has both negative and positive effects. Since neither I, nor my partner, who is also an academic, have careerist goals, the peripatetic aspect has not constrained us. Not following a traditional academic pathway is liberating in another way, in that one's interests and approach are not subject to the imposition of rigid disciplinary knowledge and methodological boundaries. This is the background to my engagement with economic sociology in an attempt to understand society, through an approach critical of the view that capitalism is the best of all possible systems. No longer being tied academically to a single disciplinary boundary leaves me free to analyze in this manner. Although I've stopped going to conferences and academic events, I've succeeded in editing the journal and book series as a space where people like me, who do not adhere to traditional disciplinary boundaries, can do interesting work. I see this as liberating, because of not wanting to be party to the kind of education pushed down their throats. You struggle and make do with your intellectual agenda.

Raju Das: In the light of your own experience, what would you suggest to someone wanting to study poverty? How should one go about this?

My understanding of poverty drew on my own intellectual background, a combination of mathematics, statistics, economics, and sociology. What I learned was that students never challenge the way the question itself is framed, thereby missing the underlying issue. In my earliest work on inequality and poverty, done with a colleague, we analysed government data and population surveys, converting figures into family income differentiated according to its source in terms of interest, labour, and property. We demonstrated how in the mid-1970s the income of households in the lowest quintile, based on labour, remained flat, whereas that of top quintile households, derived not from labour but interest and capital, grew. With my students I do a similar budgetary exercise, starting with the elements composing household income, subtracting taxes, and then dividing expenditure on a monthly and yearly basis. Turning gross household income calculated at between US$90,000 and US$120,000 per annum into disposable income reveals that those in the lowest quintile rapidly lose all sorts of things the students themselves take for granted: less food, worse housing, no health care, no insurance, making them realize the meaning of poverty, and that our notion of middle class is really a fantasy. Statistical and mathematical skills enabling the decomposition and recombination of data make the figures something more than simple information. It's one thing to display data, another to explain them, and it is the latter that matters. My early work on poverty came out of an ability to deal with data, an approach that gave me new insights and allowed me intellectually to move onto other questions that were not themselves data driven. Anyone wanting to research poverty, therefore, has in my opinion to begin with what one knows, with the community in which one grew up. Take, for example, W.E.B. Du Bois, who critiqued traditional (and White) sociologists who conducted 'drive by' sociology which consisted literally of driving around a Black neighbourhood to see what was going on there. He observed that until we understand a community in careful detail it is impossible to make sense of it. Equally, poverty must be experienced, not necessarily by living it but by unpacking the lived experience. What, for instance, is going to happen to the five million households losing Medicaid when COVID exemptions end? What does it mean for those no longer possessing health care, or housing? Research into poverty, or related issues like homelessness, begins with such questions, from which we can then build answers.

Robert Latham: *This poses in turn the following question, which concerns the nature of the connection between your critique and a project of social change. Does the latter take the form of a struggle against capitalism and for socialism, and, if so, how do you situate your own editorial work in relation to this largescale project?*

Although not a pessimist, I think no one individual can formulate major social change required by society. However, I'm optimistic that things can be achieved at a local level. In practical terms, I've helped those struggling with major projects in Detroit, community groups which had rejected development incentives because these provide no benefit to the grassroots, pointing out that such funding could be directed instead towards local improvements (housing, street lighting, etc.) that benefit middle and low-income communities. Because there are always other ways of spending the money, they were advised to examine closely the details of what is on offer, and always to challenge this, warning that a Detroit project linking the construction of a hockey arena to the provision of affordable housing and jobs yielded only a parking lot for those attending hockey games. My political goal is to effect social change locally through these kinds of intervention. With regard to positioning my editorial work in the same process of struggle, because *Critical Sociology* was a journal beset with problems, I was asked to become editor. Since its focus specifically on Marxism restricted the sorts of submissions received hitherto, I broadened the range of issues covered, no longer restricting them in terms of disciplinary or theoretical approach, increasing the number articles submitted and published. Many contributors are from countries where library admittance is difficult, so the journal is accessed electronically. At the same time Brill agreed to produce a spin-off book series, *Studies in Critical Social Sciences*, attracting interest from scholars both within and, later, outside the English-speaking world, whose research was not mainstream in a disciplinary sense. Together with Alfredo Saad-Filho, we have established a separate book series, *New Scholarship in Political Economy*, providing a platform for early career researchers and recent doctoral students. These publishing endeavors correspond to what I envision as my intellectual contribution to the larger project identified above, my job being to promote critical scholarship not hampered by disciplinary or locational constraints. Over the years, I have honed my editorial skills, knowing what to stress as important and what to cut out as unnecessary.

I have a follow-up question regarding the dissemination of knowledge generated in this fashion. Can you tell us something more about that?

Over the last four or five years both the journal and the book series has enabled me to make international connections. There is now a book produced by Japanese Marxists at the Institute for Social Theory and Dynamics, and other volumes from Eastern Europe, Latin America, and Korea. This creates not just a space but linkages which, at the end of the day, will become even more important, as scholars become aware that they are not working in isolation. Opening out these communication networks will contribute to an understanding and recognition of the different intellectual traditions in Europe, Africa, and Asia.

Raju Das: *As you note, progressive knowledge is a necessary precursor of progressive change. We accept it's not sufficient, but it's necessary. Since this knowledge also has to circulate on a global scale, can you tell us how you go about your editorial work, and what kind of changes you've seen in the nature of submissions both to Critical Sociology and to the book series. Furthermore, how is such editorial work regarded by the university? that is to say is editing generally an underrated aspect of academic work?*

Regarding change, progressive and otherwise, my focus currently is on the reactionary upsurge in anti-liberal populism of a neo-fascist sort, leading me to consider the example of Mussolini in Italy. He, rather than Hitler, is the model for what is happening, and the kind of danger facing Austria, France, Germany, and the United States. Fascism has to be understood as an anti-Enlightenment ideology, interested in reversing progressive change. Turning to my role as editor, and what this involves, every discipline has its top journals, which act as standard bearers and defenders of the canon. They are the places where, if there is an intellectual shift, it is in them that such alterations are first revealed by changes to editorial policy and journal content. Their gatekeeping role and academic influence is pervasive, an authority I've seen exercised on many occasions, not least when an unimpressive job applicant was deemed acceptable to a colleague of mine simply on the grounds of having published in a top journal, despite not having read the article in question. For these sorts of publication, universities recognize the editorial work involved by releasing those who do it from teaching and other academic tasks. But others, like me, receive no such recognition. When I requested course release on the grounds that I was spending a lot of time editing the journal, I was told no, because the work did not count as university business, thereby underlining that journal editing is not considered productive in the way universities assess value. So no, there is not a lot of institutional support for the role of editor, this despite the additional tasks it involves. Thus, many journal and book submissions require lots of careful attention, since editing includes not just dealing with the work in question but also with the allocation of reviewers. Many years ago, I sent an article to a good friend and senior scholar, who rejected the submission and told me it occupied two hours of his time he would never get back. This indicated to me that I should not request reviews of submissions of poor quality,. This underlined the extent to which an editor has to do a better job of filtering, and sending out for review only submissions that are serious and warrant careful assessment. At present *Critical Sociology* gets close to 300 submissions a year, but if everything was sent out for review, I'd be looking at deploying 800 to 1,000 reviewers, so 40% of what is submitted is previewed and rejected.

In terms of what is submitted over time, have there been changes in the kind of interest exhibited, in the approach broadly to issues of political economy?

I don't think the interest has changed, but the quality of submissions has increased. We get lots of good articles, partly due to an expanded word limit. The limit used to be 8,000 words, whereas now submissions fall into the range of 9,000–10,000, and even 12,000 words if necessary. The analyses we receive, now from around the world, are better in depth and more considered in approach. Nowadays more research is leading to articles sent in from Scandinavian countries, Central Europe, and Latin America. Have these people always been writing, but without a publication in which to place the results? Or have they been encouraged to write because currently there is a space for the result? Whatever the cause, I'm pleased to see that the journal has a global reach, and that more scholars are being encouraged to contribute, thereby creating the dialogue we want.

Robert Latham: *You've raised and covered a lot of very interesting issues, among them the work that has to be developed which addresses concerns about the direction taken by capitalism, where this leads, and that a progressive socialist outcome cannot be taken for granted. How do you see your continued role in this process?*

I will soon turn 75, and I've been the editor for quarter of a century, which has both an upside and a downside. Some of the work submitted these days is a challenge because I'm not familiar with relatively newer scholarship. What I do know is that I will not die in post, so now we're in the process of bringing in mid-career Marxist scholars who are more attuned to the times. The associate board is also being expanded, and I'm working on a sharing arrangement with a younger scholar who will take over from me in the next two or three years, when the journal will continue with someone else's vision. My hope is that I've built enough of a foundation that will carry the journal forward on a secure footing, as others become involved in continuing that work.

Raju Das: *Thank you, David, for taking us on this illuminating journey with you.*

CHAPTER 3

Thank You David
A Tribute to a Mensch

Lauren Langman

Let me first begin by noting that I have probably known David Fasenfest, longer than most of his other academic friends and colleagues, since his early academic career began at Loyola University Chicago, where I had just become a junior faculty. I should perhaps begin by noting that while we are extremely secular, we both come from Jewish backgrounds and indeed, David's parents were holocaust survivors, disposing a highly critical perspective on authoritarianism of any kind at any level. Between our shared cultural backgrounds, and our common normative values, critical of domination, rooted in Marxist and humanist traditions, we shared an outlook not widely embraced in our discipline in its attempt to be "value free" which of course becomes a basis to elide critical perspectives. Thus, we hit it off immediately and thus began a long and valuable friendship that has endured to this very day. While our foci may very well differ, given my concerns with social movements and Frankfurt School critical theory, and his with economic sociology, especially urban economics, nevertheless, there is a great deal that we share, especially the critique of capitalist domination in its many forms at many levels, and the values of universalism, toleration of difference, equality, democracy, freedom, and autonomy. To briefly summarize my perspective on his life and work, David is a *mensch*.

But what exactly does that mean? The term *mensch*, the German word for a man has a particular connotation in Yiddish that is not easily, directly translated; loosely it means a decent person, a good person, someone who does good, for the sake of doing good for others as opposed to narcissistic gratification, assertion of power. Perhaps the most important aspect of his work and amazing service to the profession has been his 20+ years of leadership as editor of *Critical Sociology,* the forerunner of which, *Insurgent Sociology,* was a product of the progressive movements of the 1960s, challenging seemingly uncritical structural functional sociology, implicitly hegemonic, by moving toward a more radical critique. The context was opportune, given the events of the times, primarily mobilizations for civil rights, feminism, even environmentalism and perhaps most of all, the massive protests in the streets and campuses against the war in Vietnam seen then, and for many people now, as a tragic, ill-fated consequence of America's long-standing traditions first of settler colonialism, then imperialism and conquest.[1] The adverse consequences of that ill-conceived incursion were again repeated in Iraq and Afghanistan resulting in hundreds of thousands if not millions of deaths.

In the many years of that leadership, *Critical Sociology* has become one of the top sociology journals and indeed, *the primary journal for theoretically informed, empirically based, critical sociological analyses.* Unlike many other leftist, progressive journals, *Critical Sociology,* tends to be more open to a variety of perspectives, while maintaining the highest standards of scholarship. We progressive scholars well know how many of the other left, often Marxist perspectives, tend to be highly partisan to the point of fragmenting what is in many cases a marginal position. But under David's leadership, *Critical Sociology* has ascended to a top ranked position among sociology journals and yet managed to maintain an openness to a variety of progressive perspectives, with first-grade scholarship and steering clear of highly purchasing biases.

It becomes important to note how time-consuming and tedious editorial work can be: just think about our own papers, and how much time we spend on their construction. And the work we've had to put into editing and getting just one paper or book ready for publication. Imagine reading hundreds of papers and/or books a year, deciding which ones may be suitable for publication, then deciding on who to send those papers for review – then the process of getting on the cases of reviewers, at least those like me, that are invariably late. To devote so much time and effort in support to other scholars in the progressive voice sociology, a task inevitably detracting from his own time spent on his scholarship – is the mark of a *mensch*.

Moreover, in addition to editing *Critical Sociology*, he was also the founding editor of *Studies in Critical Social Sciences* (published by Brill, with 250 books in print and 70 manuscripts under contract), and in July 2019 became the founding co-editor (with Alfredo Saad-Filho) of the series *New Scholarship in Political Economy* to promote innovative scholarship by new Ph.D.s with further books in print and 32 manuscripts under contract. Indeed, David was more than helpful, above and beyond the call of duty in marshaling two books that I did, the critical theory of American character and essays on Thomas Piketty's book *Capital.*

I should perhaps also note, one of his latest perhaps most important contributions to scholarship has been his book, *Marx Matters*, a collection of

---

1 David encouraged and shepherded the publication of a book I did with George Lundskow on American character, *God, Guns, Gold, and Glory,* with Brill and subsequently Haymarket.

essays on the current state of Marxist perspectives and sociological theory and research that won the *Choice Award: Outstanding Academic Title of 2022*. I was indeed very honored to have been invited to make a contribution to that collection: my paper on social movements, unlike most American social movement research, places much emphasis on the role of political economy and legitimation crises as fostering various social movements progressive or reactionary. I think that David spent as much time helping me getting that paper ready for publication as I spent writing it.

It is amazing how much time editing these many publication feats require, over and above the editorial job itself. David has been extremely generous and helpful in aiding and guiding many authors like me through the process of publication, from proposal to print. And yet notwithstanding the time required for such activity, rooted in kindness of heart, he has still been able to produce first rate empirical research in Marxist sociology, especially urban economics and generally with a broad international perspective. He has also been active in the International Sociological Association and has been invited to participate and/or present papers in such varied locales as Norway, People's Republic of China, Russia, and England.

The recognition of David's contributions to sociology as a first-rate editor, a respected scholar, and mentor, has been especially evident in his long career, especially his service and scholarship to Marxist sociology for which indeed he was awarded the honor of lifetime achievement award by the Marxist section of the American Sociological Association. Perhaps most notably, are the many friends and colleagues who are more than happy to contribute to this *Festschrift*. Truly we must recognize David as a major influence in academic critical sociology: it is on scholarship, and most of all the kindness, generosity, and devotion to helping other scholars, that are truly the mark of a *mensch*. Thank you, David, for all that you've done: you deserve recognition of those efforts, by so many.

CHAPTER 4

Critical Evaluation of a Critical Scholar
David Fasenfest

Rodney D. Coates

The critical scholar faces a daunting task as they are attacked from almost all sides. If they are honest and do not shy away from controversy, they will be equally critical of both the progressive and the conservative viewpoints, policies, and practices. Their critical perspective should be versed in theory and praxis, history and reality, subjectivity, and objectivity. A comparative focus leads one to analyze and understand from multiple vantage points while maintaining clarity and substance. For most scholars, the challenges are not worth the effort or the cost. While the effort is understandable, few comprehend that the cost typically is associated with being marginalized, criticized, and ostracized by all sides. But these costs go with the turf, and we are honored, enlightened, and empowered for those who dare to walk this path. Such has been the path taken by David Fasenfest, a career that has stretched the horizons of our discipline, demonstrated the possibilities of critical sociological imagination, and remained true to both the craft and the purpose by which we are driven. In this chapter, I shall highlight the significance and the contributions made by this humble giant.

1 The Sword of Truth – for the Love of Money

David's journey into sociology was circuitous. He actually started off to become a professional in Chinese Studies, then into Economics, and finally Sociology. One of the reasons he left Economics was that it had shifted from a social and economic analysis of society, to one that was increasingly microeconomic analysis based on mathematical modeling. He had no love for a discipline that had become centered on econometrics, and a data analytical understanding of society. It was not so much that it was based on mathematical modeling, but one that interpreted and mathematically constructed the social realities. And so rather than a critical understanding of the political economy, social reality becomes a biproduct of data analysis. Sociology, similarly, had drifted into an analysis of such things as poverty or homelessness because of societal ills. The remedy, better social policy, and other interventions (Fasenfest, 2010b. Sociology is not an abstract perspective, but rather is integrated into our very being. It reflects the lived experiences of the subject and object. Therefore, the sociology that one practices, pursues, and engages in is reflected in the realities that they have experienced. Fasenfest's lived experiences were dictated by the social injustices that he had experienced, and his desire to produce radical social change. He emerged during a time when sociology was being challenged by radical intellectual scholarship. One of the chief vehicles that he utilized, the journal *Critical Sociology*, ultimately emerged. Through this vehicle, David aimed to extend the work of Marx, Durkheim, Weber, and Du Bois by decolonizing the curriculum, and understanding how systems of oppression are generated by a market structure predicated on the accumulation of capital at the expense of justice, human rights, and people. The product of privilege, and the dominant assumptions and intellectual orientations the capitalist market ideology supports is at the core of the problems created in the system.

The truth should be at the core of what we do as both academics and sociologists. And what is that truth? Intersecting systems of oppression associated with race, class, gender, sexuality, and ability have often been rationalized by social theorists, particularly within sociology. To be honest to our calling and canon, we must understand how society and social inequalities manifest and persist across history and geography. This would require us to analyze society by challenging and critically analyzing how systems of oppression are rationalized by 'economic, political, and social systems' (Fasenfest 2010b). This journey begins by understanding the significance of global imperialism.

The forces of global imperialism have wreaked havoc on multiple nations, groups, economies, and ecologies. Neither developed nor developing countries have been able to avoid the climatic upheavals orchestrated by imperialism and continued by bourgeois capitalism. At the core of David Fasenfest's approach is a determined program of analyzing these debilitating outcomes while articulating progressive strategies, social movements, and policies of resistance and persistence. These truths, expressed as early as 1997, provide an alternative to a market-driven approach and social activities. Instead, Fasenfest explores an 'emancipatory social vision' derived from a social justice framework. Such a framework would lead to a re-evaluation of the worth of individuals in that they are no longer measured by their consumption potential but rather by their human potential.

Consequently, the intrinsic worth of the individual is not measured by the role in the corporate structure but in the community, a system defined by networks of family, friends, and neighbors. Fasenfest argued for valuing non-utilitarian activities such as birthing and raising children, caring for aged friends and family, and organizing the community. This recognizes that these non-monetized, yet essential activities support our economic and political institutions.

Sociology and social activists have been engaged for decades, if not longer, in attempting to provide long-term social change, particularly for the most disenfranchised. But, while we have written millions of pages and published thousands of reports and articles, little actual change has occurred. Fasenfest et al. (1997) explained that while many individual success stories exist, limited fundamental social change has taken place. In 2009, he (Fasenfest 2009) would again argue that the cracks in the system, pointed out by social protests from the early 1960s to the 1980s, demonstrate that the fundamental social ills, social dislocations, and disempowerment structures, systems, and practices remain unchanged. What is needed is a focus on systemic, not individual change.

Programs that focus on the individual rarely produce any real change. The issue, for example, when we consider how to support female ex-inmates, is not how they must change but how such things as post-release environments, racial and gendered discrimination in employment, access to substance abuse and psychological counseling, childcare. As explained by Fasenfest and colleagues (in Case et al., 2005), real change can only come about by adequately funding the system that would provide access to the full range of services, transforming the inequitable structures, and then working to reintegrate the individual into an equitable system.

Modern world history, according to Fasenfest (2010a) can be divided into two basic periods. The first, occurring during the first half of the 20th century, was marked by European expansion into Asian, Africa, and Latin America. In many ways the first World War, initiated by the scramble for Africa, was associated with a determined attempt by France, England, Germany, and Italy to control the vast natural resources necessary for industrial development and capital accumulation. World War II established what can be called the new world order, as France and Britain solidified their colonial rule.

Eisenhower, over three decades ago, warned of the danger if we did not control the behemoth that he labeled the 'military industrial complex' (Fasenfest, 2010a)). Today, the Pentagon and nuclear weapons under the Department of Energy, cost billions. The Pentagon, alone, consumes over half of the federal discretionary budget, while public health, environmental protection, job training and education must scramble for what is left. The concentration of the 'Big Five' -Boeing, General Dynamics, Lockheed Martin, Northrop Grumman, and Raytheon – account for more than 20 percent of the total Pentagon budget, or more than US$150 billion (Hartung and Freeman, 2023). What would happen, asks Fasenfest, if these funds were directed into a 'university-industrial' complex. And rather than watching our institutions of higher education become institutions of occupational credentialism, maybe we could create a new 'knowledge economy' which would provide research and policy initiatives that would provide innovative ways of supporting the public good. Maybe we could solve our problems and pave the way to a more progressive future (Fasenfest, 2010b).

Discontent among numerous marginal groups – blacks, women, LGBTQ+, native Americans, immigrants, and youth – notes Fasenfest (2009), fomented the various social movements of the 1960s. These movements, individually and collectively, challenged the neoliberal state and demanded substantive and social justice orchestrated change. Such challenges soon spread to Africa, India, and the Middle East, as liberation struggles challenged the corporate, economic, and political apparatus of the former colonial empires. As the 1980s came into view, scholars and student protests led to the formation of centers and programs of race and ethnicity, gender, and global studies, challenging the status quo. Liberation sociology and radical economic movements appeared, and scholars offered counter-theories of modernity and how capitalism promoted poverty, oppression, and exploitation across the globe. This period, referred to as neoliberalism, only served the financial interests of hegemonic powers, now under the control of U.S. foreign policy. Globalization, enshrined in regional trade associations like NAFTA, the European Union, and the increasingly imperial goals of China and Russia, which ensured hegemonic control more efficiently. Operating on a global state, neoliberalism served to destabilize nations, attack welfare and social programs, increase militarism and the prison industrial complex, and undermine labor unions and organizations (Fasenfest, 2009).

2   Neoliberal Challenges, Institutional Change: When Social Justice Is Replaced by Economic Rationalism

The United States and much of the world took a hard right turn in 2011. In that year, spurred on by the Tea Party, Conservative Republicans took over the US House of Representatives. The Tea Party claimed that 'illegal immigrants' and other minorities were bringing the country down, arguing that, suffering from a 'plantation mentality,' they were welfare-dependent. The solution was to reduce governmental spending dramatically (Huntington and Glickman, 2021). Determined, as Fasenfest (2011) points out, to put America back on track, this refusal to negotiate almost led to the US being unable to cover its debts for the first time. That year, markets went over the cliff as borrowing reached

US$1.3 billion (Obstfield and Zhou, 2023). As we approach a similar scenario today, his observations seem prescient. Strange then, that 'Conservatives, long the champions of "freedom and democracy" around the world (but perhaps not in Florida!) find themselves critical of Obama's stance calling for change and respect for the wishes of "the people" of Egypt'. And so, support for Taliban-like governments, not democratic ones, flourished. Similarly, by choosing to fund the Contra war against the Sandinistas in Nicaragua, the US backed the wrong side (Fasenfest, 2011).

When the global markets crashed in 2007–2008, and COVID-19 struck, academic institutions responded by doubling down on managerialism. Fasenfest (2021) maintains that academia responded by accelerating the push toward managerialism and the progressive decline of post-secondary education. In keeping with this, universities became the tool of corporations, leading to the downgrading of the liberal arts and social sciences, together with the heightened presence of business managers running the university. Faculty governance gets replaced by bureaucratic organization and administration that controls hiring and promotion, curricular priorities, and conditions of employment. Equally, faculty research productivity and value are determined by impact factors rather than critical analysis of social problems. And rather than big ideas, we have theoretical conformity, intellectual laziness, and the loss of critical voices. In the mix, public fiscal support has shifted the burden of paying for this bureaucratic bloat to the student.

Consequently, student debt has inflated, while academic standards are reduced to bureaucratic posturing. The decline of higher education, the erosion of scholarship, and the inability to prepare the next generation of citizens have never been so apparent. Democracy or any progressive future requires that each generation is equipped with the critical skills to understand, write, and research complex problems and issues. They must lead the vanguard that challenges the hegemonic systems that are unfolding.

If the 1960s were marked by populism from the left, then the current era is marked by populism from the right. In the US this took the form of extreme anti-democratic forces associated with MAGA ('Make America Great Again') and Trumpism, while analogous hardline, neoliberal populist forces took control of the government apparatus in Austria and Italy. Similar results were evident in France and Germany. Our current neoliberal moment is very clearly associated with a radical right-wing shift over the past decades. Using the global economic crisis of 2008, right-wing extremists opposed social justice policies, immigration, and liberal criminal justice reform. These all led to unprecedented inflation, governmental deficits, loss of jobs, and structural paralysis. The result, David argued in 2019, has been a direct challenge to the basic stability and health of liberal democratic principles and the institutions that they maintain.

We live in a world where extreme, right-wing populism, supercharged with aggressive libertarianism, has thwarted real reforms in health care, election refinancing, education, or public policy for decades. Caught up in denial and obstruction, climate change, immigration, gender, and sexual equality, as well as racial justice, are stalled. Whether it was the Tea Party two decades ago or the MAGA movement today, the constant political and social disasters have been carefully orchestrated. So, while marginalized individuals and their communities are marginalized yet further, corporations and special interest groups find that their powers have been enhanced and often enshrined into law. US Supreme Court rulings set a clear pattern, as we consider that corporations have legal rights, that women have no rights to their bodies, that affirmative action in college admissions is unconstitutional, and that racial profiling is legal. With each of these rulings, the political landscape is tilted to favor corporate interests and racial elites at the expense of all others. Thus, democracy becomes limited, 'free speech' becomes stifled, and we all suffer (Fasenfest, 2010c). Most imperial states in the past century mirror each other.

It would be dangerous to suggest that only Western nations created neoliberal challenges to democracy. Historically, the Japanese State essentialized the ethnic distinctiveness and superiority of the Japanese people. It did this by creating a racial elite linking Japanese identity to nation, family and culture, a combination that was central to Japanese imperialism. These developments coincided with Japanese geopolitical efforts to dominate the East Asian regional states, utilizing colonialism as its chief method of expansion. The next phase was made possible by export-oriented production that benefited from the devastation left by World War II. The result of this drive toward Asian dominance, characterized by some as an 'economic miracle', was a cascading crisis marked by prolonged and recurring recessions, conflict, and turmoil. After decades, Japanese capitalism found itself with a major competitor for Asian dominance in the upsurge of China in the region (Gottfried and Fasenfest, 2021).

Japan, particularly from 1979 through 1990, soon challenged America. This challenge resulted in major shifts in how US automakers operated, their response being what became known as Japanese 'lean production' procedures. These served to increase competitive advantages while eliminating waste and coordinating workflow. Such methods were further enhanced by computer technologies that further streamlined Japanese production, so much so that within a decade Japanese auto imports captured over quarter of the US markets just for passenger cars (Fasenfest and Jacobs, 2003).

One of the most important features of Fasenfest's approach has been an ability to connect global productive forces with local labor displacements. Labelling these as *glocal,* he (Fasenfest, 2010d) emphasized repeatedly the impact of globalizing processes on local systems. Specifically, glocal articulates how global productive forces, reflected in the competition between regional market systems (not only between East and West, but North and South), results in displacement, disinvestment, and disengagement from local market systems. Fasenfest points out that 'McDonaldization' disrupted local economies by creating a fast-food restaurant chain that displaced local business and producer networks, thereby setting a global standard based on 'the race to the bottom', as the quality of all things was reduced to a normative mediocrity.

Operating at the local levels, neoliberal agendas called for the creation of financial sites able to generate profits by participating in a range of financial instruments. The latter generated huge profits, masking the toxic debt that produced a crisis undercutting social policies and generating huge local governmental deficits. What resulted was an assault on the poor, as they increasingly bore the brunt of the ideological shift that would follow (Fasenfest, 2009). Municipalities, caught in this vice grip, were unable to deal with the effects of these structural and political strains. Barack Obama road the waves of political discontent, promising to be the President of 'Hope', able to bring about 'Change We Can believe in' and, despite all that had happened, 'Yes We Can' because we were all 'Fired Up!' and 'Ready to go!'

Fasenfest (2010d) demonstrated, however, that Obama faced some of the most extreme racist vitriol that had been heard in the past 50 years since the civil rights era. And while many presumed that his election marked the beginning of our post-race era, in fact it only highlighted the racial undertones that were deeply embedded in US society. Racialized discourse, often underlying our racist policies, systems, and structures, are often obscured if the targets are urban, poor black residents. In these instances, sociologists and news outlets naturally assume that it was their class, not their race that marked them for such treatment. But when prominent blacks, such as Harvard professor Henry Louis Gates, was arrested for apparently breaking into his own home (having mislaid his key) then we are forced to understand that this is indeed racist. And contrary to the post-racial myth, non-whites are frequently confronted by forces of racial control aimed at keeping them in their place (Fasenfest, 2010e). Thus, we have 'driving while black', 'jogging while black', 'housing while black', 'banking while black' – let's just say 'living while black'. Local efforts to combat these processes have resulted in limited change, but what is needed, Fasenfest repeatedly points out, is a national strategy for change.

3   Where Is There a Progressive Future?

Each election cycle, in the US, France, or Great Britain, promises change, job creation, enhanced rights for the workers, and investment in social justice programs. Each post-election reality is that excuses, failures, and frustrations abound, as presidents and administrators obfuscate, avoid, and minimize anything close to a progressive agenda. Legislative bodies and executive branches repeatedly enhanced the military-industrial complexes and fostered capital accumulation and corporate agendas. What results is a pro-business agenda funded by the working classes within society. Race, gender, sexual, class, environmental social change become reduced to campaign slogans. Investment flows and political outcomes continue to protect corporate interests even while these problems (both nationally and internationally) are exacerbated. If indeed we are to create a progressive future, then we need to employ progressive strategies.

So often, progressives end up going in circles. The revolution revolves around the revolutionary interests of the proletariat. As those interests coalesce globally, we will see the dawn of the revolutionary age. This age will culminate in the revolution to end all revolutions, as the revolutionary interests take center stage. Neither Marx nor Fasenfest was so circular. The latter provides a very clear and remarkably powerful Marxian analysis of the problems that beset us and points to what various progressive futures would look like and the multiple paths we can take to get there. In response to global structural and systemic problems, one such way is to reorganize and reimagine locally innovative solutions. Locally produced social practices that engage local suppliers and consumers can be good environmentally and economically.

Left on the corner of globalization and profits were the originality and creativity of local producers and merchants. Community building and development require focusing on how local networks of production and consumption can be empowered. Nothing demonstrated the prophetic message more than how various communities responded to COVID. According to the U.S. Chamber of Commerce (Thau, 2023), '55% of consumers patronize neighborhood stores or buy from locally sourced products'. Moreover, 75% of consumers have left the supersized stores and the billion-dollar brands, having instead discovered and liked the 'mom-and-pop' shops. And, as poetically declared by Gil Scott-Heron (1970), 'The revolution will not be televised; it will be live.'

Liberal democracy must move past technical problem-solving and address the real problems of the Third World, the Global South, and the local communities we all live in. This starts with recognizing that wealth accumulation, focusing on short-term financial gains at the expense of everything else, is at the heart of our current crises (Fasenfest and Das, 2021). These strategies have been facilitated by social policies that have reduced fiscal regulations on banks and financial institutions, as well as a shift in corporate restructuring favoring outsourcing and increased compensation for corporate officers. This means that inequality is increased, global production systems are enhanced, and local systems are destabilized. Such processes have resulted in the most devastating economic crises of the 21st century. For example, the global financial Crisis 2008 was the largest one since the Great Depression. It was generated by a policy that allowed for billions of loans associated with properties and borrowers that were shaky at best. High-leveraged mortgage bonds were marketed to corporations, retirement systems, and individuals. The promises of high yields did not materialize, as inflated properties lost value, and investments plummeted. Insurance companies and banks looked toward the US government for bailouts. Major European economies linked to the US markets soon felt the sting as their economic systems plummeted (Reuters, 2023).

The cycle of fiscal crises, of which 2008 is only one, demonstrated that the premise and the promise of everyone benefiting from the expansion and growth of global markets rested on faulty grounds. As Fasenfest (2009) reminds us, Marx first explained the economic collapse so endemic with capitalist centers of power and wealth. What is happening not only in the so-called Western states but also in the Global South, East, and throughout Africa. China and Japan demonstrate what happens when we promote profits above the interests of people. The world's economies were disrupting local social safety nets at the encouragement of international organizations such as the World Bank and the International Monetary Fund. These disruptions were at the heart of financial institutions' moral and economic bankruptcy.

Over the past few decades, across Western Europe (particularly Great Britain, Germany, and France) and the United States, we have seen ultra-right wing social movements increasingly gaining support at local and national elections. This has been extremely vicious in the United States since 9/11, as Muslims have been particularly and aggressively targeted. This is at the same time when right-wing Christian Nationalism has blossomed almost as a state religion. Added to the targeted groups list are immigrants from Latin America, Haiti, and other Caribbean countries. Antisemitism, homophobia, and blacks have also been targeted with hate crimes and mass attacks. The Western World turned a deaf ear to the cries of millions of displaced persons from Syria, Iraq, the Middle East, and North Africa as war, destruction, and madness consumed the land. The genocides were only made more virulent as the so-called democratic states refused to see, hear, or act. Women and persons of color across the world faced a human rights crisis as the plight of child labor and human trafficking escalated, and clean water, health care, and safety were not to be found (Fasenfest, 2016).

If indeed, as explained by Fasenfest and articulated by Marx, there is a right to equal liberty, right to security, and right to pursue happiness – then we must ensure that workers have a right to their labor. They have a right to redress. They have the right to advance human rights agendas. Those of the public must balance corporate interests. Human emancipation must dictate our policies and offer new opportunities that promote the common cause as a basic condition of democracy.

Strange, as I write this, we are more than two years after the election of Joe Biden, yet we are still dealing with the debacle of Trump's refusal to admit defeat. As Fasenfest (2010b) argues, some of the problem is that many Americans have difficulties differentiating 'alternative' facts from truth. Trump utilized to his advantage labor discontent and other kinds of dissatisfaction accumulating in the decades of social unrest linked to neo-liberal policies and globalization. The MAGA movement challenged the idea of the richest country in the world being unable to feed large numbers of Americans who experience food insecurity. Absent from the left has been a consistent and limited political message.

At its core, that message should generate alternatives to despair, and boost economic strategies to combat resource scarcity. Democratic public policy must be merged with democratic financial strategy so as to mobilize resources, activate international alliances, and utilize the law to make democracy accountable to the people. A global democratic movement embracing the local communities must work to maximize employment, livable wages, and access to health care, public goods, and services. These should be used to overcome the centuries of oppression, imperialism, racism, homophobia, classism, and ableism that undergird our societies. Hegemonic structures that reify race hierarchies, male supremacy, and classism should be supplanted by programs of action that empower, invest in, and strengthen local communities and people (Fasenfest, 2021).

4 The Humble Giant – Accolades from the Bleachers

David Fasenfest has worked to promote truth and reason in a world where power and oppression rule the airwaves, publishing houses, corporations, educational institutions, and religious places of worship. Scholars who would never have made it in the academy owe their very start, if not their continuance, to the publishing instruments he has created and sustained over the past few decades. David has done this while being marginalized and castigated by the official organizations within the academic disciplines of both sociology and economics. However, the thousands of pages he has edited and authored, the hundreds of issues he has researched, and the solutions he has offered, have not gone unnoticed. But as in the days of old, we ignore and kill our prophets, shy away from the truth, and hold on to our collective amnesias, myths, and fallacies. But while the revolution will not be televised, it will be live. And it will be even more so because David Fasenfest came this way.

References

Case, P., Fasenfest, D., Sarri, R., & Phillips, A. (2005). Providing Educational Support for Female Ex-Inmates: Project PROVE as a Model for Social Reintegration. *Journal of Correctional Education* (1974 -), *56*(2), 146œ157. http://www.jstor.org/stable/23282840.
Fasenfest, D. (2009). *Engaging Social Justice: Critical Studies of 21st Century Social Transformation*, edited by David Fasenfest. Leiden/ Boston: Brill Publishers.
Fasenfest, D. (2010a). Neoliberalism, Globalization and the Capitalist World Order. *Critical Sociology*, *36*(5), 627–631. https:// doi.org/10.1177/0896920510372861.
Fasenfest, D. (2010b). A Political Economy of Knowledge Production. *Critical Sociology*, *36*(4), 483–487. https://doi.org/10.1177/00113921110374694.
Fasenfest, D. (2010c). Government, Governing, and Governance. *Critical Sociology*. *36*. 771–774. 10.1177/0896920510378192.
Fasenfest, D. (2010d). The Glocal Crisis and the Politics of Change. *Critical Sociology*, *36*(3), 363–368. https:// doi.org/ 10.1177/ 0896920510365199.
Fasenfest, D. (2010e). A Touch of Class, with Layers of Race and a Sprinkling of Gender. *Critical Sociology*, *36*(1), 5–8. https:// doi.org/10.1177/ 0896920509347135.
Fasenfest, D. (2011). Terrorism, Neo-Liberalism and Political Rhetoric. *Critical Sociology*, *37*(3) 379–382.
Fasenfest, D. (2016). Marx, Marxism and Human Rights. *Critical Sociology*, *42*(6), 777–779. https:// doi.org/10.1177/ 0896920516645720.
Fasenfest, D., Ciancanelli, P. and Reese, L.A. (1997), Value, Exchange, and the Social Economy: Framework and Paradigm Shift in Urban Policy. *International Journal of Urban and Regional Research*, 21: 7–22. https://doi.org/10.1111/1468-2427.00055.
Fasenfest, D., & Das, R. J. (2021). Constructing the Conceptual Tools for the Global South. In *Constructing Social Research Objects*. Leiden, The Netherlands: Brill. https:// doi.org/ 10.1163/9789004450028_006.

Fasenfest, D. and Jacobs, J. (2003). An Anatomy of Change and Transition: The Automobile Industry of Southwest Michigan. *Small Business Economics*, 21(2) 153–172.

Gottfried, H., & Fasenfest, D. (2021). Understanding the Trajectory of Japanese Capitalism. *Critical Sociology*, 47(1), 149–161. https:// doi.org/ 10.1177/0896920520944465.

Hartung, W.D and Freeman, B., 2023. "Not Your Grandfather's Military-Industrial Complex." Antiwar.com. Not Your Grandfather's Military-Industrial Complex - Antiwar.com

Huntington, John, S. and Lawrence Glickman (2021). America's Most Destructive Habit. *The Atlantic*. https://www.theatlantic.com/ideas/archive/2021/11/conservative-backlash-progress/620607/.

Obstfeld, Maurice, and Zhou, Haonan. "The Global Dollar Cycle." National Bureau of Economic Research. https://www.nber.org/system/files/working_papers/w31004/w31004.pdf.

Reuters, 2023. "Morning Bid: Markets turn risk-averse after bumper month." Morning Bid: Markets turn risk-averse after bumper month | Reuters.

Scott-Heron, G. 1971. "The Revolution Will Not Be Televised". RCA Studios, New York City.

Thau, Barbara, 2023. "Hyper-Local Commerce and Smaller Brands Benefit From Post-Pandemic Consumer Trends." U.S. Chamber of Commerce. Pandemic Consumer Trends: Hyper-Local Commerce & Small Brands | CO- by US Chamber of Commerce

CHAPTER 5

Marxist Sociology in Asia

David Fasenfest's Engagement with the Global South and China

Ngai Pun

1   Marx Matters

Since the global financial crisis of 2008, the capitalist world has grappled with significant upheavals. The public voice has risen in protest, even major investment firms and magnates have begun to address environmental concerns, global inequality, wealth concentration, and above all, the continued relevance of Karl Marx. Yet, this hasn't always been the norm. The decline of communism worldwide has forced Marxism into a struggle for its existence. Meanwhile, the global Right advances under the banner of neoliberalism, whereas the Left appears fragmented, a phenomenon reflected not only in intellectual spheres but in political systems worldwide. In this context, the work of David Fasenfest becomes critically important. His scholarly contributions over the last four decades, including his roles as the editor of *Critical Sociology* and the Brill book series, his commitment to promoting Marxist ideas, and his efforts to stimulate critical social analysis, especially in the Global South, are significant. Fasenfest's unwavering dedication has greatly contributed to the advancement of Marxist scholarship.

Fasenfest has endeavoured to explore how Marx's ideas retain their significance in understanding and addressing contemporary social, economic, and political dilemmas. In *Marx Matters*, a book examining the continued relevance of Marx's ideas, Fasenfest underscored the systemic nature of crises and the opportunities they present for change, the inherent collective aspect of human society that shapes the social structure of work and the environment, and the crucial role of historical understanding in interpreting social, political, and economic transformations within any epoch (Fasenfest, 2022: 3).

Through his emphasis on the applicability of Marxist theory, together with the exploration of their practical implications, recognition of intersectionality, scholarly dialogues, and efforts to demystify Marxist thought, Fasenfest has played an important role in spreading and interpreting Marxist ideas in Hong Kong, Mainland China, and in other Asian societies. He has stimulated critical thinking and encouraged greater engagement with Marxist thought in contemporary society. His persistent engagement with topics such as globalization, neoliberalism, the capitalist world order, the global working class, and social inequality, along with his structural analysis of social changes from a Marxist viewpoint, and his more recent focus on human rights issues, all testify to an enduring contribution to Marxist sociology. They also highlight new directions for critical sociology, an achievement only possible through a relentless commitment to his discipline.

2   Championing the Global South through Critical Sociology

As the editor of *Critical Sociology*, a flagship journal in the field, Fasenfest has made significant contributions to the advancement of an investigative scholarship, offering the Global South a guide to much-needed conceptual tools. The journal has been instrumental in moulding the field and pushing the boundaries of sociological inquiry, challenging mainstream sociology's orthodoxy, combatting elitism, questioning oppressive structures, and advocating diverse perspectives. In recent years, *Critical Sociology* has broadened its international scope and confronted Eurocentric viewpoints prevalent in sociological discourse. It has become a premier outlet for global scholarship, actively seeking contributions from scholars outside North America and initiating special issues focused on specific regions (Fasenfest, 2014).

Approaching issues and problems from a classic Marxist perspective, Fasenfest underscores the importance of the Global South, particularly its workers, in scrutinizing the global capitalist system. In collaboration with scholars such as Raju Das, Fasenfest illuminates the perils of 'world-regional exceptionalism' and Eurocentric universalism. Though Marx initially analysed the emergence of capitalism in Europe, his ideas found wider acceptance and application in Asia and the Third World. His concepts, based on social relations and geography, encompass all forms of class society, including advanced capitalism. As capitalist relations evolve in the Global South, Marx's insights into advanced capitalism in Europe remain pertinent. This understanding helps elucidate the South's material challenges, contradictions, and its position within the imperialist system, countering postcolonial and postmodern scepticism and providing a philosophical foundation to critique prevailing perceptions of the South. Fasenfest and Das's work re-emphasizes Marx's global approach to analyzing capitalism, underscoring the necessity of understanding countries in the Global South in terms of class, taking into account their historical struggles against feudalism, imperialism, and failed anti-capitalist revolutions (Fasenfest and Das, 2021).

More recently, in a co-authored article with Alfredo Saad-Filho, Fasenfest addresses the issue of global poverty, linking its reproduction to global capitalism and neoliberal policies (Fasenfest and Saad-Filho, 2021). Particularly in the case of developing countries, neoliberal policies and globalization have intensified issues surrounding benefit appropriation, exploitation of the working class, surplus value extraction, and systemic inequality on a global scale. Stabilization and structural adjustment policies, championed by entities like the International Monetary Fund and the World Bank, primarily reflect the interests of a societal minority. These policies, often enforced as conditions for access to financial aid, have led to the misappropriation of social surplus and wealth concentration among a select few. Hence, Marx's ideas illuminate how the fruits of development in developing nations are often appropriated by a small elite, rather than contributing to the welfare of the masses. A critical analysis of power dynamics and class relations is crucial to any consideration of the persistent poverty issue in the Global South.

The Global South has been a focal point in Fasenfest's work. In 'Globalization and its Discontents', he highlights the region's struggle with underdevelopment, marked by seemingly ineradicable poverty linked to economic difficulties (Fasenfest, 2012). This he aligns with Marx's analysis of the relationship between capitalist countries and the rest of the world, wherein capitalism extracts resources, and maintains low wages to maximize profits. Hence the practices of international financial institutions, such as the IMF and World Bank, perpetuate dependency and exploitation in the Global South by offering loans for rapid modernization. The expansion of global markets and the integration of national economies into the global capitalist system further corroborate Marx's analysis of capitalism's global expansion tendencies. Issues of debt in the Global South underscore the ramifications of imposing austerity measures on countries unable to sustain significant debt burdens.

3 Engaging with China through a Marxist Lens

Given his concerns regarding the Global South and the exploitative nature of global capitalism, Fasenfest also turns a keen eye towards China. Actively participating in international dialogues and conferences, including the second and third World Marxism Conferences in Beijing and a series of seminars at Shanghai University, Fasenfest's engagement with Chinese issues is unwavering.

In the article 'Is Marx Still Relevant,' he broaches China's relevance and the significance of Marxism (Fasenfest, 2018). Given the global economic landscape's evolution, with industrial production shifting from West to East, particularly to Asia and China, he argues for a re-evaluation of Marx's ideas and their applicability to the contemporary economic milieu. Marx's insights, he maintains, may serve to illuminate China's economic development and its relationship with capitalism. He also urges serious consideration of China's pursuit of 'socialism with Chinese characteristics,' particularly how the surplus generated in China contributes to poverty alleviation, advanced infrastructure construction, and citizen service.

Fasenfest further explores the possibility of a development path in China, in the context of the Belt and Road Initiative (BRI), that avoids the abuses associated with colonial and neo-colonial expansion. He suggests that the BRI could present an alternative to the exploitative relationships historically linked to European capitalism and colonialism. China's efforts to establish partnerships with Global South countries based on mutual benefit might be able to steer clear of these earlier one-sided relations. While the debate continues whether China, with the BRI, can effectively counter the traditional industrial and financial capitalist world, Fasenfest indicates that Marx's fundamental concepts and ideas have the potential to guide us in repeating during in the 21st century the exploitation and harm of 19th-century global capitalism.

China's unique history with Marxism is undeniable, having adopted the ideology under Mao Zedong's leadership and established the People's Republic of China in 1949. Marxist theory played a crucial role in shaping the Chinese Communist Party's policies and governance. However, the implementation of Marxism in China has evolved over time, incorporating elements of state capitalism and market-oriented reforms while preserving a socialist political system. Marx's discussions of exploitation and commodification have gained renewed relevance as China transitioned from socialism to capitalism (Pun, 2021).

Hence the reform and opening up of China led to the emergence of a new working class, primarily composed of migrant laborers from rural areas working in industrial zones. This transformation, however, represents a paradox—a departure from the socialist past and a recategorizing of class politics. Accordingly, the reform process led to increased class inequality in China, with the private sector growing rapidly while state-owned enterprises diminished in importance. Various aspects of Chinese society became commodified, including land, natural resources, labor, and public services. Ironically, the state played a pivotal role in managing this process, inviting foreign capital investment, constructing special economic zones, providing infrastructure, and ensuring the supply of low-paid but skilled workers.

This shift from the fundamental form of politics in Maoist China—based on class—challenged the official ideology of 'socialism with Chinese characteristics' and led to a resurgence of grassroots agency, labor struggles, and class consciousness among workers and students. In this context, Marx's theory can further illuminate China's role, especially as it transitioned from competitive capitalism to state-monopolized infrastructural capitalism through initiatives like the Belt and Road Initiative.

4 Engagement, Inspiration, and the Power of Collaboration

Reflecting on my own interactions with David Fasenfest, it is the dialogues, encouragements, and insights drawn from his writings that have immensely enriched my research and understanding. The intellectual sparks that ignited during our collaborations were illuminating, propelling us to delve deeper into our investigations. Indeed, it is his commitment to critical inquiry, embodied in his editorship of *Critical Sociology*, challenging existing paradigms, dominant power structures, and promoting inclusivity and diverse perspectives that inspired our recent special issue of that journal (Volume 48, Issue 7–8). The values embodied in this environment fostered a productive and investigative approach, prompting us to challenge our presuppositions and stretch our intellectual horizons.

The most important lesson taught us by *Critical Sociology* is to engage with debates on Chinese capitalism critically. Moving beyond the stage theory which usually takes development of capitalism as linear temporality or teleology of historical progress, the special issue positions post-socialist China as a late comer joining global capitalism, embodying multiple forms of capital and operating as a variegated form of capitalism when compared to both the Global North and Global South. Taking Hong Kong as part of China's capitalism project, the simultaneous operation of multiple capitals in China (including Hong Kong) creates its own 'third world' in its hinterland, in its internal regions of the country and across the border to its neighbouring regions. This specific mode of operation of capitals, understood from a Marxist perspective, enables us to capture the features of contemporary Chinese capitalism and to tease out its complexity; in short, its coordination of all the overarching forces that shape the formation of the trans-border working-classes in Hong Kong and mainland China.

A critical sociology also facilitates the conceptualization by us of the contemporary moment of Chinese capitalism as a form of infrastructural capitalism (Pun, Siu and Gottfried, 2022). The current variant illustrates a Chinese development trajectory characterised by strategic moves from competitive capitalism in the early reform period to the advent of monopoly capital and an emerging imperialist rivalry. Regardless of whether we understand infrastructural capitalism as a kind of state capitalism, its variegated nature includes features of both physical and digital infrastructures, resulting in sustaining and speeding up expansive manufacturing, logistics and e-commerce industries.

Debates over the past three decades on the nature of Chinese capitalism tended to stress deviations of the Chinese economic system from western capitalism, licensing the conclusion that China is not in fact a capitalist system. The role of the redistributive state, coordination between the state-private business, the mixture of the role played by the party in management control over corporations, and the ambiguity of private property rights all stand out as distinguishing the China model with its 'special characteristics'. Notwithstanding, the heated debates on whether China can be viewed as capitalist or as 'socialism with its special characteristics' miss the role the working class plays in significantly defining its form of capitalism. More specifically, it is largely the conflicts and contradictions between capital and labour, the production and reproduction of these conflicts, and the enduring contradictions that define capitalism, while at the same time sowing the seeds of capitalism's future destruction.

5 Concluding Remarks

For scholars in the Global South, Fasenfest's unwavering commitment to exploring the complexities of such contexts, together with his innovative application of Marxism to understand these dynamics, have been a beacon of inspiration. His insights have not only guided our work but also encouraged us to confront and question existing narratives critically. On a personal note, the discussions we've had, the constructive feedback we received on our drafts, and the mutual respect we cultivated throughout our collaboration are experiences I deeply cherish. In an important sense, the intellectual journey we have traversed has itself been as rewarding as the final output. Because of this positive influence on my own research, enabling it to develop by asking searching questions that need rigorous answers, it is a privilege to have worked alongside David Fasenfest.

References

Fasenfest D (2012) Globalization and Its Discontents. *Critical Sociology* 38(3): 343–46.
Fasenfest D (2014) Critical Sociology after 40 Years: Looking Back, Looking Forward. *Critical Sociology* 40(1): 3–6.
Fasenfest D (2018) Is Marx Still Relevant? *Critical Sociology* 44(6): 851–55.
Fasenfest D (2022) The Once and Future Marx. In Fasenfest D (ed) *Marx Matters*, Leiden: Brill, 1–13.
Fasenfest D, Das RJ (2021). Constructing the Conceptual Tools for the Global South. In Leiulfsrud H, Sohlberg P (eds) *Constructing Social Research Objects: Constructionism in Research Practice*. Leiden: Brill, 59–83.
Fasenfest D, Saad-Filho A (2021). Global Poverty: a Marxian Analysis. *Вопросы Политической Экономии*, *1*, 65–77.
Pun N (2021). Turning Left: Student-Worker Alliance in Labour Struggles in China. *Globalizations*, 18(8), 1392–1405.
Pun N, Siu K, Gottfried H (2022) Global Capitalism and Labour in the Age of Monopoly: Hong Kong and Mainland China. *Critical Sociology* 48(7–8): 1115–1122.

CHAPTER 6

The Politics of Coercion, the Coercion of Politics
Thought Conversion in Pre-war Japan

Hideo Aoki

1   Introduction

I was a student at a Japanese university in the early 1960s. Our home-room professor was a liberal during the war. He was arrested, interrogated, tortured, and stabbed in the calf muscle with a red-hot implement by (police) authorities. One day, he rolled up his trousers and showed students the scars, still raw after more than 20 years. He was converted and then sent to the battlefield. He told us: "It's embarrassing, but my only anti-war achievement was keeping my troops alive. As we crouched in the trenches with bullets flying above, I told my soldiers to stay down and hide. I kept them where they were." No, it was a brave act that even if he survived, he would be court martialed and sentenced to death for avoiding the enemy. Born in Kanazawa, a city in Northern Japan, he graduated from the Fourth High School (presently Kanazawa University) and studied at the Imperial University of Tokyo. He came into contact with liberal thought, engaged in anti-war activities, was arrested, renounced his thought, was released, and then sent to the battlefield. He was one of many students who walked a similar path. In his words, I saw a part of the anguish of 'conscientious converts' who were still suffering after the war and could not be easily liberated. This paper examines the experience of communists in pre-war Japan when they were forced to convert to patriotism, the ideology or thought of their opponents, due to the harsh oppression of the fascist state.

Elsewhere I have analysed the worldview of Japanese soldiers during the war, especially the *Kamikaze* (special attack). The conversion of communists is deeply related to the process of creating the ideas held by *Kamikaze* soldiers. Many of the latter were former university students who had accepted communism and liberalism. When they were drafted into the army, they became *Kamikaze* soldiers in an environment of overwhelming patriotism; they experienced a serious conflict between ideals of communism/liberalism and those of patriotism. It was directly connected to the issue of why they lived and died. Facing inevitable death when diving on enemy warships with planes and submarines, some stuck to communism/liberalism, others clung to patriotism, and others were confused and stopped thinking. Their experiences give important clues to understanding the thought conversion of communists in pre-war Japan.

Many people living in the world today are experiencing or are subject to various forms of conversions resulting in harsh political and thought crises. People branded as religious extremists, ethnic extremists, or political extremists, are considered 'terrorists' destroying society, arrested, interrogated, and imprisoned, and are forced to renounce religious beliefs, ethnically assimilate, renounce political thoughts, and succumb to their rulers. Muslim jihadists, for example, were branded as terrorists committing a *Holy War*, and so were arrested, forced to recant as a result of re-education, a process of deradicalization and rehabilitation carried out in the Guantanamo Bay Detention Camp, to prevent them from returning to jihadism. Max Ward referred to the similarities between this case and the conversion of Japanese communists (Ward, 2019: 9–14), writing, "I utilize the particular history of the Peace Preservation Law in order to consider the various modes of power that state, not just the interwar Japanese state, use to police political threats, thus reproducing and redefining their respective national polities in the process" (Ward, 2019: iv).

In the contemporary world of conflicting nationalities, ethnicities, and political beliefs, the human drama of conversion and non-conversion is ubiquitous. The conversion of the communists in prewar Japan provides many lessons about such a process, and raises the following question: Who is living in the current harsh political and thought crises, and how are they managing? What do we need to do to defend freedom of thought by defying the compulsion to convert? For example, the Chinese government, in dealing with the Xinjiang Uyghur Autonomous Region, apply detentions and other efforts at cultural assimilation, is not unlike how the Japanese government-imposed conversions during its military expansion in East Asia. The analysis of the experiences facing communists in pre-war Japan helps provide an answer to these questions and is the focus of this chapter. "The dynamics that gave rise to both Marxism and fascism in Japan were shared across much of the world", write Hayter, Sipos and Williams (2021: xxv). Even more importantly, we live today in a period of rising reaction and right-wing politics in which people are rejecting views of community and casting aside their prior liberal and progressive values. At the heart of it is thought conversion.

2 Japanese Conversion

The conversion of communists in pre-war Japan serves as a model case for conversion around the world, and vividly illustrates its essence. Here the Japanese-style conversion is called the *tenkō* (changing direction), and its characteristics are as follows. Whereas Jihadists were required to renounce Muslim extremism and were rehabilitated to prevent them from returning to it, Japanese communists were required to undergo both external *tenkō* (renouncing communism) and internal *tenkō* (accepting and defending patriotism). *Tenkō* required communists to accept their opponent's thoughts, to actively defend them, and to put them into practice daily.

Second, after the Sino-Japanese War of 1937, the thought issue was elevated to the 'Thought War' and the scope of thought control was expanded from Japan to colonial Asia. Japan aimed to establish *Greater East Asia Co-Prosperity Sphere* in East Asia. Therefore, "the nation-state of Japan was explicitly created against the principle of ethnic nationalism ... Imperial Japan was a multiethnic nation-state, an ostensibly integrative and integrating polity." (Ward 2019: 156). *Tenkōsha* (convert) included those who aligned with Japanese communists and fought for national independence in colonial Asia. In Korea, Taiwan, and Manchuria, many communists and independentists were arrested, and *tenkōed* (converted) due to the oppression of the Japanese authorities.[1]

Third, *all* of the over 60,000 Japanese communists[2] were arrested. The State (together with its related authorities) placed itself in the *state of exception* (Agamben, 2005) and pursued communists by any (lawless) means, including shadowing, warning, intimidation, espionage, and family persuasion (Ogino, 2012). Arrests were followed by grueling interrogations and torture. Officials interrogating arrestees knew that they could torture arrestees to death with impunity. In practice, no officials who killed arrestees went punished. Arrestees were the literal *homo sacer* whom "anyone can kill without being stained by sacrilege" (Agamben, 1998: 73).

Fourth, almost all communists *tenkōed*. This is because there were systematic and detailed policies (laws and institutions) from arrest to *tenkō* in

---

[1] Here the term 'authorities' extends from the Ministry of Justice to Special Higher Police which arrested and interrogated thought criminals.
[2] Communists consisted of members of the Japanese Communist Party (hereafter the Party) and Marxist scholars of *Lecture School*, and non-Party members and Marxist scholars of *Workers and Farmers School* (Aoki 2021). They debated over how to understand Japanese capitalism. But the controversy was interrupted when all the participants were arrested by the authorities.

operation throughout the state. "Japanese government authorities adopted, and encouraged, conversion as a way of reintegrating leftists into Japanese society" (Hoston, 1983: 98). There was no other alternative powerful thought to communism in Japan. Through interrogation, torture, and persuasion by authorities, they finally became patriots who actively defended *Kokutai* (polity of Emperor State). Those who renounced communism had no other choice.

3 *Tenkō* Studies

There are many previous studies on the prewar *tenkō* of Japanese communists, including the following: Beckmann and Ōkubo, 1969; Fauconnier 2021; Fujita 1997; Hayter, Sipos and Williams 2021; Higuchi 1972; Hofmann 2020; Hoston 1983, 1985, 1987; Ishidō 2001; Itō 1995; Kobayashi 1987; Kunimatsu 1989; Linkhoeva 2018; Maruyama1995, 1996; Matsuo 1971; Miyaji 2019; Nakajima 1980; Nakazawa 2012; Ogino 2000, 2012; Okudaira 2006; Shisō no Kagaku Kenkyūkai [Science of Thought Study Group]1962; Steinhoff, 1969, 1988; Toike 2014; Tsurumi 2012; Ward 2014, 2019, 2021; Yoshimoto 1990.

The themes covered are wide-ranging: *tenkō* policy and thought control of authorities, the form and process of *tenkō*, the mentality of *tenkōsha*, media *tenkō* reports; the Party, including thought control in the post-war era, specifically the 'Red Purge' from public offices by Allied Occupation Forces in 1949–50 (Fauconnier 2021: 39), and debate on war responsibility and subjectivity. In particular, the works of Shunsuke Tsurumi and others marked a turning point in *tenkō* study in post-war Japan (Shisō-no-Kagaku-Kenkyūkai 1962). All of these studies delineated the uniqueness of Japanese *tenkō*.

Ward analyzed the development of the *tenkō* policy targeting communists and summarized the main points as follows: "First, *tenkō* was completed from abandoning communism to reaching to voluntarily practicing the idea of *Kokutai*. Second, the emphasis on control shifted from thought suppression in the 1920s to the prompt of *tenkō* in the 1930s. Third, *tenkō* expanded from *tenkō* of thought criminals to a national indoctrination movement in which *tenkōshas* (converts) who were dramatically awakened to the Japanese Spirit was used as a model for *imperial subjects*. Fourth, it was a thought apparatus of public mobilization to the war effort. Fifth, Japanese *tenkōshas* became ardent adherents of the idea of the *kokutai*" (Ward 2019: 159).

From the *tenkōsha's* point of view, Patricia Steinhoff analyzed the mentality of *tenkōshas* focusing on human relationships with their families and within the Party (Steinhoff 1969:159–160). Focusing on the distance between *tenkōshas'* thoughts and their class status, family background, and status within the

Party, she classified *tenkō* into political *tenkō*, civic *tenkō*, and religious *tenkō*. And she characterized each in terms of patriotic awareness, family ties, other relationships, and consciousness of self (Steinhoff 1988:88–91). She considered *tenkō* to be a phenomenon deeply related to group belonging and individual identity.

Germaine Hoston, following Steinhoff, classified three forms of communist *tenkō*. "A political (*seiji-teki*) *tenkō* was one based on political differences of opinion with the Communist Party, as in the Sano and Nabeyama prototype (Sano and Nabeyama 1957). Citizen (*shimin-teki*) *tenkō* involved a desire to return to normal life as a good Japanese citizen. In religious (*shyūkyō-teki*) *tenkō*, one gave up communist ideology because of a new belief in something else, though not necessarily an organized religion" (Hoston 1983: 99–100).

In this way, Ward focused on the external factors (*tenkō* policy) that urged communists to *tenkō*, while Steinhoff and Hoston focused on internal factors (*tenkōsha*'s belief system). Referring to these studies, this chapter focuses on *the thoughts or ideologies of communists, especially the Party members*. There are two reasons for this focus. First, authorities regarded communism as the most dangerous thought, and made its control the cornerstone of thought control. Second, communists were *tenkōed* for various reasons, but the central one was the renouncement of communist thought. All other aspects were reduced to thought *tenkō*. The transformation began with thought *tenkō* and ended with it. Because of this, *tenkō* analysis begins with the study of the selection and change of thought.

The next section looks at the external factors of communist *tenkō*, such as *tenkō* policies, laws, institutions, and treatment of detainees and the protected. Section 5 analyzes the internal factors of *tenkō*, or the thinking processes of communists, such as situational awareness, beliefs, and attitudes. Section 6 discusses the contemporary meaning of this *tenkō* case-study.

4 Authorities and *Tenkō*

4.1 Law and Institution

The Imperial State harshly oppressed communists, whom authorities derogatorily called *Shugisha* (Ist). The legal basis for its control was the *Peace Preservation Law* (PPL)[3] enacted in 1925, which followed the promulgation of the *Extremist Social Movement Control Bill* in 1922 and of *Matters on Penalties*

---

3 In 1941, the PPL was completely revised and expanded from 7 articles to 65 articles, including the provision for preventive arrest. Communists were arrested as persons in need of

for Peace Preservation in 1923. Article 1 of the PPL stipulated that it aims to protect Kokutai and the private property system and to punish groups and persons involved in challenging these institutions, not least by engaging in activity. Authorities deemed communists first, liberals second, and then some religious sects to be 'dangerous extremists', all of whom denied Kokutai and the private property system.

Thought criminals were not only cracked down on by means of arrest, prosecution, and imprisonment. In 1936, the government enacted the Law on the Protection and Observation of Thought Criminals, which aimed to educate and surveil thought criminals released after prison sentences, released on parole, given a suspended sentence, under postponement of the indictment, or preventative detention to prevent them from returning to extremism, by putting them in internment facilities (Internment Facilities 1943). "The former thought criminals are placed in 'formless prisons' under supervision and observation for two years, where they are accommodated and released into society only after they have re-established their lives, been introduced to jobs, completed their thought, reached out to the Japanese Spirit, and have become respectable human beings" (Osaka Mainichi Shinbun September 1, 1936).[4]

4.2 Control in Practice

How many people were arrested, interrogated, and imprisoned under the PPL? The number varies depending on the material. One document counted hundreds of thousands of people arrested under the PPL, and some 75,681 were sent to trial between 1928 and 1945, including more than 1,500 religious people arrested, of whom 5,162 were prosecuted (Matsuo 1971: 11). The number of the prosecuted is small compared to those tried because many *tenkōed* before the actual prosecution took place. There was strong *tenkō* coercion there. Another document indicated that between 1925 and 1943, 67,223 persons were arrested, 6,024 were prosecuted, 65 died under torture, 114 died later as a result of torture, and 1,503 other cases with illnesses that may have been caused by torture or imprisonment (Misuzu Shobo 2004: 646–649). Most of these victims were communists. The death by torture of Takiji Kobayashi, a famous novelist, is

---

indoctrination for pre-*tenkō* based on the prediction that they might break the law even if they did not do so.

4   There was the Teikoku Renewal Society (founded in 1926), a semi-official rehabilitation organization for (former) 'thought criminals'. In 1931 it began a rehabilitation program for them. This also worked to educate *tenkōshas* and stabilize their lives (Kobayashi 1987:28–30). Its management policy was rehabilitation and reconciliation through familial ideology.

well known, but 64 more persons lost their lives in this way, and another 114 persons later.

Tenkō in practice was as follows (Itō 1995:134). Between 1928 and 1938, 12,145 persons were punished for violations of the PPL. 93.5% of them were released after *tenkō*, and of them, 7.5% were punished again. That is to say, 92.5% of those released did not re-embrace their original views. It was the successful result of the authorities' persuasion of *tenkōsha* inside the prison, and indoctrination and surveillance outside the prison. Most of these *tenkōshas* were communists. This is corroborated by other sources. Between 1925 and 1945 the Party had 2,300 members, all of whom were arrested and prosecuted, and 98 to 99% of them *tenkō*ed. Only 9 to 20 members maintained a non-*tenkō* position (Miyaji 2019). While there is no way to verify these figures, all data show almost the same trend. Prisons played a significant role in *tenkō*: they accepted 8,710 internees between 1936 and 1944, and asked for 5,353 of them to be inspected by the Probation Review Board (Nakazawa 2012: 159). Internees consisted of released prisoners, paroled prisoners, prosecuted and suspended sentence prisoners, and preventive detainees. In 1943, these corrective institutions surveyed internees (Probation Office 1943 in Tsurumi 2012:52–54), providing an overview of current and former inmates:

1. *Characteristics of internees.*
   Male-93.8%, female-6.2%, 2,888 persons in total — Among them, 248 were persons mostly from Korean Peninsula.[5]
2. *Criminal thoughts (risk factors).*
   Communism-90.0%, anarchism-2.1%, extreme religion-5.7%, ethnic movement-2.2%, and 2,671 persons in total. — Those classified as adherents of 'Extreme religion' were few, while 'Ethnic movement' referred to the Korean, Chinese, and Taiwanese independence movements.
3. *Motives for tenkō.*
   National awakening-31.9%, family reasons-26.9%, regret at being detained-14.4%, discovery of theoretical fallacies-11.7%, personal anguish-9.6%, religious faith-2.1%, others-3.3%, and 2,671 persons in total. — 'Family reasons' refer to being the family breadwinner, or concern for the family. 'Personal anguish' refers to problems such as age, health, and psychosis. Political *tenkō* was due to patriotic awakening and the discovery of the deficiency of communism accounted for 43.6%, and other motives also were related to political *tenkō*.

---

5 In the pre-war era, many colonial Koreans, including students studying in Japan, were arrested for belonging to the national independence movement.

Manabu Sano and Sadachika Nabeshima, executives of the Party, issued a *tenkō* statement, *Letter to the Co-Defendants*, in prison in 1933, when mass *tenkō* of communists occurred. According to the above survey, motives for *tenkō* were commonly in the order of personal anguish, family reasons, then social group (Tsurumi 2012:54). However, in 1942 motives were in the order of national awakening, family reasons, then personal anguish. This order change of *tenkō* motive indicates how thought control was strengthened over time, thereby reducing the influence of communism. Shunsuke Tsurumi identified three characteristics of Japanese *tenkō* (Tsurumi:53–54). First, very few did *tenkō* for religious reasons. Neither faith nor other kinds of thought acted as a bulwark against fascism in Japan. Second, many *tenkōed* due to the patriotic awakening, underlining the extent to which nationalism had become influential. Third, many *tenkōed* due to family reasons, since those who did so had strong family ties. These characteristics were rooted in Japanese culture and society (Tsurumi 2012: 54): "The group orientation predominant in prewar Japan is by far the most cogent explanation for the proportions and dynamics of the *tenkō* phenomenon. *Tenkō* reflected both solidarity with the *kokutai* and solidarity with the subgroup of fellow Marxists" (Hoston 1983:103). Thus, almost all communists *tenkōed*. "Today, it is said there are around 60,000 persons all over Japan, who have a history of left-wing thought crimes and have expressed so-called *tenkō*. From this point of view, this can be said the *era of mass tenkō* of leftist thought criminals" (Higuchi 1972:1). *Tenkō* in Japan generally occurred from top to bottom, with Party leaders Sano and Nabeyama *tenkōing*, followed by rank-and-file members (Ishidō 2001:105–106). "Within one month after the Sano-Nabeyama statement, a third of all detainees – and 36 percent of all those convicted (548 *tenkōsha*r) under the 1925 Peace Preservation Law – had issued similar declarations of *tenkō*" (Hayter, Sipos and Williams 2021: xx).

The background of mass *tenkō* included not only coercion and indoctrination by authorities, but also Party infiltration by espionage, repeated warnings, and strict surveillance including tailing Party members. And many Party members were arrested by repeated mass round-ups; these included the First Japanese Communist Party Incident in 1923, the March 15 Incident in 1928, the April 16 Incident in 1929, and the Atami Incident in 1932. The number of arrestees ballooned; "68,000 for 18 years (1927–45), or an average of 3,600 a year. The vast majority of those arrestees were identified as 'leftists.' This accounts for a total of 64,000" (Fauconnier 2021:31). Similarly, "Mass defections brought about the complete destruction of the Communist movement in Japan by the end of 1935. Such mass arrests were the precondition for mass *tenkō* after 1936. By 1940 virtually all JCP members had *tenkōed*" (Hoston 1983:98).

4.3 Tenkō *Criteria*

Tenkō occurred within the cut and thrust of communism and patriotism. The Authorities' aim of *tenkō* was not just to get people to renounce their thoughts, but also to reorient their thoughts in the 'correct direction.' This was the authorities' mission: to destroy dangerous thoughts. Even if cruel and merciless violence was practiced, they could not be sure that 'thought criminals' would succumb to a complete *tenkō*. Since violence is only ever an external driver of *tenkō,* The Authorities honed their skills in inducing *tenkō*, working to persuade and encourage communists to 'reintegrate' (Tsurumi 2012:55–57). They emphasized love of family, showing compassion for the circumstances communists faced and using words of sympathy and solidarity to manipulate their innermost emotions. At times, authorities won communists over by promising to arrange jobs for them or to look after their families if they *tenkōed*.[6]

Authorities judged and decided whether a communist *tenkōed*: using both violence and persuasion, it was they who had the power to decide the extent of *tenkō*, and so what *tenkō* constitutes. In 1933, the Head of the Penal Bureau issued 'A Notice on the Degree of *Tenkō*' (Okudaira 2006: 174–175). It was the first attempt to categorize thought criminals; *tenkōsha*, semi-*tenkōsha*, and non-*tenkōsha, albeit* still a rough classification. The criteria for *tenkō* became ever-stricter over time (Steinhoff 1988: 84–86). As indicated, in Article 1 of the PPL 'anyone who *organizes* a group to change *Kokutai* ... who *denies* the private property system', .and 'who *serves* as an officer or other leader of the said group' was liable to be punished. Its object was to punish 'acts' of thought criminals, such as being involved in associations for the reform of *Kokutai*. However, in 1933 not only acts, but also the eradication of communist thought became part of the criteria for *tenkō*. Moreover, in 1936, authorities classified five stages of *tenkō*, starting with non-*tenkō* and proceeding until reaching a complete thought change (Moriyama, 1937: 62–5).

> Stage 1. A person who asserts the legitimacy or approves of Marxism.
> Stage 2. A person who, although still uncritical of Marxism, renounces liberal and individualist attitudes.
> Stage 3. A person who reaches the point of criticizing Marxism.
> Stage 4. A person who completely understands and acknowledges the Japanese Spirit.

---

6 'Back home, your parents are crying' was an argument that authorities used against thought criminals. Higuchi (1972) and Misuzu Shobō (2004) provide insights into the methods and role of interrogators such as prosecutors and judges.

Stage 5. A person who reaches the point of applying the Japanese Spirit in practice.

It stipulated that *tenkō* was completed only after becoming *Shinmin*, the Imperial Subject, of Stage 4 and practicing *Nihon Seishin*, the Japanese Spirit, in the daily life of Stage 5. "The official definition of *tenkō* had shifted from negating one's communist affiliation in 1933 to the proactive demonstration of imperial ideology by the time of the outset of the Asia Pacific War", notes Ward (2021: 10). Masaru Higuchi, Tokyo Criminal District Court Judge, wrote the following in 1933: "*Tenkō* from Marxism is the destruction of Marxist consciousness itself. Western modern consciousness, which is also the consciousness of life in modern Japan, which eventually became Westernized, must be a straightforward destruction of itself. And yet, for the Japanese, as Japanese Subjects, it is possible only by sticking to the morals of the Empire" (Higuchi 1972: 8–9). "The essence of *tenkō* is an awakening of one's true nature. It is not limited to a mere symbolic awareness about *Kokutai*, but a holistic coalescence with it, i.e., *satori* (to clear mind and to understand the truth-quoter) as spiritual enlightenment" (Higuchi, 1972:42). According to Hirata Isao, the Chief of the Thought Section of the Tokyo Procuracy, out of the 60,000 suspects arrested under the Peace Preservation Law since 1928 (to 1936), roughly 10 percent still believed that Marxism was correct, while another 10 percent had 'truly overcome Marxism' by 'grasping the Japanese spirit' (Hirata 1938: 206). The remaining 80 percent were thus at various stages of moving towards 'completing *tenkō*'. To 'overcome Marxism', Hirata argued, was to return to a more fundamental consciousness of oneself as an *imperial subject* (Ward 2014:471).

It was only in Stage 4, and especially Stage 5, that detainees were released from the prisons. The ultimate aim of *tenkō* was to change a communist into a person who actively puts the Japanese Spirit into practice. After 1936 when the Law on the Protection and Observation of Thought Criminals was passed, authorities began to change thought criminals outside the prison system too. Thought criminals released after sentences, released on parole, given a suspended sentence, being under postponement of the indictment, or being in preventative detention were accordingly held in internment facilities, and re-educated so as to induce a patriotic awaking.

5 Communists and *Tenkō*

5.1 *Isolated Party*

Mass *tenkō* of communists, as outlined above, was primarily due to authorities' coercion (violence and appeasement). The Party itself was founded in 1922

(First Party), disbanded in 1924, and reformed in 1926 (Second Party). Mass arrests of Party members in 1928, 1929, and 1932 took the Party to the brink of ruin, and finally, the arrest of a Central Committee member (Hakamada Satomi) in 1935 ended the Party's political activities. Again, as noted, most Party members *tenkō*ed. In 1933, Sano and Nabeyama issued a *tenkō* statement while in prison, which was the forerunner of the *tenkō* issue. This brought about the 'era of *tenkō*' in which many Party members followed them. As well as coercion by authorities, therefore, mass *tenkō* was a result of circumstances within the Party.[7].

The Party's political line was led by Comintern (Communist International), the international communist movement organization that started under the lead of Lenin in 1919. At the first Congress, more than 50 representatives of communist political parties and revolutionary organizations from 30 countries gathered, each national party featuring as a branch of the Comintern. After Lenin's death, Stalin introduced his theory of One Country Socialism, which required all national parties to defend the Soviet Union from imperialism. As a result, the independence of revolutionary movements in each country was curtailed. During World War II, Comintern was unable to implement the 'From Imperialist War to Civil War' as it did during World War I because nationalism was on the rise in all countries, and the organization was disbanded in 1943.

In 1932, Comintern issued *The Statement on the Conditions in Japan and the Japanese Communist Party's Mission* (*Thirty-Second Thesis*) to the Party. It defined the coming Japanese Revolution as a bourgeois-democratic revolution, first to achieve bourgeois democracy and then to carry out a socialist revolution. To this end, the overthrow of the Emperor System, which had brought Japan's semi-feudal *Kokutai*, was considered the first step in the future socialist revolution. In the words of Hoston (1983: 113): "The Comintern had pressed the JCP to oppose Japanese imperialism and to call for the abolition of the Emperor System". Kenji Miyamoto, a Party executive, issued an appeal: "All Party members must fully grasp the program and statutes of Comintern, especially the Thirty-Second Thesis, as guidelines for daily struggle" (Miyamoto 2012: 386). This meant direct conflict with the PPL, which stipulated in Article 1

---

7 "Normally, *tenkō* was 'completed' by testimony or declarations as per the scenario authorities envisaged. *Tenkō* was not acknowledged until an expression was made of taking the same aggressive, reactionary stance as the authorities. The testimony or declarations of people committing *tenkō* were all very similar, within the same prescribed range" (JCP 1976:60).

the protection of Emperor-centered *Kokutai*. Here was the reason why authorities deemed the Party the most dangerous opposition group in Japan.

This instruction by Comintern was confronted by the fact that Japanese people had been thoroughly inculcated with the Emperor System. The idea that the Emperor was sacred, a living god, whether truly believed or merely spoken, had deep roots in the population. Those who doubted or denied it were deemed 'unpatriotic' and 'non-national', and consequently watched by authorities. Indeed, people themselves took the lead in accusing those who questioned this nationalist ideology.

In such circumstances, how realistic was the Party line in aiming to change *Kokutai* and overthrow the Emperor System? What prospects did the Party have for realizing them? The prestige of the Party was absolute among the communists, and criticism of the Party was tantamount to the betrayal of the Party itself. Nevertheless, such doubts were inevitable among Party members. At the Second Congress of Comintern in 1920, before the First Party was founded, the following letter was sent from Japan: "The Emperor is personalized as the divine, and Japanese people are very proud that the Imperial Household has continued uninterrupted since 600 B.C. For Japanese people, the Emperor is a focus of religious worship, and they are resolved to die should the Emperor so order. ... The concept of the Emperor's holiness is drilled into the Japanese from when they are children" (Murata 1986:8). After that, however, such situational awareness was not utilized in the Party's movement. There was no condition for carrying out a bourgeois-democratic revolution, let alone undertaking a socialist revolution.[8]

In this way, the Party's views had no basis in the population at large, and the sense of isolation from the people deepened among Party members. Moreover, there was an additional reason that fuelled their sense of isolation: namely, that the Party was subordinate to the Soviet-controlled Comintern, which itself was ignorant of the Japanese political situation. The Thirty-Second Thesis was the Japanese version of Stalin's global strategy, which Party members interpreted in the following manner: "If the Soviet Union seeks to build One Country Socialism in Russia, the Party should aim to build its socialism based on Japanese circumstances." Thus, an identity debate arose among Party

---

[8] On the contrary, the Party believed that the revolutionary situation in Japan was imminent. After the war, the Party acknowledged such an error of overoptimism about the desired situation. "For example, in the 1932 Thesis, there was a subjective overestimation of the revolutionary situation in Japan, such as 'we may be in a situation of the revolutionary crisis soon'" (JCP1976: 62).

members over whether the Party belonged to the Soviet Union or the Party itself. Such a sense of isolation and identity crisis came to a head when the Sino-Japanese War broke out, and the momentum for *tenkō* spread among Party members. Many members thought that they could resolve the isolation and upset by changing the Party line (Hoston 1987:192). Thus, the Party perished by a combination of the authorities' oppression and internal line turmoil.[9] The political crisis was in effect an ideological one.

5.2 Agency and Tenkō

Tenkō is essentially a thought (ideological) transfer. Therein lies the *agency* that changes thought, since *tenkō* "means a subjective change in one's perception of the situation" (Fujita 1997:5). *Tenkō* is thus "a phenomenon produced between coercion and spontaneity – between external state power and the internal thoughts and decisions of an individual" (Ward 2021: 14). Therefore, *tenkō* does not arise for a person who has no inner tension between self and thought. "*Tenkō* would never become an issue for an individual who takes an attitude that the circumstances are predestined or simply happen by chance, and who always just adapts to the situation in his/her sphere of activity" (Fujita 1997:5). "In practice, cases of *tenkō* always have both voluntary and coercive aspects" (Tsurumi 2012:30). That is, *tenkō* is always the result of agency following on from and determined by thought choice. Hence an individual has the option of not *tenkōing* no matter how harsh the authorities' coercion may be: as Yoshimoto (1990: 290) puts it, "I think that we must distinguish between oppression and *tenkō*, and that without spontaneous will we cannot form any kind of opinion".

So how does the individual change his/her thought? "Thought is first understood as a composite of beliefs and attitudes" (Yoshimoto, 1990: 290), to which can be added situational awareness. Awareness is a perception of reality, belief is an interpretation of that reality, while agency is the practice linked to that perception. Generally speaking, therefore, agency/action is justified by the notion that belief is itself correct. As a result, what might be termed the correct

---

9   In 1926 *Kyūshū Levelers* (KL), an organization of *Burakumin*, the biggest minority in Kyūshū, Southern Japan, protested against discrimination in the Imperial Military asserting "We also are children of the Emperor. How can you discriminate against the same children of the Emperor?" The military officers could not refute it, because KL invoked the absolute norm that all Japanese were children of the Emperor. In effect, KL criticized the Emperor's military for bypassing the Emperor System itself, so to speak (on which see Gramsci's *Trench Warfare*). Significantly, KL carried out the only organized mass anti-military activities in fascist Japan (Shindō 1974).

thought is selected. However, when conflicts between these processes occur, one or other component of the chain may be discarded.

The acknowledged distance between Party and population led members to question their beliefs, and eventually to renounce them: this was the trajectory of *tenkō*. Amid the fascist storm, all people, whether workers or farmers, accepted the Emperor and *Kokutai*, and cooperated in the war, either reluctantly or by choice. How realistic, therefore, was it to advocate the overthrow of the Emperor System? *What did it mean to hold on to belief when there is no popular support and no prospect of revolution?* It was no surprise that Party members asked themselves this question.

On the other hand, it is the power of thought that keeps communists believing that people will abandon false consciousness and take up the struggle for socialism, even if they are now entangled in state power. However, this is a difficult position to hold, between an actually hostile population and the belief that it will come round to the opposite view. It was this negative/positive tension, seemingly irresolvable, that led many Party members to *tenkō*.

5.3   *Trap of* Tenkō

Tenkō is different from just shaking or modifying the original thought. It means nothing less than replacing the core part of the original thought with the core part of the new thought. When people *tenkō* (convert), they feel frustrated and guilty for betraying the group they belong to, and their human pride is damaged. Because of this, people do not easily renounce their original belief. Confirming the justice of the old idea, people gradually mix it up with the new. They disbelieve that changing the original thought is *tenkō*, and then secretly slip the new into the core part of the old. *Tenkōshas* follow just such a re-education process, which amounts to a form of self-deception. What works then is the rhetoric or chicanery that bridges the original thought to the new one: "The precursor to *tenkō* facilitates *tenkō*" (Toike 2014: 174). Communists moved from the original thought process to the new one by persuading first themselves and then others through these various stages of ideological transfer. The rhetoric that Sano and Nabeyama used in their *tenkō* statement provided a skillful means of negotiating apostasy for the communists who were frustrated by the discrepancy between the Party line and people's reality. This was how many communists followed Sano and Nabeyama (Beckmann and Ōkubo 1969), the authorities' policy that tempted them to *tenkō* achieving the end result. The rhetorics of Sano and Nabeyama's statement, which reconciles communism

and the Japanese Spirit, can be summarized in three points.[10] It is the defense of *Kokutai*, Emperor, and war using Marxist terms.
1. Capitalism originating in Western nations is a class society, in which capital exploits workers and landlords exploit farmers, a system that should be abolished.
2. Japanese socialist revolution is possible only under the Emperor-centered *Kokutai*, based on the Japanese Spirit cultivated over its long history.
3. Western imperialism should be expelled from Asia, and Asian socialism centered on Japan, that is, the *Greater East Asia Co-Prosperity Sphere* should be established. War for that purpose is the Asian Liberation War and should be justified in these terms.

5.4 Trap of Non-tenkō

Non-*tenkō* means sticking to original thoughts without changing them. After the war, non-*tenkōshas* were praised as persons of strong conviction who endured the authorities' harsh treatment. However, the story is not so simple. Non-*tenkō*, like *tenkō*, is located in same kind of dynamic, involving an interplay between perception, belief, and agency. Some people stick to their original beliefs, avoiding confronting the reality that deviates greatly from their beliefs, a situation in which the meaning of sticking to one's beliefs is not questioned. Others transfer to new beliefs submitting to the new reality. The meaning of transferring to the latter is not questioned either.

Under authorities' coercion, very few Party members resisted, going through to non-*tenkō*. Notably famous were Miyamoto Kenji, Tokuda Kyuichi, and Hakamada Satomi, executives of the Party, who adhered to non-*tenkō*, and were released from prison after the war by the Supreme Commander for the Allied Powers (SCAP).[11] They were praised as 'people's warriors' for their resilient thought and unyielding spirit.

However, the question of the exact meaning of what is *tenkō* and what is non-*tenkō* remained. Many Party members were arrested and *tenkōed*. Authorities'

---

10 It was "a fascist vision of a Japan in which national harmony would replace class struggle and, in so doing, enhance state power and Japan's place in Asia" (Hofmann 2020:403). It was almost the same as the right-extremism of Ikki Kita (Kita 1923). The latter advocated Japanese National Socialism to remodel *Kokutai* by restricting private property and private land based on the idea of not 'Emperor's People' but 'People's Emperor.' His thought had a great influence on the young military officers who staged the coup d'état (February 26 Incident) in 1936. He was also executed along with the young officers.
11 Around 3,000 Party members remained in prison until Japan's defeat in 1945 and were released by the SCAP (JCP 1976:25). Most of them had *tenkōed* in prison but had not been released.

coercion was *the next burden*. Rather, *the harsh coercion itself is proof that the Party was isolated from the people*. The Authorities knew that whatever they might do to the 'thought criminals', they would not be punished. Hence the communists' sense of isolation was amplified, amid a fear of interrogation and torture, knowing from others that no help would come from the population. The Party offers the following post-war account of this process. "Even if the policies and activities of the Party had historical limitations and immaturity in the pre-war era, and even if there were many *tenkōshas*, the Party was composed of highly disciplined fighters, and as a single public institution, it did not *tenkō* at all" (JCP 1976: 72). Here, 'highly disciplined fighters' refers to non-*tenkō* Party members. However, why were there so many *tenkōshas*? How did it relate to the Party's 'historical limitations and immaturity'? There existed the issues of thought and Party line. People became Party members, a serious decision to make in the fascist situation. Thus, it was not a matter of ethically condemning them as 'not very conscientious.' There still is no explanation for the gulf separating the Party from the people, which means that it is difficult to explain the discrepancy between the Party line and reality: as Toike (2014: 170) observes, "Sano and Nabeyama yielded to the Japanese feudal system. Miyamoto avoided confrontation with the feudal system". It is a disconnect between what might be described as true consciousness (*tenkō*) and false consciousness (non-*tenkō*). Both are, in the sense that neither confronted reality, on the same plane: *tenkō* and non-*tenkō* are not that different. Takaaki Yoshimoto went as far as to call Miyamoto's stance 'a non-*tenkō*-like *tenkō*' or 'an indifferent *tenkō*' (Yoshimoto 1990:287). "It was nothing more than a logical cycle of ideology without considering reality's trends or people's trends" (Yoshimoto, 1990: 304). If so, simply ethically asserting that non-*tenkō* is right and *tenkō* is wrong solves nothing.[12]

5.5   Tenkō *and Development*
Tenkō and non-*tenkō* were similar because each avoided confrontation with reality. What do *tenkō* and non-*tenkō* look like when confronting reality? Tsutomu Toike (2014:25) wrote about *tenkō* as follows: "As a general category,

---

12   In 1956, Maruyama Masao criticized the Party as follows: "Before indulging in self-praise of their resistance such that 'we would rather die than betray our comrades,' it would be reasonable to conduct an open and honest scientific analysis of why they surrendered leadership of Japanese politics to fascism, why they failed to prevent an aggressive war against neighboring countries, why they did not effectively organize against fascism and imperialist war, release the results of that analysis to the Japanese people, and admit their responsibility as the Party" (Maruyama 1995:164).

I do not think of *tenkō* as a bad thing in and of itself. Rather, I believe that the methods and distinctive paths taken in individual cases will determine whether it goes in better or worse directions". What does a 'better direction' for *tenkō* mean? Here, Yoshimoto (1990:313–314) inserted the concept of *development* between *tenkō* and non-*tenkō* as the third way and called it Nakano-style *tenkō*. Yoshimoto did so because he perceived in Nakano's *tenkō* 'a third model of thinking way of Japanese intellectuals' going beyond both the *tenkō* of Sano and Nabeyama and the non-*tenkō* of Miyamoto.

Shigeharu Nakano, a famous novelist and poet in Japan, was arrested in 1932, and in 1934 he admitted that he was a Party member, and promised to withdraw from communist movements (Nakano 1988:34), leading to his release on probation. However, after *tenkōing*, Nakano chose "not to be a martyr, but emphatically the path of refusing to become an apostate" (Kunimatsu 1989:285). And he chose a path of resistance and rebuilt his internal logic grounded in reality using a sense of shame at having submitted to power and a sense of atonement at having betrayed the Party and people as steppingstones. Nakano (1998:764) wrote, "If we flesh out the intricacies of the social and personal factors of the self-identified shame of surrender into a literary narrative, and if we can join the revolutionary critique of the traditions of Japanese revolutionary movement, the past will still be the past, but with that indelible flaw on our cheeks, we will continue to pursue our priority as human beings and writers." Kiyotomo Ishidō (2001:108) wrote that the desirable *tenkō* would be "not renouncing the Party's theory and principle, but constructing alternative theory", which means that "if a person *tenkōed* should be blamed, it is not for renouncing the Party's path of revolution, but rather because he/she was responsible for not using alternative tactics." Moreover, Toike (2014:189) wrote. "Principles and philosophies are honed while struggling robustly against reality. Bearing in mind other principles, this approach criticizes the rigid non-*tenkō* by Miyamoto and his comrades which ignored reality and also develops the various fundamental principles while achieving a balance between the principle of non-*tenkō* and other principles.".

According to these writers, Party members should have remained non-*tenkō*, faced reality, and created an alternative theory that transcends the original position, an argument that is plausible as being neither *tenkō* nor non-*tenkō*. However, the following question remains: was there an alternative path possible before the war, and would it have borne fruit? Party members, non-Party communists, and previous studies have yet to provide an answer. Why could Party members not stick to the non-*tenkō* by endorsing an alternative path? For its part, the Party condemned critics as betrayers of the Party, and expelled them. Under such hard political conditions both internal and external Party members had only two choices: *tenkō* or non-*tenkō*. It was difficult for them to choose the alternative path of revising the Party line.

6   Dictums and Prospect

Tenkō is a choice of ideas. It is the product of perception, belief, agency, subject as such a process is to consistency, inconsistency, or merely confusion. This pattern gives rise to various *tenkō* forms:.

Non-*tenkō*: adhering to the original thought (communism).
Tenkō: transferring to new thought (patriotism).
Quasi-*tenkō*: pretending to transfer to new thought.
Semi-*tenkō*: transferring partially to new thought.
Reverse-*tenkō*: returning to original thought after transferring to new thought.
Development: rebuilding critically original thought.
De-*tenkō*: withdrawing from original thought and the new one.
Tenkō is, in short, a complex ideological and political transition, effected to preserve not just the self but also self-esteem. Non-*tenkō* oscillated between the old and the new, opting eventually for recidivism.

The linkages between *tenkō* and non-*tenkō*, together with the processes involved, are set out in Figure 6.1. Using only five basic linkages as a method of analysing their various relationships. On the horizontal axis it takes 'Keeping the original thought or accepting new thought', while on the vertical axis it takes 'Either criticizing or accepting reality.' Here, 'reality' refers to Emperor, *Kokutai*, and war. De-*tenkō*, or the rejection of all views, is left out of the figure.

(1)   From non-*tenkō* to *tenkō*. Non-*tenkō* means staying in the original thought. False-*tenkō* is substantially non-*tenkō*. As long as the original thought is not entrenched (like in the case of Miyamoto), non-*tenkō* is also the result of the ideological twists and turns Communists anticipate a better prospect beyond the hopeless situation, believing in future support from a population that currently rejects them. Remaining no-*tenkōsha* requires such power of imagination and reasoning. *The richness of imagination underpins the strength of the will.*

(2)   From non-*tenkō* to semi-*tenkō*. Semi-*tenkō* is a partial change of the original thought, halfway to *tenkō*. The core of original thought has not yet been renounced. However, facing the discrepancy between thought and reality, the trust in the thought is shaken.

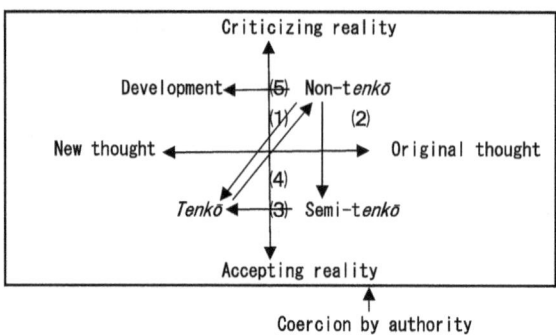

FIGURE 6.1 Process and form of *Tenkō*

(3) From semi-*tenkō* to *tenkō*. A communist renounces the core of the original thought and kneels to the reality that should be criticized. Here he/she *crosses the line* of thought choice. But even then, in many cases, *tenkō* is not total, and the peripheral parts of the original thought remain. Then the original thought and reality are fused, gradually shifting to a complete *tenkō*. At that time, the rhetoric that connects and fuses the original and new thoughts functions effectively.

(4) From *tenkō* to reverse-*tenkō*. It is a case of returning to the original thought after *tenkō*ed to the new thought: such a case would be rare. But it is not like there were no communists that overturned *tenkō* after *tenkō*ing once. Nakano's case is close to this.

(5) From non-*tenkō* to development. It is the case of holding the original thought and developing its core part. It is the way to grapple with reality and "develop the basic ideas together, while also considering other ideas and maintaining a balance between them" (Toike 2014: 189).

7 Conclusion: Lessons and Prospects

The contemporary world is changing in a politically rightwards direction. Neoliberal globalization has transformed world's economic and political systems. It has brought hierarchical polarization among people and produced a vast 'new poor' in the Global North and has intensified the exploitation of workers and farmers resulting in many immigrants and refugees in the Global South. As "politics always obediently follows economics" (Hammond 1957:21) cross-border capital and human flows have lowered the walls of national borders, increasing nationalism in the receiving countries. Xenophobia has intensified, generating support for stopping immigration, a process fuelled not just by poverty and unemployment but also by war. War used to be an extension of politics. "War is nothing but the continuation of policy with other means" (Clausewitz 1976:9). But in contemporary times, politics has become an extension of war. War occurs first. "Politics itself is increasingly becoming war conducted by other means. War, that is to say, is becoming the primary organizing principle of society, and politics merely one of its means or guises" (Hardt and Negri 2004:12). World politics began to move around war. Right-wing governments have emerged in many countries. And of these, ultra-right-wing governments persecute communists, liberals, minorities, and foreigners. Democracy has fallen to the ground. Ethnic cleansing and xenophobia intensified. The state has increasingly placed itself in a state of exception (outside the legal order) and strengthened its system of control, surveillance, and imprisonment of people. "In our age, the state of exception comes more and more to the foreground as the fundamental political structure and ultimately begins to become the rule" (Agamben 1998:20). More oppressive control has become the political principle of the world. "The state of exception, which was essentially a temporary suspension of the juridico-political order, now becomes a new and stable spatial arrangement inhabited by the bare life that more and more can no longer be inscribed in that order" (Agamben 1998:20.:175). "We are all virtually *homo sacer*" (Agamben 1998:20:115). We are becoming prisoners in our own societies.

This is the contemporary world we live in. *The present age is an era of conversion.* Conversion has two meanings: broad and narrow. First, there is the conversion for state rule. War and governing have turned many peoples into vanguards of mutual surveillance and alien exclusion. Foreigners are forced to assimilate, and those who refuse are deported. Forced to conform to this political system, people renounced democracy and became patriotic. Foreigners renounced their ethnicity and became alien citizens. Second, there is the conversion in the narrow meaning. Those who deviate from this political system are surveilled, arrested, detained, corrected for their deviations, and forced to become patriots. Some have indeed become patriots. Others have refused to renounce democracy and their nationality, and have been sentenced to imprisonment and expulsion. Still, others are lost and confused between democracy and patriotism, alienated from family, friends, and society, isolated, and becoming yet another *homo sacer*.

This chapter considered the *tenkō* of communists in pre-war Japan, a process that can be summed up as follows:

1. Oppression is an external factor that triggers *tenkō*.
2. More important is the internal factor of *tenkōsha*.
3. The biggest internal factor is a sense of isolation from the people.

4. It is the will of the individual that ultimately decides on *tenkō*.
5. *Tenkō* is the product of complex sets of situational awareness, belief, and attitude. They are changed independently. Sometimes consistent, sometimes discontinuous.
6. *Tenkō* and non-*tenkō* are partly opposed and partly overlapped.
7. Between *tenkō* and non-*tenkō*, there may be an alternative way of thought development beyond both.

Tenkō of communists in pre-war Japan occurred in the world conditioned by the political situation, and the circumstances of the Party, and its members. However, the lessons of conversion obtained from this case-study can be extended universally to human societies in crisis.

The present age can be described as an era of global conversion. Between democracy and patriotism, state rule and resistance, people in Global North and South are forced to make choices and respond to strong-State concepts of national sovereignty. People struggle with this choice and go through the processes outlined above.

There can be no doubt as to the current shifts in social and political ideology of traditionally liberal societies? Much of Western Europe is experiencing significant shifts in national politics. Italy's current ruling party has fascist roots, far-right elements could become part of Spain's government, and right-wing parties are in governments in Sweden and Finland. In the last French election, the center-right Emmanuel Macron defeated the far-right Marine Le Pen, though her party appears to be gaining support after recent riots. Germany, where the history of the Holocaust kept right-wing extremism at bay the reactionary Alternative for Germany is rising in the polls as the second most popular party in the country. Conversion need not be a result of force, but these shifts require more analysis to understand what is happening.

Thus, *tenkō* analysis in this chapter, *all its lessons*, is fully applicable as a tool for analyzing contemporary oppression, and for analyzing the ideological processes of the captured and imprisoned on one hand, and more generally on national consciousness on the other.

References

Agamben, G. (1995 = 98) *Homo Sacer: Sovereign Power and Bare Life*, translated by Daniel Roazen, Stanford, CA: Stanford University Press.

Agamben, G. (2003 = 05) *State of Exception*, translated by Kevin Attell, Chicago, IL: University of Chicago Press.

Aoki, H. (2021) Marxism and the Debate on the Transition to Capitalism in Prewar Japan, *Critical Sociology*, 47(1): 17–36.

Beckmann, G. and Ōkubo, G. (1969) *The Japanese Community Party 1922–1945*, Stanford, CA: Stanford University Press.

Clausewitz, C. ([1832] 1976) *On War*, Oxford: Oxford University Press.

Fauconnier, B. (2021) The Historical Origins of *Tenkō* as an Intellectual and Social Issue: Marxism Thought Control – Media, in Hayter, Sipos and Williams, 23–46.

Fujita, S. (1997) Tenkō no Shisōshi-teki Kenkyū [Study of Thought History into Conversion], Fujita Shōzō Chosakushū 2 [The Collected Works of Fujita Shōzō, vol. 2]. Tokyo: Misuzu Shobō.

Hammond, T. (1957) *Lenin on Trade Unions and Revolution 1893–1917*, New York: Columbia University Press.

Hardt, M. & Negri, A. (2004) *Multitude: War and Democracy in the Age of Empire*, New York: Penguin Press.

Hayter, I., Sipos, G. and Williams, M. eds. (2021) *Tenkō: Cultures of Political Conversion in Transwar Japan*. New York: Routledge.

Higuchi, M. (1907 = 72) Sayoku Zenrekisha no *Tenkō* Mondai nitusite [Regarding the Conversion Issue of Leftist Antecedents]. *Shisō Kenkyū Shiryō* [Thought Study Materials], special edition no.95. Criminal Investigation Bureau of the Ministry of Justice. *Shakai Mondai Shiryō Sōsho* [Social Issues Materials Series]. vol.1. Social Issues Materials Research Institute. Tokyo: Tōyō Bunka Publishing. 1–234.

Hirata, I. (1938) 'Marukishizumu no kokufuku' [Overcoming Marxism]. In Shisosen koshukai kogi' sokki [Thought War Lecture Shorthand], Naikaku jōhōbu, ed. Tokyo: Naikaku johobu. III: 14: 205–236.

Hofmann, R. (2020) What's Left of the Right: Nabeyama Sadachika and Anti-communism in Transwar Japan, 1930–1960. *Journal of Asian Studies* 79(2): 403–427.

Hoston, G. (1983) Tenko: Marxism & the National Question in Prewar Japan, *Polity*, Northeastern Political Science Association, 16(1): 96–118.

Hoston, G. (1985) Emperor, Nation, and the Transformation of Marxism to National Socialism in Prewar Japan: The Case of Sano Manabu, *Studies in Comparative Communism*, 18(1), 25–47.

Hoston, G. (1987) Between Theory and Practice: Marxist Thought and the Politics of the Japanese Socialist Party, *Studies in Comparative Communism* 20(2): 175–207.

Internment Facilities (1943) 'Shisōhan Hogo Taishōsha ni kansuru Shochōsa' [Various Surveys Related to Thought Criminals Subject to Protection] in (Tsurumi, 2012).

Ishidō, K. (2001) *20 Seiki-no Imi* [Meaning of the 20th Century], Tokyo: Heibonsha.

Itō, A. (1995) *Tenkō to Tennōsei: Nihon Kyōsanshugiundō no 1930 Nendai* [Conversion and the Emperor system: Japanese Communist Movements in the 1930s], Tokyo, Japan: Keisō Shobō.

Japanese Communist Party (*Akahata* Party History Team) (1976) 'Inu ha Hoete mo, Rekishi wa Susumu: Anmoku Jidai no Tōdai Nihon Kyōsantō' [Even if the Dog Howls, History Continues: The Japanese Communist Party, a Beacon in the Dark Ages], *Bunka Hyōron* [Cultural Criticism]. Tokyo: New Japan Publishers, 180. extra expanded edition, 18–75.

Kita, I. (1923) *National Restructuring Proposal Principle Outline*, Tokyo: Kaizōsha.

Kobayashi, M. (1987) *Tenkō*-ki no Hitobito: Chianijihō kano Katsudōka Gunzō [People in the 'Age of Conversion': Activist Groups Under the Peace Preservation Law], Tokyo: Jidaisha.

Kunimatsu, A. (1989) Shōsetsuka Nakano Shigeharu niokeru Tenkō Taiken: 'Mura-no Ie'-o chūshin nishite [The Converted Experience in Case of Novelist, Shigeharu Nakano Centering 'Family in the Village'], *Area and Culture Studies*, 39: 274–290.

Linkhoeva, T. (2018) The Russian Revolution and the Emergence of Japanese Anticommunism, *Revolutionary Russia* 31(2): 1–18.

Maruyama, M. (1956 = 95) Sensō Sekinin no Mōten [Blind Spots in Responsibility for the War] *Maruyama Masao shū* [Maruyama Masao Collection], vol. 6. Tokyo: Iwanami Shoten,159–165.

Maruyama, M. (1961 = 96) Nihon no Shisō [Japanese Thoughts] *Maruyama Masao shū* [Maruyama Masao Collection], vol. 7. Tokyo: Iwanami Shoten,191–244.

Matsuo, H. (1971) *Chianijihō: History of Oppression and Resistance*, Tokyo: Shin'nihon-shuppansha.

Misuzu Shobō (1973 = 2004) Chianijihō Ihan Jiken Nendobetsu Jin'inhyō [Table by Fiscal Year of the Number of People in Incidents Violating the Peace Preservation Law]. *Gendaishi Shiryō 45: Chianijihō* [Archives of Modern Japanese History, vol.45: The Peace Preservation Law]. Tokyo. 646–649.

Miyaji, K. (2019) *Tenkō* to Hi-*Tenkō* no Atarashii Mikata to Kangaekata: Senzen Tōin 2300 nin to *Tenkō* to Hi-Tenkō Mondai [A New Way of Seeing and Thinking about *Tenkō* and Non-*Tenkō*: 2,300 Pre-war Party Members and *Tenkō* and Non-*Tenkō* Issue] http://www2s.biglobe.ne.jp/~mike/tenkou.htm (accessed June 29, 2023).

Miyamoto, K. (1934 = 2012) *Tetsu-no Kiritsu-niyotte Busō seyo – Tō Borusheviki-ka-no tameni* [*Arm Yourself with Iron Discipline: for the Bolshevikization of the Party*]. *Miyamoto Kenji Chosakushū* [Collected Works of Miyamoto Kenji], vol.1 (1927–33), Tokyo, Japan: New Japan Publishers, 385–393 (*Communist Party Newspaper Akahata*. number 170).

Moriyama, T. (1937) *Shisōhan hogo kansatsu-hō kaisetsu* (An Explanation of the Thought Criminal Protection and Supervision Law), Tokyo: Shōkadō Shoten.

Murata, Y. (trans. and ed.) (1986) 'Nihon-no Jōsei Shōkan' [Brief Observations on the Conditions in Japan] (J・K, 1920), *Shiryōshū: Cominterun to Nihon* [Documents Collection of Comintern to Japan] (1) 1919–1928, Tokyo: Ōtsuki Shoten.

Nakajima, M. (1980) *Tenkōron Josetsu: Senchū to Sengo o Tsunagumono* [Introduction to Conversion Theory: Linking Wartime and After the War]. Kyoto: Minerva Shobō.

Nakano, S. (1959–88) 'Bungakusha ni tsuite ni tsuite: Kishi Yamaji he' [About 'about Being a Literary Scholar': To Kishi Yamaji], *Shōwa Bungaku Zenshū* [Complete Works of Shōwa Literature], vol.6, works by Murō Saisei, Hori Tatsuo, Nakano Shigeharu, and Sata Ineko. Tokyo, Japan: ShShōwa Bungaku ZenshūSh [Complete Works of ShShōwa Literature], v. Tokyo, Japan: Shōgakukan, 758–764.

Nakano, S. (1959 = 98) *Nakano Shigeharu Zenshū* [The Complete Works of Nakano Shigeharu], Separate volume, Annuals, Bibliography, Index. Edited by Matsushita, Y. Tokyo: Chikuma Shobō.

Nakazawa, S. (2012) *Chianijihō: Naze Seitō Seij wa 'Akuhō' o Unda ka?* [Peace Preservation Law: Why Did Party Politics Create 'Bad Law'?], Tokyo: Chuōkōron-Shinsha.

Ogino, F. (2000) *Shisō Kensatsu* [Thought Prosecutors], Tokyo: Iwanami Shoten.

Ogino, F. (2012) 'III Sono Seitai ni Semaru' [III Approaching the True State] *Tokkō Keisatsu* [The Special Higher Police], Tokyo: Iwanami Shoten, 57–98.

Okudaira, Y. (2006) *Chianijihō Shōshi* [A Short History of the Peace Preservation Law], Tokyo: Iwanami Shoten.

Probation Office (1943) Surveys on People Protected as Former Thought Criminals.

Sano, M. and Nabeyama, S. (1933 = 57) 'Kyōdō Hikoku Dōshi ni Tsuguru Sho' [Confession to Comrade Co-Defendants]. *Sano Manabu Chosakushū* [The Collected Works of Sano Manabu] vol. 1. The Collected Works of Sano Manabu Publishing Association, 3–20, (*Kaizō* (1933),191–199, Tokyo: Kaizōsha), Science of Thought Research Group, Tokyo: Heibonsha.

Shindō, T. (1974) *Document: Fukuoka Regimental Incident*, Tokyo: Contemporary History Publisher.

Shisō-no-Kagaku-Kenkyūkai (1959–62) *Kyōdō-Kenkyū Tenkō* [Joint Research *Tenkō*] vol. up and down, Tokyo: Heibonha.

Steinhoff, P. (1969) *Tenkō: Ideology and Societal Integration in Prewar Japan*, University Microfilms, Harvard University.

Steinhoff, P. (1988) *Tenkō* and Thought Control, in Bernstein G, Fukui H (eds), *Japan and the World: Essays on Japanese History and Politics in Honour of Ishida Takeshi*, London: Palgrave Macmillan, 78–94.

Toike, T. (2014) *Tenkō-ron* [Theory of Conversion], *Seikei Ronsō* [The Review of Economics & Political Science], Meiji University School of Political Science and Economics, 82(5–6): 167–192.

Tsurumi, S (1959 = 2012) Jogen: *Tenkō no Kyōdō Kenkyū nitsuite* [Introduction: About *Tenkō*'s Joint Research], *Kyōdō Kenkyū: Tenkō* [Joint Research: *Tenkō*], vol.1A: Prewar), 19–68.

Ward, M. (2014) Crisis Ideology and the Articulation of Fascism in Interwar Japan: the 1938 Thought-War Symposium, *Japan Forum*, 26(4):462–484.

Ward, M. (2019) *Thought Crime: Ideology and State Power in Interwar Japan*, Chapel Hill, NC: Duke University Press.

Ward, M. (2021) Ideological Conversion as Historical Catachresis: Coming to Terms with *Tenkō*, in Hayter, I. et al.: 3–22.

Yoshimoto, T. (1958 = 90) Tenkō-ron [Theory of Conversion], *Machiu Shoshikiron: Tenkōron* [Matthieu Preliminary Theory: Theory of Conversion], Tokyo: Kōdansha, 285–314.

CHAPTER 7

Profile of an Insurgent Sociologist

Ricardo A. Dello Buono

In January of 1969, an academic newsletter arose out of the intensifying ferment of the anti-war, new-left student movement, giving birth to what eventually developed into a high-impact, international journal of critical sociological thought. The consolidation of this publication project is inextricably tied to David Fasenfest, *Critical Sociology*'s editor since 1998. In this chapter, I explore David's journey from both a personal vantage point, having known him for over 35 years as a close friend and colleague, and as a highly public figure in the discipline.[1] Like other chapters in this tribute volume, I argue that David's unique journey has paid rich dividends to the development of critical, alternative scholarship within the field of sociology. As my exploration suggests, this was not a necessary or even likely outcome given his early formation as an economist and years of tepid and declining institutional support from his eventual affiliation at Wayne State University. But looking back at how things unfolded, tenacity and creativity in confronting adversities composed the fortuitous path that David took and in so doing helped change the discipline of sociology for the better.

1   Birth of a Radical Journal

Initially founded under the name *The Insurgent Sociologist*, the history of the prestigious international journal that we now know as *Critical Sociology* began in the turbulent period of 1969–70. Indeed, the first three issues of *The Insurgent Sociologist* were essentially the newsletter of the Sociology Liberation Movement. At the time, anti-war sentiments were raging, and radical movements flourished across the US. In academia, radical caucuses were being formed in various disciplines, including in the ASA, where a Union of Radical Sociologists was forged to challenge the political complacency of the larger association.

---

[1]   A good deal of the primary information for this chapter came out three detailed interviews I conducted with David Fasenfest in Melbourne, Australia in 2023 at the XX ISA World Congress of Sociology.

The founding editor of *The Insurgent Sociologist* was Albert Szymanski, who was based at the University of Oregon where the Department of Sociology was already making a name for itself as a bastion of radical sociological thought. Szymanski was an overarching figure and the driving force of *The Insurgent Sociologist* who relentlessly confronted the mainstream posture of the American Sociological Association (ASA) and its stultifying effect on critical analysis.

By its third volume, *The Insurgent Sociologist* was beginning to consolidate its place as a radical alternative to mainstream sociology, calling on the discipline to assume the form of an insurgency in order to forge a critique of and ultimately nourish the transformation of existing institutions in the US and elsewhere. My first professional publication in 1979 was in *The Insurgent Sociologist* which provided me with an enormous sense of satisfaction as a graduate student, feeling fortunate to be published alongside of so many well-known radical sociologists. At the time, the journal had an editorial collective of mostly graduate students with a few strategic faculty mentors that worked along with Szymanski.

I would only come more directly in contact with the journal in the mid-1980s. I remember vividly the period of *The Insurgent Sociologist* when it struggled for its survival as a university-based journal with an excessively modest budget. The perennial discussions included "how can we increase the number of subscribers" and "who will attend the table" at the various professional meetings in order to sell individual copies of the journal (see Photo 7.1). This of course was not unusual for radical journals of the time. It was well before the internet and social media, so hard copies had to be managed in a world of dot matrix printed originals and folded, 11X18 photocopied binding. Even still, creative imagery still managed to prevail (see Photo 7.2). Special issues of *The Insurgent Sociologist* were particularly popular, featuring symposia on pathbreaking works such as Harry Braverman's *Labor and Monopoly Capital* and various Marxist authors of the times, such as Poulantzas, Althusser, Erik Olin Wright, and many others..

The Insurgent Sociologist inspired a community of radical/critical/Marxist academics throughout its existence, sharing much in common, but never formally linked to the Marxist Section of the American Sociological Association (ASA). Even as Marxist scholarship gained acceptance into the ASA, the lingering suspicion of mainstream sociology kept the editorial board members of *The Insurgent Sociologist* wary of assimilating into its establishment.

PHOTO 7.1   Al Szymanski (on left) selling the journal

2   Academic Insurgency and Its Discontents

In 1979 at the age of 43, Nicos Poulantzas, the famed Marxist structuralist theoretician, committed suicide. While accounts differ of the reasons for his demise, Michael Löwy recounts that a close friend of Poulantzas who was present at the fateful moment related that the renowned theorist began to swear that the work he had written was worthless and that he had failed the revolutionary cause (Löwy 2015). He began throwing his books out of the Paris high rise and then threw himself out the window behind them. So, for many, it was the political frustration of a sociologist and revolutionary that was the underlying cause of his demise. To be clear, other accounts point to personal factors, such as his wife's affairs with other men, including Etienne Balibar, contentious relations with his own extended family, and so on (Wilk 2018:1).

Poulantzas death at the age of 43 was something of a metaphor for a dying spirit of revolutionary fervor that had erupted in Paris in 1968 and reverberated around the world. At the same time, it placed the personal and public contradictions of radical sociologists plainly in view. Poulantzas was reportedly frustrated above all by his own inability to write more accessibly for a broader

PHOTO 7.2   Artwork from the journal

mass of readers (Wilk 2018). The shock waves were far more intense than the period following the abrupt death of another insurgent sociologist, C. Wright Mills, who in 1962 died at the early age of 45 following a series of heart attacks. As a graduate student during the late 1970's, I managed the C. Wright Mills Memorial Library at the University of Maryland. We published a periodic graduate student run newsletter that I started entitled *Listen Yankee!* (*1960*), named after Mills' famous account of the Cuban Revolution's early days, including a meeting with Fidel Castro. The Library had been established and maintained exclusively by graduate students and I vividly recall the local legend of how Mills experienced a rocky road while at Maryland.

As Mills wrote to Thomas McCormick, one of his former professors at the University of Wisconsin:

> about my present job: It was very nice when I first took it three years ago. But it is not so good now. Carl Joslyn, one of the finest men I've known, resigned over the unhappy administrative situation and because he had a way out: inherited money. Well, now there is no head and probably won't

> be. The Business Administration dean—of all people—seems to want to gobble up the department as one aspect of business training! Then sociology would be geared to community and business services, and there would be no sociology as a science. The entire administration is quite badly handled; the men that run it are, well, they're just not very intelligent men. I work my head off recruiting graduate students and expanding sociology here. I get no raise after three years, during which I've held, and in some instances upped, enrolment in the department despite the sharp decline in total enrolment in the university this past year. There is no money for research, not even for a typist! I taught the Army for four semesters without one cent of pay, and teach all summer—last year and now this one—without any compensation, even though the basic contract of $3,000.00 a year does not include summer session, much less a full summer quarter! And now they mutter about sociology being put under Business Administration. Really it's too much.
>
> MILLS 2000: 69

This sort of scenario may sound familiar to many sociologists. Mills wrote to Robert K. Merton just a few days later, indicating the following:

> Dear Bob: As you may have heard, the University of Maryland is a sinking ship. Since Joslyn left, matters have deteriorated to such an extent that were the war not under way as an excuse, I do not believe the institution could or should be accredited. I will not bore you with the details, for I am sure these things follow regular patterns, and I am sure that you are acquainted with the pettiness, the inequities, [the] personal despotism and humor of such messes. Anyway, if you run into a decent job, I should appreciate your letting me know about it. I am on the market.
>
> MILLS 2000: 70–71

We now know that Merton responded favorably to Mills and helped broker an entry into Columbia University, despite Mills' preference for the Midwest, and he settled into New York in what would become his permanent intellectual home in Spring, 1945. Merton clearly realized the tremendous talent that Mills wielded and is largely responsible for landing him into a much better institutional venue.

Unlike Poulantzas, the insurgent Mills was both theoretically sophisticated and extremely talented in his ability to write for a broader public, indeed, becoming one of the first truly "public sociologists" (Scimecca 2021). The preferred medium of Mills was the ten cent "mass market paperback" which he viewed as a key opening for critical sociologists to address public issues. Works like *The Causes of World War Three* (1958) and *Listen, Yankee: The Revolution in Cuba* (1960) that used this venue reached deeply into a far broader audience and influenced public opinion.[2] The structural Marxism of Poulantzas that was popular among many Marxists in Western Europe and North America displayed an entirely different character, seemingly striving to be unintelligible to any who were not already socialized in Marxist theory. Hence, the insurgent style of Mills in the 1940's contrasted sharply with the style of committed leftists such as Poulantzas and Louis Althusser of the 1970s who focused their efforts towards influencing the Communist Parties of their era. In November 1980, Althusser's mental meltdown that resulted in the murder of his wife, Helene Rytman, once again shook the radical academic world and vividly underscored the contradictions of personal troubles by insurgent theorists who confronted public issues.

Unfortunately, this syndrome of intellectual meltdown, fatigue, illness and despair was destined to visit *The Insurgent Sociologist*. In 1985, its founding editor Al Szymanski (Photo 7.3) took his own life with a firearm in his home, a suicide that seemed to echo that of Poulantzas. As *The Insurgent Sociologist* collective wrote:

> *The Insurgent Sociologist* has the sad responsibility of reporting the untimely death of our friend and comrade Al Szymanski. Al died at his home in Eugene, Oregon on March 9, 1985. After a long struggle with recurrent episodes of depression and physical exhaustion, Al took his own life. Al was an early supporter and editor of the *Insurgent Sociologist*, which he and Sue Jacobs brought to the University of Oregon, where he remained a member of the editorial collective until his death. The inception and the continuation of this journal is in good part attributed to Al's undaunted commitment, *even under pressure from the university administrators to remove the Insurgent from the University of Oregon campus.* (italics added) ... Al was hired to teach sociology at the University of Oregon where he remained until his death. Al earned the recognition as a high caliber Marxist professor who became known for his hard work and expertise. This made him one of the most sought-after lecturers by serious university students regardless of political orientation. Al's commitment to education, however, did not end in the classroom. He

---

2 See Mills, C.W. 1958. *The Causes of World War Three*. New York: Simon and Schuster; Mills, C.W., 1960. *Listen, Yankee: The Revolution in Cuba*. New York: McGraw-Hill.

PHOTO 7.3   Al Szymanski 1941–1985

bridged the gap between esoteric-neutral academia and political action as he stepped from the halls of academia to the streets. After years of prolonged struggle to keep alive what Al referred to as "orthodox" and "imaginative" Marxism through his prolific writing, extensive teaching, frequent lectures and political activism, Al exceeded the human capacity of physical and mental strain. In failing health and with a burdened heart, Al Szymanski took his own life.

The Insurgent Sociology Collective 1987: 1

3 The Making of a 21st Century Insurgent Sociologist

David Fasenfest was not a conventional red diaper baby. As noted elsewhere in this volume, he was born in Germany into a family of Nazi Death Camp survivors. So, when his family emigrated to the United States, he did not come with Marxist "primary socialization" but as a young boy, he was anti-Fascist by concrete circumstances. He knew perfectly well through family experience in Germany what Nazis were all about. He went to summer camps as a young boy where many of the families were concentration camp survivors. He learned to speak and socialize with his peers in Yiddish. In Middle School, he had friends whose parents changed their name during WWII because Jewish names were a substantial liability. Growing up in the Bronx, he flirted at the local diner with a diverse and dynamic mixing ground of European and Puerto Rican youth.

As he left high school and headed towards undergraduate study, his political awakening began to take shape. In the Vietnam War era, he began to read about imperialism in Indochina and it all really hit home when his military draft lottery number came up as number 4! David's father, given his experience in Nazi detention, carried an understandably palpable fear of authority and worried when David began to openly challenge authority and suggested that he would prefer to go to Canada rather than serve in the US Army.

The 1960's counterculture era spawned an ever-greater politicization for David and offered a suitable backdrop by the time he experienced Marxist professors in the classroom. While he started out pursuing Chemical Engineering, his early experience in an economics course with Rick Wolff, one of his early Marxist professors, worked to re-shape David's academic interests. Upon graduation from undergraduate study at City College of CUNY in June 1971, he travelled through Europe for a couple of years on a motorcycle with Marx's *Theories of Surplus Value* in his backpack. Having read about the French Revolution with enthusiasm in college, he was now becoming more interested in the Russian Revolution. Although he didn't actually manage to visit Russia, he travelled through much of Europe during the summer months (Photo 7.4). He went to Israel for one winter where he worked on a Kibbutz and tried to learn Hebrew, but many of the resettled Jews there spoke Yiddish. During that period, a kind of socialism was still espoused in the Kibbutzim of Israel in the form of collective, communal living values. Interestingly, this led David to begin seeing China under Mao at the time as a more authentic socialist ideal than Russia. This led him to pursue China Studies in graduate school.

Funding opportunities proved to be scant in his chosen field and for practical reasons, he shifted back into the graduate study of economics while at the University of Michigan. It was there that David met his partner-to-be, Heidi Gottfried, in a Marxist study group. David reports that they argued politics relentlessly for the first year and a half of their relationship and were therefore, arguably, in love! When pressed on this issue, David has told me that he was considerably more structuralist while Heidi was more historical and "agency aware".

Like for many of us at this stage of study, financial pressures began to weigh down and David's progress on his Ph.D. in Economics stalled a bit during this period as he turned to consulting as a China Economist. This was during the time where the Soviet Russia-China split was widening. The US move closer to China was a lucrative, strategic move for Washington, but David failed to appreciate the political aspects of the rapprochement. At a party in Ann Arbor,

PHOTO 7.4   David Fasenfest, mid-1970s

he met his future academic advisor in sociology who misheard him when he introduced himself as "an economist," and replied, "So, you're a communist?" Out of that encounter, with economics becoming increasingly mainstreamed and apolitical, David was finding a receptive ear to his interests and gravitated towards sociology at the end of the 1970s into the following decade. As a graduate assistant, he began to engage students as the discussion leader in 100 + sections of sociology courses while academically discovering Marxist discourse via Althusser, Eric Olin Wright, Michael Burawoy, Jeffery Paige, and other critical sociologists.

After nine years in graduate school, David defended a topic in Urban Renewal which initiated a lifelong academic engagement with Critical Urban Development Studies. His dissertation argued that Urban Renewal was not a failure, but rather a great success in accomplishing exactly what it was designed to do, namely, putting poor communities at the service of middle-class professionals in universities, medical centers and so on. His first publication was a paper written for a sociology seminar in which he explored the case of Poletown, Detroit (Fasenfest 1986). Poletown was the residential settlement area of Polish immigrants that became displaced by a huge General Motors Assembly plant in 1981, enforced by eminent domain by local authorities at the service of big capital. David's doctoral thesis was a critical social policy analysis of the social impact of capitalist urban expansion and the lost opportunities of public expenditure.

David's first teaching opportunity was at the University of Wisconsin-Parkside and then the University of Wisconsin-Milwaukee. He then took three consecutive one-year appointments at Loyola University-Chicago in 1985–88 (where I first met him after taking a position at Dominican University in Chicago in 1987). Wherever David landed, he engaged the local dynamics, whether it was Kenosha or Chicago. After leaving Loyola, he briefly worked as a local economic development director at an Urban Research Center in Louisville and grappled with the problems of the homeless, while commuting to his partner Heidi who had settled into a position at Purdue University in West Lafayette, Indiana by 1987. By 1990, David himself managed to close the 180-mile gap and landed a position at Purdue in the Department of Sociology. There is some controversy as to whether it was Heidi who got him the job by threatening to leave or whether it was David's own merit as a research sociologist with an urban specialization in a rural college town raising corn puppies. David's official version at the time was that he was committed to make love with his partner Heidi once more before turning 50 and Purdue was his best option to not have to leave town the next morning!

In 1998, David was offered two jobs, one at a head researcher for The Urban League in Chicago and the other was as Director of the Center for Urban Studies at Wayne State University. He opted for the latter and was joined there by Heidi, who obtained a post in Labor Studies in 1999. Unlike so many academics perpetually plagued by geographical separation from their partners, David and Heidi had finally cracked the code.

4 *Critical Sociology* Moves to the Midwest

Following the death of Al Szymanski, *The Insurgent Sociologist* began to replicate the path of many radical publications that originated in the 1960s-70s. The collective was running out of steam, trying to keep up with its own publication schedule while plagued with financial shortfalls and the lack of a solid sponsorship. In 1987, the decision was made by the Editorial Board to change the journal's name to *Critical Sociology*. Some of the old guard in the journal's circle saw this as a "softening" of its radical political orientation but the majority saw it as broadening out to be more open to Feminist, Critical Race analysis and other radical currents within the discipline. The name change notwithstanding, *Critical Sociology* maintained its largely Marxist approach, led by a collective that shared tasks, invited guest editors for special issues, and somehow continued to publish.

To address the dwindling support from the University of Oregon, the Board decided to sign a deal with Humanities Press, a commercial publisher. The idea was to secure a resource base that could guarantee regular publication of the journal without sacrificing any editorial control. In 1998, a concerted search for a chief editor was initiated by the Board to put the journal more on a "standard footing" with other academic journals and ultimately, Morton Wenger was selected to fill the post. Wenger was a committed Marxist even if unorthodox in the view of some and seemed open and well suited for the intended broadening of the journal to other radical and critical currents.

The transition from the University of Oregon to a commercial publisher was a big step for the journal. In many ways, the journal was struggling to keep up with its own calendar of publication, falling behind in issues and having trouble recruiting contributions. So, Wenger had his work cut out for him. On 10 March 1999, however, tragedy reared its head once more as Wenger died a natural death unexpectedly just months after he had been selected as the journal's new editor. Speaking for the Board, Martin Oppenheimer announced in Volume 24, Issue 1–2 of the journal that "With this issue of *Critical Sociology*, we mourn the death of our editor Mort Wenger" (Oppenheimer 1998: i).

To this, Associate Editor Alan Spector added: "As an activist, his [Mort's] energy, enthusiasm, insight, and hard work have left a broad and deep legacy not just on Marxist sociology, but on the whole struggle for social change of which Marxist sociology is a part" (Spector 1998: ix). Regardless of rising expectations for expansion, the journal by all estimates was now more than a little demoralized and passing through dire straits. To make matters worse, Humanities Press was sinking into financial difficulties during this period right after signing with the journal (although this soon stabilized when they were bought out by the Dutch-based Brill Publishers).

By this time, I had become part of the *Critical Sociology* inner circle that continued to operate loosely as a collective which included Rhonda Levine at Colgate University, Martha Gimenez at the University of Colorado, Marty Oppenheimer at Rutgers and Val Burris serving as business manager of the non-profit corporation that owned the journal in Oregon. As we opened the search for a replacement for Mort Wenger, David Fasenfest entered the discussion. Having now settled into his new position at Wayne State University, he stepped forward and expressed interest in the editorship. David had a clearly established reputation for program building and management, wielding several years of editorial experience with another successful radical journal of the Union for Radical Political Economists (URPE). Given his new, high level administrative post, he could offer staff support to help catch the journal up on its production backlog. In addition, many of us knew David and appreciated his high energy style, excellent political credentials and fearless capacity for negotiation. The fact that he was willing to serve as editor of a radical journal while just assuming a new administrative was itself a political statement.

For all of these reasons, making the final selection of editor at the time proved to be easy. There was no term of appointment, so David didn't know if he was an interim, fill-in editor or a permanent replacement. In reality, nobody did, and he was effectively coming on as the "next Editor." Martin Oppenheimer spoke for the Editorial Board as he wrote in Volume 24 (1–2) of the journal that the new search for editor was "mercifully brief" as David Fasenfest, Director of the Center for Urban Studies at Wayne State University in Detroit, has agreed to take on this project (Oppenheimer 1998: i). As David took the reins of the journal with a watchful Board looking over his shoulders, his first task was to negotiate with Brill, the new publisher of the journal, on how to bring the journal up to date with its production calendar having fallen two years behind. Of course, the paramount task was to maintain the critical edge of the journal. Upon appointment, David sensed that the journal's inner circle was worn out and tired, completely ready to turn over the project to a trusted editor and so he began to bring in substantial new blood into what was now a bona fide editorial board. The journal was now situated like never before, having preserved its political character but taking on an ambitious, administratively savvy editor with an ability to garner resources. Anyone who knows David is aware of his tenacious drive, meticulous attention to detail, and capacity for creative problem solving. He embraced the editorial challenge, working closely with Brill to promote the journal and to rapidly bring it up to speed with a series of double issues and special issue editors. Submissions began to click higher, and the journal seemed to be reborn, allowing the Board to begin to step back further and let David operate unfettered.

One of the early and unexpected administrative issues that he had to confront was the "ownership" of the journal. While Brill was supportive in principle, the resource base it offered the journal was good but not great. Even though Humanities Press had respected the non-profit collective ownership of the journal, Brill purchased the entire operation of the faltering press with the assumption that they were becoming the owners of the entire line of the journal. I recall when sitting in a *Critical Sociology* Board meeting in San Francisco that the collective was thrilled that Brill was now going to promote the journal worldwide. Little thought was given to the question of ownership and the non-profit corporation continued to exist, albeit with Brill assuming the entire cost structure of production and distribution based on a respectable royalty model that could fund various projects that the journal would like to sponsor.

After several years of operation, however, David began to compare notes with other journals and their arrangements, ultimately concluding that there were more advantageous royalty arrangements available on the journal market. He worked his networks and managed to gain access to several other academic journal contracts with rival publishers which offered more generous royalty structures. When he approached Brill to negotiate the issue in Leiden, he hit an impasse. This prompted David to begin negotiating with other academic publishers and before long, publishers interested in acquiring the journal made attractive offers.

When David indicated that he was inclined to take the journal elsewhere, negotiations with Brill stalled due to Brill's proprietary posture. Undaunted by this scenario, he skilfully engaged in negotiations with Sage UK that ultimately led to a deal where Brill offered to release the journal in exchange for three Sage journals. Sage accepted, offering *Critical Sociology* a more attractive royalty scheme and a ten-year commitment to publish the journal.

The transition to Sage UK was the key element in the expansion of the global readership of the journal, incorporating it into their library packages and creating a reliable royalty scheme that increased when the journal went from four to six issues a year, and later to eight issues a year. The increased number of pages available to critical scholarship was nothing short of spectacular as Sage progressively reduced the limits on space in the journal. The arrangement that David negotiated also helped set the stage for a significantly greater flow of revenue that helped support graduate staff while enabling the journal to sponsor academic conferences, book awards, travel support, translation subsidies and so on. Four geographical Area editors including myself as the Latin American and Caribbean editor, were added in addition to an expanding Editorial Board, an International Advisory Board with prestigious members, in addition to an expanding list of associate editors, and most recently, a Senior Associate Editor designed to point the way to eventual editor transition. It should also be mentioned that the technical platform used by Sage allowed for more efficient processing of articles and online first publication in advance of the print copies.

For his part, after leaving his position as Director of the Center for Urban Studies, the college of which he was part was ultimately closed by Wayne State University. He along with Heidi Gottfried were tenured, and so moved over into the Sociology Department full time. Almost unbelievably, David remained locked into the Associate Professor rank for the years that followed despite being one of the most prolific and productive members of the department. He wore this title as a badge of honor and a marker of dignity in the face of petty politics, reactionary academic prejudice, closet jealousies, and chronic malpractice on the part of department and institutional administrative figures. This of course is nothing new, particularly in public universities in the United States where radical scholars remain frequently penalized and marginalized within the status distinctions and pecking orders of departmental politics. In 2022, David initiated a phased retirement plan with Wayne State and began to circulate more prominently at other institutions, including York University, while at the same time laying the groundwork for an eventual transition of the editorship that is still in process at the time of this writing.

5 Concluding Thoughts

David is a remarkable individual in every sense. He has generously dedicated his time and energy, not only to the journal, but to mentoring generations of graduate students at Wayne State and elsewhere. At the same time, he effectively advised many early career sociologists and most recently, has worked literally across the globe to help scholars publish their research. His creation of several book series (discussed elsewhere in this volume) has provided a venue to critical social scientists from around the world and has helped subsidize the translation of promising scholarship in foreign languages into English, making it available to a larger audience.

Under his direction, the journal has sponsored innovative events, projects and conferences, such as the annual Left Forum in New York City, a South-South Dialogue of noted Third World Scholars in Toronto, a Critical Sociology conference in solidarity with Cuban Sociologists in Boston, the Rethinking Marxism (RM) Conference in Amherst, co-sponsored sessions in the International Sociological Association (ISA) and numerous special sessions in various professional associations, just to mention a few. He is an active international scholar whose expertise and role in promoting critical scholarship makes him a frequent invitee to a wide range of international conferences (see Photo 7.5) regarding critical thought that implores progressive change.

When I was elected President of the Society for the Study of Social Problems (SSSP) in 2012, the most essential role among those I needed to fill was the Chair of my program committee. Despite an enormous workload, David affirmatively responded to my request for this largely thankless and laborious task, putting all of his organizational talents to work for a NYC conference venue. His tremendously successful execution of the program led to the largest SSSP conference in the history of the association in 2013, with keynote addresses by Australian Raewyn Connell as well as US Feminist Charlotte Bunch. It was a

PHOTO 7.5   Mark Rudd and David Fasenfest, Shanghai University, 2018

fantastic testimony to his unique combination of skills and networking. Given my positionality, I look back at this successful project as a metaphor for what he accomplished with the journal.

I would be remiss if I neglected to highlight David's delightful sense of humor. When he introduced me for my presidential address to the Society for the Study of Social Problems (SSSP), he couldn't resist injecting his signature comicality into the occasion. Before a diverse crowd of scholar-activists with a significant number of social practitioners in attendance, including a delegation from the Danish School of Social Work at Alborg, he highlighted my short-lived career as a social worker in Boston, Massachusetts. He quickly indicated that this explained "my caring attitude and my overwhelmingly controlling behavior." He proceeded from there with even further audacity to quip that "As the English say, the difference between social workers and pit bulls is that parents have a better chance of retrieving their children from the latter." To a mixture of laughter and groans, I proceeded to deliver my prepared address. After badly exceeding my allotted time, he quipped that he forgot to mention in his introduction that I graduated from the "Hugo Chavez school of public speaking".[3]

---

3   The audiotape of these quips can be found on https://www.ssspi.org/index.cfm/pageid/1686.

Holding my lingering bitterness at bay, I maintain that all of David's varied talents form part of an indelible, 21st century, insurgent sociologist. In one of the last (unpublished) articles that Al Szymanski wrote before his death, he stated: "[T]he future prospects for a rebirth of Marxist theory are thus great. As difficult as it might be in the absence of significant mass movements when we are facing strong counter currents wherever we turn, we must keep the seed grain from rotting." Thanks to David Fasenfest, that seed so firmly planted in *The Insurgent Sociologist* was nurtured and ultimately flourished, branching out globally in ways that never could have been imagined.

References

Fasenfest, D. 1986. Community Politics and Urban Redevelopment: Poletown, Detroit and General Motors, *Urban Affairs Quarterly*, 22:1(Sept): 101–123.

Löwy, M. 2015. "The Nicos Poulantzas I Knew." Interview by Mike Watson. London: Verso. https://www.versobooks.com/blogs/news/1908-michael-lowy-the-nicos-poulantzas-i-knew.

Mills, C. W. 2000. *C. Wright Mills: Letters and Autobiographical Writings*. Edited by Kathryn Mills with Pamela Mills. Berkeley: University of California Press.

Oppenheimer, M. 1998. *Critical Sociology* 24 (1–2): i.

Scimecca, J. A. 2021 Public Sociology and the Lost Legacy of C. Wright Mills, in *The Routledge International Handbook of C. Wright Mills Studies*, Frauley, J. ed. London: Routledge.

Spector, A. 1998. Morton Wenger 1946–1999, *Critical Sociology* 24 (1–2): vi–ix.

The Insurgent Sociologist Collective. 1987. Al Szymanski 1941 – 1985. *Insurgent Sociologist* 1985 13:1–2, 3–4.

Wilk, C. 2018. *A Biography of the State*. Newcastle: Cambridge Scholars Publishing.

PART 2

CHAPTER 8

Decolonizing Canons

A Conversation with Chinese Sociologists[1]

Michael Burawoy

As I recall, the first time I met David Fasenfest was in 1976 when I took up a position at the University of Wisconsin, Madison in anticipation of being denied tenure at Berkeley. All I remember of our meeting was David turning me upside down. When I think of David, I always think of him turning things upside down, and that indeed is what he has done with *Critical Sociology*. Louis Althusser once said in regard to Marx's inversion of Hegelian philosophy – a person on his head is the same person when they are walking on their feet; it is a change in perspective but following the same problematic. Over the last 25 years, David has changed perspectives while holding on to the Marxist problematic of the old *Insurgent Sociologist*. He has molded *Critical Sociology* to the new post-1980s context of a more professionalized sociology by encouraging new critical stances, whether it be feminism, environmental justice, critical race theory or trans studies. With the help of trusted allies, David not only brought *Critical Sociology* back from the brink of collapse but turned it into a thriving journal with 8 issues a year. His genius was to give *Critical Sociology* professional recognition without sacrificing radical imagination, without losing sight of visions embedded in social movements, without sidelining the fundamental problems of our neoliberal age. He has created a safe and supportive space for challenging currents of the mainstream. There's been a no more important contribution to the marriage of Marxism and sociology. Throughout he has had a keen eye for the global, and insisted on the unusual recognition that US sociology is not the only sociology in the world. I know he has a special interest in China which is why I offer this trans-continental conversation with Chinese sociologists as a small appreciation of his tireless devotion to a progressive agenda.

∴

---

1   Thanks to Yan Long for inviting me to give this talk and to Wen Xie, Xiaohong Xu, Jing Li, and Zuoyo Zheng for their critical commentaries.

Decolonization is spreading across US academia like a wildfire. Every university has to examine its past for collaboration with white supremacy, whether the university was constructed on land expropriated from indigenous people or from the proceeds of slavery, whether it consecrated propagators of racism in statues, portraits, or in the names of buildings. There is a rising chorus demanding reparations for past oppression through the redistribution of material and intellectual endowments. Within academic departments there is a call for decolonizing syllabi and curricula, and specifically decolonizing canons.

History has been at the heart of the decolonization movement. A debate was fueled by the 1619 Project that originated in the pages of the *New York Times*, tracing the nation's history to the beginning of slavery rather than the declaration of independence. Historians were thrust into the public sphere, defending or disputing claims about the legacies of slavery. Outraged by this dark history, US President Trump created the 1776 Commission to give a rosier view as the basis of 'patriotic education.' The Commission was terminated by President Biden but the political struggle over 'decolonization' continues in the banning of 'critical race theory' from schools, including documents from the 1619 project.

Disciplines have been compelled to examine their own history. While anthropologists have been in the business of 'decolonizing' for half a century, recognizing their complicity with colonialism and its dehumanizing views of the colonized, those social sciences with a more scientific pedigree, such as economics, have been slower to examine their own history. Disciplines that are rooted in claims about the universality of Western thought, such as philosophy or political theory, have also been reluctant to disinter their past but they, too, have not been unaffected. The decolonization movement peters out as one moves from the social sciences and humanities to the natural sciences, technology, engineering and mathematics – though even here there is increased sensitivity to the limited diversity of its scholars and students.

Sociology has not escaped critical self-examination. From the beginning sociology has either endorsed or ignored the wider context of the 19th century, especially the context of Empire. As the discipline has come to focus on social inequalities, it has had to become ever more self-conscious about the inequalities it has sustained or overlooked. Inevitably, the debate swirls around the relevance of the canonical figures that have conventionally defined the foundations of our discipline. Marx, Weber and Durkheim were white European men whose writings straddled the nineteenth and early twentieth century, marginalizing questions of race and gender. Arising within an imperial order they left too much unproblematized. A battle rages over what to do with these canonical figures.

1 Strategies of Dealing with the Canon

To decolonize, then, is to recognize, critique and expunge the presence of colonial presuppositions in canonical texts, exposing flawed universalistic claims that are rooted in metropolitan experiences, claims that overlook patterns of colonial domination, the relations between center and periphery. There are, I believe, four contending responses to the decolonization movement: restoration, rejection, revolution and reconstruction.

Restoration still holds a powerful place, not only in the United States, as many continue to make Marx, Weber and Durkheim the reference point and foundation of sociology. Having been schooled in the works of these figures, having taught them for years, many sociologists are invested in their continuity. But there's more to their persistence than inertia. They emerged with civil society in the second half of the 19th century, taking a stand against the overreach of the state and the market. As we return to the bourgeoning economic inequalities of the late nineteenth century and recognize that the period from World War I to the 1970s was a progressive blip that has been fast disappearing (Piketty 2014); as we see the sprouting of authoritarian regimes across the globe; as we continue to face the renewal and deepening of marketization of labor, nature, money and knowledge; as we enthusiastically participate in the commodification of daily life through digitalization, social media, thereby aiding and abetting surveillance and control; in short, as markets and states encroach on an autonomous civil society so the canon, far from being irrelevant, assume ever greater significance as a dam as well as an inspiration for counter-movement. In this sense, sociology is inherently an anti-colonial movement, opposing the colonization of civil society by state and market (Polanyi 1944; Habermas 1985)

Marx, Weber and Durkheim don't have a monopoly on elevating the importance of civil society and the restorationists are ready to recognize others who have always hovered on the periphery of the canon – Simmel, Mead, Freud – and today courses on classical theory include feminists such as Harriet Martineau or scholars such as W.E.B. Du Bois who, as we will see, can be appropriated in different ways. These concessions are how the restorationists accommodate to the pressing demands of those who want to abolish the canon.

So let me turn next to *rejecting* the canon – a move that comes along two opposed paths. On the one hand, there are postcolonial theorists who center the importance of Empire as the context within which sociology emerged, but also its entanglement with race and gender. So, the canon is subject to critique for failing to adequately address that context, but they also consider the very idea of a canon, associated with some key writers, as problematic. Any foundational thinking is exclusionary, and decolonization must be inclusionary. Julian Go (2016), for example, advocates what he calls a perspectival realism which embraces a multiplicity of perspectives that are not identified by the race or gender of authors but by the standpoint they adopt. Epistemic justice replaces epistemic rigor. There are no criteria for the soundness of theories built on competing perspectives. It does not mean that the canonical thinkers are swept aside; they are just brought down from their pedestal. Let a hundred flowers bloom.

The postcolonial critique is one avenue to rejecting the canon, the other avenue is followed by scientists who would embrace Alfred North Whitehead's (1916) dictum: 'A science that hesitates to forget its founders is lost.' These positivists dismiss Marx, Weber and Durkheim not because of their white masculine Eurocentrism but due to their antiquated methodologies and outmoded theories. These figures may be of historical interest, but of no relevance to the contemporary practice of sociology that has eclipsed its origins. These scientists who model sociology after the natural sciences, now given a boost by the advent of big data, have a powerful influence within the discipline. Though otherwise bitter enemies, the postcolonialists and the positivists are enjoined in their rejection of the canon.

But let me turn to a third response to the canon, what I call the *revolutionary* response. Here the idea is to replace the old canon with a new canon. There have been many candidates but, at this moment, none match the credentials of W.E.B. Du Bois – the first African American to receive a PhD from Harvard in 1895 – a historian, a philosopher and sociologist who wrote professional articles, lyrical essays, poetry, novels, and dramas. He was an academic, but also a public figure of global renown, who played a leading part in civil rights and Pan-Africanist movements and was a socialist and peace activist. Aldon Morris in his *The Scholar Denied* (2015) anointed Du Bois as the true but unrecognized founder of US sociology – true because the Atlanta School founded by Du Bois ante-dated the Chicago by 20 years, unrecognized because of the racism within our discipline. No less important, his last 50 years of writing not only centered race and class but also imperialism. Following the lead of Morris, Jose Itzigsohn and Karida Brown (2020) have advanced a Du Boisian sociology under the rubric of a 'racialized modernity'. Here the project is to clear the decks and start afresh by rooting sociology in the oeuvre of Du Bois.

I consider such a revolutionary move to be premature. We are in danger of throwing the baby out with the bathwater. Even if we grant that Marx, Weber and Durkheim had limited perspectives on questions of race and gender, of colonialism and imperialism, they still have redeeming importance not only as a political stand against markets and states but, as Arthur Stinchcombe (1982) once wrote, as exemplars of scientific research, as developing an understanding of complexity to replace clichés, as a source of puzzles and hypotheses for empirical work. Foundational figures are bound to have blindnesses to issues that subsequently become salient – the test of their resilience lies in how they can adapt to new challenges, how they can be reconstructed to meet the exigencies of the present. A discipline, like a science, has foundational assumptions out of which develop research programs that are continually reconstructed to accommodate and absorb both internal contradictions and external anomalies. This is the *reconstructionist* position that I will defend and elaborate here.

2 A Theory of the Canon

Before reconstructing the canon we need a theory of the canon. I believe it is defined by four attributes: it is foundational, historical, geographical and relational. I'll tackle each in turn as it applies to sociology.

2.1 The Canon Is Foundational

What are the foundational principles that underlie the canon of yesterday, principles shared by Marx, Weber and Durkheim. I tentatively propose four. First, they possess a theory of history and, thus, provide a prognosis of the future. Second, they possess moral foundations that offer a distinctive perspective on the world and its possibilities. Third, they possess original methodologies that allow sociologists to grasp the world in unique ways, illustrated in exemplary studies. Fourth, they possess a conceptual framework that defines sociology's object – society – together with theories of its reproduction and transformation. I believe that these principles continue to inform the sociology of today. Even if the connection is not always visible or direct, the substantive themes we pursue in our inter-connected sub-disciplines can be traced to the way canonical theorists enact foundational principles.

But why might Marx, Weber and Durkheim be regarded as foundational? Why should we rely on figures that were writing over a century ago? First, they were living through and reflecting on a period when capitalism, the world in which we live today, became hegemonic, that is when finally, the old (feudal) order was extinguished and the seeds of a possible new (socialist) order could not yet be successfully sown. As I have already stated, in many ways we are returning to that early period. Second, they each were originating a new field of inquiry and as such they had to justify their existence against hostility of competing disciplines, they had to spell out philosophical and scientific principles that have been easily lost in a century of professionalization and specialization. Third, Marx, Weber and Durkheim give sociology a moral compass as well as scientific foundations. The standpoint of these writers opposed the alienating, commodifying, exploitative, exclusivist tendencies of market and state, and, in different combinations, defended ideals of freedom, equality, solidarity.

2.2   The Canon Is Historical

These foundational principles are not fixed. They change over time. The canon has a history. It possesses not only a history but also a prehistory of scattered empirical projects without any obvious unifying core. The canon was first established by Talcott Parsons' (1937) theory of voluntaristic action that was based on a serendipitous convergence in the writings of Marshall, Pareto, Weber and Durkheim. These became canonical figures, but only for a short time as Parsons himself dropped Marshall and Pareto as he developed structural functionalism and its associated modernization theory. Durkheim and Weber were welded together to create new foundations built on the premise of an underlying value consensus and a set of four functions that all societies have to perform. The premises of structural functionalism came under heavy fire during the 1960s, with the emergent struggles not just in the United States but across the world. Marxism, feminism and critical race theory dislodged and then ended the reign of structural functionalism. A new canon was created – but one based on contention rather than harmony. Durkheim and Weber were not cast out but reread in competition with one another and with Marx, a figure Parsons had dismissed on the politically motivated and dubious claim that his ideas were limited to the 19th century.

2.3   The Canon Is Geographical

If the canon is historical, i.e., it changes over time, then we have also to consider whether it is geographical, whether it changes with positions in a global order. On the one hand, there are those who consider the canon as 'Western' or 'Northern' and thus largely irrelevant for the rest of the world. They may subscribe to the development of an 'indigenous' sociology, unsullied by the Western canon. In an important elaboration of this perspective, Raewyn Connell (2007) argues for 'Southern Theory' demarcated from Northern Theory, by reflecting the specific conditions in the global south. She compiles a list of scholars, some self-proclaimed sociologists but most not, who have been ignored by Northern academics. An important corrective to the narrowness of Northern sociology to be sure, nonetheless the theorists she assembles spent much of their time in the North, often educated in the North, and certainly engaging Northern theory, thereby problematizing the bifurcation Connell advocates.

On the other hand, we can speak of a global field of sociology within which Western sociology, particularly from the US but also from Western Europe, is hegemonic but not to the exclusion of alternative sociologies, wrestling for a place within the global field, defining their own national sociologies. In this view the struggle is not between 'indigenous' and 'dominant sociologies,' between 'Southern Theory' and 'Northern Theory' but takes place on the terrain of the dominant sociologies. In other words, the point is not to reject the canon, but to reinterpret it for specific contexts, even to the point of 'provincializing' the Northern canon by rooting it in its own political and economic context (Chakrabarty 2000). In this way different national sociologies will draw on different selections from Weber, Durkheim and Marx, leading to different interpretations of their works, leading to different reconstructions of the canon.

2.4 The Canon Is Relational

The canon is not only foundational, historical, and geographical but the canon is also relational. Reconstructing the canon is not simply a matter of adding another theorist. The canon is not additive; it is composed of relations among its constituent theories. Thus, Talcott Parsons' vision of the canon was based on the derivation of principles based on the *convergence* of theorists, making up a common theoretical framework, rooted in a specific reading of Durkheim and Weber and a deliberate exclusion of Marx. However, when Marx was recalled, it was not to dissolve Durkheim and Weber but to put them into a conversation with Marx. This involved new readings of Durkheim and Weber. Instead of reading Durkheim through the collective consciousness, we began to read him through the abnormal forms of the division of labor. Out of the ashes of a conservative Durkheim arose a radical Durkheim that projected a socialist future, a guild socialism centered on occupational groups. Instead of reading Weber through his different types of action and the centrality of values, we began to see him as a theorist of domination and the state. Weber's history became the realization of rationalization – a distinctive combination of domination and efficiency. The discipline was no longer seen as unitary; it became an arena of competing research programs. The foundational principles of the canon were the basis of divergence rather than convergence.

Parsons' idea of a singular research program that would define sociology from here on out, and indeed in his wildest imagination define the social sciences, had a totalitarian feel to it. In a pluralist society, such a totalizing vision of sociology could not last for long. Its successor has been a rowdy discipline of contesting visions, with no single one dominant, which, ironically, has been more stable than the singular framework of its predecessor. Still, it is coming under severe bombardment from the decolonization movement, and W.E.B. Du Bois is the Trojan horse of a reconstructed canon.

3 Reconstructing the Canon with the Entry of W.E.B. Du Bois

The canon is not static, but moves with the times. Marx and Engels appeared in the 1970s in response to social movements that problematized the assumptions of value consensus, harmony, end of ideology, modernization theory. It did not involve casting aside Weber and Durkheim, but rereading them under the influence of Marx and Engels. Today we are living through social movements – not only in the US – that draw attention to racial inequalities and racial injustices as well as global challenges, such as climate change, pandemics, financial crises. W.E.B. Du Bois is a major contender for canonization as a social theorist largely because his life and theory was so heavily influenced by his race. But Du Bois was much more than a 'race man'; he was a Pan Africanist, a socialist, a peace activist; he was much more than a sociologist, trained as a historian and philosopher; he was more than an academic, being a poet, a dramatist and a novelist. Canonizing Du Bois by bringing him into a conversation with Durkheim, Weber and Marx will transform sociology in a dramatic fashion. Let me sketch what those conversations might look like and with what consequences for sociology.

3.1 *Durkheim and Du Bois*

Aldon Morris (2015) focuses on the early Du Bois of *The Philadelphia Negro* (1996[1899]) and the Atlanta School – this is Du Bois aspiring to be a professional sociologist, conducting meticulous community studies, historically situated empirical research of the sort he learned from Gustav Schmoller, one of his teachers at the University of Berlin. This is the Durkheimian Du Bois not just in method but also in embryonic theory. Du Bois presents the seventh ward of Philadelphia, densely populated by African Americans, as a scene of urban pathologies reminiscent of Durkheim's forced and anomic divisions of labor, capturing the disorganization resulting from migration and discrimination. Du Bois makes a Durkheimian moral appeal, urging whites to recognize the black upper crust. Du Bois claims that the black 'talented tenth,' as distinct from the submerged tenth, share a common civilizational consciousness with white elites. In forging his sociology of stratification Du Bois, like Durkheim, places a lot of weight on education as a progressive force in history, in particular the progress of African Americans.

In addition to *The Philadelphia Negro* sociology has embraced Du Bois's moving essays in *The Souls of Black Folk* (1903), especially the notion of 'double consciousness' – how African Americans living within the veil nonetheless are forced to see themselves through the eyes of their white oppressors. Karen Fields (2002) has drawn parallels between Durkheim's *Elementary Forms of Religious Experience* and the *Souls of Black Folk,* arguing that both Du Bois and Durkheim experienced the world as the discriminated other – the one an African American and the other a Jew. Too often, this is where sociology's engagement with Du Bois has ceased, overlooking the next 60 years of his prolific career.

Concerned with the violent racism deployed against African Americans, despairing of Booker T. Washington's compromise with white elites, finding it difficult to accumulate research resources but also losing confidence in the liberatory effects of science, and more generally his failure to convince whites that African Americans are humans, Du Bois leaves Atlanta University in 1910. He turns to politics, cofounding the famous civil rights organization (the NAACP) and becomes the editor of its magazine, *The Crisis* – a position he will hold for the next 24 years. In 1909 Du Bois (1996 [1909]) pens a biography of the militant abolitionist John Brown – an endorsement of the failed insurrection against slavery at Harpers Ferry, a dress rehearsal for the American Civil War. Du Bois' message in the celebration of John Brown is that the cost of liberation will be high but not as high as the price of repression. This is a new Du Bois, one that recognizes that African Americans cannot rely on others for their emancipation, but they will have to emancipate themselves.

3.2 Weber and Du Bois

We now come to Du Bois's implicit critique of Weber in *Darkwater* (1999[1920]). This collection of literary sociology opens with the famous essay, 'The Souls of White Folk' – a deliberate counterpoint to the *Souls of Black Folk.* Du Bois has given up persuading white folk that African Americans are *human* and instead demonstrates to African Americans that white folk are *inhuman,* displayed in the brutality of World War I – a struggle between European nations for the control and exploitation of Africa. If Western civilization is superior, he argues, then it is because of violent appropriations from the rest of the world – appropriation of human beings, artistic treasures, raw materials and ideas. Du Bois' history of the West is so different from Weber's account of rationalization and its religious origins. For Weber, violence may be important in the rise of merchant capitalism but this is firmly demarcated from the reproduction and expansion of modern capitalism that is based on formally free labor, accounting, separation of home and work, a legal system and the application of science. For Du Bois the violence of capitalism, and particularly racial violence, never ceases.

The essays in *Darkwater* insist that the solution to humanity's problems lies with socialism, conceived of as the public ownership of the means of production, participatory democracy and the equalization of wealth. His essays on 'The Ruling of Men,' 'The Damnation of Women,' and 'Of Work and Wealth' all point to the socialist transcendence of capitalism, but only if the race problem is solved first. He criticizes the professed socialists of his time for not taking the race problem seriously. They will never achieve an alternative egalitarian world on the backs of the majority of the world's population – 'the darker races'. Max Weber was even more skeptical of the promises of socialism – freedom, equality and democracy. For Weber socialism is neither feasible nor viable. Any attempt to bring about socialism will only bring about the opposite, the intensification of rationalization and bureaucracy, the diminution of freedom and democracy. In his view socialism would become the dictatorship of officials not the democratic rule of workers. Du Bois and Weber both question the possibility of socialism, but where the one embraces socialism the other dismisses it.

3.3   *Marx and Du Bois*

Darkwater represents Du Bois as a utopian socialist. He projects a vision of socialism but has no way of realizing it other than through a voluntaristic act by a unified working class. How that could come to pass is unclear. Not only is there no theory of class formation, Du Bois has no theory of the dynamics of capitalism that will lead in the direction of socialism. This will have to wait for his Marxist moment. Although Du Bois had spent time in meetings of the Social Democratic Party while a student in Germany, 1892–94, and although he imbibed a commitment to the state-led socialism of his professors at the University of Berlin, he never seemed to have taken the writings of Marx, let alone Marxists, seriously. It was only after his first visit to the Soviet Union in 1926 that Du Bois plunged into *Capital*, *The Communist Manifesto* and Marx's writings on the American Civil War. This led to Du Bois' intellectual transformation in the 1930s that would inspire his masterpiece *Black Reconstruction in America* (1998[1935]). So opposed to the mainstream historiography, it would take historians another 30 years to catch up with Du Bois' account.

The period of Reconstruction (1865–1877) that followed the Civil War (1861–65) had always been pictured by historians as well as in the (white) popular imagination as an unmitigated disaster. The emancipation of African Americans from slavery could only lead to corruption and chaos. Du Bois took a courageous stance against this conventional wisdom. In an article in the *American Historical Review* Du Bois (1910) had already pointed to the benefits of the Reconstruction after the Civil War – the extension of the franchise led African Americans to become major figures in public and political life and to progressive legislation including the expansion of education for all. In *The Gift of Black Folk* (1925) Du Bois wrote of the contribution of African American fugitives from the plantations to the Northern Armies. These claims would reappear in *Black Reconstruction in America* but within an entirely novel theoretical framework.

Black Reconstruction opens with a Marxian theory of the origins of the civil war. The rising demand for cotton from the largely English textile manufacturers put pressure on slavery to move into new lands and to organize the regeneration of a slave population – an expansion that threatened the ongoing capitalism of the North. That was the provocation of the Civil War, but its prosecution, in the final analysis depended upon a significant proportion of the enslaved population undertaking what Du Bois calls a General Strike, leading them to enlist with the Northern Armies and turning the war in their favor. In recognition of the significance of the African American contribution Lincoln announces the Emancipation Proclamation in 1863 which anticipates the period of Reconstruction after the War. Under Reconstruction Du Bois examines, state by state, the development of an inter-racial democracy – that he also calls an abolition democracy – and how capitalism itself can create the possibility for transcending the racial order. Progress was halted and then reversed when Northern capital, having conquered slavery, lost interest in advancing the interests of African Americans in the South, instigating a withdrawal of Northern troops. Thereafter, the South was handed back to the erstwhile planter class who set about establishing the racial order of Jim Crow, drawing white workers to the side of white capital through the creation of the 'public and psychological' wages of whiteness. Throughout the treatise Du Bois undertakes a class analysis of the forces at work in undermining and then reimposing a racial order. Du Bois effectively shows how the ideas of Marx can be fruitfully reconstructed and applied to this critical moment in US history. Rather than an unmitigated disaster, Du Bois considers Reconstruction a splendid failure – from the imaginary utopia of *Darkwater* Du Bois moves to the real utopia prefigured by the African American struggles under Reconstruction.

Du Bois' engagement with Marxism continues during the New Deal when he proposed that the African American community exploit the reality of segregation to build their own cooperative commonwealth within the United States. After World War Two Du Bois takes his Marxism in a global direction, joining his ideas of Pan-Africanism to the burgeoning anti-colonial movements in Africa. At the same time, he becomes a leader of the international peace movement which puts him on the Soviet side of the Cold War. He becomes an enemy of the US state and indicted as an undeclared agent of a foreign principle. At the trial in 1951 the case is thrown out for want of evidence. The state department exacted its revenge by denying Du Bois his passport for the next 8 years, at the end of which he becomes the celebrated guest of the Soviet and Chinese States. Du Bois openly sides with the growing strength and influence of the Soviet Union and China in promoting an international socialist project, and supporting the anti-colonial struggles in Africa and Asia. His position in the US becomes untenable and in 1961 he thumbs his nose at the US state by finally joining the Communist Party and departing for Ghana where he died in 1963 at the age of 96.

4 Sociology for Today: Reconstructing the Canon and Decolonizing Society?

This has been a rapid tour through the extraordinary life and works of W.E.B. Du Bois. We have seen how Du Bois can be read successively through a Durkheimian, Weberian and Marxian lens, compelling a more systematic theorizing of his enormous oeuvre as well as leading to rereading the erstwhile canon – something that I cannot do here. Instead let me suggest five challenges Du Bois presents to the conventional sociology canon:

1. An explanatory science that takes a global and historical perspective on capitalism, centering race as well as class, beginning with the slave trade, and continuing through colonialism and imperialism;
2. A moral science offering a utopian dimension and calling forth an anti-utopian analysis of the changing limits of the possible;
3. A reflexive science that places social scientists within the world they study as well as within contested fields of inquiry;
4. An interdisciplinary science that recognizes disciplinary boundaries in order to cross them, in particular a cross fertilization between social science, history and the humanities;
5. A public science that forces sociology out of its academic cocoon, entering the public arena by framing public debates and public issues.

Bringing Du Bois into conversation with the canon could revolutionize sociology, but only if we take in the entire gamut of Du Bois' life and work. There is always the danger that entry into the canon will come at the cost of his more radical and critical works, blunt his effect by confining him to his early empiricism.

To take such a radicalized sociology seriously is to recognize that the perspective developed here, although presented in a universal register, is in fact a perspective from the North, specifically the standpoint of US sociology. What does the entry of Du Bois mean from the standpoint of Chinese sociology? It's an open question as to the relevance of this reconstruction *for* the study of China and more specifically *from* China. Is the reconstruction I've outlined a manifestation of academic imperialism? Chinese sociologists may have no interest in the consecration of Du Bois, preferring to develop their own canon, suited to their own conditions. Notwithstanding his global perspectives, his identification with the Soviet Union, with Maoist China, with independent Africa, his hostility to the US state, Du Bois' sociology is still an American project, albeit undertaken from a subaltern position. Chinese sociologists may, indeed, question the relevance of Du Bois to China, past and present. They may be more committed to development of an indigenous sociology that would dispense with Western canon. Decolonized or not, the canon is still Western. Alternatively, Chinese sociologists may want to get on with the empirical examination of pressing social problems, unhampered by any concern or interest in foundational works whether from the West or the East. To them, all this talk of the canon is beside the point, lighting matches while Paris burns.

Western hegemony, however, is not so simply turned aside. It is backed up by institutional resources distributed by states with interests in that hegemony. Let us not forget that the Shanghai Jiao Tong ranking system was designed to measure the quality of Chinese universities against the so-called best universities in the world, deemed to be the most prestigious universities in the US, populated by scholars that win Nobel prizes, academic medals, scholars with high citation counts in 'high impact' 'international' (largely American) journals. States across the world evaluate their universities by their position in global rankings, the famous top 500, and allocate rewards accordingly. Faculty positions in top Chinese universities are largely reserved for scholars with US credentials, US PhDs, books published in the US, articles published in US refereed journals. These are just a few ways in which US hegemony is consolidated.

But the global hegemony of US academia reproduces itself within the field of national sociology. Thus, Chinese sociology is itself a contested field giving rise to divergent interests in Western sociology. Those who have profited from their training in the US or Europe have access to the best jobs in Chinese universities. It might be said they have an interest in US hegemony, and the perpetuation of its canon. Such well-rewarded 'cosmopolitans' may seek alliances with sociologists in other countries, especially BRIC countries, leaving behind locals embedded in sub-national communities, writing in Chinese languages, sociologists who have a limited interest in the trappings of Western credentialing. As Sari Hanafi once wrote, the hegemony of the West, leaves the rest caught between two alternatives: publish globally and perish locally or publish locally and perish globally. Only a few manage to straddle these two worlds.

In the welter of rankings, evaluations, and audits, we mustn't lose sight of the meaning of sociology. *Decolonizing the canon* – becoming self-conscious about the colonial origins of sociology and how they are carried forward into contemporary sociology – is a progressive, indeed exciting and overdue development, but it should not distract us from *sociology's role in decolonizing society*. As I write this, the US is fighting a proxy war in the Ukraine, pouring arms into the Ukraine to fight the Russian invasion. This is a struggle of imperialisms undertaken at the expense of a smaller but resolute nation. How different is this from Du Bois' account of World War One which was also fought over imperial control of weaker nations. How different is the Russian assertion of control over Ukraine different from the Chinese state's domination of Hong Kong? Is race so irrelevant to the Chinese state – whether it be ethnic groups or the hukou system that divided rural from urban? Ultimately what binds sociologists together within a single global field, despite its hegemonic organization, is the creation and defense of civil society – local, national and global – against the global aggression of markets and states. Marx, Weber, and Durkheim reread through the lens of Du Bois is still a potent foundation for a sociology for today.

References

Chakrabarty, D. (2000) *Provincializing Europe: Postcolonial Thought and Historical Difference*. Princeton: Princeton University Press.

Connell, R. (2007) *Southern Theory: The Global Dynamics of Knowledge in Social Science*. Cambridge, UK: Polity.

Du Bois, W.E.B. (1910) Reconstruction and Its Benefits. *The American Historical Review* 15(4):781–799.

Du Bois, W.E.B. (1989[1903]) *The Souls of Black Folk*. New York: Penguin Books.

Du Bois, W.E.B. (1996[1899]) *The Philadelphia Negro: A Social Study*. Philadelphia: University of Philadelphia Press.

Du Bois, W.E.B. (1996[1909]) *John Brown*. New York: International Publishers.

Du Bois, W.E.B. (1998[1935]) *Black Reconstruction in America*. New York: The Free Press.

Du Bois, W.E.B. (1999[1920]) *Darkwater: Voices from Within the Veil.* Mineola, New York: Dover.

Fields, K. (2002) Individuality and Intellectuals: an Imaginary Conversation between W.E.B. Du Bois and Emile Durkheim. *Theory and Society* 31(4): 435–462.

Go, J. (2016) *Postcolonial Thought and Social Theory.* New York: Oxford University Press.

Habermas, J. (1985) *The Theory of Communicative Action, Volumes I and II.* Boston: Beacon Press.

Itzigsohn, J. and Brown, K. (2020) *The Sociology of W.E.B. Du Bois.* New York: New York University Press.

Morris, A. (2015) *The Scholar Denied: W.E.B. Du Bois and the Birth of Modern Sociology.* Oakland, CA: University of California Press.

Parsons, T. (1937) *The Structure of Social Action.* New York: Free Press.

Piketty, T. (2014) *Capital in the Twenty-First Century.* Cambridge, MA: Harvard University Press.

Polanyi, K. (1944) *The Great Transformation.* Boston: Beacon Press.

Stinchcombe, A. (1982) Should Sociologists Forget Their Mothers and Fathers? *The American Sociologist* 17: 2–11.

Whitehead, A.N. (1916) The Organization of Thought. *Science* 44(1134): 409–419.

CHAPTER 9

What Does Capitalism 'Know'? The Limits and Possibilities for Advancing Socialism in the 21st Century

Robert Latham

1 Introduction

As this volume makes readily apparent, David Fasenfest has achieved and impacted much in the world of scholarship that is oriented around the struggle with and against capitalism, and to a degree the possibilities of advancing socialism. Considered in this chapter, in the spirit of David's legacy, is how two facets central to his work are connected and offer the basis to think about the difficulties we face in that struggle, in both its negative and positive aspects.

One is the attention David has given to the study of local contexts. Given the attention to national and global forces it is easy to overlook how central the local is, as we humans are anchored in corporeal existence where groups of us coexist collectively in what is often called often 'daily life,' within which those wider forces of capitalism and power are articulated and at times shaped into their real and lived forms (forms which in turn help shape those forces).

A second facet is the problem of generating knowledge and theory about our capitalist world at all its scales and depths. I write 'problem' because we cannot take such generation for granted. It requires agency like David's to facilitate and nurture it, especially in a capitalist world that rarely rewards research bearing on the critique of capitalism and certainly not the advancement of socialism. I know this first-hand as someone in a discipline that is oriented toward the liberal-capitalist center of things, having for decades to publish work where the tension between the esoteric and exoteric dimensions was pronounced.

In this chapter I want to build on those two facets to reflect on the two interrelated aims that are central to David's approach mentioned above (the struggle against capitalism and to advance socialism). I start from the assumption that capitalism has been attempting to counter the left for over a century and a half, and along the way has gained capacities and 'knows' in ways today not there in the past. Some of this is manifested in the world order it has created and is attempting to maintain (capitalist world order being a topic David started to address especially as of the 2010s). This gained capacity hardly yields an infallible capitalism, but even in its blunders it can have undermining effects for the left.

Capitalism's increasing capacity to counter struggles against it is unfolding in the context of a capitalism more overdetermined than ever, which in part reflects its growing depth and extent across planetary life. This context complicates both the struggle against capitalism and the counter to those struggles.

It will be suggested here that in the face of these pressures the left can take a more dialectical approach to strategy, adopting what is labeled a dialectical-strategic praxis that thinks in terms of multiple steps based on dialectical possibilities that also includes approaches to left organization, mass mobilization and prospective counter-struggle coming from capitalism. In this, the left could also attempt to coordinate the various, uneven forms of struggle against capitalism. I argue that the left might consider the creation of an organization of organizations, or league, focused on challenging and undoing corporate power, that could operate at multiple scales from local to global (with David's work in mind on the inter-scalar). This would not be an International nor a forum. Ideally, it would help address the great gap in socialist political presence faced since 1991 and possible paths to reach right-oriented segments of the working class. This will require forms of unification that can draw inspiration from the David's work of being a unifier across many realms but especially that of knowledge which, as I will argue, is central to the strategic possibilities going forward.

The focus is mostly on developments in capitalism's imperial center (anchored by the U.S.) but can speak also to the left more broadly. These days the label 'left' lacks precision and seems often to mean 'not the political right or center.' While written from a Marxist perspective, this essay addresses the term 'left' in a broader sense, referring at a minimum to that which acts in opposition to capitalism and more fully to undo and displace it. I will use the rubric *struggle-against-capitalism* for this array rather than anti-capitalism. Struggle-against can convey a wider range of meanings beyond the negative of only 'against' or 'anti' (e.g., opposition to). This includes the positive, intentional actions and forces that confront capitalism. Importantly, the phrase signals the class struggle at the center of things and, as David put it in 2017, 'The Struggle Continues.'

2 Capitalism's Protracted Counter-Struggle History

Central to that struggle and what makes it necessary, as is known, is the relatively long history of attempts by especially capitalist states to weaken, reverse, or destroy the forces opposing capitalism. This, it is argued here, should be regarded as counter-struggle rather than counter-revolution. Hence it is possible to view the attempt to stop or 'disrupt' (an intelligence-security sector term) revolution and revolutionary processes as a subset of the wider array of actions and programs meant to counter all struggles-against-capitalism (revolutionary and non-revolutionary).[1] For example, Jeremy Corbyn's Labour Party leadership and attempt to become prime minister was certainly not revolutionary but could be seen as the beginnings of a political coalescence that held promise as a struggle-against-capitalism (one that he recently asserted was countered in various ways by the political-intelligence realm).[2] The same might be said of radical labour unions such as Union Syndicale Solidaires in France, the Landless Workers Movement (MST) in Brazil or even the Zapatistas. Debatably, this might apply to a socialist organization that ideally desires (or projects itself) to be part of a revolutionary process but is practically focused on elections or local activism.

An argument against this broadening from counterrevolution to counter-struggle is that, ultimately, the stakes of all struggles are revolution, even if situated in the far future. While this may be so, it cannot be known in any given historical moment if it is. It also assumes the only pathway away from capitalism as the twenty-first century unfolds is revolution. It might also fail to treat revolution as a unique phenomenon, as Lenin put it involving the 'passing of state power from one class to another.'[3] Assuming revolutionary processes are a dimension of the struggle-against-capitalism – albeit a very crucial one – allows conceptual room for the various complexities of struggles in specific times and places. Many of these David has documented and analyzed. Additionally, if useful, a given action and process could be viewed in both registers, the revolutionary and non-revolutionary.

---

1 I will also use the term counter-action to represent the broader effort to undermine and destroy threats (outside of conventional war), such as those associated with international and domestic terrorism.
2 Kennard (2022).
3 I am leaving aside the use of the term revolution as a synonym for processes of transformation, which appears in historical analysis even on the left, including perhaps Gramsci's notion of passive revolution.

As we know, the most iconic counter-struggle was the Cold War, in part due to the wide range of actions and programs including coups, proxy wars, assassinations, sanctions, extensive propaganda efforts, the FBI COINTELPRO program, cultural funding programs, media manipulation, the fostering of strikes and supply-chain disruptions (e.g., against Allende's Chile). The capacity and will to use such 'instruments' remain and have been applied since 1991 to the left and beyond the left, especially in the Middle East (albeit not with the same concentration).

The pre-history to this intensive counter-struggle begins with the emergence of the organized left in Europe, occurring while semi-feudal rule was in decline as the bourgeoisie was coming into full political ascendence and capitalism developing rapidly. As is well-known, Marx faced various police actions limiting his activities, some of which led, for example, to the *Rheinische Zeitung's* shutdown. Mid-century saw the counterrevolutions of 1848 and the persecution in Germany of the Communist League, with a public trial in 1852 and jail sentences (Marx was an active member but avoided arrest in London). After 1850, the counter-struggle continued, with various forms of subterfuge, propaganda, and persecution and is marked by events such as the military repression of the Paris Commune and the 1905 Russian Revolution. The post-WWI saw counterrevolution in Germany, the Red Scare in the U.S. and a range of intrigue and battles against the left from the late 1920s on.

Two points can be made regarding this historical reminder. The obvious one is that counter-struggle has a 180-year trajectory, it has evolved with an arsenal of instruments and practices ready-at-hand. Stronger struggles-against-capitalism risks stronger counter-struggles. Counter-struggle can fail, because for example of ineffective approaches or disorder and weakness in the capitalist system or some segment of it; or because a struggle, especially in historical terms revolutionary, is able to overwhelm it.

A second, more substantial, point is the need to better understand the patterns associated with counter-struggle, not just the discernible facets in the development of its instruments and modalities, but also their deployment or appearance in the context of a contemporary capitalism that is especially complex and overdetermined, especially when seen in global scale.[4] Additionally, it means considering if patterns, forms, and forces that are not expressly designed for and maintained as counter-struggle, have counter-struggle effects.

---

4   What is needed are methods to assess such developments. However, addressing that is well beyond the scope of this chapter.

2.1 Counter-Struggle Goes Back to the Future

There are several issues to address around these two main points. To start, it is worth recalling what is axiomatic: any developed security-sector method can be applied to any supposed threat, including potential political threats thought to carry possibilities for organized violence. Counteraction is the broader rubric of practices against any organization, people, movement, or development that counter-struggle (and therefore counter-revolution) is part of. Using modes established during the cold war – counter-action can be directed at any body of actors, left or right. The Phoenix Program developed by the CIA during the Vietnam War created practices that have been applied more recently in Iraq and Afghanistan, if not also in establishing the Department of Homeland Security.[5] The continued application of counter-action to capitalism-oppressed peoples is ongoing, as Mike Davis observed, especially regarding repression in urban settings worldwide.[6] Relatedly, Peter Hallward analyzed the bold, early 2000's, U.S. and French intervention in Haiti to stop Lavalas.[7]

Also, counter-action keeps developing. Kees van der Pijl puts emphasis on counteraction in the biological sphere, exploring among other themes the implications around COVID-19 and the power of capital and the capitalist state via bio-tactics to control threats, the unruly or deemed marginal populations.[8] While some might view this as far-fetched, one can follow the development of a growing field, called 'neuro-weaponry,' helped along by the organization set up to foster security innovation, the Defense Advanced Research Projects Agency (DARPA). Notably, neuro-weaponry is about using neuro-technology to control the thought, emotions, and bodies of targeted groups and individuals. As academic spokesperson, James Giordano, put it: 'neuroweapons include drugs to degrade physiologic and cognitive functions, and/or to alter emotional states to affect the desire or capacity for aggression and combat.'[9] The inclination toward such tools is longstanding – leading, for example, to the 1950s CIA MK-Ultra experiments with LSD – but only now is the technology coming to hand.

In contrast, counter-action in the media may seem prosaic. Since the 1960s it has been widely known that mainstream media (MSM) has been a realm of counter-struggle intervention and has shown no shortage of self-directed

---

5   This is well-documented by the independent journalist, Valentine (2017: chapters 15–17), who more generally does an excellent job of conveying the range of anti-threat and counter-struggle anchored in the CIA, based on detailed interviews and document research.
6   Davis (2006, Epilogue).
7   Hallward (2007).
8   van der Pijl (2022). Some readers will find some of his assertions controversial.
9   Giordano (2017: 3).

action and complicity (apparent among large corporate, bourgeois-oriented, or fear-based compliers).

Far less known is the full nature and extent of intervention and complicity in the realm of social media.[10] Liberal observers, or what Valentine reports CIA agent Cord Meyer labeled the 'compatible left' (including political actors, journalists, and academics), frame intervention and opinion-shaping through the concept of disinformation – with the 'dis-informers' typically identified as state security threats, especially Russia, China, and Iran; or as far-right content producers critical of 'global elites', mega-corporations, and politicians associated with these (e.g., Biden). Somehow this 'compatible left' overlooks key cyber- or digital-warfare documents the US military has issued for decades, discussing its own emerging practices and programs.[11]

A perhaps broader issue here is the cultivation of left divisions. This started after WWII when order-makers argued that European 'socialist' parties could help blunt 'communism' in the region.[12] The history of the 1960s/1970s counter-struggle is full of examples of attempts to advance divisions across and within far-left movements and organizations.

Also situated along the lines of the seemingly 'soft' forms of counter-struggle (aspects of which have been thought of as 'psychological warfare') is a phenomenon that David was attuned to: the longstanding impetus to reform capitalism to mitigate or even remove the grounds for struggle, with various concepts from passive revolution to welfare or enlightened capitalism or corporate liberalism, conveying aspects of this. The impetus for this always seems to return, not just in revived rhetoric from liberal capitalist organizations like the Democratic Party, but also from capitalists like Whole Foods CEO John Mackey (advocating 'Conscious Capitalism') and today even right-wing politicians like Marco Rubio (advocating 'Common Good Capitalism'). One might also include under the soft power rubric so-called 'woke-imperialism' (trying to mobilize support for intervention, with whatever hope of success, by linking it to challenges to sexism, racism, and anti-LGBTQ+). According to one observer – who reminds us of the precedents through history going back to the nineteenth century – the 'new "woke" face of American hegemony and projects of empire is designed to project the U.S. as an international moral police force

---

10 A recent attempt to bring some of these factors together in propaganda and manufacturing consent terms is Foley (2021).
11 See, for example, U.S. Army War College (2011).
12 Latham (1997: 128–29).

rather than a conventional great power – and the result is neo-imperialism with a moral face.'[13] The possibilities of sowing left division here is obvious.

2.2 International Capitalist Order

It is not possible to mention all the elements that have historically been observed as counter-action – and more specifically counter-struggle – across the centuries, including issues David himself has explored, like national, ethnic, racial divisions or the many ways in which thinking about class has been manipulated. An encyclopedia is really needed.

One essential facet that has had important counter-struggle effects relating to the second point above, regarding the complexities tied to capitalism today, is the nature of the international capitalist order.

International liberal capitalism formed after World War II is really the first such order where conditions for accumulation, its maintenance and development, were placed expressly at the center of world institutional governance. Certainly, previous orders, as Giovanni Arrighi and Immanuel Wallerstein underscored, were vital to the existence of a developing capitalist world system; and as history moved into the nineteenth century explicit capitalist ordering increased, especially linked to imperialism and monopoly (Lenin). But these kinds of structuring and precedents are distinct from what was executed in an express way with its array of international institutions in the post-World War II order.

What is also distinct about this current order is how it put a political orientation organically compatible with capitalism (and the modernity capitalism was generating) at its center: liberalism. Previous orders could emphasize concepts like free trade, but they were mostly geared to devising a system between great powers, anchored in the hegemony of one of those powers, such as Great Britain.

It is no coincidence in dialectical terms that this type of order emerged after the rise of the Soviet Union, a power the liberal capitalists thought, mistakenly, they could rein in by bringing it into the universalizing dominion of their burgeoning order.[14] That order created, as intended, continuity with the capitalist world's past and a new range of expansive possibilities for the future. That it did, in effect fashioning the overarching context within which all struggle-against-capitalism would be situated and unfold. Marx underscored how socialism could only arise from within capitalism. But not all capitalist

---

13 Mott (2022: 2).
14 Latham (1997: Chapter 3).

contexts are the same; some might be better able to impede its arrival than others, constituting a counter-struggle force at the systemic level.

This context, we know, is most powerful in the global North, where the development of an American/European organized left occurred in tandem with that of liberal capitalist political forces. The gains in those forces manifested in such things as the growing capacity of centrist parties to mitigate or absorb left political energies. Additionally, any attempt to obtain state power had to confront a state form with all its numerous decades of entrenched interests, international penetrations, and bureaucratic logics that troubled Nicos Poulantzas. Lenin understood well that what the Bolsheviks faced was relatively thin.

This underlines how profound a loss the demise of the Soviet bloc was, its limits and faults notwithstanding. World historical dialectical processes now seem always ultimately to be situated in, or run up against, the international liberal capitalist context. When struggles-against-capitalism – which might emerge relatively distanced from the order – obtain some traction, they are drawn into the political and economic forces internal to the order. The left, of course, has no choice about this. But what does it do about it? For nearly 40 years after World War II the Soviets invested considerable resources into battling capitalism's counter-struggle in both its direct and indirect forms. Where and how to begin the battle today, when we are a long way from the capitalism of 1870?

Some may hold out hope that US hegemony appears to be weakening and perhaps has entered a spiral of decline, implying that the 'liberal world order' itself is increasingly vulnerable. For neo-cons like Robert Kagan the answer is a revamped, more aggressive US hegemony.[15] For liberals – such as the editors of *Harper's Magazine* who in a July 2022 issue declared 'The American Century Is Over' – it is a more multilateral order, with the US *primus inter pares,* of course. Both perspectives assume a conversion of the current capitalist order.

Relatedly, the language of a 'great reset' of the order has lately emerged in World Economic Forum settings that claims to be an initiative to reform the order to address 'inconsistencies, inadequacies, and contradictions of multiple systems.'[16] The familiar 'enlightened' capitalism trope is hard to miss, especially in its notion of 'stakeholder Capitalism.' But even if this order should dissolve, history suggests another capitalist order might replace it. A BRICS-centered cross-regional order would likely still be a capitalist order, and thus

---

15   Kagan (2017).
16   World Economic Forum (n.d.).

in capitalism's favor, absorbing forces that might otherwise destabilize it on a world scale. Even if the current international order is not succeeded by a new one, there is no reason why a range of coterminous, regional (capitalist) orders could not arise.

2.3 Capitalism's Cross-Development and Overdetermination

The other facet of the second point above concerns the question of how the context of a contemporary capitalism that is especially complex and overdetermined matters regarding the struggle/counter-struggle dynamic. The contemporary world capitalist order matters not only because of its counter-struggle effects, but also because keeping it in mind may help us gain some perspective on the complications entailed in the potential demise of capitalism in the twenty-first century. Factors and logics of contemporary capitalism – and its world order – bearing on its 'resilience' are central to discerning the prospects for struggles-against-capitalism.

It has been long recognized that we face a totalizing capitalism, one that David has helped us discern is not only extensive in geo-social terms (a world order not just a world system) but increasingly intensive, with a deepening reach of capitalist forms across and through social life (reflected in the much wider array of commodity and industrial forms). This creates a far more differentially multitudinous capitalism that complicates the struggle-against-capitalism.[17] Of immediate concern is the possibility that in this extensive-intensive context are growing patterns of what can be labeled cross-development. The latter is development where some social or material form that might seem initially to present a potential basis for one thing (e.g., greater popular power) turns out to also create the basis for something else relating to it (e.g., greater capitalist power). A now classic cross-development can be seen in Marx's observation that the spread of the factory system was creating the grounds for the rise of a class-struggling proletariat. However, in time, it was seen that the same factory system would also be the basis for further capitalist industrial organization and the penetration of reactionary labor organizations.

Seventy years ago, Harold Innis pointed to how the integration of Canada (especially its transport, media, laws) held promise for new forms of nation-wide democratic power, but also facilitated U.S. empire, as American corporations could exploit this integration, with easier access to uniform laws, distribution networks, and a national media.[18] A more contemporary example is the

---

17   Latham (2018).
18   Innis (1950: 171–78).

global internet. It was becoming obvious in the late 1990s that this distributed system, seen as holding so much promise (and still seen as such) for democratic communication was also an ideal realm for both capital accumulation in concentrated forms and counteraction by states and corporations.[19]

Perhaps we can look at these cross-developments not just as facets of overdetermination but as what Mao called 'non-antagonistic contradictions.'[20] Mao claimed some contradictions can transition from antagonistic to non-antagonistic or in reverse. What if they pile up and keep persisting in a non-antagonistic form, where they can reinforce one another in a system, however inconsistent and diffuse (and thereby more deeply overdetermined than ever), that helps sustain capitalism?[21] As a result old and new vulnerabilities are more numerous and distributed than ever.

Related to contradictions and cross-developments are the complications tied to the peculiar combination of what looks like effectiveness and ineffectiveness in the policies and actions associated with global capitalist power. In recent years blunders and failures have been highlighted especially by those who emphasize the waning of the current global order anchored in the U.S. imperium. The Afghanistan, Iraq, and Libya interventions, the June 2022 Summit of the Americas, and the U.S. involvement in Ukraine, are but a few recent examples. Policies such as sanctions repeatedly fail to achieve stated aims. The discourse of blunder and failure though has a long history going back at least to Vietnam. In the financial realm we see a series of crises tied to what looks like blundering policy (e.g., those leading up to the 2000 and 2008 financial crises). Yet from the standpoint of capitalist system continuity, these phenomena are but pieces of a complex array of actions and policies (including 'successes' such as the Kissinger / Nixon cementing of Sino-Soviet division by 1971) that allow not only for endurance and reproduction but also significant expansion in capital accumulation.

From the standpoint of struggles-against-capitalism, the pattern is relevant because clear lines of potential crisis that might lead to existential vulnerability of benefit to struggles may not be feasibly available. From the standpoint of capitalism's durability, the blunders and failures can be 'doing work' for the system (just as war does), especially facilitating spheres of activity for the organizational complex of capitalism. Taking short term 'best options', which

---

19 Latham (2005).
20 Mao (1937).
21 This is not inconsistent with Mao's notion, building on Lenin, of the identity and coexistence of contradictions, which by implication are not fatal to systems. Later, Deleuze and Guattari would point to something similar in their concept, territorialization.

may not achieve stated aims, can contribute to security-sector enhancement and capital accumulation (especially for the military, financial, extraction, and technology complex). Organizations of power are in place and advancing actively with ever new short-term 'best options' projects. The massive system is thereby propelled forward and what I elsewhere called the 'constitutive presence' of order-making is kept in motion across geographical, institutional, and ideational sites.[22]

Given the uneven and differentiated realms of capital accumulation it is not unlikely that there can be situations where what is detrimental (a blunder or impairment) in one sphere is seen as beneficial (a success) in another. Perhaps we can think of these as antagonistic or negative cross-developments. Some observers of imperialism (Hobson, Lenin) and the military-industrial-complex have long pointed to the uneven distribution of advantages and disadvantages to empire and conflict across economic sectors and the bourgeoisie. Recently a Bank of America memo was leaked that argues conditions of U.S. labor market weakness is desirable to keep inflation and thus interest rates in check.[23] This implies that disadvantages in the consumption realm are acceptable given the potential advantages to the financial realm (with disadvantages flowing to both retail corporations and workers). Any economic system can face what is often termed trade-offs. But in the current capitalist system they are manifold, taken as ultimately non-threatening, and even normal. There is no single ongoing and dynamic financial statement for capitalism making this visible at any given scale, local to global, but only symptoms of imbalance in existing indicators such as debt levels, the balance of payments, or GDP.

A telescopic view of these sorts of logics and patterns can be thought of as situated along a 180-degree line with two endpoints. On one end is a capitalism just coping with a wide and seemingly unending assortment of challenges, inventing new approaches to do so, and moving down the line from hyper-financialization to neoliberal authoritarianism and beyond. On the other end is a capitalism willing to go to the edge, in brinkmanship risking ecological disaster and nuclear war. Alas, humanity is subject to both ends and all that is in-between. David has engaged and helped advance much work across the decades that highlight the seriousness of elements along this spectrum.

---

22   Latham (1997: 62–66).
23   Klippenstein (2022).

2.4 What Does Capitalism Know?

Inherent in the above discussion of the complications faced by struggles-against-capitalism is a question: what does capitalism know and in what way does it know?

Knowing inheres in the body of institutions, organizations, and arrangements we often designate as an order or 'society.' What is known thereby is what can be seen as a common sense of power, situated within the institutional expectations and organizational norms and practices. From Marx on, critical thinkers have theorized such social order, frequently contrasting it to other ways of constituting social life. We have, for example, Sartre's seriality versus groups; Althusser's superstructure; Badiou's that which is 'repeatable. [which] guarantees the perennial conservation of the world' versus events; and Ranciere's police order versus politics.[24] Mainstream social scientists have also been aware of this function of social order. The system theory of Talcott Parsons stands out in this regard. Critical scholars often held it to account for its unswerving reinforcement of system preservation and journals like *Critical Sociology* have been important to this effort.

Power's common sense is situated in the body of logics that serve system continuity that subjects like state officials enact sometimes without being aware of the ultimate implications. Marx famously emphasized how capitalism as a dialectical system involves both deliberate agency (for example, the purposeful actions associated with struggle and counter-struggle) and the systemic, constitutive unfolding of relations and forces that in turn shape the conditions and possibilities of agency (surpassing the duality inherent in Hegel's 'cunning of reason').[25] Relatedly, the common sense of power manifests in and shapes dialectical processes. Responses to dialectical developments like global South movements in struggles-against-capitalism are recognized, assessed, and countered based on this common sense. As mentioned, this knowing is typically incomplete and misapprehends the real conditions and dynamics, as occurred in the Afghanistan intervention. But more important than perceived success or failure of any given project – or the 'learning from mistakes' that may occur – is continuity of the common sense and all the mobilization around it, which thereby contributes to capitalism's extension. It is sufficient if corporations and capitalist states (their organizations, personnel, and networks) can 'carry on' or even better develop through such projects (e.g., expand

---

24 Badiou (2009: 140).
25 There is no space here to explore this further, bringing in, for example, Postone's (1993: 76–77) attempt to clarify Marx conception of capitalism as subject versus Hegel's *Geist*.

the security sector, draw in local and international collaboration, or expand capital accumulation).

Misapprehension is prevalent in not just bourgeois theory and economics but in counter-struggle. This is not necessarily in the left's favour. Many counter-struggle programs do not require accurate comprehension to be effective. Most obviously, there are the blunt-force attacks via the police system that do not require knowing the complexities of real conditions. But also organizational, non-physical, destruction of any social form can occur using various tactics of subversion, where it might even be to the capitalist state's advantage to avoid recognising real conditions and needs. Even in positive counter-action endeavors often labeled 'nation-building' or 'democratization' misapprehension can serve to legitimate desired arrangements of power and logics of accumulation.

The common sense of power and capitalism's knowing may have reached its heights across the 20th and 21st centuries, with its uniquely extensive order-building and bourgeois-knowledge production anchored in the social sciences. However, that does not translate necessarily into efficiency and effectiveness, even with the development of AI. There are overarching aims of accumulation and power (for individuals in capitalist organizations and for the organizations themselves) that manifest across a widening range of contradictions and cross-developments that marks a deepening and extending capitalist totality. Given this, the fashioning of masterful policies and programs is unlikely (assuming they could ever even be desired except by exceptional idealist functionaries). But that does not stop the creation of new policies and programs that yield new common senses of power, however much they all rest on misapprehension. This additional common sense in turn, automatically, facilitates further interventions and impositions. That is, all of this occurs as a compounding of deliberate and systemic-level determinations.[26]

A recent example – and really symptom – of some of this is the concept of the 'gray zone' in U.S. security policy. A key 2015 white paper defined it as '[c]ompetitive interactions among and within state and non-state actors that fall between the traditional war and peace duality. Characterized by ambiguity about the nature of conflict, opacity of the parties involved or uncertainty about the relevant policy and legal frameworks.'[27] Rather than grounds for inaction the gray zone as a new common sense of power articulates an open

---

26   In this sense, referring to older debates, the ruling class both rules and does not rule.
27   Kapusta (2015).

door to counter-action employing a spectrum of instruments applied to all sorts of actors and in varied spheres.

The left should be attentive to the possibility that the cultivation of gray zones might be sought after by capitalist power. It is in the interest of counter-struggle efforts to create contexts of 'ambiguity', 'opacity', and 'uncertainty' not of the left's choosing. Evidence abounds for the fostering if not creation of organizations and ideational weapons that complicate spheres of conflict and even struggle since the cold war began, whether in Middle East conflicts or left struggle in Europe. The history of such effort is well-documented, for example, in the cultural sphere in Europe and the U.S.[28]

3 Organizing Struggles-against-Capitalism as a Dialectical-Strategic Praxis

It is not necessary to believe the depiction above of counter-struggle means that a significant challenge to capitalism is unrealizable. At the most basic level, struggles-against-capitalism should always be present somewhere across capitalism. In dialectical terms, struggle is inherent to it and is a part of it. Movements will emerge and sometimes sustain, like the MST in Brazil; left parties will come into government; workers will organize and at times resist; masses will assemble and overturn regimes, youth will be drawn to socialism, and international solidarity will arise. Viewed from the 2020s the question is, what can that presence amount to. Can it undo capitalism rather than just alter it? How can it scale up, cohere, and endure?

Starting points assume knowledge, and that raises the question of what does knowing capitalism entail today for strategy. Is our understanding of twenty-first century capitalism – and the possibilities of the struggle against it and what socialism can be – truly anchored in a strategic thinking that has capitalism's counter-struggle and relevant forms and complexities of capitalism itself at its foundation? I venture it is not. There is a great deal of relevant knowledge – such as the study of crisis, neoliberalism, or the history of organizing for struggle – which could be assembled in encyclopedic fashion, based on what its import for strategy today is. However, given that most relevant knowledge today comes out of the academy, the strategic import will mostly need to be extrapolated. There are numerous exceptions, for example

---

28 Saunders (2013). See the excellent review by Petras (1999) of the first edition, which supports the work but also criticizes it for not going far enough to situate the US effort regarding anti-socialism.

Samir Amin on internationalism; there is the recent work of the late Michael Lebowitz regarding the conditions and possibilities for twenty-first century socialism; and reflection on the possibilities of left social movements. There are works that explicitly draw implications for strategy today in conclusions.[29] It is a great help that David has tried to advance this via his publishing and editorship.

Can work going forward, especially with strategic and political import, place the relationship between struggle and counter-struggle at the center of analysis in specific and broad terms (that relationship typically appears as discrete issues, such as the dynamic between social movements and the right).

It is not possible to address here the questions just posed in the substantial way required. But I can as a start describe what I think – following from the discussion in the previous section – is necessary to any successful left strategic theory today. I can, to that end, focus on the following question: does assuming, for struggle, the centrality of counter-struggle forces – and especially the complexities of contemporary capitalism that is the context for those forces – engender certain approaches to strategy? There are other ways to begin, such as with the questions of what can oppose capitalism today; where the forces are to oppose it likely to come from; and how can they develop and sustain a pathway leading to capitalism's end. The 'what' refers to, on the one hand, the modes of struggle such as mass movements, disruption (in the broad sense, including general strikes), re-appropriation, or capturing political power. On the other, it is the subjects of struggle. Categories like 'workers and the oppressed' now signal a wider set than in that past, which was focused on industrial workers, peasants, and the colonized. If my point of departure expressly does not start with these questions, ultimately it leads to them.

Some may think counter forces are too negative in nature to build a strategy upon. I agree that no strategy can be built only on anticipation of negation (e.g., fear of being undermined). The obvious response is to re-emphasize the importance allocated to the (positive) conditions and forms of contemporary capitalism that are a context and force in generating struggle. However, that misses a more basic point: counter-struggle, which can be a force of negation, partly forms what capitalism is, and is thereby a positive attribute of capitalism like totalization. Thus, the struggle-against-capitalism is a struggle not just against labor exploitation, imperialism, and capitalist state power but also counter-struggle practices and the relevant conditions and complexities of

---

29   A recent example is Egan (2016). There are many others of note, such as McNally, Le Blanc and Post, whom I cannot take up here.

capitalism which (in a somewhat circular fashion) include counter-struggle as a dimension of capitalism itself.

An essential condition is international order, and it may be the most important place to start the strategic thinking advocated here, because the prevailing order potentially is in its terminal phase. Relatedly, we may have entered a period where not just global economic crisis but war, involving the most powerful states, is more prevalent. Yet today's Marxist left does not appear to have really begun to think through what this means for the struggle-against-capitalism. There is a tradition for this in Marxist thought from Lenin onward into the 1930s (regarding both the Soviet Union and the Comintern). While socialists were thrust into a long period of order transformation, thinking about it started beforehand, especially around debates in the Second International – for attention to war and order having an international is a great advantage, even if such issues can lead to tragic division. Since then, certainly individual wars (from Vietnam to Iraq-Iran) have figured into party and movement positions (especially anti-war) and strategies as have, less so, macro strategic views tied to global (imperial) order. We need to return to these to think through the challenges for struggles and advancing socialism under conditions of international instability and multiple wars. The notion that we must wait until the specific conditions emerge fails to acknowledge that we already face specific conditions bearing on world capitalist system change (e.g., China-U.S. conflict, the BRICS+). The range of questions that will need to be addressed is extensive and might include the left's relationship to the war-politics relationship, intensive assessments of the possibilities for socialist internationalism, differences in methods in geo-regions such as US/Europe, the Middle East, Latin America, and Asia, bearing on global economic crisis, best approaches to spontaneous popular uprisings, and whether or how to challenge attempts to create a new capitalist order.

Hope that one can limit the strategic view to one's nation-state or local region rests on unhistorical assumptions. As implied above, while David's own research and analysis has placed emphasis on the local, it is typically done with wider geo-scales in mind.

What compounds the strategic challenge is the necessity of both national and global strategies, along with the coordination among those and other geo-scales. A great deal of political conflict might occur at the national level, as global developments become especially crucial. Moreover, there is no established timeline for order termination – even if some feel it is near – implying the temporal site of struggle is the current moment. This is a moment complicated by the need to think strategically not just with multiple scales but multiple potential trajectories in mind: capitalism's continuity, transformation, and dissolution (the goal). Such thinking requires assessments of the current capitalist order regarding its adaptability versus its brittleness (making it more vulnerable), where entrenched interests have the power to resist challenges, and where challenges may in the end serve to strengthen the order.

Key here is the relationship between dialectical thinking and strategy. One version of this is thinking in dialectical terms about multiple negations, reverberations, and counters into the future (not only one step), guided by discernment of current developments and their negation, even at multiple scales if needed (in alterations or eliminations). This would be combined with the devising of methods, strategies, and theory (such as new approaches to party organization, which thereby implies thinking of one's own agency dialectically). These would be appropriate to the possibilities in play in the dialectical paths into the future (including even existing or emerging bourgeois divisions or new possibilities for inter-left collaboration). Pursuing this means also addressing the counter-struggle possibilities that favor capitalism, including reform, the cultivation of the right, left subversion, or state authoritarian repression.

Some might think this exceeds the strategic capacity of the left, expecting at best a muddle of disparate options thrown about, leading to confusion and inaction. Or alternatively, it might lead to esoteric ideas advanced by tiny cohorts. However, the aim is not some ultimate, integrated statement or plan, but an adaptive assemblage of strategic elements and relations that forms more of a dynamic constellation than a synchronic map: a constellation that can even be segmented. Those proposing a given action such as trying to start a new left party at the national level, for instance, might thereby be induced to think through the various strategic dimensions in a more dialectical way. Note that we already have an increasing body of relevant knowledge in place (e.g., about contemporary class composition or the history of internationalism) that can be organized (and extended) for this dialectical-strategic praxis.

If there is any credence to the claim that this is not the capitalism faced by Luxemburg, Lenin, or even Gramsci (despite the many core continuities like surplus-value), then this dialectical-strategic praxis might be seen as helping contend with the complexities associated with today's cross-developed overdetermination. If system vulnerabilities are more numerous and distributed, then strategies that work across registers might be needed such as creating cross-pressures bearing, for example, on vital junctions among the financial, production, and political realms (thus a strike shutting down transport infrastructure would be insufficient).

If there is merit in addressing more than one ensemble of linked sectors within a state or internationally, it implies the need for an extensive body of methods and sites of struggle. Elsewhere I have discussed thinking about this in uneven and combined terms: uneven in modes, sites, and orientations, combined in the shared praxis of struggle-against-capitalism.[30] In this very wide 'correlations of forces' (Trotsky's term) – the uneven and combined struggle-against-capitalism (UCSAC) – we would have Leninist parties as well as, for example, radical unions and indigenous resistance movements. Some historical precedent for this lies in the 1930s united front in the U.S. and elsewhere.

UCSAC is itself insufficient. It requires an organizational context. One that is encompassing of UCSAC, which has presence at multiple scales and sites and creates a discernible realm for it to operate in and with some unity of focus. This seems to be best advanced by creating an organization of organizations. There is precedent for this in history of the Internationals. The First International drew unions and associations together and the Third communist parties, with both including local and national chapters. One immediate advantage is the avoidance of horizontalism, which obviously is a deeply problematic form in the context of struggle and counter-struggle. It is avoided since members are organizations not individuals and thus are differentiated by definition and to a great degree contain their own internal hierarchies (e.g., that between a member organization's executive council versus general membership). What might be thought of as a league is not about coalitions and alliances but commitment to an overarching organization that has binding power, which thereby adds an additional organizational layer to the otherwise independent organizational life of any given organization-member.

The purpose of this league would be to always advance and coordinate all struggles-against-capitalism at all scales – whether that entails a socialist revolution, the appropriation of a factory in a Latin American town, a general strike, the expelling of an extractive corporation from a forest, or the mobilization of an anti-corporate bloc within an economistic union. It is distinct from bodies like a World Social Forum or from notions of a world party. It even is distinct from, although quite close to, an international (as it has appeared, historically) in that it would have fully constituted national and local leagues, not just chapters, and a nexus of organization across all scales focused on the praxis of struggle.

How to name such an entity is important. My sense is that a generic label is best given the current ideological environment, which is particularly diffuse relative to the twentieth century, and which finds expression, for example, in the embrace of the right by segments of the working class, especially in capitalism's

---

30   Latham (2018: 10–15).

center, North America and Europe. The current ideological environment in the West departs from the historical precedents of relatively clearer lines between left, right, and center. How much of this is furthered by state intervention (not just U.S.) awaits detailed research, but such activities would be very consistent with the past. It is hard to imagine that even for the right of the past there could be a figure like Peter Theil, who has been an active rightwing libertarian who founded the technology firm Palantir, which advances the security sector's surveillance agenda. Nor would it be easy to find in left history the Linke-associated Sahra Wagenknecht, who advocates a form of left conservatism. These patterns also reflect cross-developed overdetermination.[31]

Perhaps a name like the League for Human Freedom (LHF) should be sought (though I do not advocate this one per se), where the common theme is freedom from corporate power in all its forms. The advantage of this includes creating a well-known and long-established focal point that applies across the global South and North, from the fight against Cargill and Blackrock in Brazil's rainforests to John Deere and Amazon in the U.S. (one that David has engaged in his work). It also potentially cuts through the still fluid ideological patchwork, especially as a theme that might resonate with some within the working-class segments tied to the right who are critical of corporate power. The aim would be to generalize that critical attitude beyond the limited view trumpeted by corporations led by the far-right claiming – in the spirit of ideological confusion – the enemy is 'only leftist corporations' like Google. A beginning here has already emerged in the book, *Tyranny, Inc* by rightist Sohrab Ahmari. Similarly, ideological work needs to be done around the limited conceptions of the state ('deep' or 'corporate') and of capitalists who can be identified as global. The point as Lenin emphasized in *Left-Wing Communism* is to go where the masses are (and I do not just mean 'salting'), even in reactionary spaces, which today could entail engaging thinking (even about mundane issues regarding working-class life) without fear of being sullied by a 'loutish-proletariat.'

Although there are elements that connect to left-wing populism (e.g., having a focal point like corporate power) this is not an argument for it per se.[32] Populism is only one form of organization that might be included in the LHF, along with, for example, Leninist parties, socialist-oriented environmental

---

[31] There are connections here that could be made, in another context, to post-structural or post-truth perspectives – both of which might be seen as related to or even expressions of the conditions associated with cross-developed overdetermination.

[32] Lack of space prevents me from addressing in detail the relevant aspects of left populism or of debates such as that between Laclau and Zizek.

groups, and labour unions.³³ Coming back to dialectical-strategic praxis and counter-struggles, the left should gain some sway over what capitalism may see as the gray zones of contemporary struggles-against-capitalism and of ideology. As such, the left should preside over its own diversity and divisions and not leave them for capitalism to exploit – though the left will have to bear in mind the extremely likely attempt by capitalist power to draw the LHF into counter-struggle (e.g., helping generate 'blueprints' for strategy or sites for infiltration and subterfuge). But once formed the league must be many things and constantly in motion; with layers of action, program, strategy, and leadership; where what seems the tact one-year shifts or is recontextualized by a new wave of action and program. After all, seeking to dismantle corporate power raises many questions such as how far to push on it and if, when, and how to raise what comes after (questions essential to class struggle and the road to socialism). But through all this the discrete elements, actions, and programs need to make sense to everyone. Corporate power can be seen 'as the particular link in the chain which you must grasp with all your might in order to hold the whole chain and to prepare firmly for the transition to the next link.'³⁴ In so doing, the prospects for counter-struggle must be anticipated and built in from the start such that next steps include that knowledge along with the development of a new layer of action and anticipated counteraction.

4   Conclusion

However flawed some deem the extensive socialist world presence pre-1991 to have been, the left has never fully confronted in sustained, strategic terms what the gap entails for its struggle-against-capitalism – even though it has reflected on it across recent decades. Looking back to the pre-1917 world is constructive but insufficient, given how far capitalism and the relation between struggle and counter-struggle has progressed. Perhaps indicative of that difference is the absence of overarching, dialectical, historical frameworks along the lines of Kautsky, Trotsky or Mao. Instead, we have a diffusion and even splintering of framings (some inherited from a century past, others recently added), where attempts at new overarching theories seem to join the overlapping ebb and flow of their predecessors. David's intellectual leadership has nonetheless managed to help advance contemporary work in this context.

---

33   I am very aware such combination is a challenge. Elsewhere (Latham, 2022), I have put forward a strategy addressing the difficulties of sustaining left organizational solidarity.
34   Lenin (1918).

Looking at strategy through the lens of the uneven-and-combined struggle-against-capitalism is not about establishing a new framework; nor does it pretend to be anything more than a potential starting point for thinking about filling post-1991 gaps. Above all, it should be seen, dialectically, as a proposed strategic response to a contemporary capitalism not only more overdetermined than ever, but now facing the pressures of potential geo-political upheaval, with some pressures stemming from typically unavoidable longstanding historical patterns in the rise and fall of orders, others from capitalism's own doing. We will need David to continue his work, including making sure we have new Davids coming upon the scene.

References

Badiou, A. (2009) *Theory of the Subject*. London: Continuum.
Davis, M. (2006) *Planet of Slums*, London: Verso.
Egan, D. (2016) *The Dialectic of Position and Maneuver: Understanding Gramsci's Military Metaphor*, Leiden: Brill.
Foley, S. (2021) *Understanding Media Propaganda in the 21st Century: Manufacturing Consent Revisited and Revised*, Newcastle upon Tyne: Cambridge Scholars Publishing.
Giordano, J. (2017) 'Battlescape Brain: Engaging Neuroscience in Defense Operations', available at: https://hdiac.org/articles/battlescape-brain-engaging-neuroscience-in-defense-operations/.
Hallward, P. (2007) *Damming the Flood: Haiti, Aristide, and the Politics of Containment*, London: Verso.
Innis, H. (1950) *Empire and Communication*, Toronto: University of Toronto Press.
Kagan, R. (2017) 'The Twilight of the Liberal World Order', available at: www.brookings.edu/research/the-twilight-of-the-liberal-world-order/.
Kapusta, P. (2015) 'The Gray Zone', White Paper prepared for United States Special Operations Command, available at: https://info.publicintelligence.net/USSOCOM-GrayZones.pdf.
Kennard, M. (2022) 'Jeremy Corbyn on the Establishment Campaign to Stop Him Becoming PM', available at: https://declassifieduk.org/exclusive-jeremy-corbyn-on-the-establishment-campaign-to-stop-him-becoming-pm/.
Klippenstein, K. (2022) 'Bank of America Memo, Revealed: "We Hope" Conditions for American Workers Will Get Worse', *The Intercept*, available at: https://theintercept.com/2022/07/29/bank-of-america-worker-conditions-worse/.
Latham, R. (1997) *The Liberal Moment: Modernity, Security, and the Making of Postwar International Order*, New York: Columbia University Press.

Latham, R. (2005) Networks, Information, and the Rise of the Global Internet, in Robert Latham and Saskia Sassen (eds.), *Digital Formations: IT and New Architectures in the Global Realm*, Princeton, NJ: Princeton University Press, 146–177.

Latham, R. (2018) Contemporary Capitalism, Uneven Development, and the Arc of Anti-Capitalism, *Global Discourse*, 8, 2: 169–186.

Latham, R. (2022) Organizing Anti-Capitalist Internationalism in Contemporary and Historical Perspective, *Rethinking Marxism*, 34, 4.

Lenin, V.I. (1917) 'Letters on Tactics', available at: www.marxists.org/archive/lenin /works/1917/apr/x01.htm.

Lenin, V.I. (1918) 'The Immediate Tasks of the Soviet Government', available at: www .marxists.org/archive/lenin/works/1918/mar/x03.htm.

Mao Zedong (1937) 'On Contradiction', available at: www.marxists.org/reference/arch ive/mao/selected-works/volume-1/mswv1_17.htm.

Mott, C. (2022) 'Woke Imperium', available at: https://peacediplomacy.org/2022/06 /27/woke-imperium-the-coming-confluence-between-social-justice-and-neoconse rvatism/.

Petras, J. (1999) The CIA and the Cultural Cold War Revisited, *Monthly Review*, 51: 47–56.

Postone, M. (1993) *Time, Labor, and Social Domination*, Cambridge: Cambridge University Press.

Saunders, F. S. (2013) T*he Cultural Cold War: The CIA and the World of Arts and Letters*, New York: New Press.

U.S. Army War College (2011) 'Information Operations Primer', available at: https: //cyberwar.nl/d/201111_info_ops_primer.pdf.

Valentine, D. (2017) *The CIA as Organized Crime: How Illegal Operations Corrupt America and the World*, Atlanta: Clarity Press.

van der Pijl, K. (2022) *States of Emergency: Keeping the Global Population in Check*, Atlanta: Clarity Press.

World Economic Forum (n.d.) 'The Great Reset', available at: www.weforum.org/great -reset.

CHAPTER 10

The Centrality of Marx to the Global Periphery

Raju J. Das

1   Introduction

Karl Marx lived in Europe 150 years ago.[1] He engaged in political practice in Europe.[2] He read about Europe and wrote mostly about Europe. Of the thousands of pages he wrote, he wrote only about 400 pages about non-European societies (Kalmring and Nowak, 2017:331). Most of these were journalistic works on India, China and the Ottoman Empire, and they were largely from the standpoint of the state of affairs in Britain (e.g. its domestic policies). It is natural to ask: how relevant are his ideas to the contemporary global periphery (the less developed world), where most of the world's population lives now and which is economically much less developed than Europe?

Some say that his ideas are relevant, more or less, only to his time and place, i.e. to the 19th century Europe. 'Marx was not our contemporary', and he is 'more a figure of the past than a prophet of the present', Jonathan Sperber (2013) insists in *Karl Marx: A Nineteenth-Century Life*. In his new book, *Karl Marx: Greatness and Illusion*, Gareth Stedman Jones (2016) seeks to 'put Marx back in his nineteenth-century surroundings'.[3]

A specific form of the charge that Marx's relevance is limited to his own time and place is the idea that he is not relevant to the South or the global periphery. This is generally the view of post-colonial and post-modern theorists (see Chibber, 2013). The argument here is that: regions of the periphery are very different from Europe, so his ideas have no relevance or have limited relevance to them.

Others argue that Marx's ideas can be easily applied to non-Europeans societies. For example, Nimtz (2002) asserts that Marx was not Eurocentric

---

1   I originally wrote a version of this chapter in 2017 as my contribution to what would be a co-authored article (Fasenfest and Das, 2021). Parts of the 2017 version appeared in a summary form in Das and Fasenfest (2018).
2   Marx believes that science should not be for a selfish purpose and that intellectual understanding of the world and changing it radically must go together.
3   Jones is the Marxist-turned-post-structuralist and one of the authors subjected to Ellen Wood's (1998) searing criticism in her outstanding *Retreat from Class*.

(see also Arico, 2014: Chapter 3). One can indeed counter the post-colonialist type argument by saying that if Marx wrote about Europe as much as he did, that was because 'Europe was the first area in the world in which capitalism emerged', and not because Marx 'thought that there was anything inherently superior about European society' (Gasper, 2002). 'Marx was indeed a European; but it was in Asia that his ideas took root, and in the so-called Third world that they flourished most vigorously', says Eagleton (2011a: 225). And indeed, it is the periphery (Lenin's land, Mao's villages) that made Marx more famous than he would be. It is in the periphery that Marx's ideas were developed; and it is in the periphery that his ideas were put into practice, however imperfectly, to a much greater extent than in Europe.

Marx's political economic theory of capitalism leads to his political views which are focussed on the revolutionary potential of the workers (Das, 2019). Such a view could be seen as negative about non-workers (e.g. petty producers) and therefore, by implication, anti-South, because the South is often an area where the majority of direct producers may not be the wage-workers or where a massive wage-workers population coexists with a large class of petty producers. Consider Monbiot's extreme views on Marx. An anti-neoliberal critic and an environmental activist, he accuses Marx and Engels of almost genocidal intentions towards non-workers. Monbiot says: 'The peasants, aristocrats, artisans and shopkeepers ... like everyone else who did not fit conveniently into the industrial proletariat, had to be eliminated as they interfered with the theoretical system Marx had imposed on society' (quoted in Maunder 2006).[4] I respond to this charge below.

Epistemologically speaking, Marx's ideas are of different types. We can classify his ideas on the basis of social relations and geography. From the vantagepoint of social relations, his ideas exist at multiple levels of generality: all forms of society; all forms of class society; the capitalist form of class society; and specific forms of capitalism (e.g. advanced or backward form of capitalism). Marx's ideas at the first two levels are applicable to the periphery and to the center. His ideas at the other levels are, more or less, applicable to the periphery too as well as to the center (i.e. the north), to the extent that there

---

4 By assembling words of Marx from different contexts, Monbiot says that: Marx, who described the non-workers as 'reactionaries' trying 'to roll back the wheel of history', might have approved of their extermination. 'The 'social scum' ... which came to include indigenous people, had to be disposed of just as hastily in case they became, as Marx warned, 'the bribed tool of reactionary intrigue.'' (quoted in Maunder 2006). Edward Said charges, Marx with ethnocentrism, even racism, in his portrayals of non-Western societies (Anderson, 2022).

is capitalism in the periphery.[5] And, geographically speaking, some of Marx's ideas are specific to Europe (or to advanced capitalism, or the heartland of capitalism, in Europe) while his other ideas are specific to the periphery (ex-colonies of Europe of his time). To the extent that capitalist relations develop in the periphery and to the extent that there are 'islands' of advanced capitalism in the periphery which is experiencing uneven and combined development (explained below), some of Marx's ideas that are specific to the advanced capitalism of his time and place (i.e. Europe of the 19th century) may have some relevance to the periphery too.

Apart from producing scientific ideas about society and its relations and processes – the ideas that can be corroborated empirically, Marx also has insightful philosophical ideas, even if he did not write much systematic philosophical material (this is discussed in some detail in Das, 2017a: 175–211). These philosophical ideas, which inform his scientific practice, should be relevant to the study of the periphery in a way that is under-recognized.

Marx's ideas have been developed in the periphery, post-Soviet societies and other emerging market economies, in opposition to a Eurocentric understanding of social change and resistance to capitalism. The fact that there are African Marxism, Asian Marxism, Latin American Marxism, Indian Marxism, and Chinese Marxism (which is being promoted in China's various Schools of Marxism located in its major universities) as well as Marxist studies on international development, imperialism, agrarian change, etc. mean that Marx is very relevant to the issues that concern the periphery. This is also indicated by institutionalization of Marxist ideas in the form of Marxist journals from the periphery or Marxist journals that deal with the periphery (https://rajudas.info.yorku.ca/resources/).

Before we proceed, a terminological clarification is in order. I will use 'periphery' interchangeably with 'south'. The periphery is contrasted to the metropolitan center or just the center (i.e. mainly imperialist countries). In a descriptive sense, the terminology of 'south vs north', and that of 'periphery vs center' are generally the same. But from a conceptual angle, the latter terminology is better: it is indicative of the mechanisms – or what Marx (1847:55) calls the 'the selfsame relations' in which both wealth and poverty are produced -- whereby certain areas of the world have been peripheralized and under-developed, and other areas have emerged to be the center of the world economy and developed. So, the periphery vs center terminology points to the *internal* socio-spatial

---

5   This is the case until the time these ideas have been scientifically – empirically – proven to be untrue or are theoretically surpassed by superior ideas.

relation between the two parts of the world-economy and therefore to the fact that the two parts of the world are parts of one single system (i.e. imperialist world economy). The periphery vs center terminology avoids a specifically geographical problem that the south vs north framing of the world economy has: many countries of the geographical north are not developed, and many countries of the geographical south are not under-developed. By using the periphery vs center framing of the world economy, I am *not* accepting the view that the only reason why the periphery is less developed is its exploitation by the center. Marx would be against such a view.

The remainder of the chapter is divided into five sections. Section 2 discusses Marx's general ideas – his philosophical and scientific ideas—that are relevant both to the periphery and the center. Section 3 discusses Marx's ideas that are specific to the periphery. In section 4, I examine various ideas of Marx that only partly deal with the periphery but that, when properly developed and contextualized, can shed light on the periphery to a much greater extent that often assumed. These ideas include: multiple class relations; on-going primitive accumulation; economic vs extra-economic coercion; instability and inequality; the global character of capital-labour relation; and imperialism, under-development and 'super-exploitation'. The final section concludes the chapter.

2 What Are Marx's General Ideas That Are Relevant to the Periphery and the Center?

The totality of Marx's ideas as a body of intellectual work reflects, and seeks to, promote radical- democratic and anti-capitalist socialist transformation. This totality includes: a materialist-realist and dialectical ontology and epistemology; historical-materialist generalizations about all forms of society and all forms of class society, including its deeply-held prejudices and material practices against oppressed groups such as women and racialized minorities; political economy of capitalist society, including its economy, state, culture and ecological-geographical transformation; historical analysis of society; and ideas about revolutionary political practice.

Influenced by Hegel, Marx is a dialectician. But, unlike his master, he, 'the pupil of that mighty thinker', is a materialist too: in a preface to *Capital vol. 1*, Marx (1977:102) says: 'My dialectic method is, in its foundations, not only different from the Hegelian, but exactly opposite to it … [in the sense that] the ideal is nothing but the material world reflected in the mind of [human beings], and translated into forms of thought'. Marx (and Engels) would, of course, also say that ideas about the world react back – sometimes as a material force -- on the material world too. Marx is emphatic that how we think about the world now is *not* the fundamental reason why there exists the world we live in now.[6]

Marx's materialism is different from, although it connects to, natural scientists' materialism, the 'chief defect of' which 'is that the thing, reality ... is conceived only in the form of the object or of contemplation, but not as sensuous human activity, practice, not subjectively.' (Marx's first thesis on Feuerbach). Marx's materialism is about production and reproduction of means of life. It includes the idea that: humans produce/reproduce a) their bodies which have their material, sexual and other needs, b) and the material conditions of production (e.g. produced spatial organization, environment, technology, etc.), and means of subsistence (e.g. food, shelter, healthcare, etc.). Materialism also includes the idea that human produce, and can only produce, the means of subsistence and the means of production through three kinds of objective relations: metabolic or reciprocal interaction with nature; social relations of property and production, and social relations of reproductive labour (that is more or less non-commodified). Materialism implies that humans produce the things they need for the satisfaction of their material and non-material needs, and reproduce the objective social relations through which they produce these things.

A dialectical-materialist thinker, Marx emphasizes four key philosophical principles: the materiality of life/society; social relations (the idea that an object or an individual is an ensemble of multiple social relations forming a totality); the systemic – totalizing – character of society; and the fact that society changes through internal contradictions. He sees society as an ensemble of relations, a site where all things are inter-related. To him, 'The concrete is concrete because it is the concentration of many determinations, hence unity of the diverse' (Marx, 1973:34). He thinks that some of the mechanisms are not easily observable, so he makes use of the method of abstraction.[7] Employing this method, he separates what is essential from what is accidental; he looks at things from certain vantage points abstracting from other vantage-points; he adjusts the scope of a concept depending on his purpose; and he looks at things at multiple levels of generality (which are mentioned above).[8]

---

6 Of course, it is the case that certain ideas – revolutionary *ideas*, including critique of the world – are necessary to create a new world (socialist world) (Das, 2022a).

7 '[I]n the analysis of economic forms neither microscopes nor chemical reagents are of assistance. The force of abstraction must replace both' (Marx, 1977:90).

8 Ollman (2003) insightfully develops Marx's method of abstraction.

His philosophical ideas – especially, its stress on the materiality of life and his dialectical perspective on knowledge and on society – are as relevant to the periphery as to the center. Marx's dialectical-materialist perspective allows one to see the periphery in terms of its stark *material* problems (e.g. the problems of lack of food, shelter, clothing, energy, healthy climatic environment, etc.) and in terms of its various *contradictions* through which it undergoes *changes*, the contradictions that are internal to the periphery and that are also defined by its *internal relation* to the imperialist *system*. This philosophical aspect of Marx's relevance to the periphery has not been emphasized. In fact, to the extent that the study of the periphery has been shaped by post-colonialism/post-modernism, and to the extent that these perspectives are sceptical of Marx, a counter-critique of post-colonial perception of the periphery can and must be based in Marx's own philosophical ideas.[9]

Marx is against superficial generalization or overgeneralization. He emphasizes that categories and hypotheses derived from Western Europe are not to be simply transferred to other social realities:

> Thus, events strikingly analogous but taking place in different historic [and geographical] surroundings led to totally different results. By studying each of these forms of evolution separately and then comparing them one can easily find the clue to this phenomenon, but one will never arrive there by the universal passport of a general historico-philosophical theory, the supreme virtue of which consists in being super-historical.
>
> MARX, 1877; parenthesis added

However, that does not mean that one cannot make any scientific generalization, based on the deployment of the method of abstraction, about underlying

---

9 The idealistic perspective of post-colonialist theorists, who are deeply skeptical of the value of Marx for the periphery, is deeply problematic. Eagleton (2011a:223) says post-colonialism 'represents little more than the foreign affairs department of postmodernism'. If Marx encountered the contemporary post-colonialists, he would use these lines against them: 'Once upon a time a valiant fellow had the idea that men were drowned in water only because they were possessed with the idea of gravity. If they were to knock this notion out of their heads, say by stating it to be a superstition, a religious concept, they would be sublimely proof against any danger from water' (Marx, 1968).

Given that post-colonialism which stresses the perception of the periphery as constitutive of the periphery, Marx would also say the following as a response: 'one cannot judge' either a time period or a place 'by its consciousness, but, on the contrary, this consciousness must be explained from the contradictions of material life, from the conflict existing between the social forces of production and the relations of production' (Marx, 1859).

mechanisms that operate widely in time-space: if capitalism is to happen and become a dominant relation, separation of direct producers on a large scale is necessary. This is true in the USA as much as in India or Russia. As Marx says:

> If Russia is tending to become a capitalist nation after the example of the Western European countries, and during the last years she has been taking a lot of trouble in this direction – she will not succeed without having first transformed a good part of her peasants into proletarians; and after that, once taken to the bosom of the capitalist regime, she will experience its pitiless laws like other profane peoples.
> MARX, 1877

What Marx says about the Russia of his time, which was much less developed than now, applies to all other countries, including the countries of what is now the periphery or the south. Of course, whether that separation happens through class-differentiation among commodity producers or through a politically enforced way, including in today's Russia where semi-collective access to the means of production/subsistence has been privatized as a condition for the restoration of capitalism, is a separate matter.

Marx applies his method – philosophical materialism – to the study of society.[10] Human beings, as a part of nature, have material needs (needs for food, shelter, clothing, etc.) as well as cultural needs, with the material needs having a degree of priority. To satisfy these needs, humans have to interact with nature and with another. They combine their labour with the means of production that are ultimately derived from nature-human relations, on the basis of historically-specific social relations of production, to produce things to satisfy their needs. When productive forces develop, a surplus is produced, and with this, exploitative class relations as well as class struggle over surplus develop. In a class society, whether of the south or the north, if society's means of production are controlled by a small minority, the vast majority, free or unfree,

---

10 Mezzadri (2022) says that the most important reason why Marx's Capital *Volume I* should still be considered a vital reading to interpret key aspects of our contemporary global economy is Marx's *method* and that the very structure of this text offers a crucial research framework. To me, the structure of *Capital volume 1* includes, among other things, scientific-theoretical ideas about capitalism developed and presented in a way that is informed by materialist-dialectical philosophy, and empirical illustrations of those ideas on the basis of historical evidence carefully collected from various reports and newspapers.

have to perform surplus labour, the fruits of which the majority are alienated from. As Marx says in *Capital vol 1*:

> Wherever a part of society possesses the monopoly of the means of production, the worker, free or unfree, must add to the labour time necessary for his own maintenance an extra quantity of labour-time in order to produce the means of subsistence for the owner of the means of production, whether this proprietor be ... a slave owner ... or a modern landlord or a capitalist.
> MARX, 1977:344

The state arises to generally reinforce and support exploitative class relations (Das, 2022a). Ideologies play a similar role. And this is true about the periphery and the center.

The economic, political and cultural/ideological processes interact within a whole in which the economy (including especially production and exchange) is *ultimately* – not immediately – dominant. Why? We must first of all eat, drink, have shelter and clothing and medicine, etc. before we can pursue politics, science, art, religion, etc., and it is the mode of production of material life, the way we produce our livelihood, conditions our social, political and intellectual life process in general, as Engels (1883) says summarizing Marx's theoretical contribution. As Marx himself said (in *Capital volume 1*): each particular mode of production and the social relations corresponding to it at each given moment, in short,

> the economic structure of society [is] the real foundation on which arises the juridical and political superstructure and to which correspond definite forms of social consciousness ... [T]he mode of production of material life conditions the general process of social, political, and intellectual life ... [T]he middle ages could not live on Catholicism, nor the ancient world on politics'.
> MARX, 1977: 175–176

This is true about the periphery and in the center.

Human society has evolved through various forms of class society (slavery, feudalism, capitalism, etc.). In capitalism, most things are produced for the sale, so they are commodities. In pre-capitalist societies commodities may circulate but mainly to satisfy their needs, a process Marx represents by C-M-C (commodity-money-commodity). In contrast, investing money to produce commodities to make more money is a defining characteristic of capitalism

(M-C-M′), wherever capitalism is said to exist, periphery or center. M-C-M′ can be expanded into M-C (MP + LP)-P-C′-M′, where M = money; C = commodities; MP = means of production, including land, raw materials and energy, and machines/instruments, plus any normal amount of wastage; LP = labour power; P = production; C′ = new commodities produced; and M′ = M plus surplus value, which includes profit-on-production, rent, interest, tax, and revenue. Capitalists invest money (M) to buy commodities (MP, means of production, and LP or labour power) to be used in the production process (P), in which a new commodity (C′) is produced that is sold for more money (M′) than invested, as C′ has more value than in MP and LP combined. A part of M′ is reinvested in the subsequent cycle of production.

When direct producers lose access to means of production (or means of livelihood/employment) through primitive accumulation and through other mechanisms, then they must work for capitalists for a wage. The value of the wage is much less than the value of what workers produce. One of Marx's (1977: 300) most celebrated lines in *Capital* is: 'The fact that half a day's labour is necessary to keep the worker alive during 24 hours does not in any way prevent him [or her] from working a whole day'. This results in workers' exploitation. Capitalists resort to mainly two ways to increase the rate of exploitation: long hours and technical change. All this applies to the periphery and to the center.

When the rate of accumulation rises and labour market tightens (the reserve army shrinks), wages may increase, but the rise in wages is stopped as soon as it means that 'the stimulus of gain is blunted', i.e. the normal rate of profit is reduced (Marx, 1977:769–770). The rise in wages is also stopped with the help of the state's economic and disciplinary policies. There is also a permanent tendency in capitalism towards periodic economic crisis as indicated by declining average rate of profit caused by the fact that investment in the means of production relative to that in labour power rises faster than the rate of exploitation of labour in production, thus displacing the human beings as the source of fresh wealth in production (Roberts, 2016). The fall in the average rate of profit causes a fall in the productive investment, and increased unemployment and poverty. There is evidence that capitalism in India, Brazil, etc is experiencing a crisis of profitability like advanced capitalism. Given all this, there are limits to the extent to which public action and people's struggles can bring significant long-term improvements. To counter falling profitability, capitalists resort to austerity (neoliberalism), various methods of increasing exploitation and the switch of capital to non-productive sectors (e.g. financial speculation). This is true in the periphery as in the center.

In short: when all non-labour inputs into production and labour power are, more or less, commodities, and when competing capitalists combine wage-labour with means of production to produce goods and services to sell them for profit, then several consequences follow, both in the periphery and in the center. These include: concentration and centralization of productive forces in fewer hands (and fewer areas); tendency towards investment in the means of production rising relative to investment in wages, causing a long-term fall in the average rate of profit and producing economic crisis; expansion of a reserve army of unemployed and underemployed, and immiserization; rising inequality between workers and owners; proletarianization of independent commodity producers; concentration and centralization of productive forces combined with economic crisis in advanced countries needing a spatial fix (export of capital made surplus relative to the rate of profit), setting up pressure towards inter-imperialist rivalry and imperialist control over relatively less developed parts of the world with weaker states; and, adverse impacts on nature and on human bodies (unsafe working conditions), as well as alienation, and so on.[11] Just as the state is not the main reason for these problems, there is little reason to believe that the state can solve these problems: the capitalist state's fundamental role – whether in the periphery or the center -- is to protect property rights of capitalists (and other exploiting property-owners such as landowners) and to ensure general conditions for profit-making at home and abroad, so, according to Marx, workers must take state power in order to construct a society that is truly democratic.

Marx's *emphasis* in his economic theory is on production, its hidden abode, although in his view, production, distribution, exchange and consumption form a whole in which production has the ultimate primacy (Das, 2023a). There is huge exploitation across all societies -- the proliferation of sweatshops and export processing zones are all very much in keeping with Marx's account. Marx's general ideas about capitalism apply to the center and to the periphery, more or less.[12]

---

11   The totality of Marx's scientific-theoretical corpus developed by Marx's (and the work inspired by him) includes major concepts such as: productive forces; production relations; contradiction between the forces and relations; class relations, the state; ideology; capitalism; law of value; exploitation; capitalist accumulation; primitive accumulation; the reserve army; economic crisis; immiserization; imperialism; class struggle; revolution and communism (Das, 2022c).

12   Mezzadri (2022) rightly says that: Marx's analysis of the 'abode of production' developed in *Volume I* still powerfully resonates with many issues facing the labouring classes worldwide, especially the developing world, where capitalist industrialization has developed in the last 40 years or so. Those engaged in wage-labour experience unacceptable rhythms and long hours of work while remuneration is often below a 'living wage'; they also experience high occupational risk, industrial 'disasters' and health conditions linked

Capitalist production, according to Marx, creates necessary conditions for socialism. It creates the possibility of the elimination of natural scarcity and therefore the possibility of human social-ecological needs being met. Economic crisis, rising inequality, high rate of exploitation and impoverishment and alienation, and the inability of the ruling class to satisfy the needs of workers and small-scale producers prompt them to rise in revolt, overtly or covertly, from time to time. Of all the anti-capitalist agents, for Marx, the unique agent that would slowly but necessarily emerge to challenge capitalist power, is the working class, or the proletariat, given its unique position in the system of capitalist production.

Let's consider Marx's historical materialist theory of economic crisis and revolution. In his famous *Preface to A Contribution to the Critique of Political Economy*, Marx (1859) says:

> At a certain stage of development, the material productive forces of society come into conflict with the existing relations of production or – this merely expresses the same thing in legal terms – with the property relations within the framework of which they have operated hitherto. From forms of development of the productive forces these relations turn into their fetters. Then begins an era of social revolution. The changes in the economic foundation lead sooner or later to the transformation of the whole immense superstructure.
>
> No social order is ever destroyed before all the productive forces for which it is sufficient have been developed, and new superior relations of production never replace older ones before the material conditions for their existence have matured within the framework of the old society.

Is this idea relevant to the periphery? In fact, doubts *are* constantly cast on the relevance of Marx's ideas for radical changes, including the communist revolution, in the periphery. Perhaps the latter is too under-developed for it to begin a communist revolution?

Marx writes about how capitalism creates conditions for communism. For him communism is to be based on the advanced level of productive forces and on the discipline, collective traditions, education embodied in the working class (Laibman, 2013). Marxism is a theory of how well-heeled capitalist nations might use their immense resources to achieve justice and prosperity for

---

to overwork and exhaustion, imposed by the ever-increasing velocity of circulation of raw materials, goods and delivery times (Mezzadri, 2022; Das, 2023b).

their people. It is not a program by which nations bereft of material resources, a flourishing civic culture, a democratic heritage, a well-evolved technology, enlightened liberal traditions, and a skilled, educated work force might catapult themselves into the modern age (Eagleton, 2011b).

So, what relevance does Marx's theory of revolution have for the periphery? In many Third world countries, productive forces are not developed to the same extent as in advanced countries. In fact, even democratic, including anti-imperialist revolution remains incomplete. Does it mean that productive forces under capitalism should be first allowed to be developed to the extent that they enter into a conflict with social relations of capitalism, before a communist revolution can take place in the periphery (see Das, 2022d)?

It is implausible that Marx would argue for a *two-stage* theory of revolution: for a bourgeois-democratic revolution – a revolution of the type that took place in Europe – to create conditions for capitalism to be followed by a separate socialist revolution, in the periphery. As the Lenin of 1917 and Trotsky of earlier times have argued, the bourgeoisie in the countries of late capitalist development are incapable of fully completing the democratic revolution because of the fear of the working class. Therefore, they have argued, the task of democratic revolution falls on the workers and semi-proletarians, who, in the process of fighting for such a revolution, will be compelled to go on uninterruptedly to convert it into a socialist revolution: in our world, a revolution against imperialism (including its modern-day mechanisms and institutions), remnants of feudalism, and attacks on democratic rights, must grow over into a socialist struggle against capitalism itself. In fact, this idea of permanent revolution is originally Marx's (Marx and Engels, 1950): 'While the democratic petty bourgeois want to bring the revolution to an end as quickly as possible, achieving at most the aims already mentioned, it is our [i.e. communists'] ... task to make the revolution permanent' (Marx and Engels, 1850). But what does Marx mean by permanent revolution? Revolution is permanent, politically and geographically. That is, revolution is permanent:

> until all the more or less propertied classes have been driven from their ruling positions, until the proletariat has conquered state power and until the association of the proletarians has progressed sufficiently far – not only in one country but in all the leading countries of the world – that competition between the proletarians of these countries ceases and at least the decisive forces of production are concentrated in the hands of the workers.
> ibid

In other words, 'Our concern cannot simply be to modify private property, but to abolish it, not to hush up class antagonisms but to abolish classes, not to improve the existing society but to found a new one' (ibid).

It is also implausible that given Marx's internationalist approach, he would want to think about the relation between productive forces and social relations that he talks about in the famous *Preface* quoted earlier, on a country-by-country basis: there is no reason why a backward country will have to await a high level of economic development before it launches a political movement for socialism (Das, 2022d; Das, 2019). The relation between productive forces and production relations (i.e. class and intra-class relations) has to be seen at the international scale. At that scale, there is clearly a contradiction between capitalist social relations and development of productive forces under those relations. Capitalism is past its due date. It is quite possible that workers in a less-developed country can succeed in taking state power before workers in the developed countries, although without communist revolution in the developed economies, it would be difficult to successfully achieve socialism in the less developed countries.

3   Marx's 'Southern' Ideas

Although Marx's empirical examples came from Europe and from Britain, his approach to capitalism was basically global or internationalist. World commerce was the presupposition of capitalism, which makes capitalism a global phenomenon: 'The production of commodities, their circulation, and that more developed form of their circulation called commerce [trade], these form the historical ground-work from which it rises' (Marx, 1977: 247). The modern history of capital dates from the creation in the 16th century of a world-embracing commerce and a world-embracing market. And then, he argues, the development of capitalism in its heartland was crucially dependent on its interaction with the colonies. This meant an international division of labour imposed by imperialism, which is an on-going process. Marx suggests in *Grundrisse* and elsewhere that: industrial capitalism in colonizing Europe converted the colonies in Asia and other parts of the periphery into the supplier of raw materials.[13]

---

13   'By ruining handicraft production in other countries, machinery forcibly converts them into fields for the supply of its raw material. In this way East India was compelled to produce cotton, wool, hemp, jute, and indigo for Great Britain. A new and international division of labor, a division suited to the requirements of the chief centers of modern industry

Imperialism, including in the form of colonialism, driven by the need for resources, also meant a net drain of resources:

> The discovery of gold and silver in America, the extirpation, enslavement and entombment in mines of the indigenous population of that continent, the beginnings of the conquest and plunder of India, and the conversion of Africa into a preserve for commercial hunting of blackskins, are all things which characterize the dawn of the era of capitalist production. These idyllic proceedings are the chief momenta of primitive accumulation. Hard on their heels follows the commercial war of the European nations, which has the globe as its battlefield.
> MARX, 1977: 915; italics added

In other words, the development of European – and global – capitalism depended on conquest, genocide and slavery in the periphery. So, his statements about Europe are relevant to the center as well as the periphery, given the internal relation between the two. Such a relation means that the surplus appropriated from colonies, when placed in the context of already-existing capital-labour relations in Europe, was converted into capital, and this capital was invested not only in industry as in England but also in agriculture as in Scotland (Byres, 2007). And this also means that by depriving the colonies of its surplus, imperialism blocks (the European-style) economic development in periphery, i.e. a development process marked by regular tendency towards productivity-raising technical change (Brenner, 1977). Marx thus points to the exploitation of imperialized nations (colonies or the periphery) by imperialist nations (the center), a process that immense contributed to the underdevelopment of the periphery and development of the center, a process that has not ceased to exist. Imperialism allows unequal exchange to occur which leads to extra profits for the center.[14] Imperialism also creates the opportunity to increase the rate of profit in imperialist nations (i.e. to counter the tendency

---

springs up, and converts one part of the globe into a chiefly agricultural field of production, for supplying the other part which remains a chiefly industrial field' (Ghosh, 1984).

14 Pradella describes this colonialism-imposed international division of labour that Marx talks about: competitive accumulation produces uneven and combined development as it tends to concentrate high-value added production and capital in the system's most competitive centres, determining a forced specialisation of dependent countries in low-value added sectors, repatriating profits extracted in these countries, and leading to forms of unequal exchange between nations with different productivity levels (Pradella, 2017:156).

towards the falling rate of profit) by imperialist businesses being able to economize on the elements of constant and variable capital (Marx, 1894)

As compared to his earlier analysis, in his later writings, Marx seems to recognize that free trade and the destruction of the old order by colonialism do not necessarily lay the material foundation of a new order (Kalmring and Nowak, 2017: 335). He now identifies external causes of a blockage of industrial–capitalist development in these countries (ibid.).

What would be called imperialism – or the internally uneven global capitalist system – according to Marx, produces conditions for development in colonies (e.g. establishment of railways, electric telegraph, or irrigation canals, etc in colonies by the British). And imperialism produces these conditions of development mainly in its own interest:

> The ruling classes of Great Britain' or 'the millocracy have discovered that the transformation of India into a reproductive country has become of vital importance to them, and that, to that end, it is necessary, above all, to gift her with means of irrigation and of internal communication. They intend now drawing a net of railroads over India … with the exclusive view of extracting at diminished expenses the cotton and other raw materials for their manufactures.
>
> MARX, 1853

The new means of transportation and such other measures, Marx thought, even if they were introduced in the interest of the colonizing power, would have a potential positive spin-off effect on the colony: it would promote industrialization.[15] But whether the imperialized nations benefit, according to Marx, from these 'material foundations of Western society', is a contingent matter. All that the English or any other foreign bourgeoisie may be forced to do in the periphery in its own interest 'will neither emancipate nor materially mend the social condition of the mass of the people [in the periphery]'. Only a potential is created through colonialism/imperialism, i.e. through the operation of capitalism on a global scale that is based on not only exploitation of labour

---

15   Marx (1853) says: 'when you have once introduced machinery into the locomotion of a country, which possesses iron and coals, you are unable to withhold it from its fabrication. You cannot maintain a net of railways over an immense country without introducing all those industrial processes necessary to meet the immediate and current wants of railway locomotion, and out of which there must grow the application of machinery to those branches of industry not immediately connected with railways. The railway-system will therefore become, in India, truly the forerunner of modern industry' (ibid.).

by capital but also exploitation of politically subjugated nations by powerful capitalist nations. Whether the masses of the periphery will significantly benefit is a different matter. According to him, such an outcome would depend on a socialist revolution in the imperialist country which would stop the unintentionally created conditions of development mainly serving as the vehicle of transfer of the surplus from the colonies, and/or on the anti-colonial/anti-imperialist revolution in the periphery:

> The Indians will not reap the fruits of the new elements of society scattered among them by the British bourgeoisie, till in Great Britain itself the now ruling classes shall have been supplanted by the industrial proletariat, or till the [Indians] themselves shall have grown strong enough to throw off the English yoke altogether. At all events, we may safely expect to see, at a more or less remote period, the regeneration of that great and interesting country, whose gentle natives ... . have astonished the British officers by their bravery, whose country has been the source of our languages, our religions.
> MARX, 1853

Marx himself supported the freedom movement in colonies, including in India and Ireland. And, most anti-colonial movements in the periphery were inspired by Marxism (Eagleton, 2011a).

4   Marx Is More Relevant to the Periphery than He Appears to Be

Marx's relevance to the periphery can be better appreciated if he is seen as a theorist of both capitalism and of class relations as such, and not just as a theorist of capitalism. Once one emphasizes the class character of society, one can see that a given country will have multiple forms of class relation, including capitalism and pre- and non-capitalist relations, and multiple forms of capitalism itself as a class society. In the light of Marx's ideas, one can make several claims about the periphery, even if Marx's direction was sometimes less definitive. His ideas can be seen as an intellectual guide.

4.1   *Multiple Class Relations*
Countries of the periphery are not to be merely seen as having less income and more absolute poverty. Instead, they must be fundamentally seen in terms of class in the Marx sense: as countries that have suffered from aborted – or incomplete – revolutions against the propertied classes. They have suffered

from: aborted democratic revolutions, including agrarian revolutions against feudal(-type) relations, aborted national (or anti-imperialist) revolutions, and aborted or failed anti-capitalist revolutions. So, the capitalism in the periphery is not exactly like that of advanced countries.

As Patnaik says, Marx's tribune articles on India offer 'a hint of a broader perspective within which *Capital*, and the perspective surrounding *Capital*, has got to be located' (p. lvi), and these articles offer 'a perception of capitalism, as existing not in isolation but in the midst of pre-capitalist formations which it dominates and moulds to its own requirements' (p. lviii) (quoted in Byres, 2007).

In the social formation of the countries of the periphery, nominally free wage labour relations coexist with unfree labour relations employed by capitalists (and not necessarily by so-called semi-feudal owners) and as well it is the case that the capitalist class relation itself coexists with remnants of feudalism and with commodity production based on relations other than wage-labour (free or unfree). As well as indigenous-collective traditions. Marx's theoretical framework in *Capital* – especially, *Capital volume 1* – assumes that all labour involved in production of goods and services is in the form of (nominally free) wage-labour. This is a theoretical assumption, and in the work of theory, one must make such assumptions based on the method of abstraction.

While Marx (1977) does make the assumption that all labour is wage labour, he also makes a distinction between two forms of circulation (CMC and MCM) (p. 247–252) and two forms of property (property based on own labour, and property based on the appropriation of surplus labour from workers) (p. 927). He does not quite explore the implications of these distinctions though. In particular, he generally (but not entirely) under-emphasizes the fact that in the periphery, peasant labour is widely prevalent and coexists with wage labour, and is integrated into capitalist exchange and financial relations (usury) and mercantile relations. Some peasants produce for the market and provide cheap wage-labour. Other peasants are paid only for the product of their labour; their products enter the world market at very low prices for the benefit of the transnational corporations (TNCs) in the center – either to provide cheap raw materials or to be processed and then resold at much higher prices. These products from the periphery sell at much lower prices relative to the labour involved than high end products from the center.

Marx should have paid more attention to petty producers at a *theoretical* level: after all, theory can happen and does happen, at various levels of concreteness, as Marx (1973) himself argues in *Grundrisse*. Marx under-estimates the economic and political importance of non-proletarian direct producers (e.g. petty producers such as poor peasants). Petty producers are important as an *economic* category, and they are also important politically, because without an alliance with them, the working class cannot make a revolution in the periphery (Das, 2023c).

However, those who ascribe violent intentions on the part of Marx against the petty producers engage in epistemic violence on the basis of a conceptual and political conflation: a critique of petty-production is not a critique of the people who engage in petty production. When one claims that a) petty production is not conducive to a socialist order or b) petty producers can be revolutionary against merchants, state agencies, money-lenders and foreign invaders, but they ordinarily will not necessarily engage in socialist struggles against capitalists, or, conversely, c) workers, who are not proprietors (e.g. peasants), have a socialist/collectivist impulse, these claims do not mean that petty producers should be exterminated or should somehow disappear or that one is saying anything that is specifically European.[16] The approach to petty production is not the same as the approach to the human beings/grous who engage in petty production (i.e. petty producers), for Marx or for which followers such as a Lenin or a Trotsky. If Marx himself did not pay as much attention to petty producers as he should have, and if he paid less attention to peasants than to wage workers and to non-capitalist market and non-market relations than to capitalist market relations, and Marx did not, this cannot be said of his disciples such as Lenin and Mao and their followers, including recent academic writers inspired by Marx. In fact, as one of the most powerful Marxist writers on the peasantry, Tom Brass, writes: 'Peasants were – and are – central to Marxist theory about the dynamics informing the trajectory in pursuit of modernity and systemic transition: from feudalism to capitalism, and from the latter to socialism' (Brass, 2022: 271).[17]

4.2 *(On-Going) Primitive Accumulation*

The criticism that Marx should have paid more attention to petty producers should be, however, tempered with another view. This is the view of Marx about primitive accumulation (the coercive separation of direct producers

---

16 As Maunder (2006) says: 'While previous oppressed classes, such as the peasantry, could rise up, seize control of the land and divide it among themselves, workers cannot divide a factory, hospital or supermarket. If workers seize control of these things, they can only run them collectively. Their struggles have a democratic logic that can lay the basis for a different way of running society. There is nothing specifically European about these arguments'.

17 Of course, the fact that many academic writers treat the petty producers as a people, as if they are not class-differentiated, is a big problem, and Marx would not agree with such an approach (on this see Brass, 2000; 2022).

from means of production) correctly understood. For capitalism to exist, direct producers must not have direct access to means of production and subsistence (Marx, 1977).[18] Although he at times mistakenly indicated that primitive accumulation was long over, there is enough textual evidence to argue that he also thought otherwise. He would be the first one to say that primitive accumulation is an on-going affair in the context of the periphery where during his own times capitalism had hardly taken root. If primitive accumulation is continuing, then there must be people who are subjected to primitive accumulation.[19] Many of these people subjected to primitive accumulation are petty producers, by definition. The very idea of primitive accumulation has great contemporary relevance to the periphery.[20]

To the extent that Marx paid attention to primitive accumulation, he may have paid more attention to it than to class differentiation in a commodity-producing society as a mechanism through which direct producers lose access to means of production.[21] Yet, in *Capital volume 1*, in his discussion of concentration and centralization, Marx (1977) lays the basis for analyzing commodity owners going out of business. Some anti-Marxists believe that class differentiation does not exist to the extent that Marx and Marxist say it does. In the periphery, given the law of value operating at the national and global scales, small-scale farmers are subjected to class differentiation, even if that process is mediated by government policies providing some help to peasants, etc. and even if class differentiation is also slowed down because peasants under-feed themselves and their animals (Das, 2013).[22] And in many cases, the value of property that peasants own is only nominal, given their enormous debt, as Marx himself recognized.

---

18 'The capitalist system presupposes the complete separation between the workers and the ownership of the conditions for the realization of their labour' (Marx, 1977: 874).

19 If primitive accumulation is to an extent a form of pillage, it is useful to note that: 'for pillage to be possible, there must be something to be pillaged, hence production' (Marx, 1973: 31). Not just that: 'the mode of pillage is itself in turn determined by the mode of production' (ibid.).

20 Marx's idea of dispossession has inspired a new round of discussion partly thanks to the work of the geographer, David Harvey (Harvey, 2007; 2003) among others, although his theorization is very problematic, intellectually and politically (Das, 2017b; Brass, 2011a).

21 The latter is something that Lenin (1899) emphasized in his *Development of capitalism in Russia*, which can be called his version of *Capital*.

22 Lenin, who took major ideas of Marx's political economy extremely seriously, says: 'Small-scale production maintains itself on the ruins of natural economy by constant worsening of diet, by chronic starvation, by lengthening of the working day, by deterioration in the quality and the care of cattle, in a word, by the very methods whereby handicraft production maintained itself against capitalist manufacture' (Lenin, 1908).

It should be added that for Marx primitive accumulation is an international process. It occurred both within a country undergoing capitalist transition and in the colonies. The presence of direct producers with access to means of production was a barrier to capitalism and had to be broken not only in Europe but also in colonies. Marx says:

> in the colonies .... the capitalist regime constantly comes up against the obstacle presented by the producer, who, as owner of his [or her] own conditions of labor, employs that labor to enrich himself [or herself], instead of the capitalist. The contradiction between these two diametrically opposed economic systems has its practical manifestation here in the struggle between them. Where the capitalist has behind him [or her] the power of the mother country [i.e. the state of the colonizing country], he [or she] tries to use force to clear out of the way the modes of production and appropriation which rest on the personal labor of the independent producer.
> MARX 1977: 931

Marx indeed conceptualised colonialism and imperialism as constitutive elements of the development of capitalism (Pradella, 2017: 156).

4.3 Economic and Extra-Economic Coercion

For Marx, capitalism is based on a combination of economic and extra-economic coercion of direct producers. Once direct producers have been separated from means of production, economic mechanisms of exploitation are more or less sufficient to extract value, although extra-economic mechanisms are used from time to time when necessary. At the dawn of capitalism, extra-economic coercion played a crucial role. This included the fact that, as Marx suggests, wages had to be suppressed by the state to a level that was broadly suitable to a normal rate of profit. This also included slavery.

Slavery is an economic category like any other. We are dealing only with direct slavery, with anti-Black slavery in Surinam, in Brazil, in the Southern States of North America.

> Direct slavery is just as much the pivot of bourgeois industry as machinery, credits, etc. Without slavery you have no cotton; without cotton you have no modern industry. It is slavery that gave the colonies their value; it is the colonies that created world trade, and it is world trade that is the precondition of large-scale industry. Thus slavery is an economic category of the greatest importance.
> MARX, 1847

But slavery did not just happen then. It continues till date, including in the periphery. A major development in the recent Marxist literature is that capital can make currently free labour unfree in order to discipline labour, and therefore imposition of unfreedom is a form of class struggle from above (Brass, 2011b; Das, 2016).

4.4 Instability and Inequality

Marx shows 'the tendency of capitalist society to expand, polarize, destabilize, and destroy. His words could have been written today; they seem to be drawn from current world experience', says Laibman (2013). Capitalism is not only crisis-prone. It is also inequality-causing. 'With the crisis of 2007–08, for the first time in recent experience, the two understandings – of capitalism's effects on economic stability, and of its shaping of the distribution of wealth and power – came together' (Laibman, 2013:451). Now the current world experience includes that of the periphery: economic crisis emanating in the center affects the periphery (including opportunities for exports from the periphery to the center). And as mentioned earlier, when there is a crisis of profitability, advanced capitalism makes use of cheap labour and resources in the periphery to counter such crisis.

Not only is inequality increasing between poorest and richest countries but also is it increasing within fast-growing lower-income countries (so-called emerging economies as well as ex-socialist countries). The inequality between center and periphery (especially, inequalities between capitalist businesses of center and workers and peasants of the periphery) could be seen as a specific expression of Marx's statement 'Wealth in one pole and misery in another'. We now have a more or less integrated world capitalist system, with a global rich and global poor – as Marx predicted.

4.5 Global Character of Capital-Labour Relation

Marx appears to give the impression that his theory of capital-labour relation operates in a closed system, that it is perhaps more about Europe or England and about industrial capitalism than about capitalism as such, and so on. In reality, his is a theory of capitalism as it exists globally.

The capitalist class and the working class are world-classes, and the law of competition (or the law of value) is a law that ultimately operates at the global scale, although it is mediated by national and regional-level processes. Marx conceptualises 'the antagonism between wage-labour and capital as a global tendency, encompassing and reproducing relations of colonial and imperialist exploitation and oppression' (Pradella, 2017: 156). His ideas about capital-labour relation and about the mechanisms underlying what he calls the general law of capitalist accumulation (Marx, 1977: 762–801) are applicable to the world-stage now more than during his time and can be used to understand the periphery better now than during his time, as indicated in the second section.

Marx's idea in *Manifesto* that capital 'must nestle everywhere, settle everywhere, establish connexions everywhere' has become a palpable reality now, with consequences for the periphery and its relation with the center (Marx and Engels 1848; see Das, 2022d for a recent discussion on the main ideas of the *Manifesto*). These lines about the tendentially global character of capitalism are relevant to the periphery (as much as to the center):

> All old-established national industries have been destroyed or are daily being destroyed. They are dislodged by new industries, whose introduction becomes a life and death question for all civilised nations, by industries that no longer work up indigenous raw material, but raw material drawn from the remotest zones; industries whose products are consumed, not only at home, but in every quarter of the globe.
> MARX and ENGELS, 1848

Besides:

> In place of the old wants, satisfied by the production of the country, we find new wants, requiring for their satisfaction the products of distant lands and climes. In place of the old local and national seclusion and self-sufficiency, we have intercourse in every direction, universal interdependence of nations.
> ibid

Some capitalists from advanced countries have indeed shifted production to the selected regions of the periphery to take advantage of the global immobility of labor, and the subsistence (or below-subsistence) wages and despotic/authoritarian working conditions there. This produces a 'super-exploited' working class in the periphery (as explained below) and super-profit for businesses of the center, including sometimes at the expense of profits of capitalist businesses in the periphery. As well, the introduction of low-cost imports from Asia and other parts of the South by multinational corporations protects the value of money, particularly the dollar as the hegemonic currency, and thus the financial assets of the capitalist class (Patnaik and Patnaik, 2015). Such cheap imports by reducing the value of labour power in the center can actually increase the rate of exploitation in the center. Marx's reserve army has become truly a global reserve army. This forces income deflation on the world's workers, beginning in the periphery, but also affecting the workers of the center, who are increasingly subjected to neoliberal 'labour market flexibility' (Foster et al, 2011). Indeed, because of the possibility and actuality of 'super-exploitation' of workers in the periphery, their brothers and sisters in center are facing low wages and precarity: the threat of movement of jobs to the periphery has a disciplinary effect on the workers of the center. Marx's idea of the latent reserve army is relevant here. The latent reserve army of migrant labour from poor countries generates conflict within the working class, nationally and internationally (Jonna and Foster, 2016). For Marx, the reserve army or the 'surplus population also becomes ... the lever of capitalistic accumulation, indeed it becomes a condition for the existence of the capitalist mode of production' and it 'belongs to capital just as absolutely as if the latter had bred it at its own cost' (Marx, 1977: 784). Some scholars from Latin America say that a segment of the reserve army is not going to be at all employed by capital, foreign or domestic, so they call this segment the marginal mass, which lives a precarious life. Note that such a segment – racialized people with no skills – is said to exist in the center as well (Wright, 1995).

When the *Manifesto* was written in the late 1840s, most of the world's population were small-scale agrarian producers, but today, with the spread of capitalist market relations, the vast majority of people live by selling their labour power in almost every region – especially, urban region – of the world, including in the periphery. With the rise in total investment (expansion in accumulation), there is an increase in capital at one pole and increase in the proletariat at another pole, as Marx says. The periphery demonstrates this principle. The periphery actually completes the picture of capitalism that Marx begins to paint. For this reason, the slogan, 'workers of the world, unite', on the basis of objectively existing common grounds among workers of periphery and center and among workers of all countries, makes more sense now than during Marx's own times. Indeed, the situation in the periphery conforms to Marx's theory. And Marx's idea that workers will be driven to resist capitalist exploitation and that improvement in transport and communication that capitalism itself creates will enable this, is proven to be true when workers launch massive revolts in India, Brazil, South Africa, Egypt, etc.[23] The working class is a far stronger sector of the population with far more power, and this is partly

---

23   Indian workers – 180 million of them – participated in 2016 what is perhaps the largest strike in human history.

because of the expansion of the working class in the periphery. This is the case even if they are not always conscious of their power, and of the fact that their interests and capitalists' interest are ultimately irreconcilable. Such a lack of consciousness is partly because of identity politics among the working class that Marx pointed to (racism of English workers against the Irish workers) and because of the workers being misled and misinformed by their opportunistic and pro-capitalist leaders and others as well as by the sectarianism – and what Marx (1873) called indifferentism – of certain elements of the leadership of the working class.[24]

4.6 Imperialism, Under-Development, and 'Super-Exploitation'

For Marx, capitalism is a class relation, and it exists at multiple scales (city/village, region/province, nation, and the whole world). On the basis of these ideas, it would be possible to argue – although Marx does not quite do this – that capitalism seen globally operates as imperialism which signifies the exploitation of workers and small-scale producers (e.g. peasants) in the imperialized countries by the monopolistic/large-scale businesses of technologically advanced countries, an exploitation that is supported by their militarily powerful states, and reinforced by national and racial oppression. Low-cost politically/military guaranteed access to the periphery's land/resources and markets and to their pool of cheap labour -- just like the use of advanced technologies -- becomes a means of competitive advantage for capitalists of advanced nations. Imperialized countries also become dumping grounds for surplus products and sites for relative surplus capital (relative to the prevailing profit rate) as well as pollutants and wastes, from imperialist countries, and are subjected to exploitation in the sphere of mercantile and financial capital (e.g., trade; debt; speculative capital). Imperialism indeed produces a distinct stamp on the periphery of the capitalist system, a system of global uneven development.

In the *Manifesto*, Marx says:

> The bourgeoisie cannot exist without constantly revolutionising the instruments of production, and thereby the relations of production, and with them the whole relations of society. ... Constant revolutionising of production, uninterrupted disturbance of all social conditions,

---

24 Such a lack of consciousness is also because of the sectarianism – and what Marx (1873) called indifferentism – of certain elements of the leadership of the working class (see Das, 2019).

everlasting uncertainty and agitation distinguish the bourgeois epoch from all earlier ones.

If this is the case, how would Marx explain the relative economic backwardness of the periphery, where per capita income, labour productivity and the general level of living are all rather low relative those in advanced capitalist (i.e. imperialist) countries? Note that some of these countries – India and China – were relatively much more developed until a few centuries ago. Does the thesis of constant revolutionization of productive forces apply to Europe and outposts of Europeans only? I argue that it is in Marx's ideas that we can find some of the explanations of periphery's under-development. Although Marx had sometimes a more favourable view about the beneficial impact of colonialism, in his later writings he talks about its destructive impacts. In many ways, imperialism continues to block economic development in the periphery through a net drain of the surplus. Operating in tandem is another process that is rooted in the structure of class relations within the countries of the periphery. Following primitive accumulation, capitalism evolves in two stages, as Marx discusses in *Capital 1*, including in its Appendix. In the first stage (formal subsumption of labour), capital appropriates surplus value in its absolute form, on the basis of long hours (and one may add, low real wages). During this stage, systemic technical change raising labour productivity does not quite happen. In response to the struggle against long hours, capital resorts to labour-saving technical change making workers produce more value every unit of time, thus appropriating surplus value in its relative form (Marx calls this real subsumption of labour). Marx sometimes mistakenly assumes that the transition from formal to real subsumption takes place spontaneously. Much of 'western' Marxist theory, inspired by Marx, assumes that once you have capital-labour relations in a market economy, economic development driven by technical change just follows. It does not. England took almost 200 years for the transition to take place, a transition that was mediated by class struggle. Given that there is a massive reserve army in the periphery (which is partly created by imperialism/colonialism), and given that the peripheral state has much more limited ability to provide for the subsistence of the reserve army than the state in the center does (and this is also because of imperialism, to a large extent),[25] struggle

---

25   The extent to which the periphery can serve as a global platform for low-wage capitalism serving the interests of imperialist businesses and of their local allies depends on the income deflation – and reduced consumption – of the masses in the periphery. The peripheral state's welfare policies are directly controlled and restricted by imperialist financial institutions such as the World Bank and IMF (see Das, 2022b: chapter 11).

against formal subsumption is not effective enough to force capital to deploy real subsumption. Also, the on-going drain of surplus (via unequal exchange) deprives the periphery of the capital needed for investment in machinery and improved raw materials. In other words, and in terms of Marx's own theory in *Capital*, the periphery can be seen as a site of blocked transition from formal to real subsumption. There is a capitalism but it is a backward form of capitalism (for further details, see Das, 2012; Das, 2017a: chapter 8). The periphery indeed suffers not only from capitalism but also from its incomplete development, as Marx would say.

Marx assumes that wages cover the cost of reproduction of labour power (value of labour power). One wonders where in the world does that assumption hold. It certainly does not hold in most cities and villages in the periphery. To his credit, Marx himself does say that in reality for millions of people, wages fall below the value of labour power. Here is Marx from his *Wage Labour and Capital*:

> Thus, the cost of production of simple labour-power amounts to the *cost of the existence and propagation of the worker*. The price of this cost of existence and propagation constitutes wages. The wages thus determined are called the *minimum of wages*. This minimum wage, like the determination of the price of commodities in general by cost of production, does not hold good for the *single individual*, but only for the race. Individual workers, indeed, millions of workers, do not receive enough to be able to exist and to propagate themselves; but the wages of the whole working class adjust themselves, within the limits of their fluctuations, to this minimum.
>
> MARX, 1976: 27

This can happen, thanks to the over-supply of labour relative to demand, including the over-supply of labour caused by the reserve army of labour produced through technical change and primitive accumulation. Given the massive reserve army of labour in the periphery, that has been expanding since colonial times (export of machine-manufactured goods to colonies), millions of people work in absolute poverty, and millions are working poor. Partly because of the difference in the relative supply of labour in poor and rich countries, wages for a given kind of work in poor countries are much less than those in richer countries, leading to the super-exploitation (appropriation of above-average rate of profit) of workers in the periphery, something Marini from Latin America, among others has pointed out.[26] The fact that the wage of an average worker falls below the value of labour power is especially relevant to the periphery. Marx generally underestimates this fact.

Of course, all this does not mean that there is no technical change in the periphery. There is. But the level of technical change (as indicated by the ratio of constant to variable capital) is below the world average or it is below the level attained in the advancded countries. The assembly line and other techniques do not have to be invented in the periphery and can be easily adopted, thus allowing the countries with belated capitalist development to make a 'leap'. And given the average rate of profit declining in advanced countries, certain nations in the periphery with their cheap labour and resources are often attractive to imperialist capital (either through direct investment or through sub-contracting of production). Fractions of imperialist and 'national' capital operating in the periphery have to use technology to remain globally competitive. This is the case, for example, in specific sectors where, from a technical angle, machines cannot be replaced by living labour (e.g. oil drilling). Thus, technologically backward level of economic development and lower forms of class relations (remnants of feudalism; petty production often based on 'self-exploitation', and formal subsumption of labour by capital) coexist with (urban or urban-regional) islands of advanced capitalism (real subsumption) in the periphery.[27]

---

26 This is a theme that has been taken up by Smith (2016) in his book on imperialism. A study of autoworkers showed that those in the U.S. are 18% more productive than their counterparts in Mexico, but are paid 14 times (1,400%) more (Gilbert, 2017).

27 Or, in the words of Trotsky (1932/2008: 4–5), an ardent follower of Marx's political economy and his internationalist outlook: A backward country assimilates the material and intellectual [achievements] … of the advanced countries. But this does not mean that it follows them slavishly, reproduces all the stages of their past … The privilege of historic backwardness … permits, or rather compels, the adoption of whatever is ready in advance of any specified date, skipping a whole series of intermediate stages.

  Unevenness, the most general law of the historic process, reveals itself most sharply and complexly in the destiny of the backward countries. Under the whip of external necessity their backward culture is compelled to make leaps. From the universal law of unevenness thus derives another law which … we may call the law of *combined development* – by which we mean a drawing together of the different stages of the journey, a combining of the separate steps, an amalgam of archaic with more contemporary forms. Without this law … it is impossible to understand the history of [the periphery or of the center or indeed of the world as a whole]'.

5 Conclusion

There are at least four aspects of the central relevance of Marx's ideas to the periphery. Firstly, his more abstract ideas about society (his ideas in political economy – 'natural history of society' – as well as in social theory) are widely relevant, both to the periphery and to the center, in terms of how people earn their living and how societies evolve in a crisis-ridden manner. Secondly, to the extent that capitalist relations develop in the periphery (beyond the extent he was able to observe), Marx's ideas about advanced capitalism of which Europe was an exemplar site during his time and whose *global* (i.e. center-periphery) character he emphasizes, may be applicable to today's periphery, with some suitable adjustment for the changes in the temporal-geographical context.[28] Marx's general ideas about capitalism – commodification, pre-and non-capitalist relations slowly, albeit unevenly, being supplanted by capitalist-market relations, dispossession, exploitation, crisis-proneness, masses' tendency to rise in revolt – are, more or less, applicable to the periphery, to the extent that capitalism is developing there. Thirdly, many of his ideas that are specifically about the periphery of his time have some relevance to the periphery today. Finally, his philosophical ideas – materialism and dialectics – are widely relevant to the periphery. Interestingly, many of those who deny Marx's relevance to the periphery – scholars influenced by post-isms – also have a dim view of both materialism and dialectics.

Marx's thinking helps us understand the specificity of the periphery and its historical and on-going relation to the Core, on the basis of his general concepts (class-exploitation, commodity, accumulation, and other concepts) and his ideas that are specific to the periphery. We need to see Marx's ideas or 'Marxism of Marx' in terms of it:

> a) being relevant to the understanding of economy, politics, culture and nature in the abstract and at the level of the world-market, and b) as comprising bodies of work (various Marxisms) that i) critically capture the 'unique' ways in which capitalism develops in, and impacts, specific world-regions, including in the periphery, and ii) demonstrate how the different world-regions of the periphery are developing unevenly relative

---

28 All these general ideas of Marx discussed in this section – commodification, pre-and non-capitalist relations slowly, albeit unevenly, being supplanted by capitalist-market relations, dispossession, exploitation, crisis-proneness, workers' and peasants' tendency to rise in revolt – are, more or less, applicable to the periphery, to the extent that capitalism is developing there.

to one another and relative to the imperialist countries, within the framework capitalist imperialism.

I have advocated a dialectical view of Marx's relevance to the global periphery. There is a need to avoid two dangers in assessing Marx's relevance. One is world-regional exceptionalism, which absolutizes the specificity of the regions of the periphery (see the critique of such intellectual tendency by Chibber, 2013). Then there is Euro-centrist universalism, which mechanically applies Marx's ideas that may be valid only/mainly for Europe to the periphery, as if regions of the periphery are just climatically warmer Europe or the regions which will eventually become developed like those of today's Europe. Not everything Marx says is relevant, but a lot of it is. If he says something about the periphery that is empirically false or that is inconsistent with his overall social theory or political economy that is defensible, one must be sceptical of it (Das, 2017a; Das, 2012). To Lenin, Marx's greatest disciple (and to many others, including Samir Amin), Marx was/is a starting point, a great beginning, but not inviolable. His ideas can be developed and used in order to shed light on today's challenges, in a way that is geographically sensitive to the periphery and to the center:

> We do not regard Marx's theory as something completed and inviolable; on the contrary, we are convinced that it has only laid the foundation stone of the science which socialists *must* develop in all directions if they wish to keep pace with life. We think that an *independent* elaboration of Marx's theory is especially essential for ... socialists [of different countries, including in the periphery]; for this theory provides only general *guiding* principles, which, *in particular*, are applied in England differently than in France, in France differently than in Germany, and in Germany differently than in Russia'.
> LENIN, 1899; italics in original; parenthesis added

References

Anderson, K. 2022. No, Karl Marx Was Not Eurocentric. *Jacobin*. https://jacobin.com/2022/07/karl-marx-eurocentrism-western-capitalism-colonialism.

Arico, J. 2014. *Marx and Latin America*. Chicago: Haymarket.

Brass, T. 2022. Marxism, Peasants, and the Cultural Turn: the Myth of a 'Nice' Populism, in D. Fasenfest (ed.), *Marx Matters*, Leiden: Brill.

Brass, T. 2000. *Peasants, Populism, and Postmodernism: the Return of the Agrarian Myth*, London: Frank Cass.

Brass, T. 2011a. Unfree Labour as Primitive Accumulation? *Capital & Class*, 35(1), 23–38.

Brass, T. 2011b. *Labour Regime Change in the Twenty-First Century*, Leiden: Brill.

Brenner, R. 1977. The Origins of Capitalist Development: a Critique of Neo-Smithian Marxism, *New Left Review* I/104 (Jul–Aug), 25–92.

Byres, T. 2007. Karl Marx on India, *Journal of Agrarian Change*, 7:1, 128–132.

Chibber, V. 2013. *Post-colonial Theory and the Specter of Capital*. London: Verso.

Das, R. 2023a (Forthcoming). Marx's *Grundrisse*: Introduction to political economy and historical materialism. *World Review of Political Economy*.

Das, R. 2023b. Capital, Capitalism and Health. *Critical Sociology*, 49(3), 395–414.

Das, R. 2023c. On the worker-peasant alliance in India (and other countries of the Global South). *Links*. https://links.org.au/worker-peasant-alliance-india-and-other-countries-global-south.

Das, R. 2022a. Theory and class struggle: A dialectical approach. *Links*. https://links.org.au/theory-and-class-struggle-dialectical-approach.

Das, R. 2022b. *Marx's Capital, Capitalism, and Limits to the State*. London: Palgrave.

Das, R. 2022c. What Is Marxist Geography Today, or What Is Left of Marxist Geography? *Human Geography*, 15(1), 33–44.

Das, R. 2022d. On *the Communist Manifesto*: Ideas for the Newly Radicalizing Public. *World Review of Political Economy*, 13(2), 209–244. https://www.jstor.org/stable/48687800.

Das, R. 2019. Politics of Marx as Non-sectarian Revolutionary Class Politics: an Interpretation in the Context of the 20th and 21st Centuries, *Class, Race and Corporate Power*: Vol. 7: Iss. 1, Article 8. DOI: 10.25148/CRCP.7.1.008319. Available at: https://digitalcommons.fiu.edu/classracecorporatepower/vol7/iss1/8.

Das, R. 2017a. *Marxist Class Theory for a Sceptical World*. Leiden: Brill.

Das, R. J. 2017b. David Harvey's Theory of Accumulation by Dispossession: a Marxist Critique, *World Review of Political Economy*, 8:4.

Das, R. 2013. Agrarian Crisis as the Crisis of Small Property Ownership in Globalizing Capitalism. *Monthly Review Online*. https://mronline.org/2013/10/01/das011013-html/.

Das, R. 2012. Forms of Subsumption of Labour under Capital, Class Struggle and Uneven Development, *Review of Radical Political Economics*, Vol. 44:2, 178–200.

Das, R. and Fasenfest, D. 2018. Marx and the Global South, *Global Dialogue*. https://globaldialogue.isa-sociology.org/articles/marx-and-the-global-south.

Eagleton, T. 2011a. *Why Marx Was Right*. New Haven: Yale University Press.

Eagleton, T. 2011b. In Praise of Marx, *The Chronicle of Higher Education*; available at: https://www.chronicle.com/article/In-Praise-of-Marx/127027.

Engels, F. 1883. Speech at the Grave of Karl Marx. https://www.marxists.org/arch ive/marx/works/1883/death/burial.htm.

Fasenfest, D. and Das, R. 2021. Constructing the Conceptual Tools for the Global South, in H. Leiulfsrud and P. Sohlberg (eds) *Constructing Social Research Objects*, Leiden: Brill.

Foster, J., McChesney, R. and Jonna, R. 2011. The Global Reserve Army of Labor and the New Imperialism, *Monthly Review*,63: 06; available at: https://monthlyreview.org /2011/11/01/the-global-reserve-army-of-labor-and-the-new-imperialism/.

Gasper, P. 2002. Is Marxism Relevant in the Third World?; available at http://socialis tworker.org/2002-1/405/405_08_MarxismRelevant.shtml.

Ghosh, S. 1984. Marx on India, *Monthly Review*, 35:8, 39–53.

Gilbert, D. 2017. Is Marxism Relevant? Some Uses and Misuses, available at: https: //abolitionjournal.org/is-marxism-relevant-some-uses-and-misuses-by-david-gilb ert-political-prisoner/.

Harvey, D. 2003. *New Imperialism*. Oxford: Oxford University press.

Harvey, D. 2007. Neoliberalism as Creative Destruction. *The Annals of the American Academy of Political and Social Science*, 610(1), 21–44. https://doi.org/10.1177/00027 16206296780

Jones, G.S. 2016. *Karl Marx: Greatness and Illusion*, Cambridge, MA: Harvard University Press.

Jonna, R. and Foster, J. 2016. Marx's Theory of Working-Class Precariousness: Its Relevance Today, *Monthly Review*, available at: https://monthlyreview.org/2016/04 /01/marxs-theory-of-working-class-precariousness/.

Kalmring, S. and Nowak, A. 2017. Viewing Africa with Marx: Remarks on Marx's Fragmented Engagement with the African Continent, *Science and Society*, 81:3, 331–347.

Laibman, D. 2013. On the 130th Anniversary of the Death of Karl Marx: Answers to Questions from China's People's Daily, *Science and Society*, 77:4, 451–458.

Lenin, V. 1908. Marxism and Revisionism. https://www.marxists.org/archive/lenin /works/1908/apr/03.htm.

Lenin, V. 1899. *The Development of Capitalism in Russia*. https://www.marxists.org/arch ive/lenin/works/1899/devel/.

Marx, K. 1977. *Capital volume 1*. New York: Vintage.

Marx, K. 1976. *Wage Labour and Capital*. New York: International Publishers.

Marx, K. 1973. *Grundrisse*. https://www.marxists.org/archive/marx/works/downl oad/pdf/grundrisse.pdf.

Marx, K. 1968. *German Ideology*. https://www.marxists.org/archive/marx/works/downl oad/Marx_The_German_Ideology.pdf.

Marx, K. 1894. *Capital volume 3*. https://www.marxists.org/archive/marx/works/downl oad/pdf/Capital-Volume-III.pdf.

Marx, K. 1877. Letter to Editor of the *Otecestvenniye Zapisky;* available at: https://www.marxists.org/archive/marx/works/1877/11/russia.htm.

Marx, K. 1873. Political indifferentism. available at: https://www.marxists.org/archive/marx/works/1873/01/indifferentism.htm

Marx, K. 1859. A Contribution to the Critique of Political Economy: Preface https://www.marxists.org/archive/marx/works/1859/critique-pol-economy/preface.htm.

Marx, K. 1853. The Future Results of British Rule in India https://marxists.architexturez.net/archive/marx/works/1853/07/22.htm.

Marx, K. 1847. *Poverty of Philosophy,* available at: https://www.marxists.org/archive/marx/works/1847/poverty-philosophy/ch02.htm.

Marx, K. and Engels, F. 1850. Address of the Central Committee to the Communist League, Available at: https://www.marxists.org/archive/marx/works/1847/communist-league/1850-ad1.htm.

Marx, K. and Engels, F. 1848. *Communist Manifesto.* https://www.marxists.org/archive/marx/works/download/pdf/Manifesto.pdf.

Maunder, J. 2006. Marxism and the Global South. *Socialist Worker.* https://socialistworker.co.uk/features/marxism-and-the-global-south/.

Mezzadri, A. 2022. *Marx in the Field.* Cambridge: Cambridge University Press.

Nimtz, A. 2002. The Eurocentric Marx and Other Related Myths. In: Bartolovich C and Lazarus L. (eds) *Marxism, Modernity and Post-colonial Studies.* Cambridge: Cambridge University Press, 65–80.

Ollman, B. 2003. *Dance of the Dialectic,* Urbana-Champaign: University of Illinois Press.

Patnaik, U. and Patnaik, P. 2015. Imperialism in the Era of Globalization, *Monthly Review,* available at: https://monthlyreview.org/2015/07/01/imperialism-in-the-era-of-globalization.

Pradella, L. 2017. Marx and the Global South: Connecting History and Value Theory, *Sociology: The Journal of the British Sociological Association,* 51:1, 146–161.

Roberts, M. 2016. *The Long Depression.* Chicago: Haymarket.

Smith, J. 2016. *Imperialism in the 21st Century,* New York: Monthly Review Press.

Sperber, J. 2013. *Karl Marx: A Nineteenth-Century Life,* Liveright Publication.

Trotsky, L. 1932/2008. *The History of the Russian Revolution,* Pathfinder Press.

Wood, E.M. 1998. *Retreat from Class,* London: Verso.

Wright, E. 1995. The Class Analysis of Poverty, *International Journal of Health Services,* 25:1, 85–100.

CHAPTER 11

Crises in Neoliberalism

Towards a Democratic Alternative

Alfredo Saad-Filho

1   Introduction

It has become commonplace to insist that our generation is confronting unprecedented challenges.[1] David Fasenfest has addressed several of these challenges, from different angles, both in his own scholarly work and as editor of *Critical Sociology*. There were, of course, grave dangers confronting humanity in general, and the working class specifically, when David started his academic career, in a post-colonial world bitterly divided by the Cold War. However, that was also a time of hope, when it seemed that different paths to political freedom and economic equality were possible. David has probed these paths and their limitations with penetrating insight and in a spirit of solidarity with the poor and the exploited everywhere. He has continued to do so, even as circumstances have become increasingly difficult for the left since the transition to neoliberalism and the subsequent rise of authoritarian modalities of governance. It is fitting that we should reflect, in the spirit of David's work, on the current challenges to human freedom, and even to our survival as a species.

The argument in this chapter is organised around the contradictions and crises in the dominant system of accumulation, that is, the current phase, configuration or mode of existence of capitalism: neoliberalism. Examination of these contradictions helps to contextualise the tensions in global neoliberalism in the domains of the economy (marked by a long stagnation punctuated by finance-driven implosions); politics (marked by the erosion of democracy and the rise of specifically neoliberal forms of fascism); health (most obviously through the disastrous outcomes of the COVID-19 pandemic, but also the epidemic of addiction, the mental health crisis, growing resistance to antibiotics, and more); social reproduction (leading to crippling pressures within

---

[1] This chapter draws upon Ayers and Saad-Filho (2015, 2020), Boffo, Saad-Filho and Fine (2019), Fine and Saad-Filho (2017) and Saad-Filho (2011a, 2017, 2020a, 2020b, 2020c, 2021b, 2021c, 2023).

households); and the environment (with severe implications for life as we know it). This is, of course, only a sample of the multiplicity of crises afflicting contemporary societies, which also include food provision, water supplies, soil erosion, pollution, 'forever chemicals', microplastics, geopolitical tensions, and much more.

The complexity of these issues implies that a comprehensive picture is impossible; instead, this chapter offers a set of observations that, hopefully, David might find interesting. This is not about some bland generalisation about 'polycrisis', which would recognise the multiplicity of challenges but bypass the relations of determination between them. We can do better than this, and a Marxist approach can offer valuable insights towards an integrated analysis. The systemic approach in this chapter suggests that neoliberalism is changing, and its evolution points towards distinctive forms of state intervention seeking to contain the crises in social reproduction and in our basic conditions of living. The prospects for human freedom at this point are unfavourable (to put it mildly), although several positive experiences exist, and they can help to inspire the mobilisation of the working class and the poor as they press for their own political emancipation.

This argument is developed in eight sections. This introduction is the first. The second reviews the foundations and the economic crisis in neoliberalism. The third examines the rise and decline of neoliberal democracy, and the fourth charts the rise of authoritarian neoliberalism in the wake of the Global Financial Crisis (GFC), that started in 2007. The fifth reviews the health crisis driven by the COVID-19 pandemic. The sixth examines the crisis in social reproduction, and the seventh summarises the environmental crisis and the relevant policy option. The eighth section concludes.

2   The Economic Crisis in Neoliberalism

Neoliberalism is often conceptualised either as an ideology, or as a set of economic and social policies. In contrast, this chapter focuses on neoliberalism as the current configuration (instantiation, phase, or mode of existence) of capitalism as a (global) mode of production; in other words, as the dominant system of accumulation today.[2] Neoliberalism emerged tentatively and spread around the world from the mid-1970s, in response to the challenges to

---

2 For a detailed examination of different conceptions of neoliberalism, see Fine and Saad-Filho (2017) and Saad-Filho (2017, 2021a).

capitalist reproduction after the disarticulation of the Keynesian-social democratic consensus in the advanced capitalist economies (AES), the disintegration of developmentalism in the developing economies (DES) and the collapse of the Soviet Bloc.

The most significant feature of neoliberalism is the financialisation of production, exchange and social reproduction, that is, the intensive and extensive accumulation of what Marx called interest-bearing capital (IBC) or, more colloquially put, the growth of activities geared to making profit out of investments in money and paper assets, including certificates of ownership of 'real' property and purely financial instruments (what Marx called fictitious capital), rather than the employment of people to produce goods or services for sale.[3] The extended range, reach, influence and resourcing of finance has been closely related to the development of new instruments, the growth of a well-rewarded sphere of speculation, and the appropriation of an expanding share of the value produced in the economy by IBC. These transfers of value have given a significant contribution to the polarisation of incomes in recent decades, that has been captured, most famously, by Piketty (2014). Financialisation has also underpinned the transnationalisation of production under neoliberalism, which is usually summarised as 'globalisation'. Neoliberalism, financialisation and globalisation have contributed to an extraordinary recovery of profitability since the crises of Keynesianism, developmentalism and Soviet-style socialism, and led to rising inequality almost everywhere (Boffo, Saad-Filho and Fine 2019).

The state always plays a key role driving the transition to neoliberalism, building the new (financialised and globalised) institutional framework, and legitimising that transition by recourse to claims about the 'superior efficiency' of the market, the (invariably) 'difficult' state of the public finances, the imperative of privatisation and commercialisation of public services, the requirement to roll back the welfare state, the imposition of private sector performance indicators on public institutions, and the need to repress the opposition. In this way, government policies have dismantled state capacities and public services in most countries, reformed public institutions to serve capital in general (and finance specifically), and led the transformation of social reproduction under neoliberalism. The transition to neoliberalism also led to profound changes in institutions, ideologies, rules, policies and practices, seeking to restructure production and social reproduction and shield market processes

---

3 There is a vast literature on financialisation; see, for example, Ashman and Fine (2013), Christophers and Fine (2020), Fine (2010, 2013–14), Fine and Saad-Filho (2017), Mader et al. (2020), Sawyer (2022), and van der Zwan (2014).

from any form of wider accountability. They have also led many social groups, especially the working class in the Anglo-Saxon countries, to become deeply enmeshed into financial circuits through their bank accounts, overdrafts, savings, credit cards, mortgages, pensions, and payments for education, health, and other areas of social provision (Montgomerie 2020).

The technological, economic, institutional, ideological and political changes outlined above, and the restructuring of production and social reproduction under neoliberalism, created an array of economic 'losers' centred on the traditional working class in the advanced capitalist economies. In particular, millions of skilled jobs were eliminated through deindustrialisation in the Global North, and following debt and balance of payments crises in the Global South and the former Soviet Bloc. As a result, entire professions vanished or were exported, employment opportunities in the public sector worsened because of privatisations and 'retrenching', job stability declined, and pay, conditions and welfare protections tended to deteriorate in most countries. Similar pressures were felt by an indebted, impoverished, anxious and vulnerable middle class. In some of the wealthiest countries in the world, and in the wealthiest regions of most developing countries, formerly privileged social strata lament their inability satisfy the material aspirations stressed by the consumption-oriented cultures of neoliberalism. Many have also become unable to bequeath improved material prospects to their offspring, breaking a generational contract of continuous improvement ('we sacrifice so our children will do better than us') that had helped to legitimise the privations imposed by capitalism since the 18th Century.

Instead, accumulation under neoliberalism has tended to take the form of finance-driven bubbles that are parasitical on the exploitation of the workers (through the global restructuring of production and the expansion of precarious forms of labour, culminating in the 'gig economy'), exactions from the periphery (via unequal trade, financial extraction, rents, and so on), and the plunder of nature. These bubbles invariably collapse with destructive implications, and their containment always requires expensive state intervention. Beyond growing instability and periodic crises, accumulation under neoliberalism has been sluggish. Despite the recovery of profitability and rising inequality, and technological innovations, rates of investment and GDP growth have tended to decline for several decades, especially in the AEs, despite the unprecedentedly favourable conditions for accumulation created by neoliberalism itself (Boffo, Saad-Filho and Fine 2019). In fact, between 2007 and 2020, the West suffered the longest economic calamity and the weakest and most regressive recovery on record, which was followed by the COVID-19 pandemic and the subsequent economic crisis (that has often, and misleadingly, been blamed on the Russia-Ukraine war).[4] This is *the economic paradox of neoliberalism:* the transition to neoliberalism created the most favourable conditions for accumulation since the late 19th Century; yet, economic performance has worsened in terms of GDP growth, rates of investment, employment creation, volatility and vulnerability to deeper and more long-lasting economic crises, in addition to a staggering concentration of income and wealth.

For example, Gabriel Palma (2023) shows that, if the USA had its current GDP, but the same share of income of the top 1% as in 1980, that group would earn US$2 trillion less than they currently do. Similarly, if the distribution of income in the USA had remained as in 1980, the top 1% would have only about half its wealth. The top 0.1% would have only one-third, and the top 0.01% would have only one-fifth. This implies that the top 1% would own US$20 trillion less than they do. The other side of the coin is the decline in investment: if the share of investment in US GDP had remained stable since 1980, investment would be US$1 trillion higher than today. Today, non-residential private investment in the USA barely meets depreciation: it is no wonder that infrastructure is literally falling apart. Productivity growth has declined so much that, if the USA had kept its pre-neoliberal productivity growth rate, its GDP could (notionally) have been US$10 trillion higher today. Similarly, since the early 2000s, Germany embarked on a deliberate strategy of construction of inequality, including a badly paid working class encompassing around 20 per cent of the population. In taking this destructive course, Germany converged not only with Latin American levels of inequality, but also with Latin America's collapsing rates of investment and productivity growth.

Similar tensions between rising inequality and falling investment exist in other advanced economies; for example, in Japan, where the income share of the top 1 per cent increased by 4.2 percentage points, while the investment rate fell by 6.2 percentage points of GDP. In turn, in Latin America, the share of investment in GDP started from a relatively low level of 22 per cent in the 1970s, and it fell by another 3 percentage points since 1980, despite the inflow of US$3.6 trillion in constant dollars of 2019. Palma (2023) shows that the decline in GDP growth rates in Western Europe and Latin America since 1980 can be attributed to the collapse of productivity growth, which fell in both regions from over 3 per cent per annum to zero. This was avoidable: since 1980, labour productivity tripled in Indonesia and Malaysia, quadrupled in Thailand, multiplied by 5 in South Korea, Taiwan and Vietnam, by 6 in India, and by 20 in

---

4   See Aglietta (2016), Ivanova (2016), Parboni and Tridico (2018) and Tcherneva (2015); for current data and analysis, see UNCTAD's *Trade and Development Report.*

China. In the meantime, the US lost half its manufacturing jobs, and Western Europe lost one-third of them.

3 Democracy in Crisis

The transitions to neoliberalism have been associated with a wide variety of political paths. They range from constitutional means in most AEs, imposition by dictatorships in Turkey and in several Latin American and sub-Saharan African countries, to coeval transitions to neoliberalism and democracy in Brazil, South Africa, South Korea and Eastern Europe. Despite this diversity of paths of transition, a 'typical' democratic form of neoliberalism had become established by the 1990s.

While these neoliberal democracies satisfied the elementary requirements of political pluralism and (limited) respect for human rights, their political processes were effectively constrained to the choice between shades of neoliberalism in a tightly regulated political market. There, the friendly duel between parties with similar programmes was policed, daily, by a plutocratic right-wing media and, constitutionally, by a nominally 'independent' judiciary: Clinton Democrats versus mainstream Republicans in the USA; New Labour versus moderate Tories in the UK; centre-left versus centre-right in Canada, France, Germany and Italy, and so on. In addition, the institutional framework introduced with the neoliberal 'reforms' insulated economic decisions from the political process and from potential 'interference' by the majority, in order to secure the political hegemony of finance and the neoliberal elite. As a result, neoliberalism was locked in institutionally: it became virtually impossible to shift the system of accumulation following the regulations that neoliberalism itself had imposed. Outcomes included the contraction of the scope for legitimate opposition, and the reduction of the policy space for states, societies and political systems to shape economic policy and even to find negotiated solutions to the limitations and crises in neoliberalism.

While the economic changes imposed by neoliberalism created large numbers of 'economic losers', the parallel transformation of social structures, institutions and the law tended to evacuate the political sphere, rendering these losers increasingly unable to resist against neoliberalism, demand changes of course, and even conceptualise alternatives. These processes also led to the decline of most forms of collective representation and working-class sociability: left parties and organisations, trade unions, community organisations, clubs, and so on. While these outcomes helped to consolidate neoliberalism in the short term, they also fostered long-term political disengagement and created powerful tendencies towards apathy and anomie, severely undermining the legitimacy of neoliberalism (Ayers and Saad-Filho 2015, 2020).

Given the fragmentation of society, the ideological hegemony of neoliberalism and the choice of what would count as 'legitimate' opinion by the mainstream media, the 'losers' increasingly tended to perceive their predicament through the lens of 'corruption' among the elites, and 'undue privileges' gifted by the state to the undeserving poor, women, self-identified minorities, foreigners, and foreign countries. While these groups were deemed to be favoured by public policy, the state institutions seemed to have become hostile against the 'losers', who found it increasingly difficult to make end meet. Everything seemed to be upside-down, with the undeserving cutting ahead of the 'morally upright', in sharp contrast with the misty olden days when people of good character, strong discipline and sharing 'our' values (essentially, males with the correct ethnic background) could count on steady employment, rising incomes, good promotion prospects and generous pensions. In mature neoliberal societies, the demands and expectations of the 'losers' tend to be framed by simplistic discourses drawing upon 'common sense' and a universalist (classless) ethics founded on identity (demanding acceptance within the system of accumulation), meritocracy (demanding that the rules must be followed), and revulsion at corruption (aiming to fine-tune neoliberalism, since replacing it seems impossible).

Nationalism and racism (grounded on presumably shared values and background) offer familiar frameworks to articulate these narratives. In other words, in contemporary neoliberalism, the losers are invited to frame their disappointments, resentments, fears and hopes by means of ethical conflicts between 'good' against 'bad', and 'insiders' against 'outsiders', in a moral universe in which there is no systemic exploitation nor structures of reproduction of inequality. Instead, members of 'our' group must defend themselves against predatory non-members while, within the group, 'honest' individuals are besieged by dishonest characters: 'our' values of honesty and hard work are undermined by politicians stealing 'our' money, immigrants crowding 'us' out of 'our' houses and hospitals, and distant countries stealing 'our' jobs.

The *political paradox of neoliberalism* is that the institutionalisation of neoliberal democracy has undermined the foundations of democracy itself: the structures of representation became increasingly unresponsive, public policy became increasingly indifferent to the majority, and the state signalled more and more clearly that class-based collectivities would not be recognised and that cash-poor individuals were either 'failures' or 'crooks'. Given the disarticulation of the left, these circumstances fostered the rise of anti-systemic forces dominated by the far right, and polarised by authoritarian nationalist leaders vouching to confront the neoliberal state, finance, globalisation, the elites, foreigners and so on, to garner the votes of the losers – while, simultaneously, enforcing policies leading to the intensification of neoliberalism.

4   The Rise of Authoritarian Neoliberalism

The GFC and its aftermath opened a third phase of neoliberalism, distinguished by the need to manage the consequences of the crisis in a context of loss of legitimacy due to the widespread realisation of the enormity of the shock, the astronomical cost of saving finance, the perception that neoliberalism had concentrated income and wealth and imposed unpopular patterns of employment, and that it had failed to deliver rapid and stable accumulation. The policies imposed in the wake of the GFC also contributed to the loss of economic dynamism in the AEs, while the inability of neoliberal states to address the concerns of the losers undermined the legitimacy of policies, practices, institutions, parties and leaders that were, previously, unassailable.

Given the faltering ideological hegemony of neoliberalism and financialisation, the policies imposed after the GFC required the intensification of political repression and the introduction of new forms of exclusion. The effort was made, but it proved to be excessive: political control slipped from the traditional neoliberal elites in several countries, leading to the emergence of anti-systemic forces polarised by 'spectacular' authoritarian leaders and a new generation of far-right movements. The malaise reached even the 'core' NATO countries, when Brexit won in the UK and Donald Trump was elected in the USA. The policies pursued by those administrations converged around more or less overtly repressive and racist forms of neoliberalism, justified by unwieldy combinations of 'national' values, racism, the imperatives of austerity, and the whims of the 'leader'. This is *authoritarian neoliberalism*. This political form of neoliberalism partially breaks away from its earlier democratic shell, exacerbating the authoritarian tendencies of neoliberal capitalism, in order to sustain the system of accumulation despite its inability to deliver any form of shared prosperity.

Seen in this way, authoritarian neoliberalism is neither a transitory blip which, after inevitable failure, will lead to the restoration of 'normal' neoliberal politics, nor a marker of the 'end of neoliberalism'. Instead, it is a symptom of the decomposition of neoliberal democracy, an indirect outcome of the crisis of restructured economies, political systems and institutions of representation under neoliberalism, and evidence that mass discontent has been hijacked by the far right. The *paradox of authoritarianism* is that the crises in neoliberalism foster the personalisation of politics and the emergence of 'spectacular' leaders untethered by stabilising institutions such as party structures, constitutional checks and balances, trade unions, social movements and the law.

In general terms, these leaders tend to be committed to both neoliberalism and the expansion of their own personal power. Although they campaign against specific aspects or consequences of neoliberalism, when they reach power they invariably implement policies intensifying neoliberalism and financialisation while attacking all forms of opposition and rendering even more power to the neoliberal elite. These policies are likely to hurt their own electoral base: wages tend to decline, taxes tend to become more regressive, social protections tend to be eroded, economies tend to become more unbalanced, poverty tends to grow, and society tends to become more divided. Mass frustration is likely to intensify: authoritarian neoliberalism is intrinsically unstable, and leads to a politics of permanent crisis, while opening spaces for modern forms of fascism.[5]

5   Health in Crisis

The previous sections outlined the contradictions of neoliberalism as they appeared until early 2020, when the world was overwhelmed by the COVID-19 pandemic. While the pandemic did not change anything fundamental about global neoliberalism, it intensified the existing tensions, and revealed the limitations of neoliberalism like never before.

The global capitalist economy was already glowing sluggishly, then it collapsed into the deepest economic contraction in the history of capitalism (Roubini 2020; Saad-Filho 2020b): 'globalisation' seemed to go into reverse; long supply chains, that were previously the 'rational' way to organise production, collapsed and hard borders returned; trade declined and international travel was severely constrained. Tens of millions of workers became unemployed in a matter of days, and millions of businesses lost their employees, customers, suppliers and credit lines. A long line of industries rushed to the

---

5   'Neoliberalism ... has helped create the conditions for the re-emergence of the far-right whilst, at the same time, the far-right has focused on attacking what it sees as the symptoms of neoliberalism through racializing its social, political and economic effects ... It is not then that neoliberalism *causes* racism ... in the sense that racism is an organic dimension of it, but rather that neoliberalism is grounded on a *collective socio-economic insecurity* that helps facilitate a revival of pre-existing racialized imaginaries of solidarity' (Davidson and Saull 2017, pp.715–716).

closest government for a bailout. In turn, many political systems were already drifting towards authoritarianism and, in the pandemic, they often become spectacularly perverse, imposing health policies that killed millions, and that entrenched COVID-19 so it can never be eliminated. The cases of the USA, UK, India and Brazil are especially significant in this respect (Saad-Filho 2021b).

The pandemic highlighted three important contradictions in neoliberalism: first, the more the state had been reconstructed along neoliberal lines, and the more social reproduction had been marketised, the less expertise and spare capacity these states and economies tended to have in order to respond to emergencies. Second, neoliberalism had hollowed out, fragmented and part-privatised health systems in several countries, while also creating a precarious and impoverished working class that was highly vulnerable to disruptions in their earning capacity and to health scares because of their low savings, poor housing, inadequate nutrition, and work patterns incompatible with healthy lives (Solty 2020). Third, the privatisation and disarticulation of national health systems expanded the scope for unco-ordinated intervention by the private sector, often in corrupt arrangements with prominent civil servants and politicians (Coburg 2020; Kinder and Plimmer 2020).

Neoliberal discourses about the imperative of 'fiscal austerity' and the 'limits' of public policy were shelved as soon as the pandemic hit. The goal of neoliberal governments, as in previous crises, was to shelter capital as efficiently as possible. However, the policies implemented after GFC rapidly proved to be insufficient (Sandbu 2020). Unprecedentedly, Central Banks started providing finance directly to large companies, essentially handing 'helicopter money' to selected capitalists who, in some cases, immediately passed those resources to their shareholders as dividends, in a scandalous robbery of public resources. This policy was also symptomatic of the growing role of Central Banks in the completion of individual the circuits of capital, while finance focused narrowly on the enrichment of itself. In order to disguise the unseemly spectacle of billionaires, often tax exiles, receiving subsidies from the same exchequer that they had previously evaded and publicly maligned, some governments offered support to the workers too, but generally as an afterthought, miserly, often through the employers, and seeking primarily to avoid the collapse of demand rather than aiming to support people in need.

In the meantime, already in a context of disintegrating democracy, states used the pandemic to reinforce the apparatus of repression, with greater legitimacy and regardless of their performance against the coronavirus itself, across systems to control movements, trace contacts, intercept communications, monitor health, suppress protest, and decide what output and services should be available to the citizens. This power-grab took place at the same time as the largest Big Tech companies (Amazon, Apple, Facebook, Google, Microsoft), as well as relatively new entrants (Zoom) profited mightily from the pandemic while, also, hoovering up data to be monetised later (Zuboff 2019).

6 The Crisis in Social Reproduction

Under capitalism, the working class is separated not just from the means of production, but also from the means of life more generally: historically, the process of separation starts with land (for the classical account, see Marx 1976, Part VIII), but it eventually includes housing, transport, food, healthcare, and so on, leading the working class to a position where it can have only conditional and mediated access over everything that makes life comfortable, or even possible.

This implies that, under capitalism in general, and neoliberalism specifically, the majority of the population has a material interest in securing access to the means of life, in order to protect an existence that is, structurally, saturated with stress, anxiety and unfreedom. For example, 66 per cent of the US population worries about accessing basic healthcare; 31 per cent were struggling to pay their energy bills even before the price spike due to the war in Ukraine; and 60 to 80 per cent of Americans literally live paycheck to paycheck. In 2018, 40 per cent of Americans could not cover a US$400 emergency expense (Huber 2022, p.170). These numbers are similar in the UK,[6] and it seems reasonable to assume that, in the DES, the equivalent figures must be worse.

In their work, Arruzza, Bhattacharya and Fraser (2019) stress that the global working class includes not only white men working in factories: most workers are in fields, private homes, offices, hotels, bars, restaurants, delivery services, hospitals and schools. Especially at its low pay and precarious extreme in the AES, the working class is disproportionately female, migrant and racialised. There, and in their lives and experiences, is where the Global North and the Global South truly meet. Arruzza, Bhattacharya and Fraser (2019) also highlight that capitalism tends to claim as much reproductive labour as possible, without any concern for its replenishment. This extractive process has become especially acute under neoliberalism, because of the weakness of the organised workers and, closely related, because low-waged, precarious service work has tended to replace secure unionised industrial labour in most countries;

---

6 See, for example, https://www.independent.co.uk/news/business/news/uk-households-no-emergency-savings-pensions-insurance-policies-accounts-a8199201.html.

unsurprisingly, wages have tended to stagnate in the AEs, with global implications. Moreover, under neoliberalism, the social wage has also tended to decline, as services that used be provided publicly were externalised as the state divested from them – in practice, service provision was transferred primarily to racialised and immigrant women, both at home and at work.

The consequence in the Global North and the Global South is that many workers have been forced to take on multiple jobs and borrow in order to survive, while they must also take up increasing responsibilities at home. This has led to a growing crisis of care that particularly exhausts women, damages families, and strains people's capacities. Not surprisingly, the crisis of care is closely linked to a global mental health crisis. The ensuing stresses and frustrations have helped to feed right-wing movements that identify real problems in neoliberalism, but twist legitimate grievances in order to blame poorer countries and the weakest and least protected members of society, in order to deflect blame away from capital and profit.

7   The Environmental Catastrophe

In addition to the disasters outlined above, our economic and political systems are being increasingly overwhelmed by the unfolding environmental crisis. There is conclusive evidence that the Earth's climate is warming up, and that global warming has been accelerating. Human greenhouse gas (GHG) emissions have already raised temperatures by around 1.5 degrees Celsius from the pre-industrial revolution baseline, and current trends suggest that temperatures could rise by up to 6°C by 2100 (IPCC, 2021). Disastrous consequences are inescapable, and the time available to reduce emissions in order to avoid catastrophic outcomes is declining rapidly (Saad-Filho and Feil 2023).

Climate change can be related to five sources of stress in the global economy. First, the contradictions between the limited capacity of the Earth to sustain a stable climate, the unrestrained search for profits under neoliberalism, and the more general tendency of capitalism to plunder nature for energy and raw materials and use the Earth as a free sink for the wastes of production, exchange and consumption. These contradictions imply that carbon emissions are not an unfortunate 'externality' of human production in general. Instead, they are a necessary aspect of capitalist accumulation and the boundless pursuit of profitability. Even worse, while the intrinsic capitalist drive for productivity growth expands the possibilities of consumption, it also implies the increased use of machinery and raw materials, and the generation of more waste. In other words, capitalism intrinsically tends to destabilise the ecosystem, natural resources will always tend to be overexploited, the boundary between 'sustainable' and 'unsustainable' extraction will always remain fuzzy, and nature will always serve as a sink for the wastes accompanying the production of commodities for profit: unsustainability is a built-in feature of the capitalist mode of production.

Second, the tension between the longstanding awareness of the environmental limits to growth, and the inability of governments and intergovernmental organisations to address the drivers of climate change. For example, despite the succession of diplomatic meetings, declarations and treaties, CO_2 emissions rose from 20,000 megatons in 1990, to 37,000 megatons in 2022, and the share of the dirtiest fuel, coal, rose steadily between 1999 and 2014.[7] Emissions in a small number of advanced economies have declined, but this is largely due to their deindustrialisation and the relocation of 'their' manufacturing capacity to the Global South, which, for technological and transport reasons, can be even worse for the planet.

Third, the tension between the accumulated emissions by the AEs, on which basis they grew in the past, and the rising emissions in DEs claiming the right to development today.

Fourth, the incongruous structure of the global economy, in which several countries and powerful corporations are invested in the production, export, processing and sale of fossil fuels, even though this is incompatible with climate stability. The impossibility of exploiting the known reserves of fossil fuels implies that assets worth hundreds of billions of dollars must be stranded (mines, oil platforms, refineries, ports, industrial plants, and so on). This will eliminate countless jobs, and create vast accounting losses to countries and companies. Both have been reluctant to accept these losses; some countries justify their stance by the imperative to secure jobs and incomes, others by the lack of alternative exportables, and the firms claim a duty to their shareholders. To these costs must be added the investments needed to shift the world's energy matrix away from fossil fuels while, simultaneously, retrofitting our way of life to make it compatible with net zero, plus the escalating costs of mitigating the impact of climate change, since it can no longer be avoided.

Financialisation undermines attempts at mitigation and adaptation because the financial institutions operate in highly competitive markets that impose short-termist, speculative and procyclical investment strategies. These strategies are incompatible with long-term industrial policy goals, shifts in the

---

7 See https://www.iea.org/data-and-statistics, http://www.globalcarbonatlas.org/en/CO2-emissions, and Jorgenson (2014).

composition of activity, investments in new 'green' drivers of growth, and the redistribution of income (Chesnais 2016; Heynen et al. 2007; Hudson 2010). This is why the financial institutions continue to fund environmentally damaging initiatives that conflict with internationally agreed targets and that expand the bundle of assets that must be stranded when the world finally moves away from fossil fuels (Ansari and Holz 2020; Bos and Gupta 2019). The outcome has been the exhaustion of the carbon budget (given the limits set by the Paris Agreement) and the contraction of the policy space for alternative policies, while countries fight their way towards treaties that will deliver too little, far too late. In the meantime, global businesses profit from the depredation of the Earth's conditions to support life, while they demand public guarantees of even higher profits in exchange for reducing the damage that they are poised to inflict on the planet.

If climate change is seen from the narrow neoclassical angle of 'externalities' and 'market failures', the analysis tends to become trapped into the logic of addressing the problem through the imposition of 'correct prices' by means of taxes, transfers and subsidies (Huber 2022). While this may appeal to mainstream economists and politicians, it is highly divisive, since it implies that climate change could – and should – be fixed through the compression of the standard of living of the majority, while profitability continues to drive production, pollution, adaptation, mitigation, and the clean-up. The political limitations of this approach have been revealed repeatedly, for example, by the fuel tax protests in the UK in 2000 and, more recently, by the French Yellow Vests and the farmers' movements in the EU, as well as by the platform that it often gives to right-wing populist ('pro-driver' and other) programmes.

A Marxist approach should recognise that the vast majority of emissions does not derive from decisions by individual consumers (Should I drive or take the train? How many air miles in these grapes?), just like the majority of production is neither artisanal nor for direct consumption (Bellamy Foster and Clark 2020; Huber 2022; Lawrence and Laybourn-Langton 2022; Pineaut 2023): under capitalism, the majority of production is for profit, and most products and emissions derive from webs of social relations dominated by capital, that determine the level and composition of investment, the choice of technology and energy systems, the output mix, and the dominant patterns of consumption. Shifting these parameters will require more than price changes, nudges, or advertising campaigns; instead, it will demand recognition that climate change has been driven by the profitability of capital, and that this capitalism has created a structure of production that is fundamentally incompatible with climate stability. This is a political problem to be addressed through systemic changes, including shifts in corporate structures, technologies and patterns of ownership and control. This is clearly not a problem of taxation or incentives at the margin while, simultaneously, protecting the profitability of enterprise.

By the same token, an 'austerity ecology' based on the widespread compression of living standards in the name of sustainability would be intolerable to the majority of the population. This would be the case even in the AES, not to speak of the DES, given that both groups of people have experienced neoliberal 'austerity' at least since the GFC and, in many cases, since the early 1980s. In other words, it cannot be left-wing policy to demand that those at the precarious end of society, already living in structural deprivation, should experience even worse living conditions in order to shelter the mode of production that has caused the environmental disaster in the first place. A fairer and more politically promising approach from the point of view of class mobilisation is to build links between environmental struggles and the concerns of the poor, both in production and in social reproduction, on the basis of a democratic and transformative economic, social and distributive programme. This programme should point to a new society based on equality, material security and human freedom, as well as environmental sustainability. The democratic economic strategy (DES) implied in this approach (detailed in Saad-Filho 2021c) focuses on how, and how much, the poor majority can gain by transcending neoliberalism, including the possibility of addressing climate change, since this cannot – and will not – be done in the current system of accumulation.

The challenges of leaving fossil fuels in the ground, diversifying energy supplies, securing economic stability and sustainability, and improving the distribution of income, wealth and power must be addressed simultaneously, for reasons of legitimacy, practicality and effectiveness. DES offers a potentially inspiring left alternative to neoliberalism grounded on non-mainstream traditions in economics, including the Post-Keynesian, Institutionalist, Evolutionary, Kaleckian and Marxian schools, and on the heterodox industrial policy and 'pro-poor' development literatures, while, simultaneously, addressing the environmental constraint.[8] This alternative includes policies to drive sustainable growth, diversify the economy, support green manufacturing, create employment, deliver welfare gains to the majority, foster social inclusion and the satisfaction of basic needs, and improve the distribution of income, wealth and power within and between countries.

It stands to reason that such initiatives as DES can be successful only with state planning, regulation, adequate funding and performance monitoring;

---

8 See Balakrishnan, Elson and Patel (2010), Cornia (2006), Saad-Filho (2007, 2011b, 2021c).

they must also be supported by accommodating fiscal, monetary and financial policies. State-led coordination is essential, because the state is the only institution that can influence the pattern of employment, the production and distribution of goods, services, income and assets, and the relationship between humans and nature. Only the state can limit the power of unaccountable private interests, raise sufficient funds for democratic economic reforms, implement an alternative economic strategy, and ensure that economic activity is guided by the demands of the majority. Similarly, only the state can deliver the energy transition, euthanise the rentiers, decommodify social reproduction, definancialise the economy, dismantle the fossil fuel industry, fund a new energy system, and retrofit our mode of living. However, no state will do this without significant pressure from an organised majority, led by the working class. For only the broad (male and female, immigrant and local, racialised and not, manufacturing and services sector) global working class can provide a mass base for the transformative programme in DES, since only this class has the strategic capacity to impose the economic and political changes that are essential to protect life as we know it. The political challenge for the left, especially Marxist (with has a uniquely strong attachment to, and understanding of, class and its power), is to convince masses of people in the Global North and the Global South that they have a material interest in restructuring production and society, in order to build an alternative transcending neoliberalism.

8 Conclusion

Under neoliberalism, prosperity increasingly relies on extraction, despoliation and fraud. In the meantime, and for related reasons, the system of accumulation is sliding into systemic economic crisis, fascism, and environmental collapse. A transformative agenda is urgently needed.

The changes in political and social life under neoliberalism, the declining presence of trade unions, left-wing political parties and other mass organisations, and the atrophy of collective forms of dissent, have reinforced the construction of neoliberal subjectivities and financialised social intercourse to an extent that would have been unimaginable a few decades ago. At the same time, the GFC and the 'austerity' in its aftermath were associated with the fracturing of the ideological hegemony of neoliberalism, potentially opening new spaces for contestation at different levels. Experiences of success deserve attention and replication where possible; for example, the construction of Syriza in Greece and Podemos in Spain, experience of the British Labour Party under Jeremy Corbyn, the political campaigns around Bernie Sanders in the

USA, the remunicipalisation of water and definancialisation of provision in Valladolid and in Bolivia, and so on.

In this light, what would it take to create a rupture, and turn a sequence of crises in neoliberalism into a crisis of neoliberalism as the dominant system of accumulation (Saad-Filho, 2011a)? This chapter suggests that it will be difficult to address economic stagnation, the drift towards neoliberal fascism, the health crises already in the horizon, the crisis of social reproduction, climate change and the other crises, from within neoliberalism itself. However, it can also be shown that the main constraint to the transition beyond neoliberalism is neither technical nor financial: it is political.

In this context, today's overlapping crises must be confronted together, through a democratic alternative to the depredations inflicted by neoliberalism. The difficulty is that this alternative requires new social movements, new coalitions, and new structures of representation, from parties to trade unions to community associations, corresponding to the current mode of existence of a society that has been extensively decomposed domestically, imperfectly integrated globally, that has distinct cultures but is also imperfectly connected through internet-based tools. We can see important successes in different countries, but we are not there yet.

There is nothing more important, right now, than to support these emerging movements trying to reshape our mode of existence, both in poor countries and in rich countries.

References

Aglietta, M. (2016) America's Slowdown, *New Left Review* 100, pp. 119–129.
Ansari, D. and Holz, F. (2020) Between Stranded Assets and Green Transformation: Fossil-Fuel-Producing Developing Countries towards 2055. *World Development* 130, https://doi.org/10.1016/j.worlddev.2020.104947.
Arruzza, C., Bhattacharya, T. and Fraser, N. (2019) *Feminism for the 99 Percent: A Manifesto*. London: Verso.
Ashman, S. and Fine, B. (2013) Neo-liberalism, Varieties of Capitalism, and the Shifting Contours of South Africa's Financial System, *Transformation* 81 (2), pp. 144–178.
Ayers, A. and Saad-Filho, A. (2015) Democracy against Neoliberalism: Paradoxes, Limitations, Transcendence, *Critical Sociology* 41 (4–5), pp. 597–618.
Ayers, A. and Saad-Filho, A. (2020) A Ticking Time Bomb: The Global South in a Time of Coronavirus, *Journal of Australian Political Economy* 85, https://www.ppesydney.net/issue-85-winter-2020/.

Balakrishnan, R., Elson, D. and Patel, R. (2010) *Rethinking Macro Economic Strategies from a Human Rights Perspective*, Manhattan: Marymount Manhattan College. https://www.cwgl.rutgers.edu/docman/economic-and-social-rights-publicati ons/20-whymeswithhumanrights2-pdf/file.

Bellamy Foster, J. and Clark, B. (2020) *The Robbery of Nature*. New York: Monthly Review Press.

Boffo, M., Saad-Filho, A. and Fine, B. (2019) Neoliberal Capitalism: The Authoritarian Turn, in L. Panitch and G. Albo (eds.), *A World Turned Upside Down: Socialist Register 2019*. London: Merlin Press.

Bos, K. and Gupta, J. (2019) Stranded Assets and Stranded Resources: Implications for Climate Change Mitigation and Global Sustainable Development, *Energy Research and Social Science* 56, https://www.sciencedirect.com/science/article/pii/S22146 29618305383?via%3Dihub.

Chesnais, F. (2016) *Finance Capital Today*. Leiden: Brill.

Christophers B. and Fine B. (2020), The Value of Financialization and the Financialization of Value, in P. Mader, D. Mertens and N. van der Zwan (edited by) *International Handbook of Financialization*, London: Routledge.

Coburg, T. (2020) 'The £5.5bn PPE scandal that goes to the core of government incompetence – and that's just for starters', https://www.thecanary.co/uk/analysis/2020 /07/11/the-5-5bn-ppe-scandal-that-goes-to-the-core-of-government-incompete nce-and-thats-just-for-starters/.

Cornia, G. (ed.) (2006) *Pro-Poor Macroeconomics: Potential and Limitations*. Houndmills: Palgrave.

Davidson, N. and Saull, R. (2017) Neoliberalism and the Far-Right: A Contradictory Embrace, *Critical Sociology* 43 (4–5), pp. 707–724.

Fine, B. (2010) Locating Financialisation, *Historical Materialism* 18(2): 97–116.

Fine, B. (2013–14) Financialisation from a Marxist Perspective, *International Journal of Political Economy*, 42 (4), pp. 46–66.

Fine, B. and Saad-Filho, A. (2017) Thirteen Things You Need to Know About Neoliberalism, *Critical Sociology* 43 (4–5), pp. 685–706.

Heynen, N., McCarthy, J., Prudham, S. and Robbins, P. (eds.) (2007) *Neoliberal Environments: False Promises and Unnatural Consequences*. Abingdon: Routledge.

Huber. M.T. (2022) *Climate Change as Class War*. London: Verso.

Hudson, M. (2010) From Marx to Goldman Sachs: The Fictions of Fictitious Capital, and the Financialization of Industry, *Critique* 38 (3): 419–444.

IPCC (2021) *Climate Change 2021: The Physical Science Basis*. Cambridge University Press. In Press. AR6 Climate Change 2021: The Physical Science Basis — IPCC.

Ivanova, M. (2016) Profit Growth in Boom and Bust: The Great Recession and the Great Depression in Comparative Perspective, *Industrial and Corporate Change* 26 (1), pp.1–20.

Kinder, T. and Plimmer, G. (2020) 'UK government paid £1.7bn to private groups for coronavirus contracts', https://www.ft.com/content/7fe7c2d5-24df-431b-9149-50417 fa0236a.

Lawrence, M. and Laybourn-Langton, L. (2022) *Planet on Fire*. London: Verso.

Mader, P., Mertens, D. and van der Zwan, N. (eds) (2020) *The Routledge International Handbook of Financialization*. Abingdon: Routledge.

Marx, K. (1976) *Capital Volume 1*. Harmondsworth: Penguin.

Montgomerie, J. (2020) Indebtedness and Financialization in Everyday Life, in P. Mader, D. Mertens and N. van der Zwan (eds.) *The Routledge International Handbook of Financialization*. Abingdon: Routledge.

Palma, G. (2023) Ricardo was Surely Right: The Abundance of "Easy" Rents Leads to Greedy and Lazy Elites, https://www.repository.cam.ac.uk/items/172750oc-a5oe-4199-a98b-b140722b1690.

Parboni, R. and Tridico, P. (2018) Inequality, Financialisation and Economic Decline, *Journal of Post Keynesian Economics* 41 (2), pp.236–259.

Piketty, T. (2014) *Capital in the Twenty-First Century*. Cambridge, MA: Harvard University Press.

Pineaut, E. (2023) *A Social Ecology of Capital*. London: Pluto Press.

Roubini, N. (2020), *Coronavirus Pandemic Has Delivered the Fastest, Deepest Economic Shock in History*, https://www.theguardian.com/business/2020/mar/25/coronavirus-pandemic-has-delivered-the-fastest-deepest-economic-shock-in-history.

Saad-Filho, A. (2007) There is Life beyond the Washington Consensus: An Introduction to Pro-Poor Macroeconomic Policies, *Review of Political Economy* 19 (4): 513–537.

Saad-Filho, A. (2011a) Crisis *in* Neoliberalism or Crisis *of* Neoliberalism? *Socialist Register*, pp. 242–259.

Saad-Filho, A. (2011b) Growth, Poverty and Inequality: Policies and Debates from the (Post) Washington Consensus to Inclusive Growth. *Indian Journal of Human Development* 5 (2): 321–344.

Saad-Filho, A. (2017), Neoliberalism, in Brennan D.M., Kristjanson-Gural D, Mulder C, Olsen E (edited by) *Routledge Handbook of Marxian Economics*, London: Routledge.

Saad-Filho, A. (2020a) *The Rise of Nationalist Authoritarianism and the Crisis of Neoliberalism*, http://ppesydney.net/the-rise-of-nationalist-authoritarianism-and-the-crisis-of-neoliberalism/.

Saad-Filho, A. (2020b) From COVID-19 to the End of Neoliberalism, *Critical Sociology* 46 (4–5), pp. 477–485.

Saad-Filho, A. (2020c) Endgame: From Crisis in Neoliberalism to Crises of Neoliberalism, *Human Geography* 14 (1), https://journals.sagepub.com/doi/abs/10.1177/1942778620962026?journalCode=huga.

Saad-Filho, A. (2021a) *Growth and Change in Neoliberal Capitalism: Essays in the Political Economy of Late Development*. Leiden: Brill.

Saad-Filho, A. (2021b) *The Age of Crisis: Neoliberalism, the Collapse of Democracy, and the Pandemic*. London: Palgrave.

Saad-Filho, A. (2021c) *Progressive Policies for Economic Development: Economic Diversification and Social Inclusion after Climate Change*. London: Routledge.

Saad-Filho, A. and Feil, F. (2023) From Climate Change to Sustainable and Inclusive Economies: A Policy Agenda, *Critical Sociology* 50 (1), https://journals.sagepub.com/doi/10.1177/08969205231160628.

Sandbu, M. (2020), *Huge Fiscal Spending is Needed to Fight the Coronavirus Downturn*, https://www.ft.com/content/9963f71e-67b2-11ea-800d-da70cff6e4d3.

Sawyer, M. (2022) *Financialization: Economic and Social Impacts*. Newcastle upon Tyne: Agenda Publishing.

Solty, I. (2020), *The Bio-Economic Pandemic and the Western Working Classes*, https://socialistproject.ca/2020/03/bioeconomic-pandemic-and-western-working-classes/.

Tcherneva, P.R. (2015), *When a Rising Tide Sinks Most Boats: Trends in U.S. Income Inequality*, Policy Note 2015/4, Levy Economics Institute.

van der Zwan, N. (2014) Making Sense of Financialization, *Socio-Economic Review* 12, pp.99–129.

Zuboff, S. (2019) *The Age of Surveillance Capitalism*. New York: Public Affairs Books.

CHAPTER 12

A Vanishing Army? Redefining the Industrial Reserve

Tom Brass

> And the migrants streamed in on the highways ... They had no argument, no system, nothing but their numbers and their needs. When there was work for a man, ten men fought for it – fought with a low wage. If that fella'll work for thirty cents, I'll work for twenty-five. If he'll take twenty-five, I'll do it for twenty. No, me, I'm hungry. I'll work for fifteen.
>
> A description by John Steinbeck of the way labour market competition operated in America during the Great Depression.[1]

∴

> In order to maintain car production [at the Renault factory] in France, the employees had to redouble their efforts, show that their expertise was more valuable than low-cost manpower abroad. The consequence of this fierce competition was an ever-greater exploitation of all workers: those who wanted to keep their jobs, and those who hoped to get one. Both sides lost.
>
> A description by David Foenkinos of the way labour market competition operated in France some eight decades later[2]

∴

---

1 Steinbeck (1939: 343).
2 Foenkinos (2020: 217–218). Although both epigraphs are drawn from writers of fiction, each nevertheless manages to encapsulate the same impact of labour market competition – eighty years apart – on workers employed by capital in different contexts.

1 Introduction: Things We No Longer Talk About

Socialists have long argued that the industrial reserve army is one of the most powerful weapons in the economic armoury at the disposal of capital in its struggle with the working class. As capitalism goes global, so too does this method deployed by producers to keep down labour costs, discourage unionisation, and the emergence or consolidation of class solidarity. Accordingly, an expanding industrial reserve army, generated as a result of globalization, enables capital to adopt a divide-and-rule policy, which involves turning workers of different non-class identities (ethnicity, nationality, gender) against one another in their attempts to secure employment. It has become a common tactic utilized by employers in a *laissez faire* economic context where capital has unfettered access to what is now a global industrial reserve army, giving additional momentum to the 'race to the bottom' in pay and conditions. This is especially true of contexts where migrants are many and jobs are few, a situation when competition in the labour market develops in a particularly intense manner.

Given this negative history in relation to the political economy of capitalist development, why then has the industrial reserve either vanished from consideration by social science discourse, or else – much the same thing – been redefined in positive terms? How is it that a concept that Marxism regards as crucial to an understanding of the way in which class struggle fails or succeeds, one that now is more relevant than ever as capitalism has become a systemically global phenomenon, no longer sparks the kind of political interest it once enjoyed? In an attempt to address these questions, therefore, the object here is to examine and account for the different outcomes of contrasting approaches to the industrial reserve, both within and outside Marxist theory.

The ambivalence regarding surplus labour, combining a recognition of its negative aspects, an acceptance of its importance for the accumulation process with an inability to dispense with this economic role, underlines the dilemmas facing liberal defenders of capitalism, extending from Beveridge a century ago to Fukuyama now.[3] For their part, those who address what Marx said about the industrial reserve, fall into one of two categories. First, upholders of the view that what Marx said originally about its negative political and economic impact on working class solidarity (= divide and rule tactic) still applies. And second, an approach that maintains what Marx really meant was the opposite,

---

3 For the difficulties facing the current attempt by Fukuyama to address – never mind resolve – issues raised by a globally burgeoning industrial reserve, see Brass (2023). On the earlier views of Beveridge, see below.

in that the surplus labour composed of migrants is not an obstacle to working class empowerment but much rather is today found to be in the vanguard of the struggle against capital: for this reason, therefore, the industrial reserve should be viewed positively.

By contrast, those who currently do not address what Marx said about the industrial reserve, subscribe instead to an epistemologically and politically different interpretation. Unlike Marxists, whose materialist analyses have been – and are still – on the disempowerment of class, exponents of 'new' populist postmodern theory associated with the 'cultural turn' focus on the empowerment of non-class identity (ethnicity, nationality). Consequently, for them the process of migration is to be defined in positive terms, as the exercise by the 'subaltern'/'multitude' from Third World nations of its human rights. Thus access to the labour markets of metropolitan capitalist nations is depicted as no more than equitable reparations for the long history of exploitation/ oppression their populations experienced as a result of colonization.

The absence of references to the industrial reserve or downplaying the analytical importance of its current role in and impact on accumulation, together with its form of class struggle, has to be seen as part of a much wider political and intellectual process. On the one hand the expulsion from the Marxist canon of key concepts, all central to its logic, while on the other attempts at inclusion within the same theoretical framework of non- and even anti-Marxist constructs, all of which negate the Marxist political dynamic. Over the recent past it has been possible to encounter claims to be following a Marxist approach by those who have in effect stripped away many or all of its main conceptual apparatus.[4] What one is left with in these circumstances is, variously, Marxism-without-value-theory, Marxism-without-a-proletariat, Marxism-without-class, Marxism-without-struggle, Marxism-without-revolution, and Marxism-without-a-socialist-transition.[5]

To this list can be added two further variants. First, Marxism-without-the-industrial-reserve: and second, the-industrial-reserve-as-a-form-of-worker-empowerment, in effect turning Marx on his head: a similar negation, albeit of a different kind. Those going down these two paths, each of which is the subject of the analysis which follows, usually signal this fact with announcements of

---

4   In the course of the last two decades, a number of book chapters, critical articles, review articles, and book reviews by me have chartered both the fact of and the reasons for this kind of shift.
5   Almost a century ago, similar kinds of approach were labelled by Trotsky (1934) as accounts of the 1917 Russian Revolution written by epigones, or 'disciples who corrupt the doctrines of their teachers'.

an intent to reinterpret Marxism, on the basis not of what Marx actually wrote but rather what he really meant, what he might have meant had he thought about it some more, and what he would undoubtedly have said or written had he not at the time fallen asleep in an armchair in front of the fire.

The following section examines why historically both Marxism and liberalism have regarded the industrial reserve as negative. By contrast, section 3 considers why more recent interpretations have redefined surplus labour as positive. It is argued here that, as long as capital has access to the industrial reserve, possessing thereby a capacity to restructure its labour process, this will continue to pose difficulties for the formation/consolidation by *all* workforce components of a uniform political consciousness and organizational solidarity.

2   Marxist and Liberal Views of the Industrial Reserve

Marxists generally, and Marx together with Engels in particular, have always been clear about the interrelatedness of the formation, the characteristics and the crucial political and economic role of the industrial reserve. Unlike other approaches, which perceived surplus labour as an unintended development (= anomaly), Marxist theory categorized the industrial reserve as the *sine qua non* of the accumulation process, a major weapon in the class struggle available to producers. Consisting of those who are either under-employed or wholly unemployed, the industrial reserve ensures that wages and conditions will always remain at levels below what they might otherwise reach.[6] Though not absolute, as Marx himself accepted, the general impoverishment (= 'immizeration') of the workforce as a whole means that the 'more extensive ... the pauperized sections of the working class and the industrial reserve army, the greater is official pauperism.' This, emphasized Marx, '*is the absolute general law of capitalist accumulation.*'[7]

---

6   On this point, Marx (1976: 790) observed: 'Taking them as a whole, the general movements of wages are exclusively regulated by the expansion and contraction of the industrial reserve army ... [t]hey are not therefore determined by the variations of the absolute numbers of the working population, but by the varying proportions in which the working class is divided into an active army and a reserve army, by the increase or diminution in the relative amount of the surplus population, by the extent to which it is alternately absorbed and set free'.
7   Marx (1976: 798, original emphasis).

2.1 19th Century Marxist Views

The industrial reserve operates in seemingly contradictory ways. On the one hand, it holds some elements that producers may never call upon as full-time replacement employees: as well as being a source of labour-power that is unfree, the category of surplus labour also contains those whom Marx described as belonging to the lumpenproletariat (vagabonds, criminals, prostitutes).[8] Despite remaining outside the labour market, such components remain valuable for capital as a potential threat – replacement workers, strike-breakers – to permanent labour that is well-paid. On the other, the rapid use-up of labour-power means that capital needs access to the industrial reserve merely to replenish its workforce, a point Marx stressed.[9] Much the same emphasis was made by Engels when observing both that 'the length of life of labour-power is immaterial to the capitalists', and that '[t]he capitalist sees only the continuously available surplus population and wears it out'.[10] The latter notwithstanding, Marx was adamant that the reproduction of the industrial reserve was not determined by population increase.[11]

These contrasting economic roles – those constantly required as replacement labour, those never to be employed as replacement workers – of the industrial reserve combine to regulate the labour market on behalf of capital.[12] Hence the presence of the industrial reserve serves multiple ends: it

---

[8] See Marx (1976: 797), who elaborates: 'Pauperism is the hospital of the active labour-army and the dead weight of the industrial reserve army'.

[9] According to Marx (1976: 795), therefore, 'the consumption of labour-power by capital is so rapid that the worker has already more or less completely lived himself out when he is only half-way through his life [and] falls into the ranks of the surplus population'.

[10] Having calculated the level of exploitation inherent in the working day, Engels (n.d.- b: 69, original emphasis) commented: 'These facts prove that capital regards the labourer as nothing else than *labour-power*, all of whose time is labour-time to the extent that this itself is at all possible at a given moment, and that the length of life of labour-power is immaterial to the capitalist [who] sees only the continuously available surplus population and wears it out … Capital is ruthless towards the health and length of life of the labourer'.

[11] 'Capitalist production can by no means content itself with the quantity of disposable labour-power which the natural increase of population yields,' noted Marx (1976: 788), since '[i]t requires for its unrestricted activity and industrial reserve army which is independent of these natural limits'.

[12] As Marx (1976: 792) notes: 'The industrial reserve army, during periods of stagnation and average prosperity, weighs down the active army of workers; during periods of overproduction and feverish activity, it puts a curb on their pretensions. The relative surplus population is therefore the background against which the law of the demand and supply of labour does its work. It confines the field of action of this law to the limits absolutely convenient to capital's drive to exploit and dominate the workers'.

keeps wages down and discourages the formation by all workers of an inclusive consciousness of class.[13] The significance of the latter objective is crucial: the industrial reserve hinders long-term goals, and how common political interests might be realized politically as a result of organization in pursuit not just of improved conditions and higher wages but also of broader systemic change, designed to bring about a socialist transition. Instead of the latter, the industrial reserve generates splits within the ranks of labour together with the privileging by workers of non-class identities as a way of protecting existing jobs. Moreover, this is a reactionary trend that becomes more important with the global spread of capitalism, the consequent internationalisation of labour market competition, and the increased levels of immigration.

As pointed out by Engels, the introduction of machinery into the industrial labour process not only enhances productive efficiency but also throws more and more people out of work who then – as members of the industrial reserve army – can be used by capital to force down the wages/conditions of those who remain in employment.[14] Current forms and pace of deskilling, plus the

---

13   Among those who recognized this was Engels, who in a letter to Schlüter, dated 30 March 1892, observed (Marx and Engels, 1934: 496–7): 'Your great obstacle in America, it seems to me, lies in the exceptional position of the native workers. Up to 1848 one could only speak of a permanent native working class as an exception: the small beginnings of it in the cities in the East always had still the hope of becoming farmers or bourgeois. Now a working class has developed and has also to a great extent organized itself on trade union lines ... [However,] immigrants are divided into different nationalities and understand neither one another nor, for the most part, the language of the country. And your bourgeoisie knows much better even than the Austrian Government how to play off one nationality against the other: Jews, Italians, Bohemians, etc., against Germans and Irish, and each one against the other, so that differences in the standard of life of different workers exist, I believe, in New York to an extent unheard of elsewhere. And added to this is the total indifference of a society which has grown up on a purely capitalist basis ... towards the human lives which succumb in the competitive struggle: "there will be plenty more, and more than we want, of these damned Dutchmen, Irishmen, Italians, Jews and Hungarians;" and beyond them in the background stands John Chinaman, who far surpasses them all in his ability to live on dirt.'.

14   'If the introduction and increase of machinery meant the displacement of millions of hand workers by a few machine workers,' Engels (n.d.- a: 307–8) noted, 'the improvement of machinery means the displacement of larger and larger numbers of machine workers themselves, and ultimately the creation of a mass of available wage workers exceeding the average requirements of capital for labour – a complete industrial reserve army, as I called it as long ago as 1845 [in *The Condition of the Working Class in England*] – a reserve that would be available at periods when industry was working at high pressure, but would be thrown out onto the streets by the crash inevitably following the boom; a reserve that would at all times be like a leaden weight on the feet of the working class in their fight for existence against capital, a regulator to keep wages down to the low level which suits the needs of capital. Thus it comes about that machinery, to use Marx's phrase, becomes

enhanced rapidity of labour-power use-up, make possible and indeed necessary the activation of hitherto unutilized elements belonging to the industrial reserve army of labour.[15] Although the latter encompasses those thrown out of work as a result of mechanization and technification, members of the reserve army can be incorporated by capital into its labour process for two distinct reasons. The first refers to a reserve to be drawn on when market demand expands, and capitalists need further amounts of labour-power. By contrast, the second refers to those who – as a mass of unemployed also part of the reserve army – are drawn on by capitalists not so much to increase production but rather as a weapon in their struggle against those still in work.[16] In this second role, members of the reserve army are no longer used simply in addition to an existing workforce but now instead of the latter.

Accordingly, it is crucial to distinguish between two kinds of migrant labour: that bought in *to supplement* the existing workforce, because the latter is insufficient to meet the needs of production. This is termed an as-well-as arrangement. The second form possesses a very different dynamic: migrants recruited in order *to displace* the existing workforce, because the latter either won't work for the low pay and conditions on offer, or – if in post – are deemed too costly to employ, the object being to replace it with cheaper foreign labour.

---

the most powerful weapon in the war of capital against the working class, that the instruments of labour constantly tear the means of subsistence out of the hands of the labourer, that the very product of the labourer is turned into an instrument for his subjection ... Thus it comes about that the excessive labour of some becomes the necessary condition for the lack of employment of others, and that large-scale industry, which hunts all over the world for new consumers, restricts the consumption of the masses at home to famine minimum and thereby undermines its own internal market'.

15 On the rapidity of labour-power use-up, Marx (1976: 789–90) commented: 'The over-work of the employed part of the working class swells the ranks of its reserve, while, conversely, the greater pressure that the reserve by its competition exerts on the employed workers forces them to submit to over-work and subjects them to the dictates of capital. The condemnation of one part of the working class to enforced idleness by the over-work of the other part, and *vice-versa*, becomes a means of enriching the individual capitalists, and accelerates at the same time the production of the industrial reserve army on a scale corresponding with the progress of social accumulation'.

16 Sweezy (1942: 99, emphasis added) recognized the importance of this distinction, observing that 'the increasing use of machinery, which in itself means a higher organic composition of capital, sets free workers and thus creates "relative overpopulation" or the reserve army. Marx stresses the point that the existence of unemployed labourers is conducive to the setting up of new industries with a relatively low organic composition of capital and hence a relatively high rate of profit ... *It would seem, however, that a more important effect of the reserve army is ... through competition on the labour market with the active labour force, to depress the rate of wages and in this way to elevate the rate of surplus value*'.

This is termed an instead-of arrangement, one that historically and currently generates huge antagonism within the ranks of the working class affected, an hostility that frequently resorts to discourse about ethnic, national or gender 'otherness'.

It is argued here that the combination of the global spread of capitalist development, the internationalization of the industrial reserve army, and the restructuring of the labour process, has been accompanied by the instead-of form. Significantly, perhaps, this does not prevent employers from insisting that they recruit migrants only because no locals are available or willing to do the work, a thinly disguised attempt to represent merely as supplementing what is actually its 'other' – displacing the existing workforce. Clearly, it is the latter form that drives capitalist restructuring, given the importance of cost considerations where accumulation is concerned. Unsurprisingly, therefore, when asked why they prefer a migrant workforce, capitalists deploy the politically less contentious addition-to version rather than the instead-of form.

The assumption that those expelled from the labour force by the application of machinery and technology would – after a brief sojourn in the reserve army – find alternative employment, is both pervasive and misplaced. It is linked to the notion that such workers would be employed as a result of investment in new enterprises by capitalists whose enhanced profits derived from the original labour-displacing strategy. This view is problematic, since it applies only when capital and labour are national in scope, and not international. Where the latter is the case, capital is able to do two things: either to invest elsewhere, in contexts where labour-power is available and even cheaper; or to employ (perhaps even to import) migrants who meet the same requirements. Whichever the instance, the outcome is the same: any new jobs created do not necessarily go to those expelled from the labour process because of technification/mechanization of production. The obviousness of this outcome notwithstanding, it is unfortunately still possible to hear – even from some on the left – the mantra that workers displaced in this manner will automatically find employment in new industries created by capital.

In the course of the Great Depression of the 1930s, the 1939–45 war, and its immediate aftermath, when Keynesianism was said to have solved the issue of unemployment, the industrial reserve army again moved to the centre of the political agenda, both for the liberalism of Beveridge and for neo-Marxism of Kalecki, and the Marxism of Sweezy and Dobb at that early conjuncture, and – much later – of Glyn. Notwithstanding their political differences, the negative perception both that the connection between unemployment and the continued access by capital to unregulated forms/sources of surplus labour, and that state intervention was required in order to break this connection, was an interpretation shared by all of them.

2.2 20th Century Liberal Views

Liberal ambivalence concerning the role, impact, and desirability of the industrial reserve structured the approach during the 1930s and 1940s of William Beveridge to the creation in post-war Britain of the welfare state. Anxiety regarding what he termed the 'glutting of the labour market', linked by him both to 'under-employment' as a form of sweating, and to the beating down of average earnings to subsistence level, was balanced against the need as he saw it of how to provide properly maintained reserves of labour. Underwriting this ambivalence was apprehension that a failure to address the economic connection between these phenomena might undermine the legitimacy of the accumulation process itself, and thus empower those advocating socialism. Beveridge himself recognized the possibility of such a link, conceding that 'the most general effect of war is to make the common people more important'.[17]

Of significance, therefore, is that Beveridge traced the perpetuation of what he termed 'the four giant evils' – Disease, Ignorance, Squalor, and Idleness – back to the presence and operation during the pre-war era of the reserve army of labour.[18] His 'perplexity' about the latter stems from what Beveridge regards as the 'central paradox of the unemployed problem': the juxtaposition between on the one hand rising remuneration of labour and on the other the 'irreducible' growth of unemployment.[19] Although as a liberal he appeared mystified

---

17   Beveridge (1943: 109). Even before the 1939–45 war, Beveridge (International Labour Office, 1924: 7) drew attention not just to the long-recognized connection between casual employment, labour market competition, economic crisis and increasing poverty, but also to the necessity of addressing this politically. Hence the observation that '[i]t has been for years now established how casual employment produces unemployment, and the remedy by what is called decasualisation is equally certain and agreed. It is little short of a scandal that, merely because of the difficulty of getting things done practically, we leave that side of the problem of unemployment practically untouched'.

18   About the link between the industrial reserve, unemployment, and impoverishment, Beveridge (1931a: 107–108) observes: 'The social consequences of this under-employment and of under-payment or sweating ... are ultimately indistinguishable. Each means the maintenance, as an integral part of industry, of a low and miserable form of life ... Here if anywhere is to be seen the beating down of the remuneration of labour under competition to bare subsistence ... By casual employment therefore real earnings may be and are driven down to a normal level far below the lowest rate possible in regular industry however plentiful the competition and unorganized the workmen'.

19   See Beveridge (1931a: 70), who concludes (Beveridge, 1931a: 95) that '[t]he system of casual employment to meet fluctuations [in business] requires the maintenance of reserves of labour at all the points at which men are engaged. A considerable part of these reserves

by this, a Marxist would point out that it corresponds to a situation in which the industrial reserve comes into its own: when faced with rising wages (a tight labour market) employers resort to cheaper forms of labour-power.[20] Hence not merely to the liking of capitalist producers, but crucially their need for the industrial reserve, plentiful and on station, to be drawn upon as and when required.[21]

As significant is that his motivation for advocating the welfare state as a solution to the impoverishment and misery inflicted by the industrial reserve during 1930s Depression, therefore, was in part due to a wish to avoid a 'from below' challenge to any attempt at a return to pre-war economic and social conditions.[22] This concern was itself signalled in the epigraph on the title page of the Beveridge report: 'Misery generates hate', not just between different components of the working population but also between the latter and employers.[23] An additional political concern was that a failure to ameliorate

---

is so irregularly employed as to be in chronic poverty. On every day some part of them is standing idle.' This describes as clearly as necessary one major economic role of the industrial reserve: merely to 'be there', to be called upon as and when necessary.

[20] Commenting on those employed in unskilled and unorganized work, Beveridge (1931a: 69–70) noted: 'The glut of labour in them is notorious. Has there ever ... been a time when employers could not get practically at a moment's notice all the labourers they required? Is not this indeed the root of bewilderment and despair in regard to the unemployed problem that there appears to be always and everywhere an inexhaustible excess in the supply of labour over the demand?'.

[21] Beveridge (1931a: 76, 80) outlines the manner in which producers operate their labour reserve: 'The general formula for the supply of labour in an industry appears then to be this: for work requiring ... at most ninety-eight men, there will actually be eighty in regular employment and twenty in irregular employment; there will be a hundred in all ... [t]he twenty, however, are as much part of the industrial system as are the eighty; the reserve is as indispensable as the regulars ... every element of chance in the competition for employment ... tends to swell the actual number of individuals between whom any definite amount of work is distributed and to decrease the share of each, down to the limit fixed by the standard of subsistence'.

[22] 'I want to be quite certain than I can change the person who governs me without having to shoot him,' argued Beveridge (1943: 92), adding: 'That is the essence of Democracy, that you can have a peaceful change of governors without shooting. To me a country is not a Democracy ... if you cannot change the Government by a perfectly peaceful method of putting your cross on a piece of paper'.

[23] The epigraph, Beveridge (1944: 15–16) explained, 'comes from the account given by Charlotte Brontë, in the second chapter of *Shirley* of the handloom weavers who one hundred and twenty-five years ago were being driven into unemployment and miserable revolt by the introduction of knitting frames.' He continues: 'To look to individual employers for the maintenance of demand and full employment is absurd. These things are not within the power of employers. They must therefore be undertaken by the State, under the supervision and pressure of democracy, applied through the Parliament men'.

the impact of the industrial reserve would fuel the rise of racism. Beveridge saw mass unemployment as leading inevitably to a war of all against all, as every person 'appears as the enemy of his fellows in the scramble for jobs.'[24] The latter in turn generates 'the growth of jealous restrictions', including controls on the free movement of labour and opposition to technology, fostering 'still uglier growths' such as anti-semitism, anti-foreigner sentiment, and hostility to the employment of women as workers. All these developments were attributed by him to a 'failure to use our productive powers' in order to solve unemployment: only when this had been done would there no longer be conflict between capital and labour.

In the opinion of Beveridge, however, the goal of full employment was not just unrealizable but undesirable. Consequently, the industrial reserve will never entirely disappear, nor did he think it desirable that it should do so. This he attributed both to seasonal fluctuations in demand for labour, and to an insistence on his part that the policies advocated 'does not mean giving to everyone security in his particular job'.[25] As a political liberal, therefore, Beveridge still viewed the market as making a positive contribution to society. Because he believed in 'citizen liberties' and private enterprise – 'on condition that those liberties are exercised responsibly' – Beveridge joined the Liberal Party.[26] Whereas the economic programme of the Labour Party at that conjuncture was premised on nationalisation of key industries, so as to enable both regulation and planning, Beveridge had 'no bias in favour of nationalisation' and was content to leave 'much the greater part of industry to private enterprise'.[27]

---

24   'So long as chronic mass unemployment seems possible', noted Beveridge (1944: 248), 'each man appears as the enemy of fellows in the scramble for jobs. As long as there is a scramble for jobs it is idle to deplore the inevitable growth of jealous restrictions, of demarcations, of organized or voluntary limitations of output, of resistance to technical advance. By this scramble are fostered many still uglier growths – hatred of foreigners, hatred of Jews, enmity between the sexes. Failure to use our productive powers is the source of an interminable succession of evils. When that failure has been overcome, the way will be open to progress in unity without fear'.
25   Beveridge (1944: 126ff.).
26   Beveridge (1946: 57).
27   Beveridge (1946: 63). His commitment to the continuation of the market is evident from an earlier defence of *laissez-faire* economic policy, where – along with co-authors to an edited volume on tariffs (Beveridge, 1931b: vi) – it was stated that 'we should all think it a disaster, if the policy of Free Trade which has served Britain so well materially, as through her it has served as an inspiration to all who in any land have worked for a good understanding among nations, were today to be sacrificed to ignorance or panic or jealousy or specious calculations of a moment's gain'.

In keeping with Keynesian demand management, what the Beveridge Report advocated was using the State to give workers more purchasing power, the spending of which would in turn create demand for commodities manufactured by capitalist producers in Britain.[28] Its object was to establish some control over an unplanned market economy, not its elimination: in the words of Beveridge, 'planned marketing and production of primary products, both agricultural and mineral, is an essential condition for the stabilization of demand for manufacturing products'.[29] His aim was to save capitalism, and he obtained the support of conservatives and employers for his programme by arguing not just that better-paid workers formed consumers for commodities but also that healthcare and other welfare costs would henceforth be met by the state.

2.3 20th Century Marxist Views

During the 1940s and 1950s, amidst end-of-ideology triumphalism accompanying claims that Keynesianism had banished recurring capitalist crises, perceived as the ability of capital actually/potentially to produce abundance, thereby providing workers with full employment and higher living standards, Marxists took a different view. Unlike liberals such as Beveridge, who thought that full employment was unachievable, Marxist/neo-Marxist economists like Kalecki, Sweezy, and Dobb argued that full employment was never going to be acceptable to capitalists. Each of them positioned the issue of the industrial reserve in relation to the need on the part of producers for enhanced labour market competition in order to impose a check on wages and boost profitability, and thus untrammelled access to the industrial reserve. The difficulty faced by producers is simply put: where capitalist demand for labour-power exceeds supply, wages tend to rise. What, therefore, asks Sweezy, 'keeps wages in check so that surplus value and accumulation may continue as characteristic and essential features of capitalist production?'.[30]

The answer to this, Sweezy indicated, was the presence of the reserve army, which 'consists of unemployed workers who, through their active competition

---

28 On the necessity of a greater role for the state in post-war Britain, see Beveridge (1943: 90ff.). His support for Keynesian theory is also clearly signalled (Beveridge, 1944: 106–7).

29 Beveridge (1944: 103). Significantly, in the 1945 British general election – which Labour won by a landslide – the programme of the Conservative Party allocated economic importance to the continued role of the market ('free enterprise'), whereas that of the Labour Party sought to bring about full employment in industry by means of state planning (McCullum & Readman, 1947: 53–54).

30 Sweezy (1942: 87).

on the labour market, exercise a continuous downward pressure on the wage level.' This was linked by him to the problem of crisis, which stems from a situation where the reserve army, for whatever reason, shrinks, thereby eliminating the check it exercises on wages.[31] The result is that '[c]apitalists are forced to bid against one another for additional workers, wages rise, and surplus value is cut into,' with negative outcomes for investment and accumulation.[32] When wages start to increase, then is when the real significance of the industrial reserve comes into its own, as can be seen currently in cases where employers and their organizations call for more access to foreign workers: this is because 'the stronger the tendency of wages to rise, the stronger also will be the counteracting pressure of the reserve army.'[33]

In a lecture at Cambridge during 1942, Kalecki highlighted the potential fact of employer opposition to contraction in the industrial reserve on the grounds that 'lasting full employment is unsound from their point of view and that unemployment is an integral part of the "normal" capitalist system'.[34] For his part, Sweezy – like Marx – reiterated the point that the industrial reserve operates independently of population levels, underlining that 'Marx's great accomplishment was ... to free [the conceptualisation of the industrial reserve] from an otherwise fatal dependence on the Malthusian population dogma.'[35] At the start of the following decade, Dobb reinforced the earlier concern expressed by Kalecki, warning against the illusion that accumulation and full employment

---

31 '[T]hrough its relation to the reserve army,' explained Sweezy (1942: 90), 'the problem of crises assumes a central position in Marx's theoretical system. Whereas for the classical theorists, the problem was not so much to explain crises as to explain them away, for Marx capitalism without crises would be, in the final analysis, inconceivable'.

32 Sweezy (1942: 150).

33 Sweezy (1942: 88).

34 'We have considered the political reasons for the opposition to the policy of creating employment by government spending', noted Kalecki (1943: 326), adding: 'But even if this opposition were overcome – as it may well be under the pressure of the masses – the maintenance of full employment would cause social and political changes which would give new impetus to the opposition of business leaders. Indeed, under a regime of permanent full employment ... [t]he social position of the boss would be undermined, and the self-assurance and class-consciousness of the working class would grow. Strikes for wage increases and improvements in conditions of work would create political tension. [The] class instinct [of business leaders] tells them that lasting full employment is unsound from their point of view and that unemployment is an integral part of the "normal" capitalist system'.

35 Sweezy (1942: 89).

were compatible.³⁶ Presciently, it was pointed out by him that, sooner or later, capitalist profitability would require the reintroduction of unemployment, and with it an enhanced industrial reserve, and this is exactly what occurred, culminating in the rise and consolidation of *laissez-faire* deregulation from the 1980s onwards.

Maintaining or enhancing profitability in this way is crucial for any accumulation project in what is an increasingly competitive world market. For this reason, the global spread of capital during the post-war era made access to the industrial reserve not just easier but necessary. From the 1960s onwards the Green Revolution drove peasants in Third World nations (India, Mexico) off the land, thereby commencing the augmentation of the industrial reserve world-wide, while from the 1990s onwards the fall of the USSR released new sources of labour from Eastern Europe available for employment by capital in the European Union. Combined with the latter is the outsourcing made possible by the expansion in the industrial reserve throughout Asia, not least that of China, a development licensing what Glyn has referred to as a contraction in labour's share of national income coupled with 'Marx's rising rate of exploitation emerging, a century and a half after he first predicted it.'³⁷

It has therefore become possible for corporations either to outsource production to far-off locations where surplus labour already existed, or else to insource labour itself, from these same and other locations closer to where production was already based. Drawing on either or both these supplies of worker meant that producers were henceforth able to compete with rival capitalists as long as they restructured their own labour process. This employers did by

---

36   See Dobb (1955: 215–25), where he argued that capitalists viewed full employment as 'a situation where the sack has lost a good deal of its sting as a disciplinary weapon, with the virtual disappearance of the industrial reserve army'.

37   See Glyn (2006: 14), who comments: 'What makes China (and India) fundamentally different is the presence of vast reserves of labour previously isolated from the world economy ... This represents an enormous potential labour supply. Estimates of the numbers who may be pulled out of agriculture, where their incomes are very low, into industrial and service jobs in the towns range as high as 150–300 million ... These, together with tens of millions of urban unemployed, constitute a reserve army of labour of quite unprecedented magnitude.' He continues (Glyn, 2006: 15): 'China is producing large numbers of highly trained but still relatively cheap workers ... This could bring intense pressure on the jobs and working conditions of northern workers [as the] bargaining chips would be in the hands of capital to a degree not seen since the industrial revolution. The stylised fact of labour's share fluctuating in the 2/3 to 4/5 range could disappear too, with Marx's rising rate of exploitation emerging, a century and a half after he first predicted it.' Further details about the post-war background leading to this process can be found in Glyn (2007).

replacing those in better-paid permanent jobs with cheaper workers, either at home or abroad. Those belonging to the latter category are employed usually on a temporary or casual basis, a transformation that in some instances also corresponds to multiple forms of workforce substitution: of foreign migrants for locals, of unfree production relations for pre-existing free equivalents, and of age- or gender-specific forms of labour.[38]

Until the 1980s this restructuring was not possible: in 1960s Italy, for example, the strength of working-class organization and struggle, plus the absence as yet of cheap migrant labour, combined to prevent producers from taking advantage of the industrial reserve. 'The main point', noted one observer, 'is whether or not secondary workers are available to act as a potential source of competition for primary workers.'[39] The neoliberal turn from the 1980s, however, involving as it did deregulation, privatisation, and the adoption of *laissez-faire* economic policies, facilitated the cross-border movement of workers and money: the transfer of capital and labour between sending and receiving countries paved the way ultimately for segmentation of the labour market within metropolitan capitalist nations themselves. Such labour process restructuring, involving workforce decomposition/recomposition, was anticipated by Marx, and is described by him thus: 'On the one hand, therefore, with the progress of accumulation a larger variable capital sets more labour in motion without enlisting more workers; on the other, a variable capital of the same magnitude sets in motion more labour with the same mass of labour-power; and, finally, a

---

38 In the words of Marx (1976: 788), 'the development of the capitalist mode of production, and of the productivity of labour ... enables the capitalist, with the same outlay of variable capital, to set in motion more labour by greater exploitation (extensive or intensive) of each individual labour-power. [Hence] the capitalist buys with the same capital a greater mass of labour-power, as he progressively replaces skilled workers by less skilled, mature labour-power by immature, male by female, that of adults by that of young persons or children.' The fact of and the importance of changes in the age and gender division of labour, together with the link to the industrial reserve, are issues emphasized subsequently (Marx, 1976: 794–95): 'Both in the factories proper, and in the larger workshops ... large numbers of male workers are employed up to the age of maturity, but not beyond. Once they reach maturity, only a very small number continue to find employment in the same branches of industry, while the majority are regularly dismissed. This majority forms an element of the floating surplus population which grows with the extension of those branches of industry ... Capital demands more youthful workers, fewer adults'.

39 See Bruno (1979: 131) who points out that 'in Italy this competition did not take place, not only because the working class employed in the core of large and medium industrial firms (primary workers) resisted it successfully, but also because the surplus population (secondary workers) did not compete in the primary market'.

greater number of inferior labour-powers is set in motion by the displacement of more skilled labour-powers.'[40]

3 Interpretations of the Industrial Reserve as a Positive

In a basic sense, this section of the chapter marks what can only be described as a fundamental epistemological and political shift in the way the industrial reserve is interpreted. This entails a change from the undeniably negative one, held both by Marxism and by some liberals, to views – held by Basso, Mezzadra, and Bradley and Norhona, among others – that regard the industrial reserve as in some way positive.[41] The resulting break extends from those who see the industrial reserve merely as unimportant, or else politically empowering for the working class as a whole, as evidence for its progressive role in challenging capitalism, to those with a different focus, who regard it simply as empowering for migrants.[42] A variant of this is Basso, who insists that over the recent past migrant workers cannot be said to form part of the industrial reserve, since 'it remains the case that the majority of immigrant workers in the EU *are within the active army of labour, not the reserve army.*'[43] Thus the element of surplus labour has not so much vanished from the development debate as been redefined.

This negative→positive shift accompanied and indeed was made possible by the wider context: the rise of the 'new' populist postmodernism (= the 'cultural

---

40 Marx (1976: 788). However, the many references by Marx (and other Marxists) to the important role of female and child labour-power in the way producers have restructured the labour process historically, and still do so today, has not prevented some current observers from continuing to claim – erroneously – that Marxism ignores the fact that not all workers employed by capital are adult males.

41 Considered elsewhere (Brass, 2017: Chapter 19; Brass, 2021: Chapter 8; Brass, 2022: Chapter 7) are two other views about the industrial reserve, neither of which name it as such. On the one hand, therefore, are bourgeois economists who, like employers, regard surplus labour as a positive contribution to economic growth. On the other is the negative interpretation held by exponents of Great Replacement theory, which regards immigration simply as a process of cultural erosion.

42 Those who dismiss the industrial reserve as unimportant extend from the 1980s, when 'a number of recent feminist writers ... dismissed the relevance of the industrial reserve army to an understanding of women in capitalist society' (on which see Collins, 1984: 52) to its present categorization as 'functionalist' by an agrarian populist (Bernstein, 2021: 26, n 21). A variant of this view simply denies that surplus labour is a political issue, for an instance of which see 'The Tories concocted the myth of the "migrant crisis"', *The Guardian* (London), 7th November 2022.

43 Basso (2021: 6–7, original emphasis)

turn') which marked a privileging of non-class identity (ethnicity, nationality) and the conceptual displacement of Marxist theory about class and class struggle. It was this as much as anything that led to a move away from the industrial reserve as a locus/cause of worker disempowerment and to its redefinition as the empowerment of 'otherness', to be accepted and celebrated as such.[44] The latter was signalled by the way in which migration into metropolitan capitalist nations now became characterized in positive terms, as a 'human right' reflecting a 'common humanity', no more than a form of reparation owed by receiving countries to sending ones for having colonized them.

3.1 Border Wars

To this category it is necessary to add yet another view, drawn significantly from within Marxist theory: a positive one that claims to reinterpret what Marx himself meant, and on the basis of this to argue that the industrial reserve is the locus of struggle to undermine not working-class solidarity but much rather capitalism itself. Unsurprisingly, given a shared positive take on migration into metropolitan capitalism, this championing of an open-door policy in the name of Marx combines with similar calls made in the name of non-class identity. Accordingly, opposition to racism within the nation state – an uncontroversial proposition backed by all Marxists – is interpreted by exponents of 'the cultural turn' as an endorsement of the unconditional right to cross-border migration simply on the grounds of being 'other'. This in turn licenses an imperceptible slide into ideological support not just for open-door policy but also and thereby for an expanding industrial reserve, which fuels the political emergence of rival populisms. To the postmodern argument emphasizing the cultural identity of the migrant-as-'other'-nationality, therefore, the far right counterposes an argument similarly emphasizing cultural identity, only this time the nationality of the non-migrant worker.

According to Basso, Marx is wrongly invoked in order to justify anti-immigrant border controls, that it is his ideas about the capitalist industrial reserve that are deployed most frequently in this endeavour (especially in Italy

---

44 This shift reproduces the earlier approach to the question of immigration of Kennedy (1964), in whose footsteps Basso *et al* seemingly follow. Accepting that immigration was 'not always a happy experience', the issue for Kennedy (1964: 67–68) was one of 'adjustment' and 'assimilation', a process amounting to 'the expression in action of a positive belief in the possibility of a better life'. For current versions of the same argument, see Marquardt (2021) and Khanna (2022), together with an opinion piece by the latter 'Borders are holding back the world's eight billion', *Financial Times* (London), 12–13 November 2022.

and Germany), and that such interpretations distort Marx and decouples it from his political conclusions.[45] In the opinion of Basso, therefore, 'those who have claimed to be drawing on Marx's analysis of the industrial reserve army ... have distorted it and severed it from his political conclusions'.[46] For this reason, opponents of permanently open-door immigration into the EU who base this on what Marx wrote about the industrial reserve are nevertheless described by Basso as Nazis and racists, a label applied to three commentators in particular: Diego Fusaro, Sahra Wagenknecht, and Wolfgang Streek.[47] A consequence of their breaking with Marxist internationalism, argues Basso, is an espousal of nationalism. According to each of them, therefore, immigration supresses national wage levels, national resources are insufficient to meet the requirements of both locals and immigrants, and immigration generates culture wars within the nation.[48]

Basso is right to blame Fusaro for thinking that the capitalist state can be relied on to regulate the labour market on behalf of workers, a view Basso correctly describes as 'empty idealism'.[49] Marx himself certainly did not believe this to be the case, although currently there are indeed purportedly leftist analyses in the sphere of development studies which maintain just this, arguing for political solutions to *laissez-faire* that simply entail a return to a 'kinder'/'caring' capitalist state.[50] For this reason Basso is also right to criticize the nationalism not just of Fusaro but also of Wagenknecht and Streek, all of whom imagine that working class political interests can safely be left in the hands of a state apparatus that is capitalist.

In defence of their core argument – that borders should be abolished – Bradley and Noronha take issue with the leftist case that such a policy would undermine both the livelihood and the organizational capacity of workers

---

45 See Basso (2021: 217–238). The references here are to a copy of the same text but with a different numbering (Basso, 2021: 1–21), kindly sent me by its author.
46 Basso (2021: 8ff.).
47 Wagenknecht is a member of the left in the Bundestag and author of a critique of identity politics (*Die Selbstgerechten*/The self-righteous), while Streek (2017) is a sociologist who has written about the political economy of German society. Each is accused (Basso, 2021: 13) of 'falsification of Marx's thought', and further 'the posture of both our heroes is of people who stand firmly on the side of the weakest, of the "lower classes", the working class, against the strong powers of global capital that inordinately swell the industrial army with migrants'.
48 For his part, Streek wishes to close borders to asylum seekers as well as economic migrants.
49 Basso (2021: 10–12).
50 Among those who advocate a return to a 'kinder'/'caring' capitalist state is Jan Breman (on which see Brass 2018).

currently in jobs.[51] It is clear, moreover, that the migration pattern they envisage is one composed of those who want the right 'to work, to join family, to access welfare benefits and healthcare, and to move freely'.[52] Border abolition and its 'struggle for freedom', they then observe, licenses nothing less than an ability 'to move and stay', which is precisely the kind of policy favoured by capitalists.[53] Subsequently they seem to recognize that this case about the desirability of open borders is in lockstep with the pursuit by capital of access to the industrial reserve: this notwithstanding, they shift blame away from capital and towards colonialism, doubling down on their original argument.[54]

Equating border controls with a colonial legacy that discriminates against ethnic 'otherness', underlines the extent to which Bradley and Noronha regard any objection to their advocacy of an open-door approach as merely racist.[55] It comes as no surprise that any questioning of – let alone expressing concerns about – immigration is dismissed by them simply as evidence of racism.[56] In what is a reductive approach, therefore, everything is presented as an effect of

---

51 Noting that 'The intensification of violent and spectacular bordering is intimately connected to the ascendancy of racist, nationalist and rightwing governments', Bradley and Noronha (2022: 2, 3) continue: 'But this is not only a problem on the right. Voices across the political spectrum assert that borders are sensible and necessary. Many political parties and even trade unions argue that borders protect the working classes from low wages caused by a surplus of migrant labour', before switching to a version of discourse about 'revenge colonialism': 'To sustain this account of borders … requires a deep historical amnesia about colonialism'.

52 See Bradley and Noronha (2022: 6).

53 Bradley and Noronha (2022: 9–10).

54 'Clearly, border abolition needs to be distinguished from … arguments for "open borders"', note Bradley and Noronha (2022: 52), 'and this requires a more critical account of the relationship between capitalism and immigration control'. Much the same contradictory procedure informs their argument regarding nationalism and racism, momentarily conceded as not simply an ideology confined to whites (Bradley and Noronha, 2022: 25–26). Although the fact of ethnic conflict in African and Asian countries after the end of colonial rule is acknowledged, this is attributed largely to the impact of newly independent nations of colonialism.

55 'Despite many successful struggles for formal rights and recognition,' insist Bradley and Noronha (2022: 54–55), 'the structural inequalities forged by colonialism remain, mediated more indirectly by immigration controls and restrictive citizenship regimes. This is one of the ways in which we might describe our contemporary world order as racial, or racist: the borders between nation-states perpetuate hierarchies made by colonialism'.

56 See Bradley and Noronha (2022: 15ff., 25, 29), whose catch-all definition of racism is so inclusive that any/every form of economic disadvantage is attributed to this identity. Despite accepting that there are 'obvious class differences' within countries, nationalism is also categorized merely as another kind of racism.

ethnicity, to which the only solution is border abolition ('anti-racists must seek the abolition of borders').

Part of the difficulty faced by Bradley and Noronha is that they conflate two distinct issues, and thus two separate problems. The undifferentiated claim that borders do not 'protect people's rights', therefore, overlooks what under capitalism are divergent interests: of workers in the receiving country, and those in the sending one. There are two ways of looking at borders in a capitalist system, ones that are not just different but potentially antagonistic. To the migrant, a border constitutes a bar to his/her empowerment, in the form of higher wages, improved work conditions, and better livelihood prospects when compared with what exists in the sending country. In the case of those already employed in metropolitan capitalist nations, by contrast, 'rights' – livelihoods, wages/conditions, secure employment that is permanent – are seen as protected by borders, insofar as the latter prevent yet more acute labour market competition.

In keeping with this, Mezzadra looks at the problem of borders simply from the viewpoint of a non-class-specific migrant (= 'the right to escape', 'the autonomy of migration'), not the migrating worker, nor the worker in the country of destination.[57] Such an approach makes it impossible to make common cause with labourers in the latter context when one is effectively in competition with them for the same jobs, the getting of which by the 'escaping' migrant at the expense of an actual/potential worker in another country is the only thing that seems to be seen by Mezzadra as a legitimate political objective.

For his part, Basso argues against '[t]hose who speak of the need to reinstate frontiers, walls and boundaries', which suggests that he, too, favours an open-door approach to the issue of borders.[58] He invokes Marx's internationalism as a justification for an open-door approach, observing that at a time when 'bosses were importing "foreign workers" and "transferring manufacture to countries where there is a cheap labour force"', the struggle against capital 'must become international. Anything but "political control of cross-border flows" and the closing of frontiers!'. Subsequently, however, although this is qualified somewhat, Basso nevertheless insists that eliminating open borders (by regulation/closure) would have no effect on 'workers' problems'.[59]

---

57   Mezzadra (2006).
58   Basso (2021: 11).
59   'As for borders,' he comments (Basso, 2021: 16–17), 'it would be naïve to think that their removal would solve everything – that is true. But we can be sure that none of the workers' problems would be solved through the closing of borders, with all the associated rhetoric and racist practices'.

3.2 Human Flourishing, but Whose?

The case made by Basso about the industrial reserve is based on a number of problematic claims. To begin with, he doubts that there are those who 'celebrate migration ... as an inherently positive model, at once integrative and emancipatory', an argument which – lacking exponents – is described by him as a 'phantom-subject'. This is quite simply wrong: not only does he himself seemingly endorse just such a positive view (see below), but the list of those who also subscribe to it is long, very long. Supportive of the positive view deemed absent are the non-economic and migrant-centric arguments of much journalistic, NGO, and academic discourse, informed as these are by concepts like justice, citizenship and human rights.[60] The latter also inform the case against borders advanced by Mezzadra and by Bradley and Noronha.

In line with the non-economic epistemology of the 'new' populist postmodernism, justice and citizenship are conceptualized by Mezzadra not in objective but subjective terms: rather than being defined by the receiving country, therefore, citizenship is said to derive simply from grassroots culture of the migrant him/herself.[61] Although misleadingly labelled by him an 'alternative modernity', this notion of citizenship, rooted as it is in a misplaced Thirdworldism, licenses an uncritical acceptance of ideological forms in the sending nation, thereby leaving intact structures advantageous to capitalism. Among the latter are kinship and quasi-kinship relations, the hierarchy and authority of which can be – and have been – used to enforce bonded labour arrangements on migrants.[62]

The object of border abolition, as perceived by Bradley and Noronha, is similarly problematic: 'new ways of caring for one another' leading to 'human flourishing'. In their opinion, 'rights for non-citizens' amounts to 'recuperating the long-unfulfilled promise of human rights.'[63] The opposition by Bradley and

---

60 For details of those holding such views, see Brass (2017: Chapter 19; and 2021: 215ff.). More recent examples in the UK press include 'Ukrainians could fill job vacancies in Britain, if only they could get visas', *The Guardian* (London), 1st June 2022; and 'Here's the best way for Britain to solve the migrant crisis: give them work visas', *The Guardian* (London), 3rd November 2022. That well-meaning NGOs which supply provisions and/or shelter to those who compose the industrial reserve without addressing the wider systemic cause merely perpetuate its existence was recognized long ago by Beveridge (1931a: 109), who observed that 'the danger of subsidising casual employment by public or private relief without improving the conditions of the casual labourer is a very real one'.

61 See, for example, Mezzadra (2011b), Balibar, Mezzadra and Samaddar (2012), and Mezzadra and Neilson (2013).

62 For the use of kinship and quasi-kinship authority to enforce bonded labour relations, see Brass (1999: 57ff., 125ff.).

63 On the centrality of human rights to their approach, see Bradley and Noronha (2022: 28, 32ff., 39).

Noronha both to citizenship and to nationalism derives from the idea that such identities legitimize and thus underwrite the existence of borders.[64] Unlike Marxism, they interpret immigration control as a relation involving not classes but nations. Since it is this imbalance between 'grossly unequal nation-states' – not classes within them – that gives rise to and sustains borders, Bradley and Noronha maintain that a national boundary together with its accompanying ideology of citizenship perpetuate 'inequality, injustice and harm.' Their case departs from analyses in which the acquisition by the immigrant of citizenship is seen as positive, as a desirable outcome of the migration process: instead, Bradley and Noronha argue that as the concept of citizen is supportive of border divisions, it must be seen as a negative identity, one that justifies barriers separating countries.[65] For them, citizenship rights attached to a metropolitan capitalist nation are exclusionary, aimed at immigrants unable to realize this sort of 'belonging'.

The absence of a sustained consideration of systemic change as seen by political economy, let alone by Marxist theory, does not prevent Bradley and Noronha from claiming that '[b]order abolition is a revolutionary politics.' On the issue of borders and immigration, theirs is a maximalist approach: no bar of citizenship acquisition should exist, and anyone from anywhere who wishes to do so must be free to migrate to a metropolitan capitalist nation. It is an interpretation that is problematic on all sorts of levels. To begin with, in economic terms it plays directly into the hands of capital, with its desire to access unlimited sources of the industrial reserve. As important ideologically is that it plays directly into the hands of those on the far right, whose claims about great replacement it appears to vindicate. To choke off the racism informing the latter, it is necessary to prevent yet more labour market competition, which in turn means denying capitalists access to the industrial reserve. Politically, it ignores that even after a socialist transition has been effected, a socialist government retains the power to plan, an executive role that extends to the movement of labour and its allocation under the socialist plan to specific economic tasks in particular areas or locations.

---

64 On this, and what follows, see Bradley and Noronha (2022: 4, 28–29) for whom 'anti-racism should centrally include people subject to immigration controls (non-citizens), without trying to resolve the problem by simply turning them into citizens'.

65 'In general', observe Bradley and Noronha (2022: 27–28), 'campaigns for citizenship for particular groups of migrants function to reinforce the notion that you have to be a particular kind of person – a citizen, an insider, someone who belongs – in order to access fundamental rights'.

As contentious is the assertion by Basso that all migration is forced, a claim which ignores the distinction made by Marx between labour-power that is free and that which is unfree. Hence the scorn poured on Fusaro for categorizing workers as 'serfs', a disdain expressed by Basso as 'the anti-Marxist one of depicting both immigrants and native-born proletarians as new serfs: the former as mere things, weak, wretched, desperate, vulnerable to blackmail; the latter as beings reified and nullified by the unfortunate arrival of new migrants'.[66] Rather than seeing it in Marxist terms, as a production relation, Basso conflates unfreedom with pre-capitalism (= serf). Consequently, overlooked is the fact that nowadays unfree labour is deployed by capitalists as part of the class struggle waged 'from above'. As such, labour-power that is not free is an important component of the industrial reserve: its acceptability to producers is determined by the very coercion/debt which makes this sort of worker 'vulnerable to blackmail', a relational form which operates against attempts to organize politically and establish common bonds with workers who are free. Bradley and Norhona also misunderstand the significance of unfree labour, and its difference from production relations that are free.[67] Consistent with their privileging of race, what they object to are views which 'define non-citizens solely in terms of their labour power.' Unfree labour is conceptualized, if at all, merely as an epiphenomenon of ethnicity/nationality.

In a similar vein, Mezzadra accepts that his interpretation breaks with Marxist theory. He advocates severing the conceptual link between the wage labour relation and labour-power, so that a 'heterogeneity of labour relations' composed of numerous other social categories and groups (undifferentiated migrants, petty traders, smallholding peasants, family farmers, sharecroppers, lumpenproletarians) can be included among those whose agency will become the deciding factor in any struggle with capitalism.[68] However, since key components of these very broad categories – labelled by him 'subaltern' or 'multitude' – occupy not just different but antagonistic class positions, and thus are usually components of the industrial reserve and generally hostile not to capitalism but to socialism, their agency cannot be seen as positive.[69]

---

66   Basso (2021: 9).
67   See Bradley and Norhona (2022: 43, 44), whose misunderstanding both of surplus labour and of the free/unfree distinction fares poorly when compared with the more rigorous analysis by Pradella and Cillo (2021) of these same issues.
68   Mezzadra (2011a).
69   The difficulty faced by trade unions in uniting local and migrant labour to form a common front against capital was underlined in the course of a 14 May 2014 interview on the BBC Radio 4. When asked why employers were recruiting workers like him in preference to locals, a recently arrived migrant replied that he was prepared to do the same job for

Perhaps the oddest claim made by Basso is that, because the majority of immigrants to the EU have now found employment in the active army, they cannot any longer be considered to form part of the industrial reserve. Much rather, the case he makes illustrates precisely the opposite: the efficacy of the economic role surplus labour performs for capital. The fact that immigrants are now located within the active army demonstrates as clearly as need be the main purpose of the industrial reserve at work. They have displaced locals who either were previously employed in the active army, or else who hoped to enter the latter.

Equally problematic is his argument that migrants are in the vanguard of the struggle conducted by the working class, a view that contrasts with that of Marxists who have long maintained the opposite: that more often than not migrants are deployed by capital in 'from above' struggle *against* working class mobilization.[70] Thus the claim made by Basso, that both Marx and Lenin hailed emigrants to the United States as uniformly engaged in the class struggle alongside fellow workers overlooks the long history, in the United States of northern worker hostility not just to yet more immigration from Europe but also to slave emancipation, both on the same grounds: each would add considerable entrants to the labour market, thereby intensifying job competition to disadvantage of the existing workforce and to the advantage of capital.

Notwithstanding the claim that immigrants are in the forefront of anti-capitalist struggles in receiving countries, therefore, not mentioned by Basso (and others) are the less positive aspects of the open-door policy. These extend from the advantages gained by employers from continued access to the industrial reserve, including as a source of surplus labour used in strikebreaking and restructuring, to evidence that currently migrants – particularly from erstwhile socialist countries – do not want to change the system itself, only to get a better deal within capitalism as it is.[71]

---

less pay. Asked, further, what he thought the impact of this would be on those currently in employment, he disavowed any sympathy for – let alone solidarity with – them, saying they would have to learn to live with such competition for jobs, and lower their wage expectations in keeping with the changed circumstances.

70   On migrants as in the vanguard of the working class, see Basso (2021: 7ff.).

71   The process of capitalist restructuring, involving the displacement of well-paid labour with cheaper foreign equivalents, was illustrated somewhat dramatically during March 2022, when in defiance of legislative procedure P&O ferries went ahead and in a single day sacked 800 British crew, immediately replacing them with stand-by low-paid substitutes recruited from Eastern Europe, an act justified by the CEO in terms of the need to remain competitive with rival companies. Significantly, this incident occurred just after the pandemic and Brexit was marked by a contraction in the industrial reserve, leading in turn to labour shortages in the transport industry, as a result of which existing workers

3.3 What Marx Really Said

Given his view about migrants being unproblematically in the vanguard of the 'from below' class struggle against capital, it is in a sense unsurprising that Basso is opposed to regulation of immigration and a supporter of an open-door approach. Attributing the latter to Marx, however, is incorrect. What Marx supported was co-operation between workers and working-class organizations located in different national contexts, which is not the same view attributed to him by Basso: namely, support for open-door migration. In fact, Marx opposed this, as is clear from his views about the political and economic link between England and Ireland.

An argument frequently invoked by current supporters of open-door migration takes the form of internationalism which, it is claimed, not only licenses untrammelled worker mobility across borders, but is also a process that Marx himself endorsed.[72] Yet the interpretation of internationalism that Marx held was very different, as he made clear in a 1870 letter to Siegfried Meyer and August Vogt.[73] There he argued that the threat an increasing reserve army posed not just to hard-won wage levels and employment conditions but also to the protection of these gains – by means of solidarity among and capacity of an existing workforce to organize – was such that serious consideration was given by him to opposing further immigration. In order to stem competition from the industrial reserve army, and the way it permitted capital to divide-and-rule its workforce, therefore, a century and a half ago Marx advocated severing the link with Ireland precisely in order to prevent migrants from competing with and undercutting English workers.[74] He referred to the latter process as being 'the secret of the impotence of the English working class, despite their organization ... a secret by which the capitalist class maintains its power.'[75]

---

were able to negotiate higher wages and better employment conditions. What this episode underlines is that as soon as the bargaining power of labour increases, so capital resorts to the industrial reserve in order to lower costs and maintain profitability.

72   Those who conflate Marxist internationalism with support of open-door migration include Bradley and Noronha (2022: 69, 176 note 19), who argue – wrongly – that 'border abolition and anti-capitalism are one and the same, and both must be global and internationalist'.

73   See Marx and Engels (1934: 289–90).

74   On this issue, Marx (1934: 288, original emphasis) stated unequivocally that '[a]fter occupying myself with the Irish question for many years I have come to the conclusion that the decisive blow against the English ruling classes ... cannot be delivered *in England but only in Ireland*'.

75   About the impact on class consciousness of this migration pattern, Marx (1934: 289–90, original emphasis) noted: 'Owing to the constantly increasing concentration of farming, Ireland supplies its own surplus to the English labour market and thus forces down

Marx insisted that working class emancipation in England depended ultimately on Ireland following its own path of capitalist development, and to this end international solidarity would take the form of support from English workers for Irish equivalents in their struggle for economic and political independence, as distinct from migrating to where this had already occurred.[76] For Marxism, addressing the presence of industrial reserve army, together with related issues of its unregulated expansion, who benefits from this and why, as a prelude to its elimination, combine to form a crucial first step in any challenge to the accumulation process. It is only after this step that a government representing all workers (of whatever ethnicity and gender) can proceed to implement regulation of wages and conditions. Unlike Marxists, however, Basso accepts the latter objective, but rejects its being conditional on the realization of the former step.

Just how far from the concerns of Marxists the attempt to redefine the industrial reserve in positive terms is clear from the claim by Bradley and Noronha that '[a]nyone genuinely concerned about labour rights needs to understand that ... border controls only strengthen the hands of bosses'.[77] Aware of leftist opposition to open-door immigration, on the grounds that it benefits capital, Bradley and Noronha take issue with such views, arguing that '[i]t is worth restating some fundamentals of left politics.'[78] Although rightly pointing out that wage levels are determined by struggle, not immigration, and that what is needed is collective resistance by all workers, including migrants, their conclusion – that '[i]mmigration controls only weaken that capacity' – is incorrect.

The inference that borders undermine collective agency, and that abolishing such regulation empowers anti-capitalist organization, is no different from the view by Basso that those in the industrial reserve form the vanguard of working-class struggle. Acknowledging that some unions oppose immigration,

---

wages and lowers the moral and material position of the English working class. And most important of all: every industrial and commercial centre in England now possesses a working-class population *divided* into two *hostile* camps, English proletarians and Irish proletarians. The ordinary English worker hates the Irish worker as a competitor who lowers his standard of life ... [t]he Irishman pays him back with interest in his own coin. He regards the English worker as both sharing in the guilt for the English domination in Ireland and at the same time serving as its stupid tool. This antagonism is artificially kept alive and intensified by the press, the pulpit, the comic papers, in short by all the means at the disposal of the ruling classes'.

76   According to Marx (1934: 290), therefore, '[t]he special task ... is to awaken a consciousness in the English workers that for them the *national emancipation of Ireland* is no question of abstract justice or human sympathy but the first condition of *their own emancipation*'.
77   Bradley and Noronha (2022; 57).
78   Bradley and Noronha (2022: 58).

much like Basso, therefore, Bradley and Noronha then argue that 'trade unions are sites of struggle and we should be fighting for and within them'.[79] This contradiction stems from a failure to understand the reason for trade union hostility to surplus labour: the combined issues of more acute labour market competition, undercutting, expanding what is now a global reserve army of labour, all of which undermine the livelihoods of those in work, whose pay and conditions are themselves the achievements of long-standing class struggle with capitalists.

3.4 Travelling the Same Road?

Seen from the right of the political spectrum, the question of borders has risen up the agenda in metropolitan capitalist nations, making inroads into conservative government policies. Not the least of the many ironies is that, instead of slowing down migration, development in Third World countries has increased this. So long as *laissez-faire* remains dominant, and is accompanied by economic growth premised on open door policy, both skilled and unskilled labour-power in less developed areas will continue to migrate in search of higher wages, better-paid jobs, and improved working conditions available in metropolitan capitalist nations. This in turn has exposed the contradictions at the heart of conservative politics, both in the UK and in the wider system of advanced capitalism.[80] The endeavour in 2015 by British conservativism to regulate immigration in order to win back electoral support lost to UKIP, and the hostility expressed by employers to this, confirms that what capitalists want, now as in the past, is deregulated/unregulated access to cheap labour provided by the industrial reserve.[81] This the UK conservative government

---

79 Bradley and Noronha (2022: 59–60, 63).
80 This contradiction – '[p]eople are arguing against immigration but it's the only thing that's increased the potential growth of our economy' – was acknowledged late in 2022 by the Confederation of British Industry when emphasizing the continuing importance to the accumulation process in the UK of the industrial reserve, and calling for closer ties with the EU in order to allow further migration. See 'Business poised to anger Brexiteers by urging Sunak to "do the deal" with the EU', *Financial Times* (London), 21st November 2022.
81 In 2015 the UK conservative administration proposed to curb immigration in the name of anti-slavery, attempting thereby to regain those of its electoral base lost to UKIP. However, two things happened next. First, the backlash from many business organizations and thinktanks (IEA, CBI, IoD, the British Chamber of Commerce) all of which complained of the adverse economic impact that would result from no longer having access to cheap migrant labour. And second, the hasty backtracking by government which assured them post-Brexit exemptions would in fact allow continued recruitment/employment of migrant workers. This episode underlines the contradictory aspects of capitalism: a

from 2022 onwards has undertaken to provide, by easing restrictions on immigration.[82]

From the left of the political spectrum, the issue of borders can – and should – be seen differently.[83] For Basso, as indeed for all Marxists, what is required nowadays is political opposition to capital by means of a joint struggle by each component of the working class – local and migrant alike – wherever the two co-exist.[84] This is uncontroversial, and a kind of mobilization all socialists can – and must – support. What Basso together with Bradley and Noronha fail to understand, however, is that as long as an open-door policy exists, capitalists will always be able to undermine – if not defeat – any such joint struggle by continuously recruiting 'green' workers from the industrial reserve. Not just locals but recently arrived migrants will, as soon as they unite and organize in pursuit of improved pay and conditions, be faced with the prospect of replacement by yet newer surplus labour drawn from this very source.

Hence the undeniably negative political impact of the industrial reserve: by its very nature (regulating the labour market on behalf of capital) it places limits on the success of any joint struggle. As one cannot emphasize too often, therefore, each component of the workforce (local + migrant) can and should unite, certainly, but – as Marx argued with regard to nineteenth century migration from Ireland to England – this unity should take the form of pushing for economic development and attacking capitalism within each context, to be followed by local/migrant unity within such contexts once the accumulation process had been deprived of continuing access to the industrial reserve. Rather than an open border or a sealed one, the object for socialists ought to

---

      disjuncture between a political objective (anti-immigration to attract working class voters) and an economic one (pro-immigration to ensure capitalist profitability).

82   For continuing disagreement within UK conservatism from 2022 onwards, between a desire to boost economic growth by easing immigration restrictions, but to stay in power also needing electoral support from workers who want to see immigration controls, see 'Liz Truss to review visa schemes in bid to ease UK labour shortages', *Financial Times* (London), 25 September 2022; 'Liz Truss plans to loosen migration curbs', *Financial Times* (London), 5 October 2022; 'Immigration policy cannot fix the job market', *Financial Times* (London), 26 October 2022.

83   As net migration has risen to unprecedentedly high levels, even the UK Labour Party has finally accepted the negative impact that the industrial reserve has on the existing workforce. See 'Starmer to call for end of "low pay and cheap labour"', *Financial Times* (London), 22nd November, 2022; 'Net migration rises to record 504,000', *Financial Times* (London), 25th November, 2022.

84   Basso (2021: 17).

be a tighter process of regulation based on planning that is no longer in thrall to a policy of enhanced labour market competition.

4 Conclusion

Historically, the impact of surplus labour on working class organization and struggle against capital has been perceived negatively by those on the left. For Marx, Engels, and other Marxists (Kalecki, Sweezy, Dobb, Glyn), the industrial reserve constitutes an obstacle not just to working class solidarity but also and therefore to the possibility of a socialist transition. Boosted by migration, it means that existing workers can be played off against incomers, and vice-versa: turning from locals then to migrants ensures that they are always in competition, generating acute hostility between different components of the workforce. Underwritten by the presence of the industrial reserve, it is a pattern of segmentation that permits capitalists not just to lower the cost of labour-power but also and thereby to compete more effectively by maintaining or enhancing profitability. This is what supporters of open borders mean when they say immigration is good for the economy.

For its part, liberalism has been more ambivalent, combining recognition of the negative aspects of surplus labour with acceptance of its positive contribution to the accumulation process. As long as unemployment exists, argued Beveridge, so also will acute competition for jobs, a result of which will be hatred of foreigners, Jews, women, and any others who seek to enter the workforce. However, he was writing largely about the UK jobs market in the 1930s, and how unemployment might be addressed by the British state, not about the labour market as a global phenomenon, as it has now become. Furthermore, Beveridge saw the solution as involving more capitalist production, generating additional employment, and consequently lessening the intensity of market competition among workers, all in a context of a nationally restricted and benign accumulation process, none of which applies currently. What he, like other liberals now, feared most was a 'from below' challenge to the capitalist system *per se*, and viewed the welfare state (and its provision) as a means of avoiding what he saw as a negative outcome (a questioning of capitalism and its replacement by socialism).

In twenty-first century metropolitan capitalist nations, the issue of the industrial reserve takes on the form of immigration control, surfacing among the working class and its representatives as one of ethnic/national/gender identity. However, this ideological shift from class to non-class identity flourishes only so long as the continued reproduction of the system which gives rise to the industrial reserve army and its effects (low wages, fierce competition for jobs, and unemployment) is not addressed. In a capitalist context, therefore, socialists have on occasion argued that controlling the level of the industrial reserve army – opposing the continued access by employers to cheap migrant labour – diminishes competition in the labour market, thereby permitting workers and their representatives to begin to settle accounts with employers from a position of strength.

Where different ethnicities/nationalities compete for the same jobs, however, antagonism generated by such economic rivalry tends to be expressed in terms of these non-economic identities, a process that marginalizes (or eliminates) class unity and benefits employers. Marxism has always recognized this outcome and its attendant dangers, but unfortunately this is not true of a plethora of faux-Marxist or non-Marxist approaches that currently emanate from or adhere to a vague politics of human rights which simply advocate migrant empowerment regardless of anything else. Accepting the negative characterization by Marx of the industrial reserve, these contrasting approaches nevertheless in effect reverse this, and perceive its components not as undermining the gains made by labour but rather as the vanguard of the working-class struggle against the capitalist system. Avoiding as they do any consideration of the economic implications of the industrial reserve for labour market competition, such notions play directly into the hands of capital and far-right populists.

Unsurprisingly, one important effect of globalization has been to place borders, who crosses them and why, at the centre of debates about 'from below' empowerment. A consequence of this is that non-class identity is now inserted (or reinserted) into the question of labour market competition. The result is that all forms of immigration now tend to be recast ideologically by NGOs, Church organizations, postmodern academics and liberal journalism largely in non-economic terms, and consequently viewed not as a labour market issue – which is how Marxists and capitalists interpret it – but simply as a humanitarian one. A variant maintains that the industrial reserve is the locus of anti-capitalist struggle. According to these approaches, shorn of its negative attributes, surplus labour is instead redefined as positive.

For a number of reasons, such views are problematic. To begin with, migrants from ex-socialist countries would not be keen on socialist political transition, nor will they see a need to organize as long as wages/conditions in the receiving context are higher/better than in the sending one. Where they are unemployed, they can be used by employers – as P&O and other examples indicate – to undermine pay/conditions of those in work. Even in instances where migrants unite with locals in pursuit of better wages and improved conditions, as long as borders remain unregulated/open capital will always be able to replace those engaged in 'from below' struggle with 'green' labour. In short, the difficulty is the perpetual nature of labour market competition licensed by open-door policy, which in turn permits access by capital to the industrial reserve, generating in turn the rise and consolidation of resistance based not on socialism but rather on populism, nationalism, and 'nativism'.

What is missed by Basso, Mezzadra, Bradley and Norhona, and others, therefore, is that ideas about opposing immigration so as to block the industrial reserve were earlier advanced by the left, and – since the left no longer appears interested in them – have now been taken over by the right. This history is overlooked by those who simply equate criticism of open-door migration with fascism and racism. Forgotten by many on the left is not just the way the industrial reserve has featured in the history of capitalism, and why socialists have viewed surplus labour negatively, as a gift to the accumulation process, but also and therefore the way it might feature in a socialist future. A crucial objective faced by an incoming socialist government is how to counter the anarchy of the market, the baleful legacy bequeathed by the capitalist system.

Because of this, socialism and socialists have always given priority to the regulation of the market – as much for labour-power as for other commodities – in order to facilitate central planning by the state. Economic planning advocated by socialists requires – indeed, depends on – strong control exercised over the element of freedom associated with the market (accurately embodied in the term *laissez-faire*), and workforce allocation by the state would of course be – inescapably – an important aspect of this. Hence the idea that cross-border free movement is in a very general sense politically emancipatory/progressive, and consequently would automatically flourish under a socialist government, is quite simply incorrect.

Hence addressing the related issues of an unregulated expansion in the industrial reserve army and who benefits from this is a first step politically, after which – in a capitalist context – a government representing all workers (of whatever ethnicity and gender) can then proceed to implement regulation of wages and conditions. Accordingly, the twofold socialist object has to be: first, to protect the existing workforce, and – of course – migrants who are already part of this; and second, to oppose strongly any attempts by capital to add to their number. Whilst most, if not all, agree on the first object, there is much disagreement about the second. Organizing and supporting all components of the workforce is an obvious aim, and as such uncontroversial. However, agency of whatever kind directed towards this end cannot but be impeded by calls either for open borders or for border abolition.

References

Balibar, E., S. Mezzadra, and R. Samaddar (eds.) (2012) *The Borders of Justice*. Philadelphia: Temple University Press.

Basso, P. (2021) Marx on Migration and the Industrial Reserve Army: Not to be Misused! In M. Musto (ed.) *Rethinking Alternatives with Marx*. London: Palgrave Macmillan.

Bernstein, H. (2021) Into the Field with Marx: Some Observations on Researching Class. In A. Mezzadri (ed.) *Marx in the Field*. London: Anthem Press.

Beveridge, W.H. (1931a) *Unemployment: A Problem of Industry (1909 and 1930)*. London: Longmans, Green and Co.

Beveridge, W.H. (1931b) *Tariffs: The Case Examined*. London: Longmans, Green and Co.

Beveridge, W.H. (1943) *Pillars of Security, and Other War-Time Essays and Addresses*. London: George Allen & Unwin Ltd.

Beveridge, W.H. (1944) *Full Employment in a Free Society*. London: George Allen & Unwin Ltd.

Beveridge, W.H. (1946) *Why I Am a Liberal*. London: Herbert Jenkins Limited.

Bradley, G.M., L. de Noronha (2022) *Against Borders: the Case for Abolition*. London: Verso.

Brass, T. (1999) *Towards a Comparative Political Economy of Unfree Labour*. London: Frank Cass Publishers.

Brass, T. (2017) *Labour Markets, Identities, Controversies*. Leiden: Brill.

Brass, T. (2018) *Revolution and Its Alternatives*. Leiden: Brill.

Brass, T. (2021) *Marxism Missing, Missing Marxism*. Leiden: Brill.

Brass, T. (2022) Great Replacement and/as the Industrial Reserve: Populism or Marxism? In D. Fasenfest (ed.) *Marx Matters*, Leiden: Brill.

Brass, T. (2023) Defending Liberalism, Promoting Capitalism: Fukuyama's Scylla and Charybdis. *Critical Sociology* doi:10.1177/08969205221104062.

Bruno, S. (1979) The Industrial Reserve Army, Segmentation and the Italian Labour Market. *Cambridge Journal of Economics* 3(2): 131–151.

Collins, J. (1984) Marx's Reserve Army: Still Relevant 100 Years On. *The Journal of Australian Political Economy* 16 (March): 51–65.

Dobb, M. (1955) Full Employment and Capitalism [1950]. In: *On Economic Theory and Socialism: Collected Papers*, London: Routledge & Kegan Paul.

Engels, F. (n.d., a) *Herr Eugen Dühring's Revolution in Science [Anti-Dühring]*, London: Martin Lawrence Limited.

Engels, F. (n.d., b) *Engels on Capital: Synopsis, Reviews, Letters and Supplementary Material*. London: Lawrence and Wishart.

Foenkinos, D. (2020) *The Mystery of Henri Pick*, London: Pushkin Press.

Glyn, A. (2006) Will Marx Be Proved Right? *Oxonomics* 1: 13–16.

Glyn, A. (2007) *Capitalism Unleashed: Finance, Globalization, and Welfare.* Oxford: Oxford University Press.

International Labour Office (1924) *Unemployment in Its National and International Aspects.* Geneva: ILO Studies and Reports, Series C (Unemployment) No. 9.

Kalecki, M. (1943) Political Aspects of Full Employment. *The Political Quarterly* 14(4): 322–330.

Kennedy, J.F. (1964) *A Nation of Immigrants* (Introduction by R. F. Kennedy). New York: Harper & Row, Publishers.

Khanna, P. (2022) *Move: How Mass Migration Will Reshape the World – and What It Means for You.* London: Weidenfeld & Nicolson.

Marquardt, F. (2021) *The New Nomads: How the Migration Revolution is Making the World a Better Place.* London and New York: Simon & Schuster.

Marx, K. (1976) *Capital Volume 1* (Introduced by E. Mandel, translated by B. Fowkes), Harmondsworth: Penguin Books.

Marx, K., and F. Engels (1934) *Correspondence 1846–1895.* London: Martin Lawrence Ltd.

McCullum, R.B., and A. Readman (1947) *The British General Election of 1945.* London: Oxford University Press.

Mezzadra, S. (2006) *Diritto di fuga. Migrationi, Cittadinanza, Globalizzazione.* Verona: ombre corte.

Mezzadra, S. (2011a) How Many Histories of Labor? Towards a Theory of Postcolonial Capitalism. *Postcolonial Studies* 14(2): 151–170.

Mezzadra, S. (2011b) The Gaze of Autonomy: Capitalism, Migration, and Social Struggles. In V. Squire (ed.) *The Contested Politics of Mobility: Borderzones and Irregularity.* London: Routledge.

Mezzadra, S. and B. Neilson (eds.) (2013) *Border as Method, or the Multiplication of Labor.* Durham, NC: Duke University Press.

Pradella, L. and R. Cillo (2021) Bordering the Surplus Population across the Mediterranean: Imperialism and Unfree Labour in Libya and the Italian Countryside. *Geoforum* 126: 483–494.

Steinbeck, J. (1939) *The Grapes of Wrath.* London: William Heinemann Ltd.

Streek, W. (2017) *Between Charity and Justice: Remarks on the Social Construction of Immigration Policy in Rich Democracies.* Danish Centre for Welfare Studies, University of Southern Denmark, Daws Working Paper – 5.

Sweezy, P.M. (1942) *The Theory of Capitalist Development* (With a Foreword by M. Dobb), London: Denis Dobson Limited.

Trotsky, L.D. (1934) *The History of the Russian Revolution* (Translated by M. Eastman). London: Victor Gollancz Ltd.

CHAPTER 13

Difference without End

Kevin R. Cox

1   Context

Prior to the sixties, the idea of difference as a category in social theory barely registered. A social order in which race and gender played key ordering roles, producing what in retrospect was a very clear hierarchy, one that permeated social life in all its aspects, was scarcely challenged; it was taken for granted. One might then talk about race or gender but not group them under the same heading of 'difference' and of a politics which shared similar features, as in 'new social movements.' This has now clearly changed. On the other hand, exploration of difference as an abstraction has tended to lag. The literature is still dominated by discussions of race and gender. Yet equally invidious, equally subject to hierarchical distinction and discriminatory allocation in the technical division of labor have been religion, most palpably, at least for advanced capitalist societies, in Northern Ireland; and citizenship, as in questions around immigration. Even that is to stop short of the full scope of difference. It is, in fact, everywhere, old forms morphing, new ones emerging. This universality should be significant in its own right.

This universality has to do with the tensions at the heart of capitalist society: tensions around material interest, status, and threats to the everyday. This necessary relationship contrasts with that of a literature in which the dominant view is of difference as interacting with capitalism only in a contingent way: racial capitalism, and the idea of intersectionality are the more obvious instances of this, where difference is theorized, that is.

The significance of difference for a Marxist understanding of the world, is then the way it often cross-cuts class and poses obstacles to labor organizing. It can divide the working class in damaging ways. The city of Liverpool in England had six parliamentary constituencies before the Second World War, but in a context of strong sectarian divides, it had to wait till 1945 to elect its first Labour Party MP.[1] In the Netherlands, the so-called 'pillarization' of society, principally along religious lines, long impeded the development of class

---

1   See Jeffery (2017) for an extended discussion of Liverpool Toryism.

politics. This dampening effect is not necessarily the case. Difference can simply reinforce existing class divisions: historically Quebec tended to divide very roughly between a French-speaking working class and an English-speaking capitalist one. In other words: 'Difference' is an important issue for Marxist geography.

The approach adopted here is to embrace difference in all its shifting manifestations, while rejecting the notion of contingency as playing any role other than a subordinate one: to see, difference, rather, as a necessary aspect of capitalism, so that while some cases might be weakened, as with gender in the advanced capitalist countries, even disappear, as in the old English aversion to the Irish immigrants, there will, *per necesita*, always be something that comes to define people as different. Capital's laws of motion mean that difference is one of its chronic features. It is then its concrete trajectory which generates its particular forms and how they change.

2   The Pervasiveness of Difference

Difference is everywhere in capitalist societies, and manifest in a quite massive range of possibilities: far broader than the usual categories of race, gender, religion and citizenship. Sometimes it is seen in regional terms, as in Northern and Southern Italians, Ossies and Wessies, even the bicoastal economy and flyover country. Urban-regional tensions have been and remain common, and currently factor into American politics over so-called 'cultural issues.' Likewise, the distinction between the established and the outsiders: something associated with a study of a small town in England (Scotson and Elias 1965; see also Damer 1974), but with vastly wider application. New ones appear seemingly out of nowhere. In the runup to the negotiations over the end of apartheid in South Africa, nobody anticipated the violence between the township residents and those in the hostels; an expression of the urban/rural, for sure, but quite unexpected, and much more complex.

Novelty is then enhanced by the way in which, even with the categories one commonly thinks of in the context of difference, the contrasts constructed can vary, sometimes nebulous and shifting. The sectarian antipathy in Glasgow is more than a matter of religion, embracing place of origin and territorial loyalties. Race often blurs into ethnicity as in African American – the term itself is ethnic: soul food, vocabulary, the celebration of kwanza, hair style, particular churches, Motown, and gospel. Anti-Muslim feeling in France is sometimes identified as racial, but there is also, just as clearly, a religious element, as in tussles with the French government about wearing the foulard in schools; and local conflicts around the construction of mosques.² Again, there is a distinct Franco-Muslim ethnicity: not just clothing and food, but also distinct words adapted to the French language while in reaction to it. With the Coloreds of South Africa, the phenotypical can be deceiving; someone like Nelson Mandela could easily have been taken for a (mixed-race) Colored. The distinction was also ethnic, combining the Afrikaner language with the (segregated) Dutch Reformed Church and perceived educational advantages.

There is little that is predictable about difference, apart from its hierarchical edge and struggles for advantage in stratification systems. Distinctions made in one country, that one might expect elsewhere, can be missing. South Africa's Coloreds find a counterpart in the equally mixed-race mestizos of Latin America. In South Africa this was reinforced by the way in which they occupied an intermediate position in the ethnic hierarchy; something continued under post-apartheid through the odd designation 'Population Group.' In Bolivia, the decision not to include 'mestizo' in the most recent census was met with outrage. In the US, the last time that mixed-race was a Census category was 1920, though since 2000 there has been a new category where someone can belong to two or more races. Yet skin tone has clearly been a criterion of discrimination in everyday life. On the other hand, difference does not have to do necessarily with attributes, like race and gender, that can easily be naturalized. Abuse is hurled at the lower orders regardless: those living in 'sink estates', 'the projects' or the French equivalent, 'les cités.' And then the lofty disdain of the chattering classes for the vulgarities and superficialities of the lower order and the sorts of distinction captured by Bourdieu (1984) in his book of the same title.

The topography of difference is constantly shifting. People from different places get aggregated in the minds of those who see them as a threat, and that imputed homogeneity is then drawn on in struggle. In South Africa, the Africans removed under apartheid from the Western Cape area to the new township of Mdantsane in the Eastern Cape had never regarded themselves as 'the Cape people', or as the highly derogatory 'bushmen', but that is what they became in the eyes of the locals in struggles over access to housing (Cox 2002: 153–154.) West Indian migrants to England, in the nineteen fifties and sixties, had never seen themselves as 'West Indian' nor even as homogeneously black. Pigmentocracy and island chauvinism ruled (James 1992.) One was from Barbados, Jamaica or St Lucia, and not from the West Indies. Skin tone determined one's position in the local racial hierarchy. But in England,

---

2 For a good critical discussion of race and ethnicity, see Davidson (1999).

it was different. The white English working class treated them as the same: as blacks and, drawing on the British colonial term, West Indians. And in subsequent struggles, they would indeed join together, though in an intriguing discursive turn, rejecting the colonial 'West Indian' in favor of the more neutral 'Caribbean'. Something else had changed. In the British colonies, whites occupied privileged positions in the social order. In England, it was more complex. Whites occupied the full gamut. There was a white working class no different in their occupations, in fact often inferior, to those who came to England to be nurses, bus drivers, and teachers; which then sharpened the sense of injustice and moral outrage still more. Difference, once arisen, therefore, is not static. It clearly gets modified and particular forms can soften and even fade away. Gender in the advanced industrial countries no longer has the intensely differentiating character, the more egregious contrasts and sense of hierarchy that it once had. Something like the exclusion acts aimed at the Chinese in the US and Australia at the end of the nineteenth century, are unthinkable today.

Whatever its substantive form, and in all its complexity, geographic and historical, difference does not stand alone. It is an emergent property: something internalized in the social process as a whole and featuring not just in the division of labor but in geography, micro- and macro-, in the living place, obviously in power relations and institutions, and in the common discourse. To the degree that there is some sort of accepted compromise, deeply internalized, then it is taken for granted. A classic case until recently, would have been gender. Nobody challenged the way in which boys and girls were channelled in particular directions; the way in which women could become town councillors, but much more rarely, a Member of Parliament; how they might be head teacher of a primary school but certainly not of a secondary one. In its everyday expressions, in the workplace in particular, difference can be quite localized. But through the media, through a discourse of national solidarity, however superficial that might be, it tends to diffuse through a country as a whole. In England, at least, Brexit was largely about immigration, and particularly those immigrants from Eastern Europe. But while there were very few in Northeastern England, a majority there voted to leave.

What rarely gets mentioned in discussions of difference is social stratification itself. It is as if, if the usual differences were eliminated, then all would be well; that people would be on an even level, and if they did not manage to be upwardly mobile, then that would be their own fault and not a result of discriminations. There is an issue here, of course. The fallacy of composition means that not everyone can be upwardly mobile at the same time; otherwise, the idea of 'upwards' makes no sense, nor, of course, resistance from the privileged. Difference in the usual senses of the word is something that can be mitigated, even eliminated, though not necessarily through legislative action. But differences in class relations, most significantly here, in social stratification cannot, by definition, be eliminated. Working class people can be upwardly mobile and those in the more affluent strata, downwardly so; but to abolish social stratification is to abolish capitalism. There *have* to be poorer people, including the unemployed, to act as a discipline on the wage demands of those immediately above them in the stratification system. There have to be the so-called improvident, the wasters, and the idlers if there is to be any meaning to the struggle to escape that world and be accepted into the values of the capitalist one: values of money, steady work, a home in the suburbs, one's own car, foreign vacations and even second homes.

3   Capital's Logic

In an important intervention, Ellen Meiksins Wood (1988) argued vigorously for capital's structural indifference to differences of race and gender. If its goal was, indeed, the extraction of surplus value with a view to its expanded accumulation, then that had to be. She then qualified this by claiming that capital would take advantage of difference if it worked to its advantage.[3]

Her claims resonate. In England, during the 1950s, West Indians had been deliberately recruited by the various bus companies, all under public ownership. The attempt to introduce them into bus crews in Bristol in 1963, however, met with union opposition, ostensibly around the prospect of wage competition.[4] On the other hand, they were employed in lower paid positions in workshops and in canteens. This would be a case in which white working-class resistance would fail. But in other instances, it would be successful. The case of the nascent gold mining industry in South Africa in the first two decades of the last century is classic (Callinicos 1981). The initial division of labor in the mines had been between a privileged white stratum that arrived from Europe, North America and Australia, equipped with a deep-mining savoir

---

3 We should note that in the prelude to capital, in acts of primitive accumulation, difference has indeed been drawn on to justify dispossession. In the colonial act, tenure in common was defined as wasteful; and waste as an expression of the nature of the indigenous people. By dividing the land into private property, and thus, incidentally, paving the way for capital, the settlers were doing indigenous peoples a service. But once capital is in motion, and to return to Meiksins Wood's first point, capital's logic has been exactly that: indifferent to difference.

4 We should also note, however, that the bus company argued that with black bus crews, white passengers would no longer use the buses: https://www.blackhistorymonth.org.uk/article/section/civil-rights-movement/the-bristol-bus-boycott-of-1963/.

faire; and a massive army of Africans on much lower wages, who took their orders. Technological development, specifically, the pneumatic drill, and the fact that the Africans were learning by observation, tempted the mine owners into replacing the white workers with Africans. This led to a period of sustained labor strife around the demand of the white labor unions – Africans were unrepresented – for job reservation: jobs requiring certain know-how would be for white workers only. Mine owner resistance led to violence in the form of the Rand Revolt of 1922, and eventually national legislation in favor of the white miners.

However, Wood qualified her claim by arguing that where circumstances were appropriate, capital might indeed take advantage of senses of difference. It is a fact that it draws on stereotypes of difference in its hiring policies. This then tends to reproduce difference in quite complex ways. It is not just through the distribution of the product, significant as home background is to the reproduction of future working classes. It is also the way in which existing hierarchies undermine confidence in assuming positions of leadership.[5] On the other hand, as circumstances change, the stereotypes can have emancipatory effects of a limited sort. Historically, women tended to be excluded from jobs requiring heavy physical labor, but the growth of service industries has filtered in their assumed advantages in dealing with people.

Gold mining in South Africa could never have taken off without the ability to super-exploit Africans: the gold ore was simply of too inferior a quality for it to have been otherwise; ultra-cheap labor was a necessity (Callinicos 1981; Jeeves and Crush 1995). The exclusion of Africans from the suffrage, in turn predicated on their supposed racial inferiority, would make all the difference to the imposition of a low wage regime. Equally, small clothing workshops in London take advantage of patriarchal relations to drive costs down: women work as much because they see themselves as subordinate to male relatives as for the wage (Mitter 1986): small firms, yes, but the major retail clothing chains that buy from them are happy to take advantage. This does not mean that the long-term logic of capital is not to do away with these sorts of discriminations, and the record shows that it does in fact happen, if slowly and unevenly, and only to be replaced by new ones.

But if, in terms of its laws of motion, capital is structurally indifferent to difference, where does difference come from? For whom is it *not* a matter of indifference? Who has an interest in constructing it? The rule of capital certainly

---

5 Something vividly portrayed in the case of African Americans in Liebow's (1967) *Tally's Corner*.

contributes to that construction, but in a highly mediated way. This is because of the existential threats that capital visits on the immediate producers. When conjoined with a technical division of labor that mitigates them unevenly, it can be seen to generate anxiety and then senses of difference. It is to the question of difference and the working class that we now turn.

4   The Working-Class Condition

The threats are threefold and tend to be jointly present, reinforcing one another. The first is obviously material: The desire not just to reproduce oneself materially, but also to achieve the material values that capitalism represents and diffuses – to realize the American dream, to acquire on an expanding scale. This applies to both workplace and living place: to be paying down a mortgage rather than paying rent.

The second is what has been called 'recognition.' This flirts with the idea of identity but the danger in that instance is, as Fraser (2000) emphasized, to miss the hierarchical nature of difference; that some assume themselves as superior to others, and the others are inclined to accept it. This hierarchy, I would emphasize, is closely related to the values of a capitalist society, even while in concrete terms, those values can shift: single motherhood no longer carries the stigma of ill-discipline and improvidence that it once did. These distinctions are so utterly taken for granted by the privileged that it can be hard to understand what is at stake for the less so. National censuses pack the official punch. The ordering of the categories in their tables is simply dumbfounding: men before women, salaried before wage, professional before skilled and semi-skilled. In apartheid South Africa the order mimicked what happened on the ground: white; Colored; Asian; African; hardly the more neutral alphabetical, therefore. On a more global scale, what to make of the distinction between First and Third World?

While recognition is increasingly recognized as an object of struggle in capitalist society, less so is what has been called 'ontological security' (Giddens, 1981: 154): a sense of order and stability in a life, in the meanings assigned to objects and events, so as to achieve a sense of coherence, not necessarily positive, but predictive and reassuring, including the way one might explain one's misfortunes; a life without the surprises that would require constant adaptation. The relation to everyday life under capital will be obvious. But capital's structural tendency, through its chronic transformation of everything, is to install a regime of insecurity: de-skilling, the threat of the industrial reserve army, and the subsequent risk of eviction through failure to pay rent or the mortgage. It is a world of constant upheaval where the verities of everyday life can be continually challenged. People can be employed, and materially comfortable but entire social worlds can be upset by all the changes going on around them, new faces, new behaviors, and senses of where one belongs, and the normative order radically challenged.

These are all anxieties which cross-cut working-class life in uneven ways and this in virtue of capital's highly developed technical division of labor. Simply put, some are better paid, less insecure and occupy more honorific roles than others. These variations are partly recognized in dual labor market theory: a unionized, better-paid, dominantly male and white stratum as opposed to the more contingently employed, non-unionized, among whom women and people of color tend to have a stronger presence. This is, of course, a highly simplified representation of labor markets, but its emphasis on their hierarchical character, ordering people by reward and, implicitly, by security and indeed difference in gender and racial terms, is surely apt.

The upshot is a working class prone to internal struggle, and to 'differentiation' in the egregious terms understood by the idea of 'difference': a divided working class where the more privileged seek to retain their privilege by resisting displacement by people of color, immigrants, women, migratory workers, and fashioning arguments to justify themselves: the merits of the national against immigrants, and the deficiencies, often 'natural' of the challengers. What is being pursued are those things most valued in a capitalist society: wage labor vs non-wage, employment vs unemployment, salaries vs wages, and the bigger the better, and control of how money will be spent. These are an object of struggle. Old conceptions of difference are drawn on, some of very long standing, like gender, some relatively more recent as in ones about race that arrived with empire; or new ones are constructed, in order to structure labor markets to the advantage of white native men, like citizen vs immigrant status. The goal is to monopolize wage labor, earnings, and employment: a struggle that then tips over into the living place and attempts to ensure that privilege in the stratification system gets reproduced as in the advantages enjoyed by the children from better-off homes,

Struggle is not always evident. Working class privilege has a geography and a history: islands and periods when expectations of income, standing in the social order, and some security against unemployment can be almost taken for granted; but a stability that will inevitably come to an end as a result of capital's ceaseless transformation of the labor process, its reaching out for cheaper, non-unionized labor elsewhere and of changes in its sectoral composition.

At the upper levels of the technical division of labor – and the word 'upper' is surely significant – salaries, job security, tend to protect from these tensions.

If they are challenged by, say, a change in the institutional order, then one has the resources, the technical qualifications to move elsewhere. Such has been the case in South Africa subsequent to the ending of apartheid and the desire of corporations to accommodate themselves to the new racial order. Cheap international airline travel and the ease of communication with those left behind, have then made this much easier. Territoriality is differentiated so that for some, as Webber (1964) argued many years ago, the mile is 'elastic.'

The other qualification is that the technical division of labor, broadly understood, is not necessarily a source of tension. It can, in fact, be a rational response to the challenges of working-class life. Brenner and Ramas (1984) have argued that the gender division of labor then practiced – the male breadwinner and the female homemaker – had a rationale. The goal was children who would, from an early age, go out to work to swell the household budget; children who would then delay marriage and continue to live at home into their early twenties, all the while bringing in money. Whatever the reasoning, the large family and the 'little worker' were features of the time. What would eventually discourage this was the introduction of mass schooling and a minimum school leaving age: something opposed by the mass of the population while vigorously pushed by middle class reformers (Zelizer 1994).

5   The Capitalist State

The capitalist state works as an illusory counter to this working-class condition. It abstracts from class by defining everyone as a citizen with an equality of rights. This sense of a shared legal status is strengthened by the fact that the capitalist state is always a national state. With respect to the working-class condition, the national then has several mitigating effects. First, through the idea of the national economy and then that of economic policy, one's material condition is attributable not just to one's class position but to the state. The significance of the buoyancy or otherwise of the economy for election outcomes is well known. Growth is the mantra because it promises to square the circle of raising wages without interfering with the accumulation process (Wolfe 1982).

'Country', through its acquired notability in various domains, from sport to scholarship, from war to peace making, then provides a vicarious sense of recognition. We may be working class, but at least the national team won the World Cup, and they represent 'Us.' The sense that 'Our' country is at the center of the universe is then enhanced through the way the media privilege the national. Finally, 'country' is a source of psychological security. Through the media, through state institutions, through others that emerge within the national frame, particular ways of doing things, particular images, particular forms of organization, and hence shared knowledge and routines, life can assume a reassuring predictability.

Capital, however, is global. It expands from particular national bases. This has two contradictory effects. First it gives the labor movement an international dimension: at one end of the spectrum, the idea that revolution, if it is to be successful, has to be international, propagated through the communist party; and at the other end the more timid idea of organizing across national boundaries so as to take wages and conditions of work out of the calculus of employers.[6] The second effect is to fortify the attempts of capitals and their states, within their national bases, to restructure for international competition and, if necessary, imperial adventure. This has to be through some sort of cross-class alliance (Harvey 1985), drawing on the national to achieve popular support: to limit wages, to subsidize firms, to allocate support in a differential manner across different sectors, and therefore regions.

In the first case, the idea of revolutionary transformation, even that of the more reformist international brotherhood of labor, has to be opposed. In his discussion of working-class movements in twentieth century Europe, Michael Mann (1995) underlined the role of the national in undermining radical challenge: in seducing the working class through appeal to a country under threat. He has not been the only one to point out the shock to national capitalisms of the revolution in Russia, the attempted ones in Germany and Hungary, and the general upsurge in working class militancy subsequent to the First World War (Eley 2021; Graham 2005; Traverso 2016.) As others have then noted, in some countries, most notably France and Germany, the threat of the international would then be defined more concretely as that of the deracinated Jew, or, in Nazi propaganda, as Judeo-Bolshevist (Brustein and King 2004; Caron 2005).

The effect of international competition, both economic and geopolitical, also introduces ethnicity from another direction. Foreigners become a threat and not just through their products, but through their presence as workers: they are defined as such, their motives suspect, their character, their skills, denigrated. They threaten 'our' jobs, are parasites on 'our' welfare state. They know no allegiance to our country and can actually be a threat to it. The national is exclusive; it comes with the idea of loyalty to a country and one that trumps all others. This is the foundational idea of the fifth column: the traitor within. In the earlier part of the twentieth century, the Irish

---

6 Jonathan Hyslop (1999) provides a fascinating case of this in his discussion of what he called 'white laborism': the endeavor of Australian, British and South African whites to exclude those of color from the more remunerative positions or even altogether.

in England and Scotland were seen as a threat since many supported home rule for Ireland, and then its extension to Northern Ireland. The current rash of far-right movements in Western Europe, blossoms on the claim that the Muslim immigrant is a force for and ally of Islamic terrorism. The sense of difference is deepened, and to the extent that the immigrant finds him or herself lodged towards the lower levels of the technical division of labor, fortifies claims demanding exclusion.

6 Questions of Geohistory

> by talking about racialization as a process you have a perspective and a concept that is inherently about process, and that opens the door to history, that opens the door to understanding the complexities of who get racialized when and for what purpose, and how that changes through time. It much more easily allows you to avoid that fundamental mistake of drawing a very clear line between what happened to the Irish in the 1850s and what happened to Jamaicans in London in the 1950s. There are fundamental aspects of those two migrations, experiences, processes and all that was consequent upon them that are very similar.
> ASHE and MCGEEVER 2011: 2019

In addressing the immensely important role of the contingent in understanding difference, this is a useful starting point, albeit requiring amendment. First, Miles (in Ashe and McGeever) is surely right about process and history, but he would have been more accurate to talk of *geo*history. The contingent is not just about juxtaposition in time, but also in space: comings together at particular places at particular times. Miles was in fact addressing the issue of racialization, but one can extend his observations to other expressions of difference. As for his remark about continuity, certainly, but also transformation, including novelty.

Doreen Massey (2005) was to the forefront in arguing for the significance of space in the way events get juxtaposed. It was not just a matter of things coming together at a particular point in time, but the geography of that coming together; how space and time could not be separated. If it happened in time, then the event had to also have a geography: a set of influences and conditions drawn in from other places and wider spaces. These geohistorical conditions and influences can extend back in time a long way, as in the rise of the Nazi party in Germany: an earlier anti-Semitism subsequent to the arrival of Jews from Eastern Europe, an empire confiscated at Versailles, even, in terms of development, how the country's latecomer status combined with feudal remnants.[7] What she did not emphasize was the way in which influences and conditions might be selected in, others filtered out, and in the context of a contradiction-driven accumulation process; and how that accumulation process might itself be the source of influences and forces experienced elsewhere. That in short, time-space juxtapositions, with all their implications, have to be seen in the context of a social process in which capitalist development is the ultimate mover. Not least, it brings workers into contact in competitive conditions, threatening those already there with diminished wages, unemployment, relegation to the ranks of the poor; and it undercuts the position of workers by outsourcing to other countries, engendering hostility to foreign 'others'.

With this as background, we can make three major claims about contingent conditions and difference. First, countries matter. They provide privileged zones of circulation, relatively isolated from the rest of the world, and subject to homogenizing forces; not least, a shared state, shared institutions, media, and way of life. In their development, these in turn draw on distinctive geohistories creating equally distinctive difference regimes. We saw this earlier in discussions of the official racial categories in South Africa, Latin America and the US. We could say the same about gender regimes. In the Scandinavian countries, gender is experienced differently than elsewhere in Europe, significantly more emancipatory as in government participation and unusually generous provision for child care. Just why this is, is buried deep in national histories (Buckwalter and Baten 2019).

Countries homogenize, and become a major influence on what is taken to be normal, accepted, always to be anticipated: a major source of ontological security, therefore, as discussed earlier. According to Giddens (1981: 154) this is a particular problem in capitalist society. Normative structures lack the moral bindingness provided by pre-capitalist societies. The organization of everyday life has neither moral nor rational basis; rather it is a matter of habit in a context of material limits. This makes people vulnerable in times of dislocation to movements that promise a return to the old certainties. There are two observations to be made here. The first is that it is in these terms that one can understand common and current reactions to immigrants: an anxiety not so much of worries about jobs and access to the welfare state, though there is that; rather it is an anxiety about the national culture, identity, and values. An alternative view is that what has been crucial is less capitalism and more the collapse of traditional political parties subsequent to neo-liberalism, and the collapse of

---

7 For a critical discussion, see Evans (1985).

the labor movement: the way they no longer provide moral guidance but have become opportunistic, opening up the way to political entrepreneurs on the far right, who then take advantage of social atomization and digitalization and mobilize support around the migration question (Borriello and Jäger 2023).

Thirdly, this is not to suggest that countries are a privileged site for the development of difference and a heightened politics. The idea of the established and the outsiders certainly applies to the intensity of feeling in Western Europe against immigrants, but the original formulation was actually about what happened in a small English town. This occurred when 'outsiders' arrived and showed indifference to the normative structure developed by the long-term resident who, while differentiated in terms of social position, were often tied together by kin relations (Elias and Scotson 1965). The fact that the outsiders came with a public housing development intensified the sense of difference. Likewise, while the pejorative 'apartheid' was developed in the context of a whole country, Montejano (1987) showed how very, very similar institutions emerged in South Texas: separate schools for the children of Mexican migrant workers, discriminatory labor laws, and customary segregation of public spaces.

In any case, the role of contingency has to be seen in the context of the social process as a whole, its geography, its institutions, divisions of labor, living and workplace. A case that commands particular interest partly because of the way it illustrates this point, but also because of its sheer novelty was the strong sense of difference, amounting to hostility, that emerged in the 1980s and early 1990s in South Africa between Africans living permanently in townships on the edge of major cities; and those living in hostels that typically existed cheek by jowl with the formal housing of the townships.

Migrant labor was, and remains, an important feature of the South African economy. Going back to apartheid days, this was typically explained in terms of urban residence rights. In virtue of a number of criteria, including being born in an urban area, some Africans had the right to live there in perpetuity. This would be in a township, usually on the edge of the city. Most Africans did not have what was called Section 10 status, but with an appropriate pass, they could live in the city for a limited time. However, they were not allowed to bring their families. Some might live with a relative in the township or even paying rent for a backyard hut. Many, though, lived in hostels, usually located in townships. There was then a difference in work experience. The migrant workers were consigned to the unskilled labor, often of the most arduous sort (Sitas 1996). Their dependents would remain in the rural areas, usually the homelands, formerly known as native reserves. The logic from the employer standpoint had always been that in that way, the dependents could self-subsist on land granted by the tribal authorities and live in whatever traditional housing they could build. As a result, the wage only had to cover the reproduction costs of the worker himself, and so could be held down. From the worker standpoint, however, there was another logic, which was patriarchal: a desire for the wife and children to be kept away from the temptations and evils of the city (Rueedi 2020). In addition, we should note that hostel living was particularly favored by Zulus from the Zulu homeland known as KwaZulu.

There had been tensions going back to the Soweto riots of the mid-seventies. There was violence, between the African youth of the townships and Zulu migrant workers who refused to obey a work stayaway called in support of them. As is related in Elsa Joubert's (1980) *Poppie Nongena*, the riots spread to the Western Cape where migrant workers were more likely to be from the Ciskei and Transkei homelands, rather than KwaZulu.[8] The heightening of the crisis in the country in the mid- to late 'eighties, intensified the polarization. The migrant workers provoked township hostility through their refusal to join in stayaways organized by the labor unions and the civic groups. But the point was, that they were more economically pressed. In the homelands, including KwaZulu, the relocation of Africans from 'white' South Africa, and a general increase in population, had increased the pressure on means of subsistence. This meant that the wage had to increasingly cover the subsistence needs of the dependents.

With the unbanning of the ANC and the growing prospect of African-majority rule, new issues came to the fore. KwaZulu had been the hearth of a Zulu-nationalist movement known as Inkatha which was suspicious of the universalistic claims of the ANC and had been more collaborative with the apartheid authorities. As it became clearer that in the 'new' South Africa, there would be an ANC-led government, rumors spread (Rueedi 2020). One was that the new government planned to abolish the homelands, which was correct. And secondly, that the land of those who held it currently, would be taken away from them, which was not. The result was that the Inkatha movement recruited heavily in the hostels, with a view to provoking conflict in the townships, creating a bloody violence which distracted from the negotiation process, as well as laying down markers for the imminent struggle over the future of the homelands.

What is one to make of this instance, this, to paraphrase Massey, particular juxtaposition of conditions and forces? It does not conform to that classic hierarchical politics of difference that is expressed through the formal

---

8 See in particular, Chapter 7: The Revolt of the Children.

technical division of labor. Clearly, it has to be situated with respect to the struggle against apartheid. The goals there, aside from a non-racial suffrage, were certainly mixed. There were reformist elements who saw the vote as a means to changing distributional outcomes. The target for many, though, was a white capitalist establishment to be eliminated through the nationalization of the mines and major industries. This was a serious concern for the latter, egged on by Cold War anxieties, further stoked by the US. This helps to explain the drawn-out nature of the crisis, in which granting the vote was out of the question. Meanwhile, the Zulu hostel dwellers refused to cooperate in the ANC program of boycotts and stayaways intended to weaken the regime and this attracted the ire of the township shock troops. The Zulus were, in effect, the traitors in the midst, identified as thus, and reviled for it.

If contingent conditions help explain the emergence of particular forms of difference, so too is that the case with their softening. Reference was made earlier to the patriarchal form of the family in the nineteenth century, but one which was functional for the survival of the working-class household. The 'little worker' figured prominently in that discussion. This would come to an end with mandatory schooling and the raising of the legal age at which children could work for a wage. Families would become much smaller. Women's labor time was increasingly there waiting to be exploited, but in a highly patriarchal society, there were limits to it; most notably women were, it was argued, physically incapable of the sort of work that men did. What would then make the difference would be the massive expansion of service employment in the postwar period, beginning with the welfare state and continuing through to the bureaucratization of the corporation. These were decidedly *not* jobs that were inappropriate for women. Rather their stereotypical attributes of attention to detail, empathy and patience with clients now came to be emphasized. The result has been a quite massive growth in female wage employment as a fraction of the total. The passage of money into female hands has then revolutionized domestic relations: a degree of economic independence has given them an independence of men; so later marriage, if at all, and higher divorce rates. This has then increased the impetus to break down remaining barriers to female employment.

• • •

From this limited point of view, the case just discussed might seem to suggest that capital's structural logic of indifference to gender, race and so on can work, even while it might be slow. Likewise, there is no disputing that the position of African Americans, while still leaving a great deal to be desired has improved relative to whites since the middle of the last century. We should, nevertheless, be careful in drawing conclusions from this about the possibility of a difference-less world. It is not just that social stratification is not going to go away since capital's own logics demand it. It is also that even while some differences can be flattened, new ones are going to appear. The structural position of the working class, the dominance of capitalist values, and the diversification of the working class in terms of the technical division of labor requires it. Some have to be subordinated, discriminated against, so that others can retain a modest position in the capitalist pecking order or even improve on it. In England, before the Indians, Pakistanis and West Indians arrived in the 1950s, it was the Irish who were the outcasts. And before that, manual laborers were regarded as a race apart, possibly inheriting their supposed improvidence, drunkenness, ignorance, over generations. In apartheid South Africa, the more urbanized African held the rural counterpart in contempt; something overlooked by more conventional understandings of that regime. Post-apartheid, it is refugees from the rest of Africa who are the threat.

One has to be impressed by the way in which old differences can suddenly acquire an enhanced significance. Capitalist urbanization has been a particular site for this sort of formation. The way in which later arrivals in the city are superposed on earlier ones has been reproduced many times, often producing a sharp politics of difference that has then been the foundation for changes in state form. There are some quite remarkable parallels between the nationalisms of the Quebecois and the Afrikaners of South Africa (Cox 2002: 195–203): an anglophone urban population in the major cities, notably Montreal and Johannesburg; a backward countryside of French-speaking and Afrikaans-speaking peoples who had been there long before; and then an urban migration which puts them at the bottom of the ladder, confronting an occupational structure in which the linguistically alien are predominant. Organization around 'difference' was, in both instances, the way chosen to usurp those in the working class above them, and achieve the dominant capitalist values.

All this suggests that capital's tendency of indifference to 'difference' has to be regarded as, indeed, 'tendential' to which will be opposed, as long as capitalism is around, that is, tendencies towards the creation of ever new 'differences': something inscribed in deeply held values of what it means to work in capitalist society and what life's purposes should be. And to the extent that success is achieved, it is to be secured by kicking away the ladder of those underneath; while those standing lower down are trying to displace you, drawing on discourses of difference, of long-standing oppression, as indeed in the cases of Quebecois and Afrikaner nationalism reviewed above.

References

Ashe, S.D. and McGeever, B.F. (2011) Marxism, Racism and the Construction of 'Race' as a Social and Political Relation: an Interview with Professor Robert Miles. *Ethnic and Racial Studies* 34:12, 2009–2026.

Borriello, A. and Jäger, A. (2023) *The Populist Moment*. London: Verso Books.

Bourdieu, P. (1984) *Distinction*. London: Routledge and Kegan Paul.

Brenner, J. and Ramas, M. (1984) Rethinking Women's Oppression. *New Left Review* I/144, 33–71.

Brustein, W.I. and King, R.D. (2004) Anti-Semitism in Europe before the Holocaust. *International Political Science Review* 25:1, 35–53.

Buckwalter, L.M. and Baten, J. (2019) Valkyries: Was gender equality high in the Scandinavian periphery since Viking times? Evidence from enamel hypoplasia and height ratios. *Economics and Human Biology* 34, 181–193.

Callinicos, L. (1981) *Gold and Workers: 1886–1924*. Johannesburg: Ravan Press.

Caron, V. (2005) The Path to Vichy: Antisemitism in France in the 1930s. Washington DC: Center for Advanced Holocaust Studies.

Cox, K.R. (2002) *Political Geography: State, Territory and Politics*. Oxford: Blackwell.

Damer, S. (1974) 'Wine Alley': the Sociology of a Dreadful Enclosure. *Sociological Review* 22:2, 221–248.

Davidson, N. (1999) The Trouble with 'Ethnicity.' *International Socialism* 2:84.

Eley, G. (2021) What Is Fascism, and Where Does It Come From? *History Workshop Journal* 91, 1–28.

Elias, N. and Scotson, E.L. (1965) *The Established and the Outsiders*. London: Frank Cass.

Evans, R. (1985) The Myth of Germany's Missing Revolution. *New Left Review* I/149, 67–94.

Fraser, N. (2000) Rethinking Recognition. *New Left Review* II/3, 107–120.

Giddens, A. (1981) *A Contemporary Critique of Historical Materialism*. Los Angeles and Berkeley CA: University of California Press.

Graham, H. (2005) *The Spanish Civil War: A Very Short Introduction*. Oxford: Oxford University Press.

Harvey, D. (1985) The Geopolitics of Capitalism, in D Gregory and J Urry (eds.), *Social Relations and Spatial Structures*. New York: Springer.

Hyslop, J. (1999) The Imperial Working Class Makes Itself 'White': White Labourism in Britain, Australia, and South Africa before the First World War. *Journal of Historical Sociology* 12:4, 398–421.

James, W. (1992) Migration, Racism and Identity: the Caribbean Experience in Britain. *New Left Review* I/193, 15–55.

Jeeves, A.H. and Crush, J. (1995) The Failure of Stabilization Experiments on South African Gold Mines. Chapter 1 in J Crush and W James (eds.), *Crossing Boundaries*. Cape Town: Institute for Democracy in South Africa.

Jeffery, D. (2017) The Strange Death of Tory Liverpool. *British Politics* 12, 386–407.

Joubert, E. (1980) *Poppie Nongena*. New York: Henry Holt.

Liebow, E. (1967) *Tally's Corner*. Boston: Little Brown and Company.

Mann, M. (1995) Sources of Variation in Working-Class Movements in Twentieth-Century Europe. *New Left Review* I/212, 14–54.

Massey, D. (2005) *For Space*. London: Sage Publications.

Mitter, S. (1986) Industrial Restructuring and Manufacturing Homework: Immigrant Women in the UK Clothing Industry. *Capital and Class* 27, 37–80.

Montejano, D. (1987) *Anglos and Mexicans in the Making of Texas, 1836–1986*. Austin TX: University of Texas Press.

Rueedi, F. (2020) The Hostel Wars in Apartheid South Africa: Rumor, Violence and the Discourse of Victimhood. *Social Identities* 26:6, 756–773.

Sitas, A. (1996) The New Tribalism: Hostels and Violence. *Journal of Southern African Studies* 22:2, 235–248.

Traverso, E. (2016) *Fire and Blood: The European Civil War, 1914–1945*. London: Verso Press.

Webber, M.M. (1964) Culture, Territoriality, and the Elastic Mile. *Papers of the Regional Science Association* 13, 58–69.

Wolfe, A. (1982) *America's Impasse*. Boston: South End Press.

Wood, E.M. (1988) Capitalism and Human Emancipation. *New Left Review* I/167, 95–107.

Zelizer, V. (1994) *Pricing the Priceless Child: The Changing Social Value of Children*. Princeton NJ: Princeton University Press.

CHAPTER 14

Capitalist Housing Regimes and Homeless People
A Relative Surplus Population of the City

Mahito Hayashi

1   Introduction

This chapter develops an extended theoretical account of urban homelessness by using Marxist and Marxian literature, with case-based illustrations to concretize this theoretical account.[1] It is hoped that this project can contribute to the explanatory power of some fundamental political-economic concepts—both classical and contemporary—combining an intensive use of a geographical area (Japan) with a topical issue (homelessness).

Currently, many critical urban researchers forcefully mobilize poststructural, postcolonial, postmodern, or posthuman concepts and frameworks, rather than those linked to classical—and even recent—Marxist research paradigms, in spite of the strengths of Marxist urban studies enumerated in earlier overviews (Katznelson, 1992; Merrifield, 2002; Tabb and Sawers, 1984). The shift in the approach of these post-Marxist paradigms may result from an interest in cultural, political, or 'material' processes that are subordinated by a hegemonic society or Euro-American (Western) civilizations. Given this, discussion of homelessness and Japan offer the possibility of revitalizing Marxist/Marxian theory in the areas of sociology, geography, and urban studies. It is argued here that these two topics help us to stretch the Marxian corpus beyond its orthodox limits, so that it can illuminate its own margins, where 'Marxism' faces constant criticism, deformation, and new intellectual creativities.

In short, these two topical/geographical areas, which have been marginalized or bracketed, can become fertile ground for harvesting new possibilities from Marxism *because of* their limited position and non-position in Euro-American Marxist discussions. To this end, this chapter draws on concepts and

---

1   This chapter draws on Hayashi (2023b) and was helped by David Fasenfest's clarification regarding Marx's texts. An earlier version was presented at the conference 'Poverty, the State and Politics in the City' at York University, Toronto, on 2 October 2023. I appreciate the stimulating discussions from Hyun Ok Park, Ken Kawashima, and Greg Albo. I also thank David Fasenfest, Raju J. Das, and Phillip F. Kelly for their generous support of the event.

arguments taken from Karl Marx, Friedrich Engels, Antonio Gramsci, Henri Lefebvre, David Harvey, Edward Soja, Bob Jessop, Neil Brenner, and Jamie Peck. Interconnecting these concepts will enable a comparison of homelessness and Japan, but without an attempt at a separation (provincialization) of the two from a hegemonic urban society or from the hegemonic Euro-American world.

2 Theoretical Orientation

The application of Marxism to homelessness in the Japanese context addresses what is an important question in Marxist urban theory: how can we locate relative surplus populations (RSPs) in capitalist urbanization? For period-specific or epistemological reasons, neither Engels nor Lefebvre—each of whom influence urban scholars—were unable to frame this question adequately as it relates to the present. Harvey (1982: 85, 88) may have closed off the question when he suggested that the 'devaluation of capital' entails the '"devaluation" of the labourer', but his urban theory did not examine how this devaluation emerges in the city or how labor can resist devaluation even after becoming an RSP. His urbanization-of-capital thesis can be reframed as the urbanization of RSPs, which have important material/political/social ramifications for urban society, not least with reference to Gramscian arguments concerning regulation and deregulation.

When it comes to the locus of homelessness in urbanization, use is made of Lefebvre and Engels in order to develop the concept of a capitalist housing regime as a city's period-specific strategy to accommodate the working class—and its different subgroups—in urban(izing) space in relation to a form of capital accumulation and labor subsumption. This conception allows us to understand that what we know as 'homelessness' is actually a period-specific form of the RSP that can come into being only after a modern capitalist housing regime has emerged in the city and has established an inclusive environment of working-class subsumption and social reproduction (see Hayashi 2022). It is also in this city, with its mature capitalist housing regime, that progressive/radical movements may emerge for homeless people, may start working for the homeless section of the RSP, and may advocate on behalf of homeless people for their 'right to the city.'

Finally, Marx's concept of metabolism (as circuits of production and consumption) is adapted to contemporary homelessness so as to illuminate homeless people's active (labor-mediated) engagement with urban space qua 'nature.' Today, a capitalist housing regime can take highly mature forms, leading to the vast formation of public spaces outside of 'housing' itself, thereby establishing the 'grid' of public/private spaces as a heavily capitalized and regulated site of working-class consumption and subsumption. In this urban landscape, homeless people must produce (before consuming) the use values of 'housing' (private spaces) out of the pregiven ('natural') use values component of public spaces. In turn, homeless people's metabolism may create disruptive moments vis-à-vis a mature capitalist housing regime, its residents, and its profit-making and regulatory agencies. This triggers a politics of 'homeless regulation' in the city, the dynamics of which show highly decentralizing—and 'rescaling' (Brenner, 2004)—trajectories of centrifugal power production for achieving 'governance.'

3   The Prehistory of Today's Homelessness

3.1   *The Relative Surplus Population and Housing: Marx and Engels*

With regard to the relative surplus population, book 1 of *Capital* (Marx, 1887 [1867]) argues that capitalism limitlessly advances the economic marginalization of the working class at the endpoint of labor–capital relations. In section 4, chapter 25 of the book, Marx discusses the RSP concept, describing not just the RSP's '*active* labour army' (emphasis added) but also the RSP's 'lowest sediment' and how it 'dwells in the sphere of pauperism' (444). The location of pauperism remains unclear, but when identifying this 'lowest sediment' in the RSP, Marx suggests that even his inclusion of this sediment, covering a breadth of pauperism, can drive an exclusion of 'homelessness' from the RSP's normal appearance. The RSP, it is suggested, must be '*exclusive of vagabonds, criminals, prostitutes, in a word, the "dangerous" classes*' (440, emphasis added).

Seemingly, Marx's exclusion of 'dangerous' people (but dangerous to what?) from the RSP category is done for social or political reasons. Marx's exclusive treatment of the dangerous concerns us because *Capital* here must mobilize the RSP category as an economic category that can reveal how capitalism (as a system of accumulation) can create and utilize divides and subgroups in the working class, and how these divides make accumulation immune to potential broader solidarities in the working class. Capitalism, in short, strives to maintain this very divided situation: 'the condemnation of one part of the working class to enforced idleness by the overwork of the other part, and the converse,' in order to accelerate 'the production of the industrial reserve army on a scale corresponding with the advance of social accumulation' (440).

Capital, at one place, suggests a tentative inclusion of the 'dangerous' people into the RSP category, calling these people 'the demoralised and ragged, and those unable to work, chiefly people who succumb to their incapacity for adaptation, due to the division of labour' (444). Another interesting suggestion is that the capitalist production of the RSP receives social and cultural elements from European civilization (relating to gender, age, and 'morals'), so that the working class's internal antagonism can propagate within civil society in 'spontaneous' ways (that is, without external political intervention).

At such points, Marx's theory of the RSP is inherently more nuanced than the simple exclusion of dangerous people. But Marx arguably could have been more sensitive to these people, and to the 'lumpenproletariat,' as described in his analysis of France. He might have deduced from his theory an understanding of how the elements of civilization can be projected onto the most 'ragged' and can amplify their negative public images (and self-images) *for* capital accumulation.

Engels, who comes closer, and perhaps is more sympathetic, to the question of 'the ragged.' His *Housing Question* (Engels, 1995 [1872]) uses the term 'reserve army,' the term *Capital* employs nearly as a synonym for the RSP category. Engels's description gives us a clue to a more nuanced understanding of how the 'the ragged' get spatialized onto the streets: 'Violent and regularly recurring industrial vacillations determine on the one hand the existence of a large reserve army of unemployed workers, and on the other hand drive large masses of the workers temporarily unemployed onto the streets.' (39; see also the discussion of roofless people and the reserve army in Engels 1845).

Engels's description is located in the dominant urban environment of his era—namely, the *non*realization of the 'bourgeois and petty-bourgeois utopia' (Engels, 1995 [1872]:12). In his terms, this means that big cities constantly fail to give each worker and their family their 'own little house and if possible a little garden as well,' which he calls 'the cottage system.'

Instead, many laborers are squeezed into the 'barrack system,' which is composed of 'large buildings containing numerous workers' dwellings' (52). This barrack system, an imperfect housing regime to accommodate laborers in the city, accompanies the phenomenon of homelessness. The essay—as well as *The Condition of the Working Class in England* (Engels, 1845), which is also full of Engels's view on street people—suggests that these people cyclically burst out from the 'barracks' and were therefore a 'natural' component of the working class in nineteenth-century European cities.

Obviously, cities in our era are different from Engels's European cities. Our cities have much advanced the realization of the cottage system, a regime that can assign many workers and their families their 'own little houses' but Engels could not see the full development of this regime with his own eyes: 'Unfortunately the cottage system is not realizable just in the centres of the housing shortage, in the big cities' (Engels, 1995 [1872]:47). Engels's description of the new housing regime's uniqueness—its form, contradiction, and politics—are thus unfinished. What are they? How can we understand 'homelessness' in this new context of capitalist urbanization?

3.2   The Housing Classes and Their 'New' City: Lefebvre, Harvey, and Soja

This question—that is, the conceptual extension of Engels's *Housing Question* to our contemporary cities—may perhaps be answered by way of Henri Lefebvre's discussion of 'habitat.' Though it is little dispersedly used in *The Urban Revolution*, Lefebvre employs this notion of habitat in relation to capitalist urbanization in the late Fordist era, when the city was achieving a highly improved and integral accommodation of workers and their families. The city, Lefebvre suggests, has now become a central site for capitalism to finalize the subsumption of the working class by providing an inclusive set of urban environments. (For a similar analysis of the city and urban settlement, see Aglietta, 1979 [1976]; Hayashi, 2022).

In this context, habitat is suggested to have both private and public spaces, or the spaces of private housing units plus their surroundings (commonly used environments and amenities). Lefebvre (2003 [1970]: 81, 98) conceptualizes habitat as the terrain of regulated housing space in the city, to which he assigns derogatory terms such as 'cages,' 'dwelling machines,' and 'switching boxes'. At the same time, he suggests the structural coupling of these private housing units with 'parks and open spaces' (Lefebvre, 2003 [1970]:27), which are publicly consumed. This public portion of the urban settlement has now expanded massively in the city and can be understood as an extension of the habitat, partly because it is the strategic site where the 'little garden' of Engels's cottage system is functionally fulfilled, even for nonprivileged workers. Of course, public spaces also can do more than play the role of a little garden, which includes the role of societalization, on which see below.

In this context, Lefebvre's notion of habitat can be reconceived of as a 'grid' or matrix of public and private spaces. This grid can sustain the regulated everydayness (what he calls the 'industrial quotidian') of workers/families against disruption by navigating habitation in the city toward 'controlled consumption' (Lefebvre (2003 [1970]: 164). This grid achieves the dissection, relocation, and 'gridding' of workers' urban (consumption) experience away from the point of production, or the 'bulk of factories' (Lefebvre (2003 [1970]: 29), so that a heightened mode of working-class subsumption permeates the city. As a result, the regulated everydayness of the working class can be maintained amid the harsh experiences of the working class at the production point—at the proximity of 'accumulation for accumulation's sake.'

It seems that what Engels understood under the banner of the cottage system in his nineteenth-century cities is now fully realized in the form of habitat (qua public/private spaces). More to the point, the (potentially) disruptive processes of unemployment, pauperism, and 'dangerous' appearances that deteriorated social homogeneity and integrity under nineteenth-century capitalism—the appearance of the 'lumpenproletariat' that Marx found, and talked scornfully about, at the margins of the RSP category—are now mostly enclosed within housing units. In the city, publicly behaving citizens (*housed* citizens) and their regulatory agents (the municipality, the police, and the like) are less likely to be disrupted by the 'danger' of pauperism.

It should be emphasized that these housed people have engaged in progressive or radical politics around the consumption of public and private spaces, clamouring for liveable and sound residential neighborhoods and housing spaces (Castells, 1983; Cox and Mair, 1988; Harvey, 2012; Hou, 2010; Logan and Molotch, 1987). Yet social relations *within* the housing classes could still be powerfully constructed by the public/private matrix despite these people's struggles from within the world of local residents and users of public space.

Now, at last, we are in the historically specific situation in which we can talk about the 'housing classes' (Rex and Moore, 1967) in a Marxist sense, as an urban category of class relations that is superimposed on, and possibly deforms, the classical class relations (worker–employer relations) and class consciousness in the city. Harvey (1976) was probably the first who clearly used the notion of the housing classes to denote an urbanized form of class relations (or urban class relations). Of course, Harvey's project in the 1980s was the 'urbanization of capital' (Harvey, 1989). What is less discussed, however, is that his extremely capital-centered thesis (Massey, 1994) had a preliminary and companion discussion about how class struggle and class relations (not just capital) also get urbanized.

According to Harvey (1976: 281), 'the early industrialists ... had to deal with workers both inside the factory and outside of it'. The factory itself was the central site where mechanisms of labor control evolved in modern capitalism (Marx, 1887 [1867]). Yet the project of labor control, if considered as an *urban* project, was also intensified outside of the factory. The built environment of private (housing) spaces, and their coupling with public spaces, had enormous power to advance 'the fragmentation that occurs within the working class as one section of it moves into homeownership and becomes deeply concerned to preserve and if possible to enhance the value of its equity.' In this context, what has happened is 'a fragmentation of the working class into "housing classes" of homeowners and tenants' (Harvey 1976: 272–273).

This world of homeowners and tenants—the world of the housing classes—was a manoeuvre of the 'capitalist class' and their 'techniques of persuasion [which] are widely used in advanced capitalist societies to ensure rational consumption' (Harvey, 1976: 277). Echoing Lefebvre on habitat, he argues that the housing classes can use public and private (housing) spaces as the site of their new struggle, 'a struggle over the definition and meaning of use values, of the standard of living of labor, of the equality of life' (Harvey, 1976: 294), which represents for him not an ephemeral (petit bourgeois) utopia but a frontier of the working class's struggle at the sites of consumption.

In effect, both Lefebvre and Harvey have virtually bolstered a new 'late capitalist' mode of Marxist enquires into Engels's cottage system, making it possible for us to trace how the Engelsian housing question has been developed into an urban geographical system (grid) of public and private spaces in the city (in the case of Lefebvre), and how this development helped the city reconstruct volatile class relations into a more stable (regulated) one (in the case of Harvey). Both suggest that housed citizens are not just a regulated, fragmented form of the working class but also a new opening of urban politics on the horizon of consumption.

And it is at this historical juncture that the 'ragged' and the 'dangerous' start to take on a clear-cut form of 'homeless people' in the city. In the city of the housing classes, homeless people are clearly delineated as the outsiders to the 'housed' and so are objectified as an 'abnormal' group. This situation is markedly different from Engels's housing question, in which the barrack system—a deteriorated regime—was rampant. Today, the perfection of the cottage system into a modern framework of habitat has been finished, and a historically new contradiction (homelessness) comes into being between habitat and non-habitat. The spatially delineated and socially divided appearance of the RSP question—the homeless question—balloons in *this* city.

Urban geographer Soja (1989: 95) may be read as critical of the concept housing classes as used here, because he emphatically contests the 'liberal' social science that makes 'efforts to separate consumption from production ... to define class, for example, primarily upon consumption characteristics'. However, it could be argued that if the historical process of capitalist urbanization is to separate the consumption experience from the (value) production experience, as Soja (1989: 70) thinks it is, and to depoliticize consumption on behalf of capitalism as a system, then this experience of urban separation can be theorized by using the notion of the housing classes. Accordingly, the latter are conceptualized here as an urban category of the working class rather than as a neo-Weberian category that is theoretically separated out from production. (For a neo-Weberian use of this concept, see Rex and Moore, 1967, or discussions of this separation in Hayashi, 2023a).

Also at this juncture, perhaps for the first time in the Euro-American history of capitalist urbanization, the new contradiction of 'homelessness' starts prompting cities to regulate homeless people (the 'outsiders' of the housed) by deploying a dense web of oppression-plus-persuasion across the streets and other public spaces, at the urban scale. It is necessary, therefore, to consider this new question of homeless regulation and how it can be related to the larger context of capitalist social formation.

4   Homelessness and Regulation Today

4.1   *Societalization in the City*

If capitalism is considered a constantly developing system of 'accumulation for accumulation's sake,' the culmination in housing classes, their formation and their habitat (public and private spaces), which Lefebvre saw in European cities around the late 1960s, should be seen as a significant progression of socialization in the urban settlement. In the regulationist vocabulary of Jessop, societalization is a social process that can stabilize or postpone, through a provision of sociocultural principles and environments useful for social integration, the crisis-prone nature of capitalist society beyond the limits inherent to the accumulation regime. According to Jessop (2002: 22), societalization is 'a pattern of institutional integration and social cohesion that complements the dominant accumulation regime and its mode of economic regulation, thereby securing the conditions for its dominance in the wider society'.

The consolidation of the housing classes and their habitat environment (public *and* private spaces) has transformed the city into a major site of societalization. Empty stomachs, untreated diseases, and housing deprivation—the 'dangerous' appearances of the RSP—have become concealed behind doors and walls and are unobservable from public spaces. As such, the grid of public and private spaces has almost limitlessly extended the housing classes to the spectrums of the working class by guarding their consumptive and semiotic (meaning-making) lives. These housed people are categorized as 'worker' or 'producer' in/around the labor market, now strongly self-identified as 'dweller' or 'consumer' of the matrix, against capitalism's continual ballooning of poverty and class division. As they were becoming so, the matrix has turned the city into a powerful framework of societalization.

In this context, people's urban encounter and society formation at and around public spaces becomes a chief process through which people form a lot of common ideas about society, life, and the nation, away from 'accumulation for accumulation's sake' and its class-dividing tendencies. This societalization role of public spaces must be defended—through various social and political actors—against homeless people's materially and culturally disruptive elements. This defense amounts to *homeless regulation*.

4.2 Homeless Regulation

In the context of societalization, homeless regulation can be theorized by reference to Gramsci's (1971: 263) argument about the 'integral state,' which he conceptualizes as a combination of 'political society + civil society'. In this conception of integral state formation, a narrower definition of the state (as political society) is distinguished from the integral state per se. The state (in the narrower sense) is epitomized by law, sanction, and sanction-based regulation/guidance as *coercion* (Gramsci, 1971: 261, 267). Civil society, in turn, is the locus of *consent* among citizens gathering around moral leaders on the grounds of religion and/or social institutions; it is the site for the 'evolution of customs, ways of thinking and acting, morality' (Gramsci, 1971: 242; see also 12). According to Gramsci, different societies developed these two sectors—the state (as political society) and civil society—without a complete overlapping, and in so doing, regularized different trajectories of civilization.

This Gramscian interpretation helps the formulation of homeless regulation as a variant of societalization that materializes around public spaces under homelessness, as depicted in Figure 14.1. The three boxes at the top of the figure, and their tripartite relationship, represent the hegemony-valorizing (societalizing) triangle of the state (in the narrow sense), civil society, and public spaces. It is within this relationship with the state and civil society that public spaces might gain their 'normal' appearance and become a strategic site for societalization in the city. Public spaces become the infrastructure of societalization. Beneath these three boxes are located 'homeless-riven public space' to show the crisis of societalization and hegemony. The two arrows extending from the 'State' and 'Civil Society' boxes to 'Homeless-Riven Public Space' indicate the roles and processes of homeless regulation in reregulating public spaces.

The hypothesis underlying this figure is that in response to homelessness, the state and social sectors in the city assemble networks and relations of regulation considered 'suitable' to these 'abnormal' people—or, more precisely, to the non-normal points of encounter between housed citizens and homeless people. From one location to another, violence and coercion create unique mixtures with agreement and consensus, producing different local arenas of

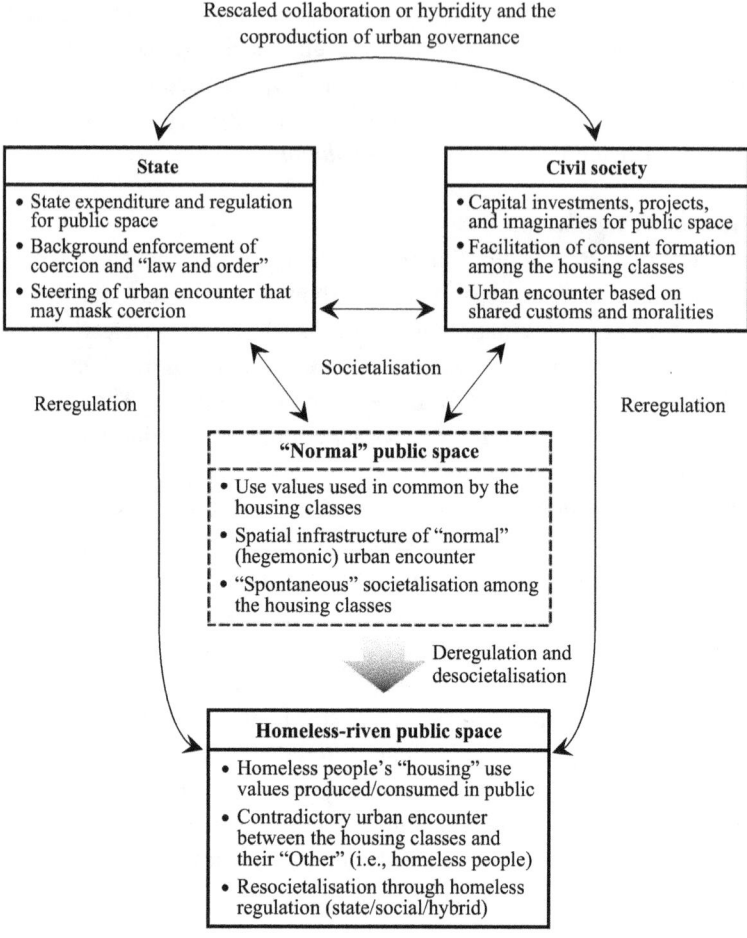

FIGURE 14.1 Regulation of public space amid homelessness
SOURCE: ORIGINALLY PUBLISHED IN HAYASHI (2023B:115) AS FIGURE 14.2)

urban governance. Yet the basic outlook of public spaces can have a more regimenting tone in defense of a hegemonic (societalized) society.

4.3 The Homeless Metabolism

With regard to 'homeless' people themselves, who must develop survival economies against homeless regulation and its societalization outcomes, the notion of metabolism can be viewed as having a broad resonance with conceptions in Marxism (e.g., Burkett, 1999; Foster, 2000; Heynen, Kaika, and Swyngedouw, 2006; Moore, 2015; Swyngedouw, 1996). A key recognition is that homeless people's consumption of public spaces to live entails their incessant production/sustenance of 'housing' through intensive labor in these public spaces (Hayashi, 2013, 2014a, 2022). Marx and Marxian authors use the term *metabolism* to refer to people's laboring capacity, directed toward (urban) nature, which can produce use values.

Homelessness—its key dimensions extended in public—can be theorized and analyzed by viewing homeless people's metabolic engagement with public spaces as urban nature in search of housing. In this process, homeless people can produce a housing space with multiple use values to make possible their living in the city. Tents, cardboard shelters, and large-scale encampment sites are the major signs of the homeless labor geared toward the production of housing. Yet even homeless people's 'minimalist' housing strategy, that is, lying on the ground, becomes possible only through a significant labor expense.

Even in this regimented approach to housing production, homeless people need to guard themselves against unpleasant meetings with the housing classes and their political guardians, find storage sites to keep important belongings, measure the length of time available for a rest, keep evacuation places elsewhere for emergencies, compete with other homeless individuals and groups for a 'good' location, and spend a considerable length of time outside of that location before it becomes available. In short, even in this 'minimalist' approach, homeless people must deploy these (and other) labor processes to consume housing use values in public spaces.

Figure 14.2 indicates homeless people's minoritarian metabolism on the left and the housing classes' majoritarian metabolism on the right. The figure shows how the metabolic process of homeless people—their production and consumption circuit of housing use values—can be conceptualized by locating it in the pregiven context of 'normal' public spaces and their 'normal' metabolic form, as envisioned and practiced by the housing classes. The figure shows how the meeting of the two groups can be seen as a contradictory encounter of two metabolic circuits. This metabolic contradiction is material, of course, but from this it develops cultural, ideological, and semiotic conflicts within the same public spaces. The homeless–housed divide, when this term is used, refers to this material and semiotic cleavage, which can burst out from the level of urban metabolism.

A methodological aspect of this formulation is inserting the 'Other' of the housing classes (homeless people) into the 'normal' metabolism mode practiced by and constructed for the housing classes in public spaces—can reveal a hidden dimension of capitalist urban regulation not much discussed in political economy. That is, the city under capitalism can acquire its significant capacity for societalization from the 'pleasant' public spaces for the housing

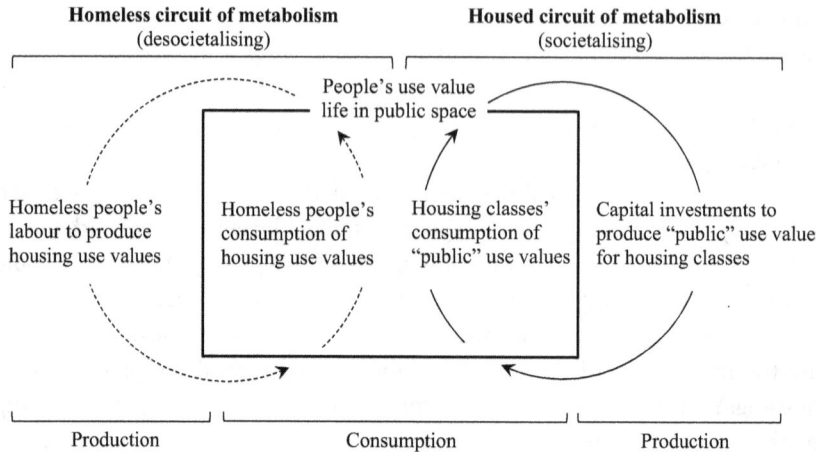

FIGURE 14.2 Two metabolic circuits in public space
SOURCE: ORIGINALLY PUBLISHED IN HAYASHI (2023B:112) AS FIGURE 14.1)

classes. In this way, homeless regulation can be considered not just as violent, less violent, and nonviolent treatments in addressing homeless people but also as an entire system of societalization at/around public spaces, which must defend the regulated terrain of the city from its (mini-)crises.

The homeless–housed opposition indicated in Figure 14.2 also reveals that the housing classes *can* enjoy (consume) the domain of urban nature without participating in the material production of public spaces. Insofar as the housing classes are thus 'dislocated' from the production process of the urban settlement per se, they can advance their consumption ontologically, not as a process or a grid given by the structure, the ruling class, or the state, but as a process that they socially, culturally, and purposefully construct. Public spaces can achieve this key societalization role in the city because public spaces allow the housing classes, through their consumption, to create and share various sociocultural imageries of 'public,' relatively away from the harsh experiences inherent in the labor process or in private life.

This urban apparatus of societalization—a modern housing regime with vast urban geographies on its public exterior—has some key historical roots in European cities, as Engels observed. Since the nineteenth century, however, the barrack and cottage systems have developed vigorously and have matured into the Lefebvrean habitat environment. The roles and characteristics of the contemporary public/private grid can be critically scrutinized, particularly when we examine cities prone to homelessness. These are the cities that have the 'outsiders' of the housing classes constantly inserted into this urban apparatus of habitat.

4.4 Redeploying Marxist Conceptions in Homeless Studies

Anglophone scholars have used the concept of the homeless–housed divide to denote the tension between the two groups in the city (Cloke, May, and Johnsen, 2010; Gowan, 2010); hence the term is not mine. Moreover, earlier research was already suggesting that homeless people bring 'private' elements into 'public,' and that this public–private contradiction creates highly disruptive moments in the world of public space users who have housing (Snow and Anderson, 1993). In these supposed situations of antagonism, notions about homeless people—about their 'survival strategies,' 'subaltern strategies,' 'agency,' and 'becoming'—have been employed to construct actor-centered versions of a homeless study focused on homeless people's identity formation, cultural creativity, and sociopolitical engagements in the face of regulatory pressure (Gowan, 2010; Snow and Anderson, 1993; Sparks, 2017; see also DeVerteuil, 2006). These 'mainstream' interests in homeless studies are said to be more attuned to complex situations (DeVerteuil, May, and von Mahs, 2009) and sometimes take positions sharply opposed to the structural understanding of homelessness proposed by Marxist geographers.

In the late 1990s, Marxist geographers Neil Smith and Don Mitchell described what one might call structural notions related to Marxism in order to denote the heightened contexts of capital-driven gentrification in US cities. They used such expressions as 'class struggle on Avenue B' (Smith, 1996) and the 'annihilation of space by law' (Mitchell, 1997), both interpreting the contradiction in public spaces under gentrification as being between the middle class plus their political guardians (regulators) on the one hand, and homeless people and their supporters on the other. This explanatory framework was appropriate to the prime urban areas of US metropolises, where the regulatory tensions around homeless people could take somewhat extreme forms.

However, British geographers have argued that the structural understanding of homeless regulation conceptualized by Smith and Mitchell does not apply to the British case, in which the regulatory tensions around homelessness can take more complex and nuanced forms than depicted by those authors (Cloke, May, and Johnsen 2010). Efforts to steer away from the Marxist formulation of homelessness and its regulation also came from US geographers, who emphasized the spatial strategies of homeless people not just to endure but also to overcome the intensive homeless regulation in large US cities (DeVerteuil, May, and von Mahs, 2009). In short, difficulties in formulating *who* regulates homeless people in the city, for *what* purposes, and *how* they do so, has provided research with reasons not to apply the neo-Marxist vocabulary of Smith and Mitchell to homelessness.

With reference to these debates, it is possible to suggest a redeployment of Marxist/Marxian concepts in homeless studies, even for the cities where the capital-driven forms of homeless regulation for advancing/regulating gentrification are weaker. This argues that the tension between homeless people and the housing classes—denoted as homeless–housed divides—can be considered as erupting from the metabolic bedrock of urban nature materially and socially constructed by the public/private matrix. From the era of Fordism onwards, this urban environmental framework has played a major role in (re-)regulating into stable urban everydayness the experience of the housing classes and their consumption of use values.

Because the housing classes and their urban environment—that is, the habitat resulting from private space plus public space—has been constructed in highly matured forms today, the homeless portion of the RSP is structurally pitted against the larger part of the working class who are housed, and their cities; therefore, the contradiction in public spaces is structural. In this context, homeless people can exhibit ever more 'dangerous' appearances vis-à-vis housed people and *their* everyday society (see Marx, 1887 [1867]). Engels's cottage system has already taken highly sophisticated forms that can subsume the various lives of the working class (both rich and poor), and this sharply delineates the contours of *non*subsumed or *less* subsumed processes of the working class in the city—homelessness.

4.5 Cyclical Homelessness and Regulation in Postwar Japan

The site of my fieldwork has been an inner-city zone within the city of Yokohama called the Kotobuki district (Kotobuki chiku) and its surrounding areas, in Kanagawa Prefecture. During the 1970s, in this locality and in other Japanese cities, homelessness grew significantly in and around a specific type of inner-city area occupied by disadvantaged day laborers, generally called *yoseba*, and the Kotobuki district is one such locale. I call this phase of homelessness the 'inner-city cycle' of postwar homelessness in Japan. Homelessness grew again after the early 1990s and into the 2000s, extending to a broader urban geography beyond the inner-city areas. In this more recent phase, labelled the 'widespread cycle' of homelessness, people who are homeless started to exist in various public spaces previously used exclusively by housed citizens. This homeless–housed proximity created significant ruptures in the 'normal' appearance of Japanese public spaces and opened numerous homeless–housed divides in cities, contributing to the bottom-up formation of (mini-)crises in urban societalization.

It should be noted that the numbers of homeless people in Japan have remained smaller than in countries within the Euro-American world. For instance, the crisis phase of Fordist urbanization in the United States, which culminated in the early 1980s, accompanied the acute growth of homeless street people, with their numbers reaching 250,000 to 300,000 (Rossi, 1989: 37). In Japan, by contrast, the number of homeless street people remained below 30,000 even during the early 2000s, when Japan experienced the prolonged downturn of the so-called post-bubble crisis and experienced a sharp growth of homelessness in public spaces (Ministry of Health, Labour and Welfare, 2003).

One might conclude from this comparison that Japanese public spaces have not been challenged by street homelessness and that the Japanese case is irrelevant for advancing a theorization of homelessness from the regulationist angle. This interpretation, however, misjudges the disruptive impact that the rise of homelessness precipitated vis-à-vis Japanese urban society after the early 1990s and into the 2000s. As outlined elsewhere (Hayashi, 2023), Japanese postwar society was founded on a highly conformist version of the societalization process that directs the housing classes toward homogeneous cultural codes of public space usage. This cultural aspect of Japanese societalization has even been *more* than cultural because it has been the reaction of this country's societalization strategy to the scarcity of public spaces available for the populace in comparison to Western countries. To make these public spaces functional as a bastion of people's social reproduction in spite of their smaller use values, postwar Japan has organized the housing classes in urban society around strict cultural codes that can powerfully homogenize behavior in public spaces.

Nonetheless, even the relatively small numbers of homeless people have created significant disruptions and conflicts with Japan's homogeneously constructed urban society. In turn, these endogenous urban regulatory (mini-)crises have led to multiple waves of anti-homeless regulation in the streets and beyond, which can effectively tame and remove the 'disruptive' impacts of homelessness, even when its quantitative volume has been minor by international standards. During the widespread rise of homelessness, starting in the early 1990s, new groups and networks of homeless regulation were quickly created across the housing classes, local businesses, landowners, the municipality, and the police—across the full spectrum of the Gramscian integral state. These local webs of homeless regulation started to severely constrain homeless people's survival economies and metabolic processes, which in turn pushed homeless people into a reflexive reconstruction of homelessness strategies, both on and off the streets, to survive the intensive pressure of regulation.

Furthermore, this haphazard dynamic of homeless regulation that erupted from cities and at the local scale would soon be followed by a rescaling of the framework of the Japanese state. This official intervention into the local regulatory dynamics would start in the 2000s, and justify and support a bottom-up process of fragmentary, haphazard, and localized homeless regulation.

5 State Rescaling

5.1 *Homeless Regulation As Rescaling*

The location of power in the process of homeless regulation is decentered, fragmented, and blurred. It is hard to claim that 'the capitalist state' or 'the ruling class' is directly responsible. However, this difficulty does not prevent us from gleaning useful categories from Marxist/Marxian literature. As outlined in Figure 14.1, some of these categories have already enabled the construction of an urban-scale understanding of homeless regulation as, for example, the relations and networks of the state and civil society.

Furthermore, the fragmented nature of a city's governance structure can be comprehended by looking at the dynamics of centrifugal power that surpasses urban governance per se, which matches the critical understanding Lefebvre (2009 [1966], 128) demonstrated with the key phrase 'a simulacrum of decentralization.' This rescaling process involves the dispersal, multiplication, and repositioning of regulatory power within a broader network of vertical power-holding entities and power-generating processes, which systemically facilitate the decentralized character of homeless regulation as it develops within the city.

To elucidate this centrifugal power restructuring process, I employ the scale concept. When employed by political-economic scholars in geography and urban studies, this concept often refers to the recurrent vertical differentiation and reordering in the scalar composition of a geography in question, known as the process and dynamics of (re-)scaling (Brenner, 2004, 2019; Collinge, 1999; Jessop, 2002; Keil and Mahon, 2009; Peck, 2001, 2002).

In particular, Neil Brenner (2004) uses the concept of state rescaling to underscore the spatially attuned strategies of the state that can, against the state's alleged 'demise' under globalization, revitalize its political and regulatory capacity through selective power devolution to urban- and local-level entities, actors, and processes. This concept of rescaling is useful to produce a broader 'territorial' and 'scalar' understanding of how decentered homeless regulation in the city can be created in combination with various decentralization strategies of the national (territorial) state.

My notion of the 'ground-up round' of rescaling refers to an early 'moral panic' phase of RSP growth in the city. It describes how the urban society of the housing classes and their guardians react to immediate regulatory ruptures by quickly inventing local networks of homeless/poverty regulation at the local scale and in a piecemeal fashion. This can start bottom-up devolutionary politics that *processually* achieve—without systematizing efforts—flexible patterns of welfare provision, conditional provision, or non-provision for the RSP's 'lowest sediment,' who may look 'dangerous' to urban societalization based on the housing classes and their urban imaginaries. In this round, the dynamics of rescaling assumes a highly spontaneous character even when it significantly advances the decentralization of welfare statism.

The 'picking-off round' of state rescaling is about a more well-organized and territory-wide phase of rescaling, which may come after the ground-up round. What characterizes this new round is the introduction of the national state and its coordinating power into the theoretical picture. More specifically, the new state capacity that Jamie Peck (2002) calls 'scale manager' starts to play an important role in streamlining and systematizing the regulatory dynamics of rescaling emerging at the local scale and from the city, which legally and institutionally supports the haphazard (ground-up) process of homeless regulation at the local scale.

5.2 State Rescaling in Britain and the United States

Before the 2000s, the British strategy of dividing the RSP populations into 'deserving' and 'undeserving' parts, and of navigating different categories in the RSP toward different policy orientations, was more fragmentary (Lowe 1997; Pleace, Burrows, and Quilgars, 1997; Watson, 1986). This earlier phase may be interpreted as a ground-up round of rescaling in Britain. In the 2000s, the state's significant effort to address homelessness on the national scale appeared with the Homelessness Act of 2002, which advanced 'a complex *rescaling* of responsibilities' (Cloke, May, and Johnsen, 2010, 34, original emphasis). This act may be considered a British case of the picking-off round of rescaling, which has advanced the re-institutionalization of centrifugal regulatory powers that legitimized the haphazard dynamics of homeless regulation already in place locally and across the city.

Historically, the United States has adhered to a loose pattern of national welfare statism (Skocpol, 1992). Federal administrators have addressed homelessness by using inherited policy tools and generating new ones, but their policies often have followed unorganized forms of subnational regulation. (For local variations of US homeless policy in this context, see Baumohl, 1996; Blau, 1992; Stoner, 1995; for a multiscalar analysis, see Hayashi, 2014b.) The

McKinney–Vento Homeless Assistance Act of 1987, a major statutory system for homelessness, was actually the federal government's powerful admission of the inherited national and subnational processes of regulatory displacement (Baumohl, 1996; Blau, 1992; Rossi, 1989). As such, the transition from the bottom-up to the picking-off round of rescaling may have appeared more like a continuity in the US case, because the US policy environment historically has been tolerant of haphazard policy dynamics in the city.

5.3 State Rescaling in Japan

In postwar Japan, local spaces for regulating new forms of homelessness started to emerge around the mid-1970s. At this time, Japan was hit by a global economic downturn, and this quickly deteriorated into homelessness among disadvantaged day laborers living in inner-city areas (yoseba). These local spaces of regulation comprised elements of both coercion and consensus—both street-level policing and local provision frameworks—that were endorsed or directly created by local regulatory actors. As of the 2000s, the Japanese state ushered cities into a new phase of homeless regulation by producing the 2002/2003 system. This system, comprising the Act on Special Measures Concerning Support for Homeless People's Self-Help and the Guidelines Concerning Support for Homeless People's Self-Help, advanced the coordination of regulation across cities.

Thus, I discern two rounds of rescaling in postwar Japan—the ground-up round starting in the 1970s and the picking-off round beginning in the 2000s. Through this transition, different policy orientations toward 'deserving' and 'undeserving' groups, which developed in each city and locality in endogenous ways, have been legally justified and discursively streamlined at the national scale, making the marginal areas of the Japanese 'welfare state' institutionally ready for local homeless regulation. The most disadvantaged and 'dangerous' sectors of the homeless population have been institutionally relegated from the poverty-alleviating mechanisms of national citizenship.

6 Urban Social Movements

6.1 Urban Social Movements for Homeless People

The rubric of 'urban social movements' addresses the ways in which social movements for homeless people can create transformative environments on the periphery of normative urban settlement (habitat) and citizenship, which are systemically reserved for the housing classes as bases of societalization. In the city, the relative separation of these transformative environments from a mainstream society of the housing classes allows activists and volunteers to escape the disciplinary imaginary of habitation so that they might conceive of urban policy for homeless people.

Located in the rescaling regulatory dynamics, the peripheries of the housing classes can be a site of new urban politics that pose fundamental questions about urban societalization organized by habitat—the matrix of public and private spaces and its meaning-shaping (semiotic) layers of consumption. Activists and volunteers can be game changers in the local (rescaled) politics of homelessness by advancing urban social movements in the city. This theory of urban social movements is divided into three themes: placemaking, commoning, and translating.

1. *Placemaking*: Activists/volunteers may overcome the colonizing power of reregulation by producing their own places at the margins of habitat. (On the place concept, see Cresswell, 2015; Leitner, Sheppard, and Sziarto, 2008; Martin and Miller 2003; Nicholls, 2009.)
2. *Commoning*: Activists/volunteers may change regulatory frameworks and create a homeless-friendly (and even prohomeless) form of urban commons whose use values and their urban circuits are otherwise closed to the housing classes. (On commoning, see Harvey 2012; Linebaugh 2008, 2014.)
3. *Translating*: Activists/volunteers may spread these transformative environments to new sites, cities, and scales beyond their birthplace and birth scale, through cultural reworking and the new production of social environments. (On translation, see Ekers et al., 2013; Ives, 2004; Ives and Lacorte, 2010.)

I argue that social movements for homeless people that address the three realms of placemaking, commoning, and translating can add a new dimension of 'homeless politics' to the inclusive domain of urban social movements that Lefebvre (2003 [1970]) expected to arise from the normative formation of 'occluded' urban settlement, namely, habiting.

Lefebvre's thesis is, of course, that the industrial quotidian in the city can be relativized and overcome in and from the streets—that a 'movement in the street' can morph the city into a 'communications space' for urban radicals (Lefebvre, 2003 [1970], 20). However, another transformative thread of Lefebvre's (2003 [1970], 21, 48, 70, 81–85, 88–89, 100, 178, 182, 188) approach is that the urban politics of the working class can also be understood in relation to a capitalist housing regime and its normative urban environment, with a focus on how the movements can actually remake the city, beyond the normalized habitat, through the ongoing politics of 'habiting'.

Lefebvre's insight that the urban settlement is itself political, and should be politicized as such, can be creatively evaluated in relation to contemporary cities by situating his habiting notion—the relativization of the 'quotidian' at urban settlements—within the urban social movements for homeless people. Each of the three realms discussed here can shed new light on the capacity of Lefebvre's habiting in our urban contexts.

6.2 Urban Social Movements in Britain and the United States

The three realms—placemaking, commoning, and translating—find good examples and suggestions in Anglophone works. Regarding placemaking, DeVerteuil (2015, 32) argues that inner-city zones in different countries have provided encouraging social spaces for activists 'through hallmarks such as density, concentration, proximity, solidarity, collectivism, irreplaceability and motivation to preserve previous gains.' Wagner (1993) finds similar placemaking spots in one US city. There, he finds that 'the streets ... constituted a community, and many service providers are a part of that community' (Wagner, 1993: 36), enabling members from the housing classes to stand with homeless people and halt the 'widespread 'not-in-my-backyard' movements against shelters and even against soup kitchens' (Wagner, 1993: 2). In addition, development of homeless advocacy at the national scale is outlined by US-based authors (Blau 1992; Hopper 2003), and this development can be interpreted as nationalization of the increased local spaces for homeless movements.

As for commoning, the everyday process of pro-homeless placemaking in the inner city must be supported by 'liminal' forms of commoning against *dis*commoning—that is, everyday struggles to unlock the use values of the commons to homeless people's survival (metabolic) economies at their thresholds, in opposition to the rampant regulatory pressure. Today, many inner-city areas are under continuous assault by profit makers and regulators who seek to reimpose the urban regulatory matrix on the niches of poverty for profit-making or regulatory reasons. The struggles of pro-homeless actors against this discommoning pressure often fail to lead to enduring mobilization for homeless people or to the stable maintenance of 'safe space' (Tilly, 2000) for radical activists. In Wagner's case study, the place of activism was internally fragile because the radical social space suffered from the scarcity of resources and the lack of political leadership, yet it achieved major success through a 'self-styled indigenous organization' that 'improv[ed] the situation of the homeless' (Wagner, 1993: 138–142). In turn, activism for homeless people in different cities is reported to have improved multiple dimensions of regulation (Cress and Snow, 2000).

Translating is a hard-to-grasp aspect of the Lefebvrean habiting movement. However, Smith's (1993) case of New York City gives us clue to how the meaning-shaping (semiotic) process of prohomeless activism can effectively advance the scale jumping (upscaling) of prohomeless discourses and politics from the local to supralocal scales. According to Smith, a piece of public art called *Homeless Vehicle* made observable to a wide range of audiences the (non-)mobility of homeless people in New York City by visualizing the difficulties that homeless people have in the city, sending prohomeless messages not just to immediate residents but also to art admirers nationwide. Smith does not suggest that this upscaling politics is an easy matter. Nonetheless, he shows that it is possible to carefully remake a locality's existing cultural elements into forms understandable to wider audiences living in different areas and residing in different scales, in order to create a larger resonance with homeless politics, outside of each locality.

6.3   Urban Social Movements in Japan

Habiting and its relationship with placemaking, commoning, and translating have undergone unique twists in Japan. To establish social cohesion with small urban use values available for people in the Japanese case (Miyamoto 1976), habiting has had to combat the pervasive, organizational, highly depoliticizing type of societalization—'hyperconformist' societalization—that has been a sociological layer of developmentalism. Because the housing classes and their urban spaces were originally co-opted into this type of social cohesion during the postwar years, it has been difficult for activists and volunteers to problematize those who suffer this urbanization at the furthest fringes of the housing classes, their use values pools, and their local societies. Simply put, any voices in support of homeless people can be erased from urban public spheres and governance. In this context, the three realms of social movements for homeless people have taken specific forms in postwar Japan.

Placemaking has happened at yoesba zones in urban Japan. These inner-city districts of disadvantaged day laborers provide rare geographies that can host placemaking actions of activists/volunteers wishing to work for homeless people. Ethnicity and race were not the prime levers for collective placemaking in the earlier years. Until the 1970s, the placemaking framework often deployed a version of Marxian class vocabulary, which was effective to organize a few day laborers but not useful in recruiting (potential) activists from the housing classes. From the 1980s forward, however, yoseba zones cultivated more diverse views for prohomeless placemaking and successfully broadened the scope of prohomeless solidarity to include the housing classes.

Commoning has also been distinctively articulated in Japan. Activists often have focused on a particular legal thread of the national citizenship framework known as *sēzon ken*, or the right to livelihood, which is detailed in article 25 of the constitution and in the Public Assistance Act of 1950. These laws determine the livelihood right broadly and inclusively, as a right of all Japanese citizens to a basic living standard, but this standard often is not maintained due to the meagre spending of Japanese welfare statism. In this national context, some activists have framed 'homeless politics' as a politics toward more genuine forms of the livelihood right. In part they have spoken out about the requirements by using law-related terms, while others have favored more anarchic ideas for framing the commoning action and have eschewed any kind of engagement with formal policy. (For this framing and its varieties, see Hasegawa 2006; Hayashi 2015.)

The translation to external areas and larger scales of socio-cultures developed in yoseba zones has been possible in Japan due to efforts of a few devoted activists who move back and forth between the inner-city areas and remote areas/scales where homelessness has newly appeared. Areas and scales remote from the inner city often were unreached by homelessness until the mid-1990s. Due to this newness, the translation of prohomeless language to new areas or scales was a daunting task. Despite this difficulty, the translating attempts to spread to broader areas/scales local cultures that were compassionate to homeless people saw some success. Aerial expansion through translation started in the 1990s; for a famous case in Tokyo's Shinjuku Ward, see Kasai (1999) and Shinjuku Renraku Kai (1997). In the late 2000s, translation for scale-jumping expansion (upscaling) succeeded in advancing both commoning and placemaking on the national scale (Hayashi 2015).

7 Conclusion

Marxist and Marxian literature can be effectively mobilized for 'homelessness and Japan.' This work can advance the redeployment of Marxist/Marxian vocabularies in urban studies and can stretch the extant Marxian corpus to its peripheries and margins, where 'Marxism' can face criticism, deformation, and new creativities.

This project, it is argued, helps to illuminate the borders of Marxist and Marxian literature, and to relativize its orthodox limits in order to find a new survival space for some useful categories and notions in classical and contemporary works. This survival space allows a performative kind of social research that can reconstruct the utility of these categories and notions within the everyday, concrete ('empirical') situations in the city and in urbanization—the open-air aspect of urban studies—in which Marxist/Marxian research projects experience a decrease in explanatory power.

To this end, I have revisited several concepts—metabolism, housing classes, habitat, the barrack/cottage system, and so on—to cultivate new Marxist threads of argument in homeless studies. I also have developed a regulationist and 'state-mediated' discussion about homelessness in terms of rescaling that addresses the rampant centrifugal power production in the 'governance' of homelessness. In addition, I have examined the implications of these discussions for urban social movements and located the historical appearances of Japan in this theory against excessive provincialization.

This approach has shown that what we know as 'homelessness' is a historically unique form of the relative surplus population that first emerged in particular historical contexts of European urbanization, where a capitalist housing regime first took on a clear appearance and grew its own contradiction. Since then, this housing regime has been vigorously updated and developed, with the help of heavy capital investments and state policy that has constructed a broad area of 'public spaces' around housing itself. This is the urban form of public space plus private space, which is now entrenched in various cities across the globe. In short, Engels' cottage system has developed into Lefebvre's habitat, and according to Harvey, the housing classes in this new regime have taken a 'displaced' form of urban class relations through the consumption of public/private in the city.

This housing regime, which today encompasses housing and its broad public exterior, has become a key geographic site for working-class subsumption in contemporary capitalism. In this context, Lefebvrean urban social movements around the urban settlement—habiting—can have a historically important (and therefore limited) role for the working class: to navigate a period-specific form of capitalist urbanization toward less destructive trajectories for the excluded—'dangerous'—part of the relative surplus population (the homeless subalterns), who are now systematically pitted against the '*non*dangerous' (the housing classes) and are surviving/laboring/metabolizing in their shadows.

In order to achieve political 'victories' for these homeless people in the city, urban social movements must take advantage of centrifugal and 'rescaled' patterns of urban governance. Today, rescaling (and rescaled urban governance) is a dominant mode of regulatory power formation to manage the border-making of dangerous/nondangerous among the RSP, which powerfully affects the RSP's access to citizenship, welfare, and housing.

References

Aglietta, M. (1979 [1976]) *A Theory of Capitalist Regulation: The US Experience* (translated D Fernbach). London: Verso.

Baumohl, J. (1996) *Homelessness in America*. Phoenix, AZ: Oryx Press.

Blau, J. (1992) *The Visible Poor: Homelessness in the United States*. Oxford: Oxford University Press.

Brenner, N. (2004) *New State Spaces: Urban Governance and the Rescaling of Statehood*. Oxford: Oxford University Press.

Brenner, N. (2019) *New Urban Spaces: Urban Theory and the Scale Question*. Oxford: Oxford University Press.

Burkett, P. (1999) *Marx and Nature: A Red and Green Perspective*. New York, NY: St. Martin's Press.

Castells, M. (1983) *The City and the Grassroots: A Cross-Cultural Theory of Urban Social Movements*. Berkeley, CA: University of California Press.

Cloke, P., May, J., and Johnsen, S. (2010) *Swept Up Lives? Re-Envisioning the Homeless City*. Chichester: Wiley-Blackwell.

Collinge, C. (1999) Self-Organisation of Society by Scale: A Spatial Reworking of Regulation Theory. *Environment and Planning D: Society and Space* 17(5): 557–574.

Cox, K.R., and Mair, A. (1988) Locality and Community in the Politics of Local Economic Development. *Annals of the Association of American Geographers* 78(2): 307–325.

Cress, D., and Snow, D.A. (2000) The Outcomes of Homeless Mobilization: The Influence of Organization, Disruption, Political Mediation, and Framing. *American Journal of Sociology* 105(4): 1063–1104.

Cresswell, T. (2015) *Place: An Introduction*. Chichester: Wiley-Blackwell.

DeVerteuil, G. (2006) The Local State and Homeless Shelters: Beyond Revanchism? *Cities* 23(2): 109–120.

DeVerteuil, G. (2015) *Resilience in the Post-Welfare Inner City: Voluntary Sector Geographies in London, Los Angeles and Sydney*. Bristol: Policy Press.

DeVerteuil, G., May, J., and von Mahs, J. (2009) Complexity Not Collapse: Recasting the Geographies of Homelessness in a "Punitive" Age. *Progress in Human Geography* 33(5): 646–666.

Ekers, M., Hart, G., Kipfer, S., and Loftus, A. (eds) (2013) *Gramsci: Space, Nature, Politics*. Chichester: Wiley-Blackwell.

Engels, F. (1845 [1887]) Condition of the Working Class in England. https://www.marxists.org/archive/marx/works/download/pdf/condition-working-class-england.pdf.

Engels, F. (1995 [1872]) *The Housing Question*. https://www.marxists.org/archive/marx/works/download/pdf/Housing_Question.pdf.

Foster, J.B. (2000) *Marx's Ecology: Materialism and Nature*. New York, NY: Monthly Review Press.

Gowan, T. (2010) *Hobos, Hustlers and Backsliders: Homeless in San Francisco*. Minneapolis, MN: University of Minnesota Press.

Gramsci, A. (1971) *Selections from the Prison Notebooks* (translated by Q Hoare and GN Smith). New York, NY: International Publishers.

Harvey, D. (1976) Labor, Capital, and Class Struggle around the Built Environment in Advanced Capitalist Societies. *Politics & Society* 6(3): 265–295.

Harvey, D. (1982) *The Limits to Capital*. Oxford: Basil Blackwell.

Harvey, D. (1989) *The Urban Experience*. Baltimore, MD: Johns Hopkins University Press.

Harvey, D. (2012) *Rebel Cities: From the Right to the City to the Urban Revolution*. London: Verso.

Hasegawa, M. (2006) *'We Are Not Garbage!' The Homeless Movement in Tokyo, 1994–2002*. Abingdon: Routledge.

Hayashi, M. (2013) Kenzō kankyō de tashaka sareru jyūtaku kiki: toshi no shizen o meguru rōdō to kanri to yume [Housing Crisis Being Othered at Built Environments: Labour, Control, and Myths Around Urban Nature]. In T Machimura (ed) *Toshikūkan ni Hisomu Haijo to Hankō no Chikara* [Forces of Exclusion and Resistance Inherent in Urban Space], Tokyo: Akashi Shoten, 25–60.

Hayashi, M. (2014a) *Hōmuresu to Toshi Kūkan: Shūdatsu to Ika, Shakai Undō, Kokka-Shihon* [Homelessness and Urban Space: Deprivation through Othering, Social Movements, and the State–Capital Nexus]. Tokyo: Akashi Shoten.

Hayashi, M. (2014b) Urban Poverty and Regulation, New Spaces and Old: Japan and the US in Comparison. *Environment and Planning A* 46(5): 1203–1225.

Hayashi, M. (2015) Rescaled Rebel Cities, Nationalization, and the Bourgeois Utopia: Dialectics Between Urban Social Movements and Regulation for Japan's Homeless. *Antipode* 47(2): 418–441.

Hayashi, M. (2022) Theorizing Regulation-in-City for Homeless People's Subaltern Strategy and Informality: Societalization, Metabolism, and Classes With(out) Housing. *Critical Sociology* 48(2): 323–339.

Hayashi, M. (2023a) Any Labour Geographies in Urban Theory? Workers Meet Lefebvre and Harvey (Yet Again). *Antipode* 55(2): 415–435.

Hayashi, M. (2023b) *Rescaling Urban Poverty: Homelessness, State Restructuring and City Politics in Japan*. Chichester: Wiley.

Heynen, N., Kaika, M., and Swyngedouw, E. (2006) *In the Nature of Cities: Urban Political Ecology and the Politics of Urban Metabolism*. Abingdon: Routledge.

Hopper, K. (2003) *Reckoning with Homelessness*. Ithaca, NY: Cornell University Press.

Hou, J. (ed) (2010) *Insurgent Public Space: Guerrilla Urbanism and the Remaking of Contemporary Cities*. Abingdon: Routledge.

Ives, P. (2004) *Gramsci's Politics of Language: Engaging the Bakhtin Circle and the Frankfurt School*. Toronto: University of Toronto Press.

Ives, P. and Lacorte, R. (eds) (2010) *Gramsci, Language, and Translation*. Lanham, MD: Lexington Books.

Jessop, B. (2002) *The Future of the Capitalist State*. Cambridge: Polity.

Kasai, K. (1999) *Shinjuku Houmuresu Funsen Ki: Tachinoke do Kiesarazu* [Records of How Homeless People Resisted in Shinjuku: Retreat, Not Disappearance]. Tokyo: Gendai Kikaku Shitsu.

Katznelson, I. (1992) *Marxism and the City*. Oxford: Oxford University Press.

Keil, R., and Mahon, R. (eds) (2009) *Leviathan Undone? Towards a Political Economy of Scale*. Vancouver: University of British Columbia Press.

Lefebvre, H. (2009 [1966]). Theoretical Problem of Autogestion (translated G Moore, N Brenner, and S Elden). In N Brenner and S Elden (eds) *State, Space, World: Selected Essays*. Minneapolis, MN: University of Minnesota Press, 138–152.

Lefebvre, H. (2003 [1970]) *The Urban Revolution* (translated R Bononno). Minneapolis, MN: University of Minnesota Press.

Leitner, H., Sheppard, E., and Sziarto, K.M. (2008) The Spatialities of Contentious Politics. *Transactions of the Institute of British Geographers* NS 33: 157–172.

Linebaugh, P. (2008) *The Magna Carta Manifesto: Liberties and Commons for All*. Berkeley, CA: University of California Press.

Linebaugh, P. (2014). *Stop, Thief! The Commons, Enclosures, and Resistance*. Oakland, CA: PM Press.

Logan, J.R., and Molotch, H.L. (1987) *Urban Fortunes: The Political Economy of Place*. Berkeley, CA: University of California Press.

Lowe, S. (1997) Homelessness and the Law. In R Burrows, N Pleace, and D Quilgars, *Homelessness and Social Policy*. Abingdon: Routledge, 19–34.

Martin, D., and Miller, B. (2003) Space and Contentious Politics. *Mobilization: An International Journal* 8(2): 143–156.

Marx, K. (1887 [1867]) *Capital: A Critique of Political Economy*, vol 1. (translated by S Moore and E Aveling). Moscow: Progress Publishers. https://www.marxists.org/archive/marx/works/download/pdf/Capital-Volume-I.pdf.

Massey, D. (1994) *Space, Place, and Gender*. Minneapolis, MN: University of Minnesota Press.

Merrifield, A. (2002) *Metromarxism: A Marxist Tale of the City*. New York, NY: Routledge.

Ministry of Health, Labour and Welfare (2003) *Hōmuresu no Jittai Nado ni Kansuru Zenkoku Chōsa Hōkokusho* [Research on the Actual Conditions of Homeless People]. Tokyo: Author.

Mitchell, D. (1997) The Annihilation of Space by Law: The Roots and Implications of Anti-homeless Laws in the United States. *Antipode* 29(3): 303–335.

Miyamoto, K. (1976) *Shakai Shihon Ron, Kaitē Ban* [The Theory of Social Capital], rev. ed. Tokyo: Yuhikaku.

Moore, J.W. (2015) *Capitalism in the Web of Life: Ecology and the Accumulation of Capital*. London: Verso.

Nicholls, W. (2009) Place, Networks, Space: Theorizing the Geographies of Social Movements. *Transactions of the Institute of British Geographers* NS 34: 78–93.

Peck, J. (2001) Neoliberalizing States: Thin Policies/Hard Outcomes. *Progress in Human Geography* 25(3): 445–455.

Peck, J. (2002) Political Economies of Scale: Fast Policy, Interscalar Relations, and Neoliberal Workfare. *Economic Geography* 78(3): 331–360.

Pleace, N., Burrows, R., and Quilgars, D. (1997) Homelessness in Contemporary Britain: Conceptualisation and Measurement. In R Burrows, N Pleace, and D Quilgars (eds) *Homelessness and Social Policy*. Abingdon: Routledge, 1–18.

Rex, J., and Moore, R. (1967) *Race, Community, and Conflict: A Study of Sparkbrook*. Oxford: Oxford University Press.

Rossi, P.H. (1989) *Down and Out in America: The Origins of Homelessness*. Chicago, IL: University of Chicago Press.

Shinjuku Renraku Kai (1997) *Shinjuku Danbōru Mura: Tatakai no Kiroku* [The Shinjuku Cardboard Village: A Record of Struggle]. Tokyo: Gendai Kikaku Shitsu.

Skocpol, T. (1992). *Protecting Soldiers and Mothers: The Political Origins of Social Policy in the United States*. Cambridge, MA: Belknap Press of Harvard University Press.

Smith, N. (1993) Homeless/Global: Scaling Places. In J Bird, B Curtis, T Putnam, G Robertson, and L Tickner (eds) *Mapping the Futures: Local Cultures, Global Change*. Abingdon: Routledge, 87–119.

Smith, N. (1996) *The New Urban Frontier: Gentrification and the Revanchist City*. Abingdon: Routledge.

Snow, D.A., and Anderson, L. (1993) *Down on Their Luck: A Study of Homeless Street People*. Berkeley, CA: University of California Press.

Soja, E.W. (1989) *Postmodern Geographies: The Reassertion of Space in Critical Social Theory*. New York, NY: Verso.

Sparks, T. (2017) Citizens Without Property: Informality and Political Agency in a Seattle, Washington Homeless Encampment. *Environment and Planning A* 49(1): 86–103.

Stoner, M.R. (1995) *The Civil Rights of Homeless People: Law, Social Policy, and Social Work Practice*. Hawthorne, NY: Aldine de Gruyter.

Swyngedouw, E. (1996) The City as a Hybrid: On Nature, Society and Cyborg Urbanization. *Capitalism Nature Socialism* 7(2): 65–80.

Tabb, W.K., and Sawers, L. (1984) *Marxism and the Metropolis: New Perspectives in Urban Political Economy*, 2nd ed. Oxford: Oxford University Press.

Tilly, C. (2000) Spaces of Contention. *Mobilization: An International Journal* 5(2): 135–159.

Wagner, D. (1993) *Checkerboard Square: Culture and Resistance in a Homeless Community*. Boulder, CO: Westview Press.

Watson, S. (1986). *Housing and Homelessness: A Feminist Perspective*. Abingdon: Routledge and Kegan Paul.

PART 3

CHAPTER 15

Postscript

On the Continuing Necessity of (Marxist) Critique

Tom Brass

1 Introduction: Paradigms, Polemics, Popularity

The importance of Marxist critique to debates within the social sciences has been emphasized, rightly, in recent analyses written by David Fasenfest, the honorand of this *festschrift*, and Raju Das, its co-editor.[1] That such observations are both timely and necessary is evident from the way in which a number of problematic developments now appear entrenched in academic discourse. First, strongly-made criticism itself – never mind that by Marxism – is now labelled 'polemical', and as such increasingly frowned upon. Second, concepts that are crucial to a Marxist framework, not to say Marxist theory itself, have been sidelined or banished from social science debates. And third, now what passes as Marxism has in many instances metamorphosed into 'Marxism'. It is these kind of developments, their political effect, together with the reason for their emergence, that are considered briefly here.

Equally in need of emphasis are the two different forms of 'going back' arising from the unfolding of a critique. On the one hand, there is criticism based on rescuing/reinstating concepts and processes (for example, class differentiation, the industrial reserve army) that not merely belong to the framework in question but are central to it, and that have been unjustifiably jettisoned in the name of 'newness', fashion or – much the same thing – the need to be seen to be 'popular'. On the other, by contrast, is the recuperation of concepts belonging to another framework altogether (for example, peasant essentialism, undifferentiated petty commodity production). This distinction, a crucial one epistemologically/politically, separates Marxist critique from various kinds of anti-Marxist equivalents: whereas the former sort of critique is engaged in restoring missing components from the *same* paradigm, the latter type of criticism has as its object the search for and installation of a wholly *different* paradigm.

---

[1] Fasenfest (2022) and Das (2020).

It is a truism, therefore, that critique must be differentiated in terms of its place of origin on a left/right political spectrum. Whereas Marxism makes no secret of why, and on what basis, it enters into a debate, much non-/anti-Marxist theory does so in a variety of disguises, attempting thereby to hide and to 'normalise' its own epistemology. This process is compounded by an additional tendency, one that is as noticeable: subscribing uncritically to a paradigm widely (and inaccurately) labelled 'new' and 'radical', simply because it is novel and increasingly popular.[2] Gathering support, the paradigm snowballs: its claims remain unexamined, all the while assuming the status of a miracle cure guaranteed to confer immunity to Marxist 'infection', a form of exorcism periodically undertaken by bourgeois intellectuals. When the political effects of the latter shift are pointed out and criticized by Marxism, however, the frequent response in academia is offence, akin to *lèse-majesté*.[3] This kind of reaction is perhaps no more than a symptom of the extent to which discussion in academia is now similar to that of a salon, governed by its codes and manners (polite conversation, eschewing controversy, avoiding politics).

This sort of response has to be linked in turn to the post-1960s fate of Marxist theory, and the way it vanished from the streets and into the academy. Over this period, many socialists had become not just ex-leftists but also senior academics, and to be reminded of how their earlier political allegiances had changed, and why, was clearly an uncomfortable experience. As revealing, therefore, are the reactions on the part of those criticized in this manner. Confronted with the extent to which they have strayed from Marxist theory and concepts, rather than addressing the critique the resort is frequently to nothing more than vituperation. The latter underlines the degree to which political debate in the academy has diminished, seen nowadays as 'unseemly' and quickly dismissed as 'polemical'. That such criticisms emanate from leftists is startling, not least because historically the term 'polemical' – referring to fierce argumentation by the politically committed – was one used by opponents of Marx, Lenin, and Trotsky whenever any of the latter challenged bourgeois ideas.

A case in point is the novelist China Miéville, whose leftist contribution to a centenary discussion of the 1917 Russian Revolution was taken to task subsequently for being suffused by an undeniable aporia (a lukewarm 'defence' reproduced also in his latest book about the Communist Manifesto).[4] Hence a Marxist critique published later noted that, given the general hostility

---

2 An instance of just this sort of process is considered elsewhere (Brass, 2023a).
3 On this kind of reaction to criticism, see Brass (2023b).
4 The contribution by Miéville to the 1917 centenary discussion is 'You say you want a revolution', *The Guardian* (London), 6 May 2017.

of newspaper articles marking the 1917 revolution, a more robust defence by Miéville would have helped.⁵ This in turn elicited an irate response from Miéville himself, who rejected the critique as 'a strain of showboating machismo within the Left that treats consideration of any revolutionary parameters other than more or less precisely those of St Petersburg October 1917 ... as effete perfidy.'⁶ It seems, therefore, that unease with revolutionary socialism is not confined to conservatives. On the nominal left, the idea of mass 'from below' agency designed to transcend capitalism by capturing its state also gives rise to misgiving.

The presentation which follows contains three sections, the first of which examines what connects academic opposition to Marxist theory/concepts, the emergence of what are claimed to be 'new' paradigms, and the role of fashion/popularity. Both the epistemology and the vehemence of anti-Marxist critiques are traced in the second, whilst a Marxist counter-critique is outlined in the third.

2 What Connects Academic Opposition to Marxist Theory?

These days the sorts of judgement made by an editor of a major social science journal – as in the case, for example, of *Critical Sociology* – include having to form an opinion about the many and varied attempts to rewrite not just whole paradigms but also – and more insidiously – undermining longstanding epistemological and politically significant concepts on which these paradigms depend.

2.1 A Return to Yesterday

In terms of voice and platforms, the left appears superficially to be well served currently by publication outlets. On closer examination, however, this turns out to be deceptive. Although there are journals with words such as 'Left' and 'Marxism' in the title, legislative enforcement of an intellectual equivalent of Trades Description legislation would quickly require them to change their

---

5 For the critique of Miéville, see Brass (2018a: 192). That the latter hit its target is evident from the response it elicited from Miéville (2022: 266–67 note 50), who complains about 'leftist revolutionism-policing' of Marxism, omitting to mention that the critique was aimed at him.

6 For this reaction, see Miéville (2022: 94), whose labelling of criticism as 'uncomradely' discloses two underlying assumptions. Not just the implied view that one should not question (a curious opinion for a leftist to hold), but also the extent to which academia ought to be no more than a present-day salon, engaged in polite conversation about unimportant subjects.

names. Thus, for example, the *New Left Review* has long since ceased to be a publication carrying serious discussion about any subject from a Marxist perspective, instead given these days to politically irrelevant salon discussions conducted by a coterie. Where the analysis of culture is concerned – and also, on occasion, politics – the *Financial Times* is more informative and more radical. The case of the journal *Rethinking Marxism* is, if anything, even worse, supporting Marxism in the same way as a noose supports a hanged man.[7]

Common to these journals is a misunderstanding as to the importance of the main concepts and systemic processes that are central to Marxist theory. One is provided with lots of favourable analysis on subjects like the body, sexuality, and non-class identities, together with the desirability of empowerment to be achieved within the confines of actually-existing neoliberalism, but little or nothing about class, its formation/consciousness/struggle under capitalism, and how the latter is connected to (or disconnected from) a socialist transition. The extent of the difficulty is evident from the way even basic concepts are being questioned or redefined so as no longer to be recognizable as such.

Where the history and presence of capitalism itself is concerned, this epistemological realignment has generated claims that can only be described as bizarre. Thus, for example, some now argue that as capitalism has in effect never existed, there is no such thing as capitalism in the sense Marx and Marxism understood.[8] By contrast, others maintain that capitalism has always existed throughout history, an ever-present and eternal systemic form.[9] To some degree, these two departures from Marxist theory coincide theoretically and politically. By extending what is termed capitalism in time and space, it ceases to be recognizable as the systemic form that Marx argued existed. To make it fit into these new times and spaces, therefore, requires a procrustean approach, discarding crucial elements and altering definitions, while at the same time adding 'new' components, concepts, and characteristics, invariably unconnected with – and in many cases opposed to – Marxism.

---

7 Other journals, that started out as Marxist or at least sympathetic to its political economy – among them *Economy and Society, International Review of Social History, The Journal of Peasant Studies, The Journal of Development Studies, Critique of Anthropology,* and *The Journal of Contemporary Asia* – have similarly abandoned this approach, to the extent of not publishing anything much that could be described as being informed by a Marxist framework. Yet others – such as *Science & Society* and *Capital & Class* – which are nominally still Marxist, do not appear any longer to endorse key concepts that are relevant to the core theory of its approach.

8 See for example Jan Lucassen, whose views are examined below.

9 This is the view of Jairus Banaji, on which see Brass (2021: Chapters 5 and 6; 2022b: Chapter 3).

Furthermore, without some certainty about the contextually-specific existence of capitalism at a particular historical conjuncture, how is it any longer possible to talk about its transcendence, or – consequently – to formulate, advocate, and promote strategies designed to bring about a socialist transition? Crisis, exploitation, and oppression are as a result deemed 'natural' and thus unalterable aspects of the economy per se. The reason either for questioning the existence of capitalism, or for maintaining that it has always existed, appear to be the same. Accordingly, an effect of no capitalism, or alternatively its eternal character, is that there is consequently either no need to oppose it (since it doesn't exist) or its historical ubiquity forbids transcendence (since it cannot be eradicated). Either way, socialism is off the agenda, economically, politically, and ideologically.

2.2 New Paradigms, Old Assumptions

Part of the difficulty is that the logic driving what are portrayed as 'new' paradigms in the social sciences is rarely problematized, let alone interrogated as to its political assumptions and agenda. It is clear, however, that one contributory factor is competition within academia for research funding: as competition intensifies, so the number of 'new' interpretations or the discovery of 'new' areas for study proliferate Brought into focus thereby is what are claimed overlooked issues which, so the argument goes, require further analysis before it is possible to be sure of anything linked to them. Social science discourse is currently awash with attempts to replace 'old' paradigms/concepts with 'new' equivalents, the latter gathering deserters from the former.

Declaring the 'old' redundant, supporters of the 'new' proclaim and celebrate its novelty amidst a growing popularity that confers on the approach a fashionable status among those conducting research.[10] Frequently, however, what is labelled the 'new' turns out to be nothing more than the resuscitation of an earlier social science or historical paradigm, itself the object of criticism by the 'old' approach now under challenge. Marxism makes no secret of its theoretical framework and epistemological lineage, originating in the nineteenth century. Unlike other paradigms, however, its claim to our attention lies not in being 'new', but rather in being politically relevant. This much is clear from what Marx had to say about the nature of popularity.

As pointed out by Liebknecht, Marx himself eschewed popularity, in the sense that he continued to pursue a radical political analysis in the face of

---

10   How such claims to 'newness' are reproduced in academia is considered elsewhere (Brass, 2017: Chapter 17; 2018a; 2018b).

criticism from bourgeois commentators ('phrase-mongers') who kept telling him that such an approach was wrong.[11] In support of this persistence, in the Preface to the first edition of *Capital* Marx invoked the words of Dante, along the lines of 'Go your own way, and let others talk'.[12] The way Marx dismissed views advanced by 'adversaries of Socialism' designed to elicit 'the applause of the crowd', echoes later warnings made against uncritical endorsement of postmodernism, simply because it is academically fashionable.[13] Lenin and Trotsky were also chary about the courting of popularity, albeit in a different form, criticizing the espousal of leftist politics by *katheder*-socialists who then diluted Marxism in order to make it respectable in the eyes of the bourgeoisie. A similar view was expressed in 1960 by Ernesto Che Guevara, who referred to Cuban intellectuals supporting the Batista dictatorship as 'simple slavishness in the service of a disgraceful cause'.[14]

3   Epistemology and Vehemence of Anti-Marxist Critiques

It is easy to overlook or ignore both the prevalence and the vehemence of anti-Marxist views – expressed not just by non-Marxists but also by some 'Marxists' – currently in circulation. Examined here, therefore, are three examples of this discourse, extending from a non-Marxist establishment historian (David Cannadine), via a couple of ex-Marxists (Ernesto Laclau, Chantal Mouffe), to post-Marxist/non-Marxist social historians (Patrick Curry, Jan Lucassen), one of whom is influenced by Laclau while the other claims to

---

11   See Liebknecht (1908: 84), who comments: 'Popularity being hateful to [Marx], he felt a holy wrath against soliciting popularity ... "Phrase-monger" was in his mouth the sharpest censure.' He continues (Liebknecht, 1908: 872): 'I have never forgotten the dangers of popularity; and if I remain unmoved ... by abusive language and the calumnies of our enemies – it is an art I learned from Marx'.

12   See Marx (1976: 93), who slightly altered the meaning of Dante's words ('*Vien retro a me, e lascia dir le genti*').

13   'For popularity Marx entertained a sovereign contempt', notes Liebknecht (1908: 82), adding that '[a]nd while socialism has not spiritually soaked through the masses, the applause of the crowd can, as a logical consequence, be bestowed only on men belonging to no party or to the adversaries of Socialism'.

14   'The role intellectuals played here [in pre-revolutionary Cuba] was far less concealed than in Argentina', wrote Guevara (2022: 215) in a 1960 letter to the Argentinian novelist Ernesto Sábato, '[h]ere, the intellectuals were nothing but toadies, who did not disguise their real position as apathy like they did [in Argentina]. Moreover, they didn't even pretend to be intelligent. It was a matter of pure and simple slavishness in the service of a disgraceful cause, nothing more'.

be politically agnostic. Whereas the former never was a Marxist, each of the latter four has seemingly metamorphosed from something akin to a fellow traveller into hostile critic. All the anti-Marxist views considered below demonstrate two things. First, the antagonistic relationship between Marxism and academia, a long-standing and ongoing conflict determined by the political antimony of a bourgeois educational institution where Marxism is concerned. And second, although Marxists are frequently accused of harsh argumentation (= polemics) in defence of their views, and taken to task for the critical nature of their tone, less attention is paid to the abrasive tenor of criticism aimed at Marxism itself.

3.1   *Class Dismissed*

The antipathy expressed by Cannadine, in the form of concentrated vitriol he pours not just over Marxism generally but also over individual Marxists, is difficult to avoid.[15] Marxism is described by him variously as 'bravura, fortissimo exhortation', a 'crusading and coruscating polemic', while references to the proletariat in *The Communist Manifesto* are dismissed as 'a transparent falsehood' and 'naïve verbiage'.[16] Marx, Engels, and Lenin themselves fare no better, each of the former being described by Cannadine as 'privileged products' of the modern bourgeois world, and the latter is dismissed merely as a 'portentous ... self-styled revolutionary'.[17] The twofold inference is that being 'privileged products' eliminates any legitimacy for opposing the system, which is anyway fatuous when it occurs, amounting to no more than a pose (= 'self-styled revolutionary').[18]

---

15 Sources used by Cannadine for his critique of Marxism suggest that he tends to rely overmuch on publications and accounts by others who are either lukewarm about or similarly hostile to Marxism, giving rise to the issue of confirmation bias. These sources, both in the endnotes and the text itself, include not just Eduard Bernstein but also Walt Rostow, Hugh Trevor-Roper, Tristram Hunt, W.G. Runciman, Gareth Stedman-Jones, George Lichtheim, John H. Kautsky, Orlando Figes, and Richard Pipes. References to their criticisms are cited approvingly, as though they correspond to opinions held by neutral observers, whereas in fact they are for the most part ex-Marxists, anti-Marxists, and/or – like Cannadine himself – establishment historians.

16 Cannadine (2013: 94–95, 102, 107). Like others (see below) who announce the death of Marxist theory about class, Cannadine (2013: 129) too makes such a proclamation: 'As a preeminent form of human identity and the most significant category of historical explanation, class has had a great fall and, like Humpty Dumpty, it seems unlikely that the pieces will be put back together again anytime soon'.

17 Cannadine (2013: 100, 107, 110ff.).

18 The latter point, it should be noted, is the same kind of criticism as that made by Miéville (see above).

Noting that others had allocated primacy to class earlier, but 'less stridently and polemically', Cannadine then asks whether 'class [has] ever been the most important and influential form of collective human identity and consciousness in the ways that Marx and Engels and their disciples, both practical and academic, repeatedly insisted that it was'.[19] This view of class as 'prime mover of change over time' could never work, he insists, because 'their attempts to explain ... all of human history on the basis of [classes] they believed to be in perpetual, sequential, and revolutionary conflict were deeply flawed'.[20] Denying the efficacy of class interests or consciousness, he invokes as an alternative the element of a 'common humanity', and laments that 'academic writing [supportive of this] has been produced by scholars whose interests are philosophical rather than historical'.[21] Given his position as part of the academic establishment, it is unsurprising that Cannadine holds the anti-Marxist views that he does; the same, however, cannot be said of others who target Marxism in a similar fashion.

3.2 *Producing Curtains*

As inescapable as that of Cannadine, therefore, is the vehemence with which Laclau dismisses Marxism. In a 1988 interview he began like the apostle Peter in the Garden of Gesthemane by observing that 'I have never been a "total" Marxist, someone who sought in Marxism a "homeland"'; he continued by asserting that 'Marxism's destiny [may be no more than being] taken over by the boy scouts of small Trotskyist sects who will continue to repeat a totally obsolete language – and thus nobody will remember Marxism in twenty years' time'.[22] Marxism was not forgotten, and two decades later in a 2010 issue of the journal *Open* celebrating *The Populist Imagination*, Laclau and others endorse the importance of myth in the mobilization of support based on populism, as

---

19 See Cannadine (2013: 96), who – together with religion, nation, gender, race, and civilization – labels class as one of these 'divisive collective' identities that 'at worst [are] reductive and misleading', leading to 'polarizing modes of thought' (Cannadine, 2013: 7, 8, 9).
20 Cannadine (2013: 101).
21 See Cannadine (2013: 7, 102), who argues that 'changes in the economy were never so momentous, straightforward, or pervasive as to bring about those homogeneous, collective consciousness ... much less the perpetual conflict that Marx and Engels and their heirs said made history go'.
22 Laclau (1990: 178–79). In a similar vein, Mouffe (2018: 2) dismisses Marxism as 'class essentialism', on the grounds that its view that 'political identities were the expression of the position of social agents in the relations of production and their interests were defined by this position'. Wrongly, she concludes: 'It was no surprise that such a perspective [= Marxism] was unable to understand demands that were not based on "class"'.

indeed does the unforgotten Marxism. Whereas the latter sees this as negative, however, fomenting as it does false consciousness among workers, the former by contrast views it as positive. A succinct account of false consciousness is provided by Adorno, who refers to it as the effect of 'curtains' produced in order to obscure what it is possible to see beyond such drapes.[23]

Unlike Marxism, Laclau regards the discourse used by populism – nationalism, ethnicity – as a benign kind of 'from below' ideology, and thus progressive, not as evidence of 'from above' political manipulation.[24] Moreover, Laclau fails to situate the rise of populism within its economic context: namely, what are the economic reasons for the success of this ideology. Rather, he and others subscribe to a form of Sorelian instinctivism, or the 'feeling' that underlies and informs the reproduction of discourse based on myth. For its part, Marxism links the success of a populist mobilizing discourse privileging ideology informed by non-class identities (ethnicity, nationalism) to a globally expanding industrial reserve, its impact on labour market competition in metropolitan capitalism (in the form of immigration), together with the concern for their own livelihoods felt by those in employment or aspiring to this in receiving nations.

---

23 Writing in the immediate aftermath of the 1939–45 war, when the capacity of the Nazi regime to generate, reproduce, and consolidate an anti-semitic discourse required understanding, Adorno (1969: 661–62) contrasted 'political ignorance' with a generally high level of awareness 'in many other matters', observing: 'The ultimate reason for this ignorance might well be the opaqueness of the social, economic, and political situation to all those who are not in full command of all the resources of stored knowledge and theoretical thinking. In its present phase, our social system tends objectively and automatically to produce "curtains" which make it impossible for the naïve person really to see what it is all about. These objective conditions are enhanced by powerful economic and social forces which, purposely or automatically, keep the people ignorant. The very fact that our social system is on the defence, as it were, that capitalism, instead of expanding the old way and opening up innumerable opportunities to the people, has to maintain itself somewhat precariously and to block critical insights which were regarded as "progressive" one hundred years ago but are viewed as potentially dangerous today, makes for a one-sided presentation of the facts, for manipulated information, and for certain shift of emphasis which tend to check the universal enlightenment otherwise furthered by the technological development of communications.' He hastened to add that such political ignorance was not attributable to 'natural stupidity [or] a basic lack of the capacity for thinking'.
24 That populism is benign is a theme encountered in most of what he has published (e.g. Laclau, 2005a; 2005b). It is an influential view among those wishing to distance themselves from Marxism, particularly in the field of peasant studies (on which see Brass 2020, 2023a, 2023b).

Asked by an interviewer what the latter terms 'ethno-populism', Laclau answers that '[e]thnic populism is important in Eastern Europe, but I don't think you will have a populism of that kind in Western Europe'.[25] From this Laclau misses the fact that discourse about ethnic 'otherness' is an ideology that operates at both a vertical and horizontal plane, and as such empowers and is empowered by populist discourse. In effect, Laclau makes the same error as that made earlier by Mudde, who asserted similarly in 2002 that populism 'plays a much more prominent role in contemporary Eastern European politics than in the West'.[26] The mistaken assumption in each case is that metropolitan capitalist nations are in some sense immune to political mobilization based on a discourse privileging ethnicity. Again, when asked by his interviewer how is it possible to describe neoliberalism as hegemonic, when in 1970s Latin America it was an economic project espoused by populist regimes but clearly imposed by 'those above' on the rest of society which opposed and resisted *laissez-faire*, Laclau responds weakly that neoliberalism 'was only hegemonic among economic and political elites', thereby undermining his own argument.[27]

Similarly problematic is the championing by Laclau and Mouffe of 'pluralistic' liberal social democratic regimes embodying what they term variously a 'national-populist tradition', a 'radicalization of democracy', or a 'radical and plural democracy', to be realized within and operated by parliamentary government.[28] In effect, theirs is an approach which leaves the capitalist system, together with its form of inequality, division of labour, class structure, income distribution, property relations, and its state intact.[29] This is because, as long

---

25 Laermans (2010: 74), who probes further by asking whether it is not the case that the anti-immigrant discourse of Dutch and French political right is also based on 'ethno-populism', to which Laclau gives an astonishingly bizarre reply. He rejects the premiss of the question, on the grounds that what is being said by the right is not that 'there exists a superior French [or Dutch] race', and that consequently the issue is 'not [about] ethno-populism but [rather] an anti-immigrant one.' Missed thereby is the fact that racism is not confined to ideas concerning superior/inferior position on an ethnic hierarchy, but also operates no less explicitly in cases where such identity is foregrounded without reference to hierarchical position.

26 See Mudde (2002: 231), whose erroneous interpretation of populism is analysed critically by Brass (2021: 10–15).

27 Laermans (2010: 82). This does not prevent Mouffe (2018: 1) from asserting subsequently that 'we are witnessing a crisis of the neoliberal hegemonic formation', the inference being – once again – that neoliberal hegemony possesses a wider base of support than in fact it does.

28 These views are expressed by Laclau in his interview with Laermans (2010: 77) and by Mouffe (2018: 2).

29 That the existing state apparatus will remain in place is accepted by Mouffe (2018: 3).

as the rich and powerful remain unexpropriated, their capacity not just to frustrate or circumvent reform, and to roll back any attempts at economic change, but also to control politics and economic policy through a combination of state capture and/or evading state regulation, remains. It is perhaps a recognition of precisely this difficulty that lies behind the unwillingness of post-Marxism to indicate either what sort of agency populism entails, or indeed what sort of end would agency itself pursue.[30] Eschewing debate with critics, Mouffe adopts a *de haut en bas* attitude: 'I would like to make clear ... that my aim is not to add another contribution to the already plethoric field of "populism studies" and I have no intention to enter the sterile academic debate about the "true nature" of populism'.[31]

3.3   Urgent Need of Renewal

Another symptomatic attack on Marxism is that by Curry, but now in the name of post-Marxist social history: it reveals the influence of Laclau and Mouffe, plus the epistemological route followed by social historiography, and why.[32] Defenders of Marxism are accused by Curry not only of 'undertaking a nostalgic retreat to the dogmas and elitism of teleology, reductionism and anachronism', but also of favouring 'empty and discredited nostrums'.[33] Dismissed by him is 'the assumption that the mode of production is a universal constant of history, and the working class therefore a privileged "universal" class', and Hobsbawm is praised for admitting in 1990 that 'the whole tradition dominated and inspired by the October Revolution has now come to an end'.[34] Much like Cannadine, Laclau, and Mouffe, therefore, Curry declares Marxism

---

30 Having proclaimed that '[t]he objective of a left populist strategy is the creation of a popular majority to come to power and establish a progressive hegemony', Mouffe (2018: 50) concedes that '[t]here is no blueprint for how this will take place or a final destination', adding that '[t]he same is true for the shape of the new hegemony that this strategy seeks to bring about'. In short, an admission that her post-Marxist populism has neither a concrete objective nor any idea how this might be achieved, were it to exist. Yet another example – were one needed – of postmodern aporia, embodied in utterances like 'struggles [will be] about different forms of subordination without attributing any *a priori* centrality to any of them'.

31 Mouffe (2018: 9).

32 The views expressed by Curry (1993) are regarded as symptomatic because they illustrate not just post-Marxist opposition to Marxism, but also – and more importantly – the theoretical underpinnings of this antagonism, and how these in turn licensed a slide into populism.

33 See Curry (1993: 172–73, 196 n58).

34 Curry (1993: 171). What is missed is that Hobsbawm was never really much of a Marxist (on which see Brass, 2021: Chapter 2).

and class redundant, but with one difference: unlike each of the former, his post-Marxist version of social history emphasizes more strongly both the from-below empowerment conferred by non-class identity, and its political legitimacy (= an authentic grassroots voice).

Curry regards the anti-Marxist case made by J.C.D. Clark, a conservative anti-Marxist reinterpretation of 17th and 18th century British history, as anti-elitist, because it claimed not only that the *ancien régime* survived but also attributed this to popular/plebeian support for monarchy, aristocracy, and religion. This is because Clark, like E.P. Thompson, shared a rejection of economic determinism and placed an 'emphasis instead on taking people's beliefs seriously'.[35] Hence the conclusion by Curry that 'English Social History [based on a Marxist approach] is exhausted', while 'some of the recent criticism by the newer historians of the Right is apposite'.[36] Because of this combined misassessment (Marxist social historiography = wrong, conservative social historiography = correct), therefore, Curry then maintained that privileging a 'from below' voice in the manner effected by these rightwing historians consequently pointed 'in the direction of greater democratic pluralism in historical practice'. In short, a view – albeit a conservative one – that Curry regarded as not so different from that of E.P. Thompson, and like him opposed to what was termed Marxist 'economic reductionism' and 'classism'.[37] This 'democratic pluralism', Curry then argued, is the way forward politically, an historiographical approach 'in urgent need of renewal', by which he means getting rid of Marxist 'accumulation of reductionist residues' and replacing them with something different.

What form this alternative to Marxism is to take Curry makes only too clear in the following manner: 'My main purpose is to offer a prescription for renewal, centred on the post-Marxism of Laclau and Mouffe', extending further this political endorsement by adding that their 'work does indeed offer a potential renewal, no less in history writing than in other respects'.[38] The

---

35 Curry (1993: 162).
36 Curry (1993: 178).
37 According to Curry (1993: 164–65), E.P. Thompson emphasized the 'cultural hegemony' exercised by rulers, maintaining that that plebeians were not unthinking accepters of their own subordination but bought into a world-view that reflected ruling class interests. His privileging of superstructural determination was criticized by other Marxists as 'culturalism'.
38 See Curry (1993: 172–73, 178), who defends both his attack on Marxism and his approval of Laclau and Mouffe by observing (original emphasis): '*This is precisely the critique of [Marxist] teleology, reductionism and anachronism – summed up in Laclau and Mouffe's work … – that we found at the heart of Thompsonian social history, and restated (for different purposes) by Clark*'.

reason for this enthusiasm is, in his words, that 'hegemony offers a hopeful way forward [in the shape of] the recent post-Marxist interpretation of Ernesto Laclau and Chantal Mouffe'.[39] Not the least persuasive argument for Curry is that for Laclau a worker 'is no longer simply fundamentally that but embodies a number of other potentially equal important identities,' the result being that 'the working class [is] no longer ... the necessary agent of global emancipation'.[40] In keeping with this view, Curry unsurprisingly defends postmodernism, denying that it is a form of relativism.[41] Rejecting the opposition expressed by some Marxists to what were now politically his new best friends, he goes on to lament 'the dreary abuse and denial that Laclau and Mouffe have elicited,' evidence Curry thinks for 'the poverty of contemporary dogmatic Marxism.'[42]

3.4 A Non-existent Capitalism

In a sense, Lucassen carries this critique of Marxism to its logical next step. Having indicated that he is not 'against Marx', Lucassen announces that he intends to compose a history of work stripped of concepts not just like class and class struggle (as do Cannadine, Laclau, Mouffe, and Curry) but also like capitalism and modernity. This strange methodology is itself compounded by his intention, nevertheless, to retain terms such as market, labour relations, social inequality, collective action and exploitation.[43] Quite how the latter set of concepts are to be defined and applied once they are decoupled epistemologically from the former group, is never revealed. Unsurprisingly, this approach generates yet more confusion and contradiction.

---

39 Curry (1993: 167–68).
40 See Curry (1993: 170, 172), who notes that the decentring of class extended from Laclau and Mouffe to include also Stuart Hall, Gareth Stedman Jones, and Gavin Kitching.
41 Curry (1993: 176, 180).
42 Marxist critics named by Curry included Ellen Meiksins Wood, Norman Geras, and Bryan D. Palmer.
43 Because 'the central concepts of capitalism and modernity are now in flux and thus have lost their precision and original analytical function,' argues Lucassen (2022: xv-xvi), it 'poses a problem for writing a long-term history like this'. He continues: 'For this reason, I have refrained from giving the terms *capitalism* (and the associated *class* and *class struggle*) and *modern* (versus *traditional*) a central place in this book [since] I believe that these terms have become so contaminated in the discussions of the last [100–150 years] that they have lost their analytical power in global labour history (original emphasis).' Instead, 'I do, however, wield [sic] the terms that are behind them, in particular *market ... labour relations, social inequality, collective action* and *... exploitation*'. This is rather like announcing an intention to swim the channel and then declaring it unnecessary first to know how to swim.

Initially, therefore, Lucassen opposed categorizing unfree labour as a residue of a pre-capitalist social order, declaring unambiguously that understanding the accumulation/unfreedom link depended in turn on how one defined capitalism itself.[44] A decade later, however, his position has shifted to one in which he denied that unfree production relations continued or increased following the abolition of slavery ('I resist the impression which is sometimes created that unfree labour since the abolition of slavery continued, or even increased, until the present').[45] Yet another decade passes, and Lucassen is now compelled to acknowledge that unfree labour does indeed persist into the present, a puzzlement expressed by the constant reference to its 'tenacious' reproductive capacity.[46]

What each of these critiques – by Cannadine, Laclau, Mouffe, Curry, and Lucassen – share is a discourse that urges historiography and/or social science generally to abandon Marxist theory once and for all. As such, it is an approach that invites – and should invite always – robust counter-critiques from those who remain Marxists.

4 Marxist Counter-Critiques

4.1 *Conversation, Collaboration, Cooperation?*

Although right about declining academic interest in Marxism, in terms both of teaching and of studying, Cannadine fails to understand the cause. According to him, it was the result of disagreement among Marxists themselves about class, its presence and meaning, an intellectual fragility which in turn led to them being overwhelmed by non-Marxist historians.[47] Overlooked by him, however,

---

44 Critical of the view that unfree production relations 'were fundamentally noncapitalist', Lucassen (1993: 17–18) argued strongly that the contrary was the case: 'All depends on the definition of capitalism of course. As we may be sure by now there is a strong relation between the occurrence of international economic development and unfree labour … and that consequently unfree labour cannot be seen as a phenomenon, restricted to some primitive or backward situations'.

45 Lucassen (2013: 14 n47).

46 Lucassen (2022: 322, 323, 360).

47 Acknowledging a renewed academic interest in Marxism over the 1960–1980 period, Cannadine (2013: 125–26) comments: 'While Marxist historians had captured the commanding heights of French academe, their British and American counterparts were less successful, especially in the universities of Oxford and Cambridge, or in the Ivy League, where class-based approaches remained essentially marginal, and where Marxism was never mainstream.' However, he misunderstands the reason for this: 'With Marxist historians unable to agree about the trajectory and trajectories of the classes they believed had

is the main reason for this waning interest: namely, that with the expansion of higher education from the 1960s onwards, Marxism (and Marxists) vanished from the street and into the universities, where it became a topic simply for study. The negative impact of this shift did not stop there, since it quickly became clear that to prosper in an anti-Marxist academic environment it was advisable quietly to jettison all things Marxist and socialist. Many leftists abandoned their political views (some turning into vehement anti-Marxists) and opted instead for the less threatening oppositional discourse then gaining hold, the 'new' populist postmodernism. This was the main reason why Marxism has declined: not because it was wrong, as Cannadine imagines, but rather because it some instances became an obstacle to becoming and remaining an academic.

Unknowingly, perhaps, his critique of Marxism is no different epistemologically from that made by Laclau and Mouffe, and for the same reason mistaken. 'For most people', argues Cannadine, 'work has only ever been part of their life … and has never been the sole determinant of how they see themselves or themselves in relation to others.'[48] Ignored thereby is that the main way in which people organize themselves and engage in agency is almost always connected to actual/potential threats to their livelihoods. That is, to protect or advance what are fundamentally economic interests (land, wages, employment), a process involving defence of or assault on property relations and institutions (the state) and structures (the law, media) connected to them. In short, action undertaken on the basis of class, promoting (or attacking) such interests as are central to this.[49]

To be sure, people do indeed have other identities and interests (for example, being competitors in pigeon racing contests, being members of a film

---

existed in the past, it was scarcely surprising that scholars who did not share their faith were strongly critical of their overall approach, and since the 1980s the flow of criticism has swollen to a flood'.

48 Cannadine (2013: 103).
49 Downgrading the historical relevance of Marxist approaches featuring concepts like class and class struggle can only be made by ignoring their centrality to an understanding of much conflict taking place over the 20th century. Episodes such as the 1926 General Strike in the UK, via the divide and rule strategy pursued by the apartheid regime in South Africa (undermining previous black/white worker solidarity), the massacre of Communists in Shanghai during 1927 and Jakarta during 1965, to 'disappearances' of workers, trade unionists, and leftists generally by far-right military dictatorships in 1970s/1980s Chile, Uruguay, Argentina, and Brazil, are all instances of class struggle waged 'from above' (by the capitalist state representing the political interests of the rich and powerful) against 'those below' on account of the latter's *class* identity – that is, workers and/or poor peasants together with their organizations and political parties.

society, supporting a particular football club) – characteristics Marxism has never denied – *but* the main kind of action undertaken (workers belonging to a trade union, joining demonstrations, or alternatively businessmen lobbying government) invariably affects what might be termed their *fundamental* interests: linked to the presence/absence of job/livlihoodprospects, the reproduction/dissolution of property rights, and thus to class position. In denying this, Cannadine sides with the post-Marxist interpretation of Laclau and Mouffe about 'equivalences', whereby a petition seeking a reduction in season ticket prices is for them no different from assembling on the street in order to oppose state oppression or a military coup, each in its own way being just another 'floating signifier' denoting a specific form of hegemony.[50]

Moreover, because he fails adequately to contextualize the decline of Marxism in academia, mistakenly attributing this to internal disagreement, Cannadine also misses the role and significance of wider societal determinants.[51] During the Thatcherite era, when *laissez-faire* was ideologically dominant, there was little institutional sympathy for leftist theory: funding provision both for university posts/courses and research projects exhibiting a specifically Marxist approach dropped noticeably. This, too, was a factor that contributed to declining interest in Marxism, leading to its replacement by the 'cultural turn'. Underestimating the acuteness of the class struggle 'waged from above' at this conjuncture, however, Cannadine egregiously declares Marx, Engels, and Lenin mistaken because 'capitalism has survived' on account of the fact that 'relations between the "proletariat" and the "bourgeoisie" have been characterized more … by conversation, collaboration, and cooperation'.[52]

---

50   Thus a landlord in Latin America or India might find himself in conflict with an alliance of tenants composed of rich peasants (small capitalists) and poor peasants (de facto workers), each of whom has a different agenda in class terms. Rich peasants want to acquire land ownership and freedom to sell its produce, while poor peasants want job security, higher wages, and better working conditions. In keeping with these different class agendas, once the landlord has been expropriated, and rich peasants become owners of the land they cultivate, as employers of labour-power they turn on their erstwhile allies whose demands are now aimed at them. In each stage of the struggle, therefore, agency by the landlord, the rich peasant, and the poor peasant is guided by their specific class identity and interests. In short, there is no escaping class, the wish by Cannadine to do so notwithstanding.

51   'The heroic narratives and broad generalizations that Marxist historians constructed have been overturned by the unprecedented research onslaught of the last twenty-five years,' Cannadine (2013: 128) asserts confidently, 'which means it is no longer possible to view the past as a succession of gigantic Manichean encounters between rising, struggling, and falling classes'.

52   'Capitalism has survived, and with it the lumpenproletariat, the peasantry, and the petite bourgeoisie,' states Cannadine (2013: 117), giving as the reason the following: 'While greed

4.2 Hegemonic Formation, Populist Moments, Floating Signifiers?

In the case of Laclau, what he cannot say is that there is indeed an additional dimension to populist discourse, one evident in the West, because to accept this would entail returning to the domain of Marxist theory and concepts, a prospect from which he is keen to distance himself. The dimension concerns the recognition that immigration is not merely an issue about national, ethnic, or cultural 'otherness' – as it is usually depicted – but also one of political economy. As Marx and Marxists have pointed out over the years, it is a question also of the industrial reserve, its enhancement, by whom or what, together with the reasons for this. As neoliberalism spreads over the globe, therefore, the inevitable result has been ever-more acute market competition, both between rival capitalists themselves and between the latter and their workers. It is an economic context that undermines consciousness and struggle based on class, and replaces them with twin forms of populism: the postmodern variant sees the cultural identity of the immigrant as empowering, on the basis of which open-door policy is to be supported politically, while the other, linked to varieties of 'nativist' conservativism, similarly privileges the nationality of the non-migrant worker.[53] Each rallies around the non-class identities wrongly perceived by post-Marxism as politically progressive.

The abandonment by Laclau and Mouffe of socialism as a desirable/feasible political objective, along with the proletariat as the universal historical subject, driving the process of class formation/consciousness/struggle, and Marxist theory in general, and its replacement with populist hegemony, leaves a space to be filled by an alternative subject and his/her agency. From this stemmed the post-Marxist claim that 'to counter the offensive of the right, it was crucial for Labour to expand its social basis ... and to incorporate the critics made by the new social movements, whose democratic demands it was essential to articulate'.[54] Into the space vacated by class Laclau and Mouffe placed a socio-economically undifferentiated category 'the people', an expansive catch-all identity beloved by populists, inside of which no significant contradiction was thought to exist.[55] In this post-Marxist framework every single occurrence – no

---

and exploitation persist, relations between the "proletariat" and the "bourgeoisie" have been characterized more in the long run by conversation, collaboration, and cooperation than by anger, antagonism, and animosity'. Painted is a scarcely recognizable history of capitalist development, a process seemingly devoid both of class and class struggle.

53 For details of these twin populisms, together with their deleterious impact on class mobilization and politics, see Brass (2022a: Chapter 7; 2022b: Chapter 1).
54 Mouffe (2018: 27, 28).
55 According to Mouffe (2018: 10–11, 24), for both her and Laclau populism is 'a discursive strategy of constructing a political frontier dividing society into two camps and calling

matter how trivial (a new way, perhaps, of combing one's hair) – becomes yet another instance of 'hegemonic formation' giving rise to its very own 'populist moment'.

Not the least of the many difficulties facing the post-Marxist populism of Laclau and Mouffe, therefore, is their interpretation of hegemony as a term lacking boundaries, exemplified by the concept 'floating signifier'. Having discarded Marxism and depriviliging class, they are unable to comprehend the way in which hegemony is structured – and thus limited – by class position, the latter bringing into consideration a positive/negative ideology that curbs any open-ended acceptance of hegemony. So class, like Marxism itself, cannot be forgotten, in that the attempt to establish hegemony will always come up against hard economic facts. Thus one cannot subscribe to any/all arguments/views regardless of political and economic interests (= the signifier on occasion refuses to float). Implausibly, however, the floating signifier of Laclau and Mouffe seems to indicate one can.

Accepting that the 1980s 'neoliberal hegemonic formation ... incorporated several themes of the counterculture', Mouffe fails to recognize its cause.[56] What the new social movements sought was autonomy, an ability to express individual choice as regards identity or lifestyle. This was an objective that was not just compatible with neoliberalism but actually central to capitalist development. In short, no contradiction existed between the neoliberal project of market expansion and the aims of the new social movements: not only were the latter neither radical nor a fundamental challenge to the system, but their desire to be accepted within it as presently constituted was much rather supportive of the accumulation process, providing it with an extra source of production so as to meet these additional kinds of consumer demand. Such compatibility notwithstanding, Mouffe appears puzzled by the fact that neoliberalism was capable of 'satisfying [new social movements] in a way that neutralizes their subversive potential', misunderstanding that – seen from the perspective of capital – these movements were never wholly 'subversive' in the first place.

---

for the mobilization of the "underdog" against "those in power"'. In a telling reveal, she then adds that '[i]t is not an ideology and cannot be attributed a specific programmatic content', but nevertheless operates contingently at specific conjunctures named by her as a 'populist moment'.

56 For this and what follows, see Mouffe (2018: 33–34).

4.3 Taking People's Beliefs Seriously?

Whilst Curry is right to argue that conservative social historiography set a trap for Marxism, ironically it is a trap into which he himself falls. This he does by signing up to all the familiar anti-Marxist tropes encountered in the conservative playbook over the years, in the belief that such backwards-looking ideology offers a politically viable alternative to Marxist theory. What is overlooked by Curry, therefore, is that 'taking people's beliefs seriously' amounts all too often to an uncritical endorsement of the 'from below' voice, simply because it is 'from below'. It is a methodology that licenses in turn the politically misleading *vox populi, vox dei* argument, on the grounds that 'there is nothing necessarily conservative or reactionary about those premises' because the latter are widely held grassroots beliefs.[57]

This approach is the cause of many of the difficulties faced by social history, equating as it has done – and does still – the 'from below' voice automatically with a progressive politics. Contrary to the view that interprets the 'from below' voice as an unmediated – and thus authentic – expression of grassroots political interests, more often than not it reproduces 'from above' ideology, resulting in the formation and consolidation of false consciousness. As such, many ideas/values which circulate at the grassroots – those which conservative and post-Marxist social historians wish to take seriously, as a 'from below' discourse – are much rather a form of class struggle waged 'from above'.[58]

Consequently, a methodologically uncritical approach to 'taking people's beliefs seriously', particularly where the element of class has been ruled out a priori, cannot but result in reification. However, swayed by a conservative historiography which methodologically based its political conclusions not on 'from above' ideology but rather on what 'those below' believed, Curry then proceeded to subscribe also to all the non-class identities that Marxism consigns to the realm of false consciousness.[59] Privileged analytically as a result of not addressing false consciousness, therefore, are not just the usual non-class forms of 'otherness' characterized by conservatives as innate, unchanging, and thus 'natural' and socio-economically non-transcendent – ethnicity, gender, patriotism, nationalism, and religion – but also 'the social history of marginalized "fringe" beliefs and people'.[60]

---

57 For this uncritical endorsement of the 'voice-from-below', see Curry (1993: 163–64).
58 Little wonder, therefore, that an establishment historian such as Cannadine (1997: 184ff.) expresses approval of social history, mistakenly labelling it 'socialist'.
59 Curry (1993: 180ff.).
60 Curry (1993: 179–80).

Significantly, Curry accepts that his enthusiasm for postmodernism and post-Marxism is tempered by its 'lending a perverse life to reaction'.[61] There is, however, nothing perverse about this connection: as has been outlined elsewhere, the link between on the one hand the 'new' populist postmodernism and post-Marxism, and on the other the political right, has deep historical roots in ideologies about Nature, the 'natural', and how these underwrite ideas about nation, tradition, race, hierarchy, and 'difference'.[62] All the latter are consistent with the arguments being deployed at that same conjuncture by the 'new' populist postmodernism, not just against Marxism as an organizing principle but also in opposition to modernity and Enlightenment discourse, grand narratives dismissed as inappropriate Eurocentric impositions on the rural 'other' in Third World nations.[63]

4.4 Where Aporia Leads

With regard to Lucassen, the problems a recognition that unfree production relations as 'tenacious' poses for his current book about the history of work are all too clear.[64] Hence the narrative about unfree labour, central to his account of work throughout history, is faced with the difficulty informing the attempt to connect – or disconnect – the presence of unfree labour to a systemic form – capitalism – which Lucassen has discarded. His earlier argument basing any discussion regarding the presence/absence of unfree labour on a prior understanding of capitalism as a system has been replaced: first, by aporia concerning when/where such a mode of production emerged; and latterly by abandoning the term altogether.[65] It is no longer possible, therefore, to pose the question of whether capitalist development entails an increase or decrease in such production relations. Having jettisoned the concepts enabling him to

---

61 Curry (1993: 180).

62 On this link, see Brass (2000).

63 Such views not only continue to inform his work but have in the process consolidated themselves. Accordingly, on his website – www.patrickcurry.co.uk – is found the following, dated 2019: 'They are all subjects that have been marginalised by, and within, mainstream modernity [which is] contemptuous of the wellsprings of life and its enchantment in the bodymind, the female, and the Earth.' About this approach he states: 'What I write out of, on the contrary, is "radical nostalgia" for what modernity mocks, marginalises, mimics and sometimes murders but which was good and worked, and (what is left of it) still is and still does. This, not reaction, is true conservatism of the kind espoused by Ruskin … And in the empire of modernity, it is under assault'.

64 See Lucassen, '"Modern Slavery": Why is Unfree Labour so Persistent?', International Institute of Social History blog, 16th November 2022.

65 For this conceptual aporia/abandonment where capitalism and modernity are concerned, see Lucassen (2022: xv–xvi).

do this, and unable as a result to decide either what characteristics define a production relation as unfree or whether or not the latter is increasing, he cannot avoid contradiction.

Its central role in his story about work notwithstanding, what unfree labour is, and thus whether or not it is increasing, are issues which remain unclear. In the case of debt bondage, uncertainty as to its relational status is evident from the description by Lucassen as a 'credit-securing strategy', a labour relation which because it is entered into 'voluntarily' is, it is inferred, free.[66] This is no different from the way neoclassical economic historians misinterpret the relation, a similarity borne out when free wage labour is defined by him as the capacity on the part of an individual 'to conclude work contracts': that is, to enter a production relation voluntarily (= freely).[67] This is the same error as that made by cliometric historians and others, who similarly overlook the fact that the freedom of a work contract lies in the ability not just freely to enter but also freely to exit from the relation (entry-into + *exit-from*). In the same text, however, indentured labour working to pay off debt – an unfree production relation – is nevertheless downgraded by Lucassen to 'shades of unfreedom' (= *perhaps* an unfree relation), which hints at the equally problematic argument that unfreedom is merely situated on a relational 'continuum', one of many locations thereon.[68]

On the question of whether there is an increase or decrease in the incidence of unfree labour, because he rejects concepts like class struggle, which links the way production relations change to the flow and ebb of conflict, Lucassen views the shift from unfree to free labour as a unilinear transformation, not unlike whig historians.[69] This is compounded by other erroneous assessments. First, that an effect of colonial expansion was that a free workforce ('Western labour relations') was reserved for their own nations by Europeans, who nevertheless imposed unfreedom on colonized subjects.[70] Reproducing the world

---

66 See Lucassen (2022: 277), who underlines his view that debt bondage does not correspond to unfree labour by putting inverted commas round the accompanying word 'enslaved' (= not really unfree). In keeping with this, subsequent references (Lucassen, 2022: 116, 196–97, 449 n57) suggest either that only chattel slaves are unfree, or that neither sharecropping and debt bondage constitute unfree labour.
67 Lucassen (2022: 196–97).
68 Lucassen (2022: 309).
69 As depicted by Lucassen (2022: 304, 362), the road of travel seems to be all in one direction, embodied in comments such as '[t]here has been an undeniable waning of unfree labour over the last two centuries', and '[d]ue to the global shifts in labour relations from unfree to free labour'.
70 Lucassen (2022: 194).

systems theory of the 1980s (free labour at the core, unfree labour at the periphery), Lucassen overlooks the widespread use of unfree production relations throughout metropolitan capitalist nations.[71] And second, the mistaken and linked assumption that unfree labour declines as the market expands, which not only reproduces the semi-feudal thesis argument that accumulation and unfree labour are incompatible, but overlooks much evidence to the contrary.[72] Unfree labour increases as the market spreads, because employers are forced to cut costs so as to remain competitive and survive as capitalists, an objective realized by restructuring the labour process where possible, so as to replace free workers with unfree equivalents.

5   Conclusion

The decentring of Marxism that ends with a recuperation of populism is a trajectory that can be explained in a large part by reference to changes in the link between leftist politics and academic institutions; how Marxism vanished from the street into the academy. Not the least of the many problems this generated have been contradictions arising from having to change one's mind as a result of initially and uncritically espousing an in vogue 'new' paradigm becoming popular in terms of teaching/research, a result of initially not having asked the necessary questions about its politics and theory. Thus a significant aspect of endorsing anti-Marxist/post-Marxist/populist discourses, together with the consequent discarding of Marxist concepts, is the nature and tone of the response to any criticism from inside the left that raises the issue of epistemological and political difficulties facing attempts to present such absences as compatible with Marxism.

Defending Marxism against these kinds of academic critiques, both from outside (Cannadine) and from within (Laclau, Mouffe, Curry, Lucassen), frequently overlooks the chronology of such interventions. Usually, therefore, it

---

71   Also overlooked is that the presence in what became colonies of unfree labour long pre-dated European expansion into such contexts.

72   References by Lucassen (2022: 12, 191, 293) to the decline of unfree labour as the market expands include the following: 'Slowly but surely, the importance for the market of domestic, independent and [,] somewhat faster, unfree labour disappeared'; 'Deep monetization of the already existing market economies has proved crucial for the development of free labour … all working for the market'; and 'In the last two centuries, labour relations – now primarily market oriented shifted radically. The share of unfree labour fell sharply'. For the compatibility between market expansion and the employment of unfree labour-power, see Brass (1999, 2011).

is the latter sort of negative appraisal which initiates and sustains debate, in effect preceding any counter-arguments made by Marxists. Where/when the latter are missing, lukewarm, or deficient, however, Marxist theory is undermined, both epistemologically and politically. Moreover, since the claims informing the sort of critiques targeting Marxism are in many respects similar – questioning and/or rejecting not just class and struggle based on this but also modernity, and even capitalism itself, in favour of vague notions like populist 'hegemony' or 'common humanity' – they contribute to and at the same time consolidate both the influence and the fashionability/popularity exercised by anti-Marxist theory and politics. It is this deleterious process that underlines the continuing necessity of critique (or counter-critique) that is specifically Marxist.

References

Adorno, T.W. (1969/1950) Politics and Economics in the Interview Material (Chapter XVII), in Adorno, T.W., E. Frenkel-Brunswik, D. J. Levinson, and R. Nevitt Sanford, *The Authoritarian Personality*, New York: W.W. Norton & Company Inc.

Brass, T. (1999) *Towards a Comparative Political Economy of Unfree Labour*. London: Frank Cass Publishers.

Brass, T. (2000) *Peasants, Populism and Postmodernism*, London: Frank Cass Publishers.

Brass, T. (2011) *Labour Regime Change in the 21st Century*, Leiden: Brill.

Brass, T. (2017) *Labour Markets, Identities, Controversies*, Leiden: Brill.

Brass, T. (2018a) *Revolution and Its Alternatives*. Leiden: Brill.

Brass, T. (2018b) The Incompatibles? Socialism, Academia, Populism, *Populism* 1(2): 173–97.

Brass, T. (2020) Is Agrarian Populism Progressive? Russia Then, India Now, *Critical Sociology* 46(7–8): 987–1004.

Brass, T. (2021) *Marxism Missing, Missing Marxism: From Marxism to Identity Politics and Beyond*, Leiden: Brill.

Brass, T. (2022a) Great Replacement and/as the Industrial Reserve: Populism or Marxism? In D. Fasenfest (ed.) *Marx Matters*, Leiden: Brill, 128–53.

Brass, T. (2022b) *Transitions: Methods, Theory, Politics*, Leiden: Brill.

Brass, T. (2023a) Critical Agrarian Studies as Populist Land Grab, *Critical Sociology* 49(3): 563–73.

Brass, T. (2023b) Academia, Marxism, and Sociology: A Warning from "The History Man", *Class, Race and Corporate Power* 11(2): Article 10. Available at: https://digitalcommons.fiu.edu/classracecorporatepower/vol11/iss2/10.

Cannadine, D. (1997) *The Pleasures of the Past*, Harmondsworth: Penguin Books.

Cannadine, D. (2013) *The Undivided Past: History Beyond our Differences*, London: Allen Lane, Penguin Books.

Curry, P. (1993) Towards a Post-Marxist Social History: Thompson, Clark and Beyond. In A. Wilson (ed.), *Rethinking Social History: English Society 1570–1920 and Its Interpretation*, Manchester: Manchester University Press, 158–200.

Das, R. J. (2020) On the Urgent Need to Re-Engage Classical Marxism, *Critical Sociology* 46 (7–8): 965–985.

Fasenfest, D. (2022) The Challenge for Sociology: The Value of the Critique, *Critical Sociology* 48(2): 189–192.

Guevara, E. C. (2022) *I Embrace You with All My Revolutionary Fervor: Letters 1947–1967*, London: Penguin Books.

Laclau, E. (1990) *New Reflections on The Revolution of Our Time*, London: Verso.

Laclau, E. (2005a) Populism: What's in a Name? In F. Panizza (ed.) *Populism and the Mirror of Democracy*, London: Verso, 32–49.

Laclau, E. (2005b) *On Populist Reason*, London: Verso.

Laermans, R. (2010) On Populist Politics and Parliamentary Paralysis: An Interview with Ernesto Laclau, in a special issue on The Populist Imagination, *Open* No 20: 70–83.

Liebknecht, W. (1908) *Karl Marx Biographical Memoirs* (translated by E. Untermann), Chicago, IL: Charles H. Kerr & Company.

Lucassen, J. (1993) Free and Unfree Labour before the Twentieth Century: a Brief Overview, in T Brass, M. van der Linden, and J. Lucassen, *Free and Unfree Labour*, Amsterdam: International Institute for Social History. 7–18.

Lucassen, J. (2013) *Outlines of a History of Labour*, Amsterdam: IISH Research Paper 51.

Lucassen, J. (2022) *The Story of Work: A New History of Humankind*, New Haven, CT: Yale University Press.

Marx, K. (1976/1867) *Capital Volume I* (Introduction by E. Mandel, translated by B. Fowkes), Harmondsworth: Penguin Books.

Miéville, C. (2022) *A Spectre, Haunting*. London: Head of Zeus Ltd.

Mouffe, C. (2018) *For a Left Populism*, London: Verso.

Mudde, C. (2002) In the Name of the Peasantry, the Proletariat, and the People: Populisms in Eastern Europe, in Y. Mény and Y. Surel (eds.), *Democracy and the Populist Challenge*, London: Palgrave, Macmillan, 214–32.

Author Index

Adorno, T.W.   275
Agamben, G.   56, 73
Aglietta, M.   170, 241
Anderson, K.   135
Anderson, L.   249
Ansari, D.   179
Aoki, H.   56
Arico, J.   135
Arruzza, C.   176
Ashe, S.D.   229
Ashman, S.   168
Ayers, A.   166, 172

Badiou, A.   123
Balakrishnan, R.   180
Balibar, E.   81, 206
Basso, P.   201 passim, 212–13, 216
Baten, J.   230
Baumohl, J.   253, 254
Beckmann, G.   57, 67
Bernstein, H.   201
Beveridge, W.H.   11, 187, 193 passim, 206, 214
Bhattacharya, T.   176
Blau, J.   253
Boffo, M.   166, 168–69
Borriello, A.   231
Bos, K.   179
Bourdieu, P.   227
Bradley, G.M.   201, 203 passim, 211ff., 216
Brass, T.   4, 6, 151–52, 154, 187, 201, 203, 206, 268ff., 275ff., 283, 286, 288
Brenner, J.   227
Brenner, N.   238–39, 252
Brenner, R.   147
Brown, K.   100
Bruno, S.   200
Brustein, W.I.   228
Buckwalter, L.M.   230
Burkett, P.   246
Burrows, R.   253
Byres, T.   147, 150

Callinicos, L.   223, 224
Cannadine, D.   272ff., 277, 279ff., 285, 288
Caron, V.   228

Case, P.   37
Castells, M.   242
Chakrabarty, D.   103
Chesnais, F.   179
Chibber, V.   134, 162
Cillo, R.   208
Clark, B.   179
Clausewitz, C.   72
Cloke, P.   249, 253
Coburg, T.   175
Collinge, C.   252
Collins, J.   201
Connell, R.   92, 102, 103
Cornia, G.   180
Cox, K.R.   221, 234, 242
Cress, D.   256
Cresswell, T.   255
Crush, J.   224
Curry, P.   272, 277ff., 285–86, 288

Damer, S.   220
Das, R.J.   7, 10, 25, 27, 29, 31, 43, 48, 134ff., 138, 140 passim, 151 passim, 162, 237, 267
Davidson, N.   174, 221
Davis, M.   116
de Noronha, L.   201, 203 passim, 211ff., 216
DeVerteuil, G.   249, 256
Dobb, M.   11, 193, 197ff., 214
Du Bois, W.E.B.   9, 10, 28, 36, 99–100, 104 passim

Eagleton, T.   135, 139, 145, 149
Egan, D.   126
Ekers, M.   255
Eley, G.   228
Elias, N.   220, 231
Elson, D.   180
Engels, F.   12, 104, 135, 137, 141, 145, 155, 189ff., 210, 214, 238ff., 248, 250, 259, 273–74, 282
Engerman, S.L.   6
Evans, R.   230

Fasenfest, D.   1 passim, 25 passim, 35 passim, 47 passim, 79, 87, 89, 134, 162, 267

Fauconnier, B. 57, 61
Feil, F. 177
Fields, K. 105
Fine, B. 166, 167, 168, 169
Foenkinos, D. 186
Fogel, R.W. 6
Foley, S. 117
Foster, J.B. 156, 179, 246
Fraser, N. 176, 225
Freeman, B. 37
Fujita, S. 57, 66

Gasper, P. 135
Ghosh, S. 147
Giddens, A. 225, 230
Gilbert, D. 160
Giordano, J. 116
Glickman, L. 38
Glyn, A. 193, 199, 214
Go, J. 100
Gottfried, H. 40, 51, 86, 91
Gowan, T. 249
Graham, H. 228
Gramsci, A. 66, 114, 128, 238, 245, 251
Guevara, E. 272
Gupta, J. 179

Habermas, J. 99
Hairong, Y. 6
Hallward, P. 116
Hammond, T. 72
Hardt, M. 73
Hart, G. 255
Hartung, W.D. 37
Harvey, D. 152, 228, 241ff., 255, 259
Hasegawa, M. 258
Hayashi, M. 12, 237, 238, 241, 244, 246, 247, 248, 251, 253, 258
Hayter, I. 55, 57, 61
Heynen, N. 246
Higuchi, M. 57, 61, 62, 63
Hirata, I. 63
Hofmann, R. 57, 68
Holz, F. 179
Hopper, K. 256
Horowitz, I.L. 3
Hoston, G. 57, 58, 61, 64, 66
Hou, J. 242
Huber, M.T. 176, 179

Hudson, M. 179
Huntington, J. S. 38
Hyslop, J. 228

Innis, H. 120
Insurgent Sociologist Collective 85
International Labour Office 194
Internment Facilities 59
IPCC 177
Ishidō, K. 57, 61, 70
Itō, A. 57, 60
Itzigsohn, J. 100
Ivanova, M. 170
Ives, P. 255

Jacobs, J. 40
Jäger, A. 231
James, W. 221
Japanese Communist Party 8, 56
Jeeves, A.H. 224
Jeffery, D. 219
Jessop, B. 238, 244, 252
Johnsen, S. 249, 253
Jones, G. S. 134, 273, 279
Jonna, R. 156, 164
Joubert, E. 232

Kagan, R. 119
Kaika, M. 246
Kalecki, M. 11, 193, 197–98, 214
Kalmring, S. 134, 148
Kapusta, P. 124
Kasai, K. 258
Katznelson, I. 237
Keil, R. 252
Kennard, M. 114
Kennedy, J.F. 202
Khanna, P. 202
Kinder, T. 175
King, R.D. 228
Kipfer, S. 255
Kita, I. 68
Klippenstein, K. 122
Kobayashi, M. 57, 59
Kunimatsu, A. 57, 70

Laclau, E. 13, 130, 272, 274 *passim*, 288
Lacorte, R. 255
Laermans, R. 276

AUTHOR INDEX

Laibman, D. 144, 154
Langman, L. 7
Latham, R. 27, 28, 31, 117–18, 120ff., 129, 131
Lawrence, M. 179
Laybourne-Langton, L. 179
Lefebvre, H. 12, 238, 241, 243–44, 252, 255
Leitner, H. 255
Lenin, V.I. 25, 64, 114, 118, 119, 121–22, 127ff., 135, 145, 151, 152, 162, 209, 268, 272–73, 282
Levien M. 6
Liebknecht, W. 271–72
Liebow, E. 224
Linebaugh, P. 255
Linkhoeva, T. 57
Loftus, A. 255
Logan, J.R. 242
Lowe, S. 253
Löwy, M. 81
Lucassen, J. 270, 272, 279–80, 286ff
Lundskow, G. 33

Mader, P. 168
Mahon, R. 252
Mair, A. 242
Mann, M. 228
Mao Zedong 50
Marquardt, F. 202
Martin, D. 255
Maruyama, M. 69
Marx, K. 9, 25, 36, 42ff., 47ff., 98 *passim*, 107, 110, 115, 118, 123, 134 *passim*, 145 *passim*, 158ff., 168, 176, 187 *passim*, 198, 200 *passim*, 210ff., 215, 238ff., 242, 247, 250, 268, 270ff., 279, 282–83
Massey, D. 229, 232, 242
Matsuo, H. 57, 59
Maunder, J. 135, 151
May, J. 249, 253
McCarthy, J. 179
McChesney, R. 156
McCullum, R.B. 197
McGeever, B.F. 229
Merrifield, A. 237
Mertens, D. 168
Mezzadra, S. 201, 205ff., 216
Mezzadri, A. 140, 143–44
Miéville, C. 268–69, 273
Miller, B. 255

Mills, C. W. 3, 82, 84
Ministry of Health, Labour and Welfare 251
Misuzu Shobō 59, 62
Mitter, S. 224
Miyaji, K. 57, 60
Miyamoto, K. 64, 68ff., 257
Molotch, H.L. 242
Montejano, D. 231
Montgomerie, J. 169
Moore, J.W. 246
Moore, R. 242, 244
Moriyama, T. 62
Morris, A. 100, 104
Mott, C. 118
Mouffe, C. 13, 272, 274, 276 *passim*, 288
Mudde, C. 276
Murata, Y. 65

Nabeyama, S. 58, 61, 64, 67, 69–70
Nakajima, M. 57
Nakano, S. 70, 72
Nakazawa, S. 57, 60
Negri, A. 73
Neilson, B. 206
Nicholls, W. 255
Nimtz, A. 134
Nowak, A. 134, 148

Obstfeld, M. 39
Ogino, F. 56, 57
Ōkubo, G. 57, 67
Okudaira, Y. 57, 62
Ollman, B. 138
Oppenheimer, M. 89–90

Palma, G. 170
Parboni, R. 170
Parsons, T. 102ff., 123
Patel, R. 180
Patnaik, P. 150, 155
Patnaik, U. 150, 155
Peck, J. 238, 252–53
Petras, J. 125
Phillips, A. 37
Piketty, T. 99, 168
Pineaut, E. 179
Pleace, N. 253
Plimmer, G. 175
Polanyi, K. 99

Postone, M. 123
Pradella, L. 147, 153, 154, 208
Probation Office 60
Prudham, S. 179
Pun, A. 51

Quilgars, D. 253

Ramas, M. 227
Readman, A. 197
Reuters 43
Rex, J. 242, 244
Robbins, P. 179
Roberts, M. 142
Rossi, P.H. 251, 254
Roubini, N. 174
Rueedi, F. 232

Saad-Filho, A. 11, 29, 33, 49, 166ff., 172, 174–75, 177, 180, 182
Samaddar, R. 206
Sandbu, M. 175
Sano, M. 58, 61, 64, 67, 69–70
Sarri, R. 37
Saull, R. 174
Saunders, F.S. 125
Sawers, L. 237
Sawyer, M. 168
Scimecca, J. A. 83
Scotson, E.L. 220, 231
Scott-Heron, G. 42
Sheppard, E. 255
Shindō, T. 66
Shinjuku Renraku Kai 258
Shisō- no- Kagaku- Kenkyūkai 57
Sipos, G. 55, 57, 61
Sitas, A. 231
Siu, K. 51
Skocpol, T. 253
Smith, J. 160
Smith, N. 249, 257
Snow, D.A. 249, 256
Soja, E.W. 238, 241, 243
Solty, I. 175
Sparks, T. 249
Spector, A. 89
Sperber, J. 134

Steinbeck, J. 186
Steinhoff, P. 57–58, 62
Stinchcombe, A. 101
Stoner, M.R. 253
Streek, W. 203
Sutch, R. 6
Sweezy, P.M. 11, 192–93, 197–98, 214
Swyngedouw, E. 246
Sziarto, K.M. 255

Tabb, W.K. 237
Tcherneva, P.R. 170
Thau, B. 42
Tilly, C. 256
Toike, T. 57, 69–70, 72
Tolstoy, L. 4
Traverso, E. 228
Tridico, P. 170
Trotsky, L.D. 25, 129, 131, 145, 151, 160, 188, 268, 272, 274
Tsurumi, S. 57, 60, 61–62, 66

US Army War College 117

Valentine, D. 116, 117
van der Pijl, K. 116
van der Zwan, N. 168
von Mahs, J. 249

Wagner, D. 256
Ward, M. 55, 56, 57, 58, 63, 66
Watson, S. 253
Watts, M. 6
Webber, M.M. 227
Whitehead, A.N. 100
Wilk, C. 81, 82
Williams, M. 55, 57, 61
Wolfe, A. 227
Wood, E.M. 223, 224, 279
World Economic Forum 119
Wright, E.O. 9, 80, 87, 156

Yoshimoto, T. 57, 66, 69, 70

Zelizer, V. 227
Zhou, H. 39
Zuboff, S. 176

Subject Index

academia   IX, 2, 8–9, 12, 39, 79, 85, 98, 109, 268ff., 282
   ANU   2
   Atlanta   100, 104, 105
   Berlin   104, 106
   Cambridge   198, 280
   careerism in   27
   Chicago   26, 32, 88, 100
   Columbia   83
   CUNY   2, 86
   debate in   3, 5ff., 50, 98, 201, 268, 277, 289
   fashion and   2, 4–5, 7, 29, 125, 267, 269, 271–72
   Hamburg   2
   Harvard   41, 100
   Imperial, Tokyo   54
   katheder-socialists   272
   Maryland   82–83
   Michigan   1–2, 25–26, 86
   Oxford   280
   Purdue   26, 88
   Shanghai   2
   SOAS   2
   student debt   39
   Wayne State   1, 25, 79, 88ff
   Wisconsin   82, 88, 97
   York, Toronto   1, 25, 92, 237
accumulation   8, 10ff., 36–37, 42, 118, 121–22, 124, 137, 142–43, 147, 151ff., 155ff., 158–59, 161, 166 *passim*, 180ff., 187ff., 192ff., 197 *passim*, 216, 223, 227, 230, 238 *passim*, 278, 280, 284, 288. *See also* capitalism, class, socialism
   primitive   137, 142–43, 147, 151ff., 158–59, 223
Africa   29, 37, 38, 43, 105, 108–109, 147, 156, 171, 220 *passim*, 232, 234, 281
   Ghana   108
   Libya   121
   Namibia   26
   Pan-Africanism   100, 108
agriculture   6, 136, 147, 150, 156, 199, 201
Asia   29, 47 *passim*, 55ff., 63, 68, 108, 127, 135, 146, 155, 199, 270. *See also* China, India, Japan
   Greater East Asia Co-Prosperity Sphere   56, 68

   Hong Kong   8, 47, 51, 110
   Indonesia   170
   Korea   29, 56, 60, 170–71
   Malaysia   170
   Manchuria   56
   Taiwan   56, 60, 170
   Thailand   170
   Vietnam   9, 32, 86, 116, 121, 127, 170

Beveridge, William   11, 187, 193 *passim*, 206, 214
   'four giant evils'   194
borders   12, 72, 174, 202 *passim*, 211 *passim*
   'the right to escape'   205
   control and   204ff., 214, 216
   open   12, 202, 203, 204, 205, 209 *passim*, 283
Brexit   173, 209, 212, 222

Canada   1, 25, 86, 120, 171
   Montreal   234
   Quebec   220, 234
capitalism   IX, 2, 3, 4, 6, 8, 10, 11, 12, 26ff., 31, 36, 38, 40, 48 *passim*, 56, 68, 101, 106ff., 112 *passim*, 125 *passim*, 135–36, 140 *passim*, 149 *passim*, 158ff., 166–67, 169, 173–74, 176ff., 187, 191, 197–98, 201–202, 204ff., 208ff., 212ff., 216, 219ff., 225, 228, 230, 234, 239, 241ff., 247, 259, 269ff., 275, 279ff., 286, 289. *See also* class, crisis, feudalism, neoliberalism, production relations, racism, socialism
deindustrialisation   11, 169, 178
deregulation   11–12, 199–200, 238, 246
financial   38, 41, 42, 43, 44, 47, 49–50, 104, 121–22, 128, 142, 150, 155, 157–58, 167ff., 178ff
Great Depression   43, 186, 193
inequality and   1, 2, 8, 26–27, 43, 47ff., 137, 143–44, 154ff., 168ff., 207, 276, 279
International Monetary Fund (IMF)   43, 49
laissez-faire   7, 11, 187, 196, 199–200, 203, 212, 216, 276, 282
privatisation   168, 175, 200
World Bank   43, 49, 158

China 2, 7, 8, 10, 25–26, 34, 38, 40, 43, 47, 49ff., 86, 97, 108–109, 117, 127, 134, 158, 171, 199
  Belt and Road Initiative (BRI) 8, 50–51
civil society 99, 110, 240, 245–46, 252
class. *See* capitalism, socialism, workers
  'dangerous' 58, 59, 62, 65, 239–40, 242ff., 250, 243–54, 259, 279
  bourgeois/middle 28, 36, 64–65, 117, 128, 145, 158, 169, 191, 201, 227, 240, 243, 249, 268, 272, 273
  consciousness 51, 63, 67, 139, 141, 157, 189, 191, 198, 210, 211, 242, 270, 274–75, 283
  formation 51, 106, 150, 189, 191, 234, 244, 270, 283, 285
  landlord 5, 68, 141, 282
  struggle 3, 10, 68, 112 *passim*, 123 *passim*, 131, 140, 143, 145, 153–54, 158, 187ff., 192, 200, 202, 205, 208 *passim*, 223, 225–26, 233, 242ff., 249, 270, 279, 281ff., 285, 287, 289
colonialism 8, 12, 33, 40, 50, 98, 101, 108, 139, 147–48, 153, 158, 204
  decolonization 9, 98ff., 104
communism 4, 5, 47, 54 *passim*, 71, 117, 130, 143–44. *See also* capitalism, Engels, Lenin, liberalism, Marx, socialism, Trotsky
  Chinese Communist Party (CCP) 50, 52
  Comintern 9, 64–65, 127
  Japanese Communist Party (JCP) 8, 9, 56, 57, 58, 60, 61, 63 *passim*, 74
conservatism 4, 35, 38, 39, 103, 130, 197, 212, 269, 278, 283, 285, 286
  British 212, 213, 278
crisis 39, 40, 41, 43, 47, 65, 66, 74, 121, 125, 127, 142, 143, 144, 154, 161, 166–67, 169, 171 *passim*, 194, 198, 201, 206, 232–33, 244–45, 271, 276. *See also* capitalism
  financial 39, 43, 47, 127, 142, 143–44, 154, 167, 181–82, 251
culture 2, 3, 4, 12, 40, 61, 86, 137, 145, 160–61, 169, 182, 203, 206, 230, 258, 270, 284. *See also* identity, populism, postmodernism
  wars 203

democracy 2, 11, 32, 39, 40, 42, 44, 64, 73, 74, 106–107, 166–67, 171ff., 195, 276
Du Bois, W.E.B. 9, 10, 28, 36, 99ff., 104 *passim*

Engels, Frederick 12, 104, 135, 137, 141, 145, 155, 189ff., 210, 214, 238ff., 248, 250, 259, 273–74, 282
Enlightenment, the 3, 30, 286
Eurocentric 3, 8, 12, 48, 100, 134ff., 286
environment 11, 47, 51, 54, 129–30, 138, 139, 167, 238, 240, 242, 244, 248, 250, 255
  climate change IX, 40, 104, 177 *passim*
Europe 25, 29, 31, 43, 48, 74, 84, 86, 103, 109, 115, 125, 127, 130, 134ff., 139, 145ff., 153–54, 158, 161–62, 170–71, 199, 209, 222, 223, 228ff., 276
  Austria 30, 39, 191
  Croatia 4–5
  Eastern 29, 171, 199, 209, 222, 229, 276
  England 34, 37, 147, 154, 158, 162, 191, 210ff., 219ff., 229, 234, 240
  France 30, 37, 39, 42, 43, 114, 162, 171, 186, 220, 228, 240
  Germany 2, 25, 30, 37, 39, 43, 74, 85, 106, 115, 162, 170, 171, 203, 228, 229
  Ireland 149, 210ff., 219, 229
  Italy 30, 37, 39, 74, 171, 200ff
  Netherlands 219
  Yugoslavia 4

far-right 74, 117, 130, 172ff., 202, 207, 215, 229, 231, 281. *See also* identity, populism, racism
fascism 11, 30, 55, 61, 69, 166, 174, 181–82, 216
  Hitler 30
  Mussolini 30
  Nazis 85–86, 203, 228–29, 275
feudalism 48, 64, 69, 101, 115, 141, 145, 150–51, 160, 230, 288

gender 2, 9, 12, 36–37, 38, 40, 42, 98, 100–101, 126, 187, 193, 200, 211, 214, 216, 219ff., 226–27, 230, 233, 240, 274, 285
  feminism 4, 32, 88, 92, 97, 99, 102, 201
  patriarchy 224, 232–33
geography 12, 36, 48, 135, 220, 222, 226, 229, 231, 237, 250, 252. *See also* historiography, social sciences
  periphery/centre 10–11, 99, 134 *passim*, 145 *passim*, 155 *passim*, 169, 254, 288
  South/North 41, 51, 72, 74, 102–103, 109, 119, 130, 135ff., 140, 169, 176–77, 181, 199, 209, 220

SUBJECT INDEX   297

Gramsci, Antonio   128, 238, 245, 251
Guevara, Ernesto Che   272

health
  COVID-19   28, 39, 42, 116, 166, 167, 169, 174–75
  healthcare   138, 176, 197, 204
Hegel, G.W.F.   97, 137
historiography   6, 106, 277–78, 280, 285
  Clark, J.C.D.   278
  cliometric   6, 287
  geohistory   229
  Hobsbawm, E.J.   277
  Thompson, E.P.   278
  whig   287
housing   12, 26, 28, 41, 175, 176, 221, 231–32, 237 *passim*, 245 *passim*, 254 *passim*
human rights   2, 36, 43–44, 48, 171, 188, 206, 215
  citizenship   12, 204, 206–207, 219, 220, 254, 258, 259
  livelihood right (*sēzon ken*)   205, 258
  reparations as   98, 188, 202

identity   4, 12, 13, 40, 58, 65–66, 121, 157, 172, 188, 202ff., 207, 214, 215, 225, 230, 244, 273, 274, 276, 278, 281, 282, 283, 284. *See also* gender, nationalism, racism
  ethnicity   12, 38, 73, 187, 188, 202, 205, 208, 211, 216, 220–21, 228, 257, 275–76, 285
  intersectionality   47, 219
imperialism   9, 33, 36, 40, 44, 48, 64, 68, 86, 100–101, 108, 109, 117–18, 122, 126, 136, 137, 143, 145ff., 153, 157–58, 160, 162
India   6, 38, 134, 136, 140, 142, 147, 148, 149, 150, 156, 158, 170, 175, 199, 134, 282

Japan   7, 8, 9, 12, 29, 40, 43, 54 *passim*, 66 *passim*, 170, 237, 238, 250 *passim*
  homelessness   35, 237 *passim*, 250 *passim*
  kamikaze   54
  kokutai (patriotism, Emperor system)   8, 57, 59, 61 *passim*, 71
  tenkō (re-education)   8, 9, 56 *passim*, 66 *passim*
  tenkōsha (convert)   56, 57, 58, 59, 60, 61, 62, 67, 68, 69, 71, 73
  Tokyo   54, 63
  Yokohama   250

journals   1, 3, 4–5, 9, 12, 30, 33, 80, 89, 91, 109, 123, 136, 269–70
  'high impact'   79, 109
  Critical Sociology   1, 5, 7, 9, 29–30, 32ff., 36, 47–48, 51, 79 *passim*, 88 *passim*, 97, 123, 166, 269
  Insurgent Sociologist   9, 32, 79ff., 84, 88, 94, 97

Kautsky, Karl   131
Keynesianism   168, 180, 193, 197

labour. *See also* capitalism, class, labour process, Marxism
  competition   11, 145, 154, 186, 191–92, 194–95, 197, 200, 205, 207, 209, 210, 212, 214ff., 223, 228, 275, 283
  deskilling   191
  division of   12, 103, 146–47, 200, 219, 222–23, 225ff., 229, 233–34, 240, 276
  free   106, 140–41, 150, 154, 192, 196, 200, 207, 208, 216, 287, 288
  lumpenproletariat   190, 240, 242, 282
  precarity   11, 156, 169, 175–76, 180
  process   189, 191–92, 193, 199, 200, 201, 288
  restructuring   43, 169, 181, 193, 200, 209, 252, 288
  surplus   11, 141, 150, 187, 188–89, 190, 193, 199, 201, 208, 209, 212–13, 214ff
  unfree   150, 208, 280, 286ff
labour-power   10, 142, 155, 156, 159–60, 190, 192–93, 195, 197, 200–201, 208, 212, 214, 216, 282, 288
Latin America   29, 31, 37, 43, 91, 127, 129, 136, 156, 160, 170–71, 221, 230, 276, 282
  Argentina   272, 281
  Bolivia   182, 221
  Brazil   114, 125, 130, 142, 153, 156, 171, 175, 281
  Chile   115, 281
  Cuba   82, 84, 92, 272
  Mexico   160, 199
  Nicaragua   39
  Uruguay   281
Lenin, V.I.   25, 64, 114, 118, 119, 121–22, 127ff., 135, 145, 151, 152, 162, 209, 268, 272–73, 282
liberalism   54–55, 117, 118, 189, 193, 214, 230. *See also* neoliberalism

Luxemburg, Rosa   128

Malthus, T. R.   198
Mao Zedong   50–51, 86, 109, 121, 131, 135, 151
Marx, Karl   9, 25, 36, 42ff., 47ff., 98 *passim*, 107, 110, 115, 118, 123, 134 *passim*, 145 *passim*, 158ff., 168, 176, 187 *passim*, 198, 200 *passim*, 210ff., 215, 238ff., 242, 247, 250, 268, 270ff., 279, 282–83
Marxism   1 *passim*, 11ff., 25–26, 29, 31, 32ff., 47 *passim*, 55–56, 61ff., 68, 80 *passim*, 94, 97, 102, 106, 108, 113, 127, 134, 136, 144, 149, 151–52, 154, 158, 161, 167, 179, 181, 187ff., 193, 195, 197, 201ff., 207ff., 211, 213ff., 219–20, 237–38, 242–43, 246, 249ff., 258–59, 267 *passim*, 279 *passim*, 288–89
media   57, 80, 99, 115ff., 120, 171, 172, 222, 227, 230, 281
Middle East   25, 38, 43, 115, 125, 127
   Afghanistan   33, 116, 121, 123
   Iran   117, 127
   Iraq   33, 43, 116, 121, 127
migrants   50, 156, 176, 192, 193, 200, 201, 202, 204, 205, 206, 208–209, 212, 213, 215, 231–32, 283

nationalism   8, 11, 43, 56, 61, 64, 72, 172, 203, 204, 207, 216, 234, 275, 285
neoliberalism   2, 7, 11, 38, 47, 48, 125, 142, 166 *passim*, 173 *passim*, 181–82, 270, 276, 283, 284. *See also* capitalism, class, crisis

peasants   3, 6, 126, 135, 140, 150, 151–52, 154, 156, 157, 161, 199, 208, 281–82. *See also* agriculture, capitalism, class, identity, populism, postmodernism
politics
   hegemony   13, 109, 110, 117, 118, 119, 171ff., 181, 245, 276ff., 279, 282, 283, 284, 289
   'hyperconformist'   257
   Labour Party (UK)   114, 181, 196, 197, 213, 219
population   12, 27, 106, 107, 116, 134, 135, 147, 156, 170, 176, 180, 188ff
   relative surplus   IX, 12, 156, 189, 190, 200, 237, 239, 253, 259, 192, 195, 198, 200, 211, 221, 227, 232, 234, 237, 239, 253, 259

populism   4, 5, 6, 13, 39, 179, 188, 201, 206, 274ff., 281, 283–84, 286, 288–89. *See also* identity, postmodernism
   'ethno-populism'   276
   agrarian   6, 201
postmodernism   4, 11, 12, 13, 48, 139, 188, 201, 202, 206, 215, 237, 272, 277, 279, 281, 283, 286. *See also* culture, identity, populism
   'floating signifier'   282ff
post-Marxism   4, 277–78, 283, 286
poverty   IX, 2, 7, 8, 26, 27–28, 35, 38, 49–50, 72, 136, 142, 149, 159, 174, 194, 195, 237, 244, 253–54, 256, 279
production relations   139, 140, 143, 144, 146, 157, 200, 208, 274, 280, 286–87, 288. *See also* capitalism, feudalism, labour, Marxism
   debt bondage   206, 287
   serfs   208
   sharecropping   208, 287
   slaves   6, 9, 98, 105, 107, 108, 141, 147, 153–54, 209, 212, 280, 286, 287
productive forces   41, 140, 143ff., 158
   machinery   142, 146, 148, 153, 159, 160, 177, 191–92, 193, 241
   technology   26, 98, 116, 122, 130, 138, 145, 160, 179, 193, 196

racism   11, 26, 37, 40, 41, 44, 98, 100, 104, 105, 106, 107, 117–18, 135, 137, 156, 157, 172ff., 176–77, 181, 196, 202, 203, 204–205, 207, 216, 219, 220–21, 224, 226ff., 229, 230, 233, 276. *See also* identity, populism
   anti-foreigner   196
   anti-semitism   196, 229, 275
   apartheid regime   220–21, 225, 227, 231ff., 281
   Jim Crow   107
religion   43, 44, 55, 58–59, 60–61, 65, 105–106, 139, 141, 149, 219, 220, 245, 274, 278, 285
reserve army of labour   11, 142, 143, 155–56, 158–59, 187, 189ff., 197ff., 201, 203, 210ff., 215–16, 225, 239–40, 267. *See also* borders, capitalism, ethnicity, migrants, populism, racism, relative surplus population
   unemployment and   11, 193, 194, 195, 196, 198, 199, 214, 215, 226, 230, 242

SUBJECT INDEX

revolution. *See* capitalism, class, Marxism, peasants, socialism, workers
   counter-struggle   114, 116, 117, 125
   Cuba 1959   82, 84, 272
   France 1789   25, 86
   Green   199
   permanent   145
   Russia 1905   115
   Russia 1917   25, 86, 228, 268–69, 277
Russia   4, 6, 25, 34, 38, 65, 86, 110, 115, 117, 140, 152, 162, 170, 188, 228, 268
   Bolsheviks   119, 228
   USSR   199

social movements   4, 10, 12, 32, 34, 36, 38, 43, 97, 104, 126, 174, 182, 219, 254ff., 259, 283, 284
   Communist League   115
   Landless Workers Movement (MST)   114
   Union Syndicale Solidaires   114
   Zapatistas   114
social sciences   1, 2, 3, 4, 5, 7, 8, 12, 25, 29, 33, 39, 98, 104, 124, 267, 271
   American Sociological Association (ASA)   2, 9, 34, 80
   anthropology   3, 98, 270
   Durkheim, Émile   9, 36, 98, 99, 100ff., 105, 110
   Eurocentrism   48, 134, 136, 286
   Frankfurt School   32
   Merton, Robert K.   83
   methodology   27, 100, 101, 247, 279, 285
   Mills, C. Wright   3, 82, 84
   Parsons, Talcott   102, 103, 104, 123
   Poulantzas, Nicos   9, 80ff., 119
   reconstructionist   101
   Szymanski, Albert   9, 80–81, 84–85, 88, 94
   Weber, Max   9, 36, 98 *passim*, 110, 243–44
socialism   3, 5, 8, 10, 11, 13, 26, 28, 50–51, 52, 64–65, 67, 68, 86, 103, 106, 112, 118, 125ff., 131, 144, 146, 151, 168, 194, 208, 214, 216, 269, 271–72, 283. *See also* capitalism, class, communism, Marxism, Lenin, revolution, the State, Trotsky
South Africa   156, 171, 220–21, 224ff., 230ff., 281. *See also* apartheid, racism
   African National Congress   232–33
   Eastern Cape   221
   gold mining   223–24
   Inkatha   232
   KwaZulu   232
   Rand Revolt   224
   Western Cape   221, 232
Stalin, Joseph   9, 64–65
State, the   8, 50, 56, 57, 73, 99, 103, 106, 108, 130, 134, 141, 143, 153, 158, 168, 172, 175, 177, 181, 195, 197, 216, 227, 237, 245, 248, 252, 281. *See also* Lenin, Marxism
   rescaling   239, 252ff., 259
   taxation   27, 142, 174–75, 179, 180
strikes   10, 115, 126, 198
subaltern, the   4, 109, 188, 208, 249, 259. *See also* identity, postmodernism

trade unions   171, 174, 181–82, 204, 208, 212
Trotsky, Leon   25, 129, 131, 145, 151, 160, 188, 268, 272, 274

United States
   Biden, Joe   44, 98, 117
   CIA   26, 116, 117
   COINTELPRO   115
   Detroit   1, 2, 26, 28, 87, 90
   FBI   115
   NAFTA   38
   Obama, Barack   39, 41
   Pentagon   37
   Reconstruction   106–107
   Red Scare   115
   Tea Party   38, 40
   Trump, Donald   44, 98, 173
urbanization   234, 238, 241, 242, 243, 244, 251, 257, 259
   metabolic   247–48, 250, 251, 256
   private spaces   239, 241, 242, 243, 244, 255
   public spaces   239, 242, 243, 244, 255
   renewal   87, 277–78

wages   10, 44, 49, 107, 142–43, 153, 155–56, 158–59, 174, 177, 189, 190ff., 195, 197–98, 204–205, 210ff., 215–16, 224, 226ff., 230, 281, 282
war   7, 8, 9, 10, 25, 32, 37, 40, 43, 54ff., 63 *passim*, 79, 83–84, 86, 99, 105ff., 110, 114 *passim*, 121 *passim*, 166, 170, 192ff., 197, 199, 219, 227, 228, 233, 275
   1914–18   37, 64, 99, 105, 110, 228
   1939–45   37, 40, 64, 108, 118–19, 219
   American Civil   105–106

war (*cont.*)
   Cold   108, 115, 116, 125, 166, 233
   Iraq-Iran   127
   NATO   173
   Russia-Ukraine   170
   Sino-Japanese 1937   56, 66
   Vietnam   9, 32, 86, 116, 121, 127
welfare state   11, 38, 49, 158, 168, 169, 180, 194, 195, 197, 204, 214, 228, 230, 233, 251, 253–54, 258, 259. *See also* Beveridge

workers   6, 10, 11, 26, 42, 44, 48, 50, 51, 56, 67, 68, 72, 106, 107, 114, 122, 125, 126, 135, 141 *passim*, 150ff., 154, 156 *passim*, 169, 174ff., 186ff., 190ff., 196 *passim*, 208 *passim*, 216, 224, 226ff., 230ff., 240ff., 275, 279, 281, 282, 283, 288. *See also* capitalism, class, Marxism, wages
'green'   213, 216
proletarianisation   140, 143, 145, 150, 208, 211

www.ingramcontent.com/pod-product-compliance
Lightning Source LLC
Chambersburg PA
CBHW070612030426
42337CB00020B/3761